chibi Vampire

VOLUME 12
CREATED BY
YUNA KAGESAKI

TOKYOPOP®

HAMBURG // LONDON // LOS ANGELES // TOKYO

OUR STORY SO FAR...

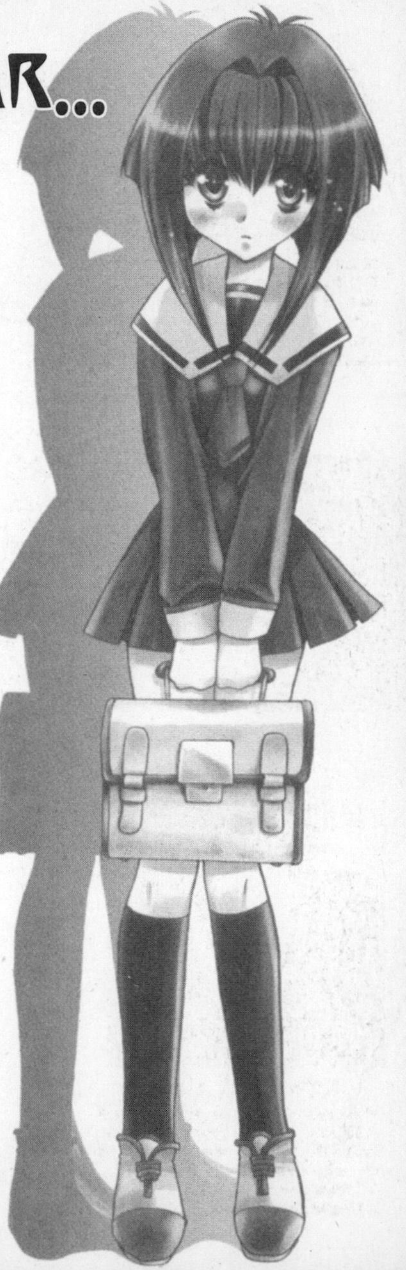

KARIN MAAKA ISN'T LIKE OTHER GIRLS. ONCE A MONTH, SHE EXPERIENCES PAIN, FATIGUE, HUNGER, IRRITABILITY–AND THEN SHE BLEEDS. FROM HER NOSE. KARIN IS A VAMPIRE, FROM A FAMILY OF VAMPIRES, BUT INSTEAD OF NEEDING TO DRINK BLOOD, SHE HAS AN EXCESS OF BLOOD THAT SHE MUST GIVE TO HER VICTIMS. IF DONE RIGHT, GIVING THIS BLOOD TO HER VICTIM CAN BE AN EXTREMELY POSITIVE THING. THE PROBLEM WITH THIS IS THAT KARIN NEVER SEEMS TO DO THINGS RIGHT...

KARIN IS HAVING A BIT OF BOY TROUBLE. KENTA USUI–THE HANDSOME NEW STUDENT AT HER SCHOOL AND WORK–IS A NICE ENOUGH GUY, BUT HE EXACERBATES KARIN'S PROBLEM. KARIN'S BLOOD PROBLEM, YOU SEE, BECOMES WORSE WHEN SHE'S AROUND PEOPLE WHO HAVE SUFFERED MISFORTUNE, AND KENTA HAS SUFFERED PLENTY OF IT. MAKING THINGS EVEN MORE COMPLICATED, IT'S BECOME CLEAR TO KARIN THAT SHE'S IN LOVE WITH KENTA... AND THIS BECOMES PAINFUL TO KARIN AS SHE SOON DISCOVERS THAT LOVE BETWEEN HUMANS AND VAMPIRES IS FROWNED UPON BECAUSE CHILDREN BETWEEN THE TWO SPECIES LACK REPRODUCTIVE ABILITIES. AS KARIN STRUGGLES WITH FEELING THAT SHE AND KENTA AREN'T MEANT TO BE TOGETHER BECAUSE OF THE DEFECTS WITH HER BODY, HER LITTLE SISTER ANJU AWAKENS AS A FULL VAMPIRE AND KARIN FEELS EVEN MORE ALONE...

THE MAAKA FAMILY

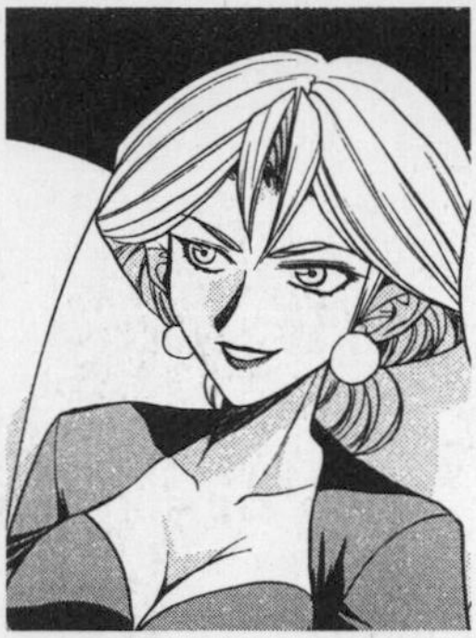

CALERA MARKER

Karin's overbearing mother. While Calera resents that Karin wasn't born a normal vampire, she does love her daughter in her own obnoxious way. Calera has chosen to keep her European last name.

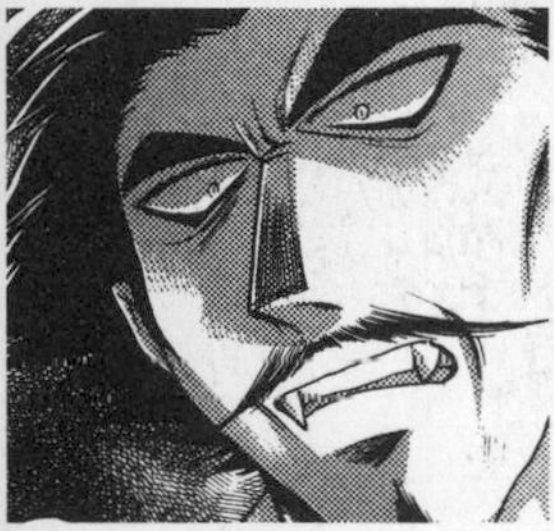

HENRY MARKER

Karin's father. In general, Henry treats Karin a lot better than her mother does, but Calera wears the pants in this particular family. Henry has also chosen to keep his European last name.

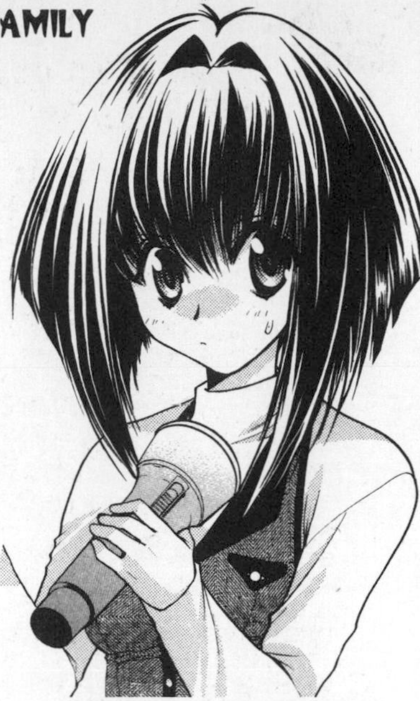

KARIN MAAKA

Our little heroine. Karin is a vampire living in Japan, but instead of sucking blood from her victims, she actually GIVES them some of her blood. She's a vampire in reverse!

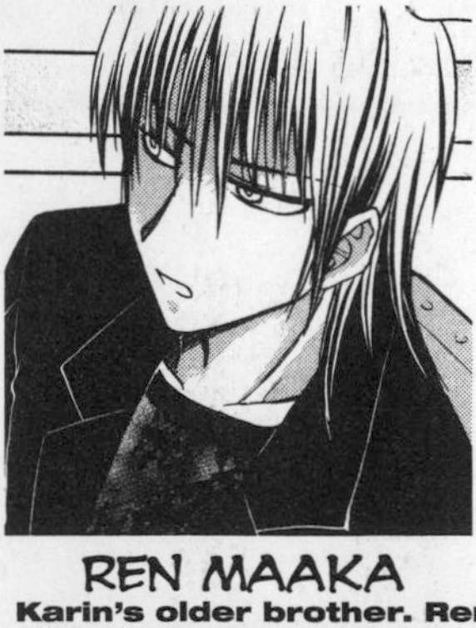

REN MAAKA

Karin's older brother. Ren milks the "sexy creature of the night" thing for all it's worth and spends his nights in the arms (and beds) of attractive young women.

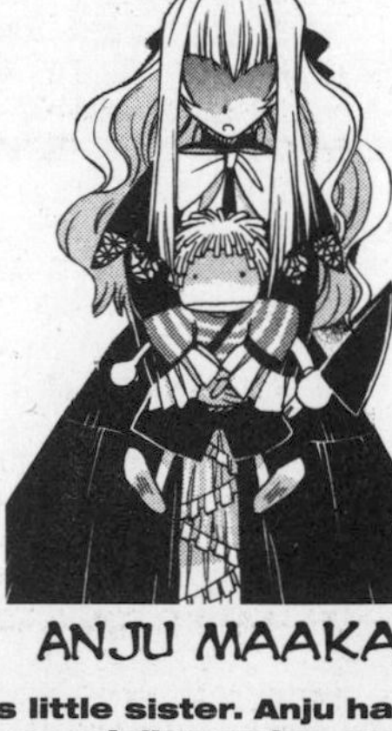

ANJU MAAKA

Karin's little sister. Anju has awoken as a full vampire, and is usually the one who cleans up after Karin's messes. Rarely seen without her "talking" doll, Boogie.

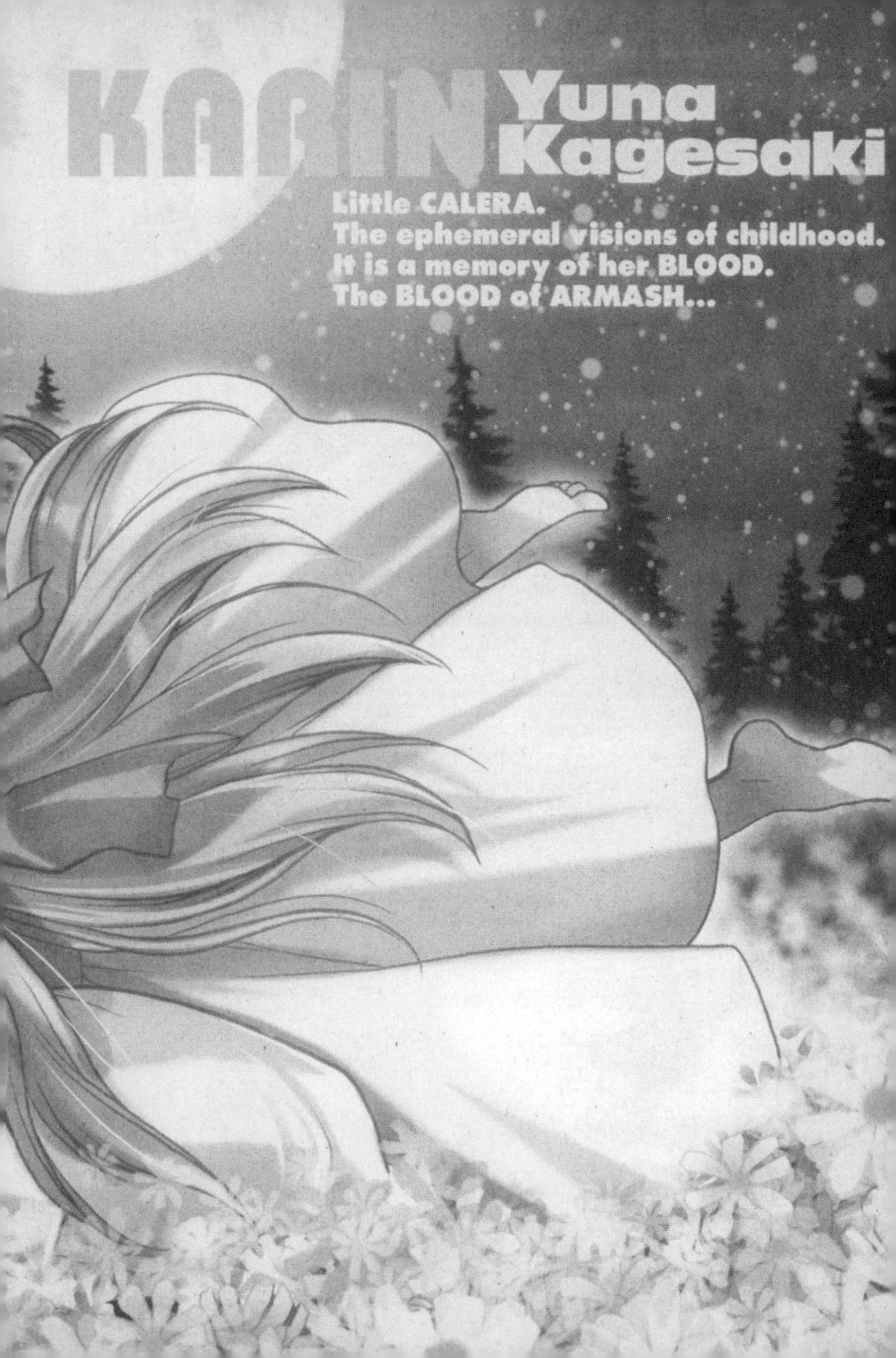
KARIN
Yuna Kagesaki
Little CALERA.
The ephemeral visions of childhood.
It is a memory of her BLOOD.
The BLOOD of ARMASH...

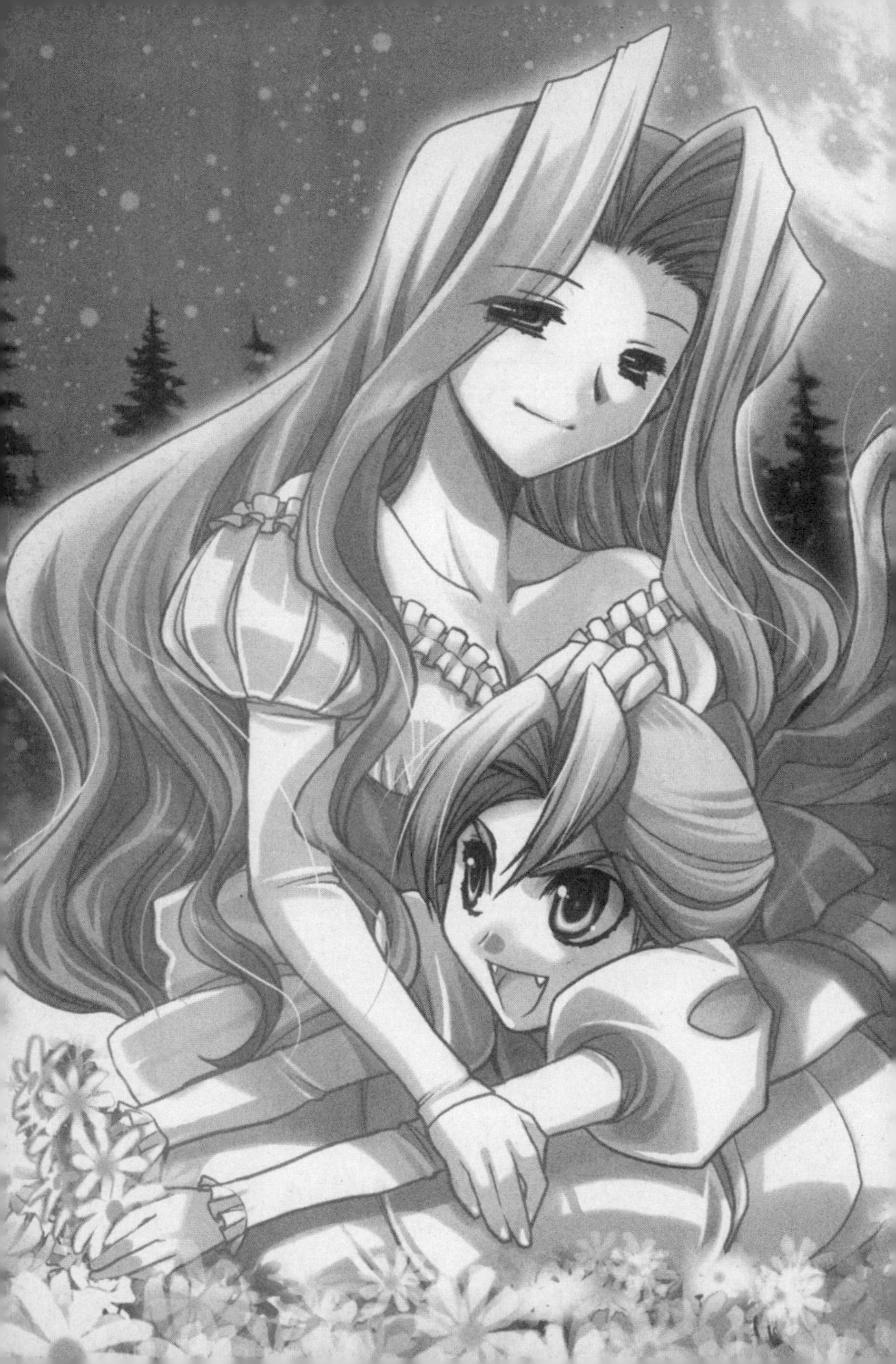

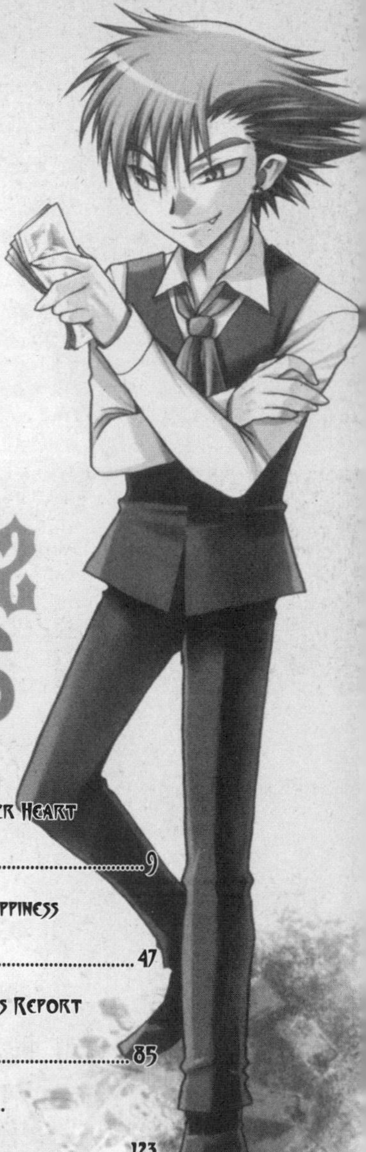

VOL. 12

CONTENTS

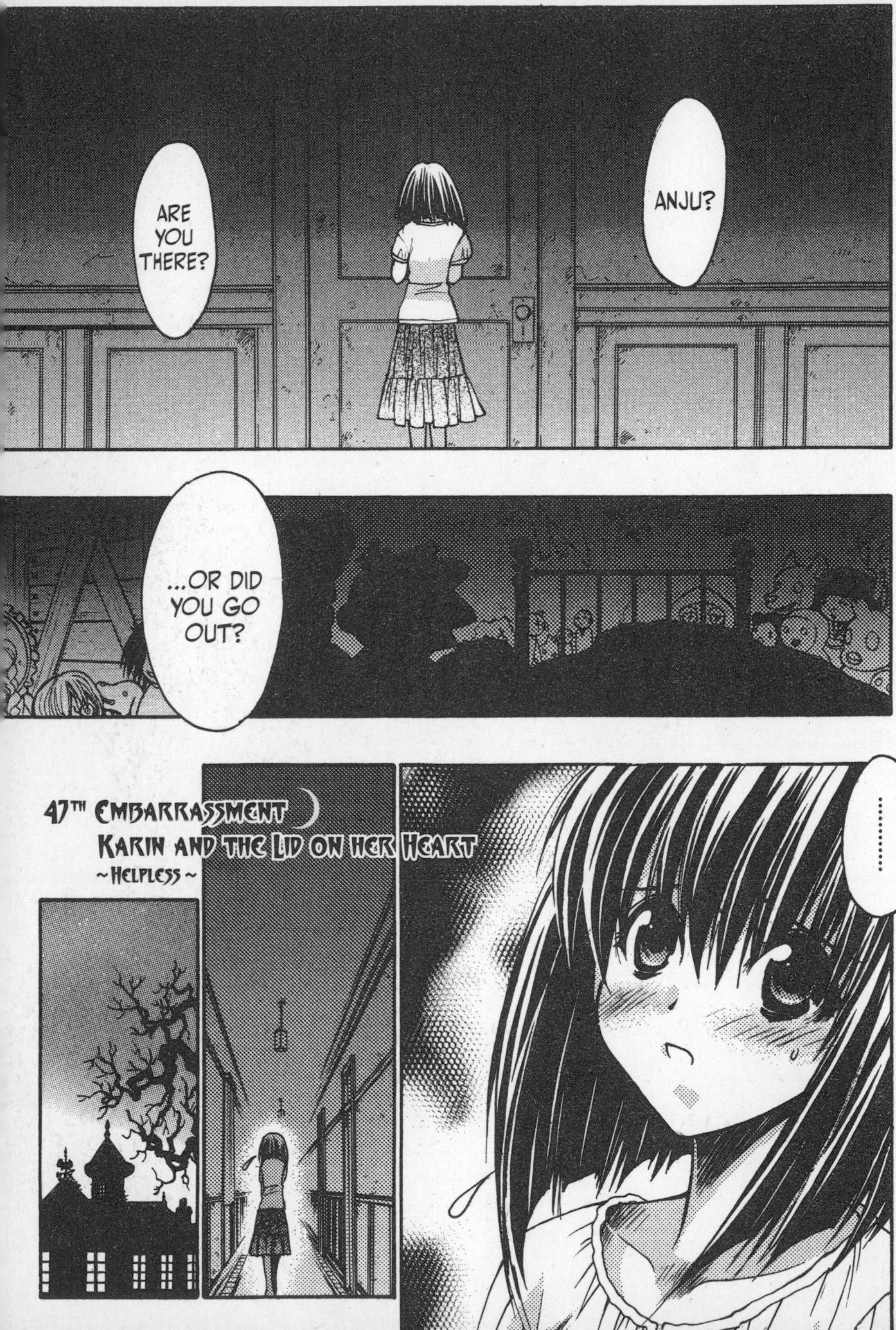
ANJU?
ARE YOU THERE?
...OR DID YOU GO OUT?
......
47TH EMBARRASSMENT
KARIN AND THE LID ON HER HEART
~HELPLESS~

47TH EMBARRASSMENT) KARIN AND THE LID ON HER HEART
~HELPLESS~

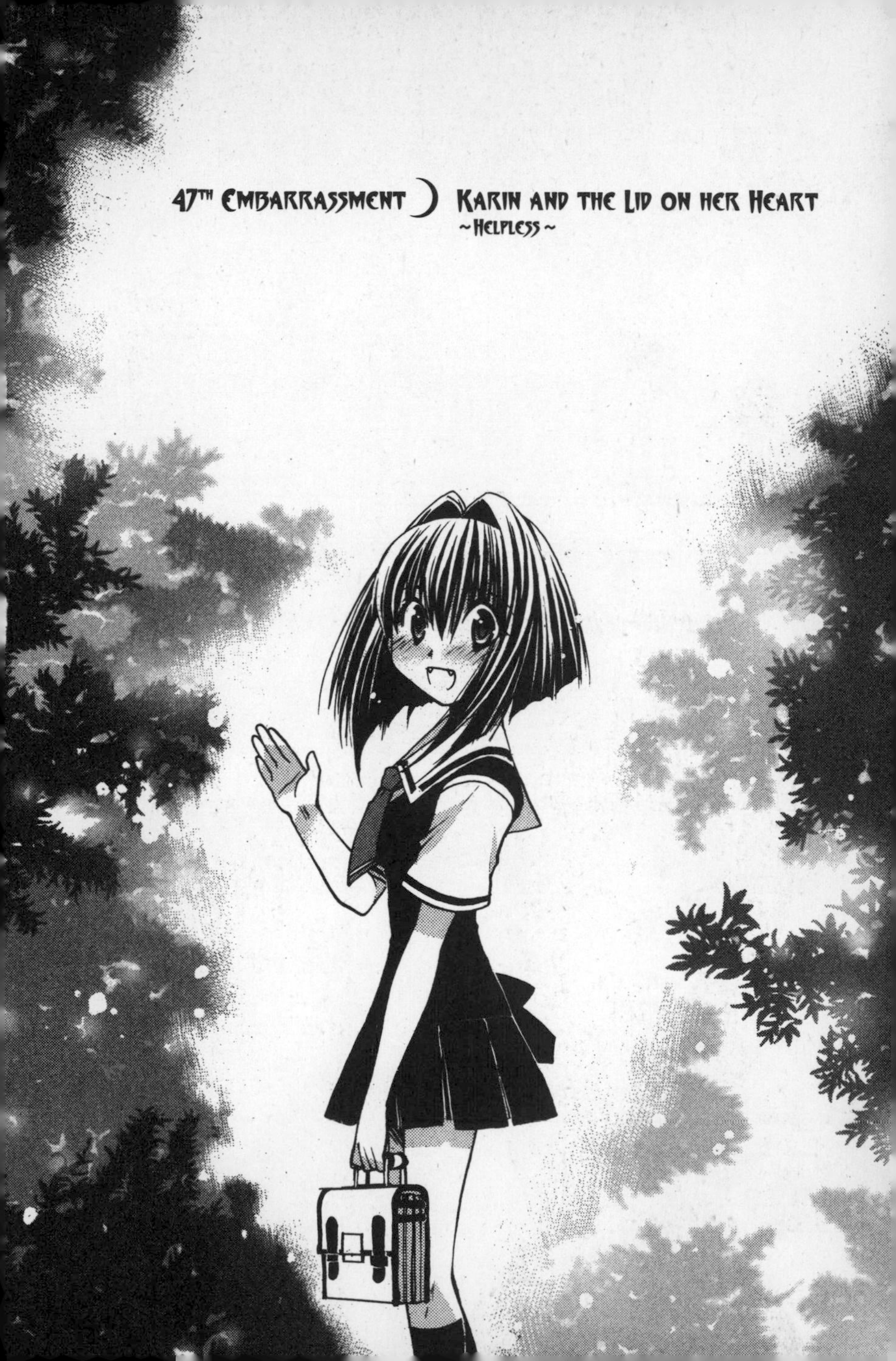

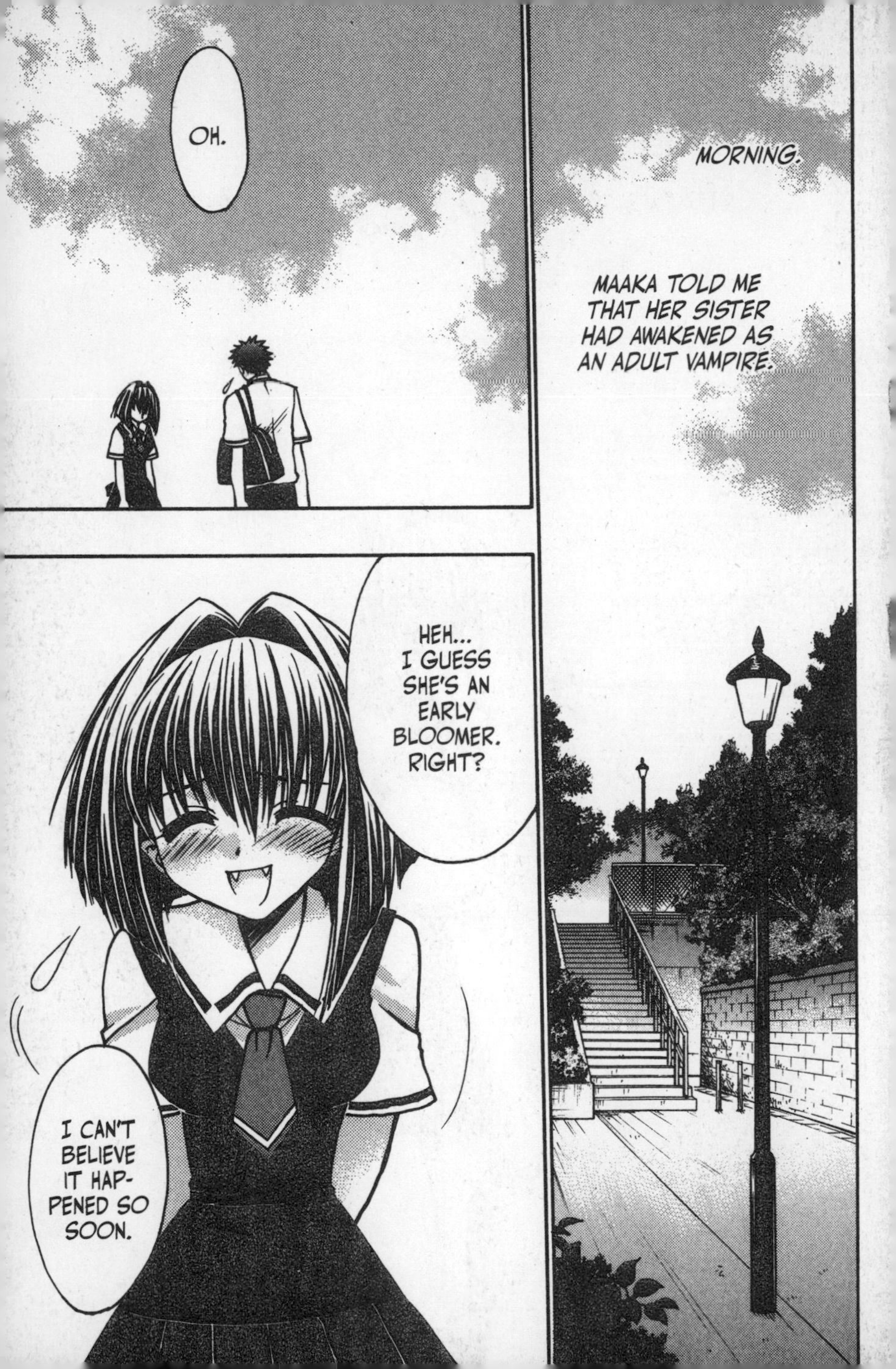
MORNING.
MAAKA TOLD ME THAT HER SISTER HAD AWAKENED AS AN ADULT VAMPIRE.
OH.
HEH... I GUESS SHE'S AN EARLY BLOOMER. RIGHT?
I CAN'T BELIEVE IT HAP-PENED SO SOON.

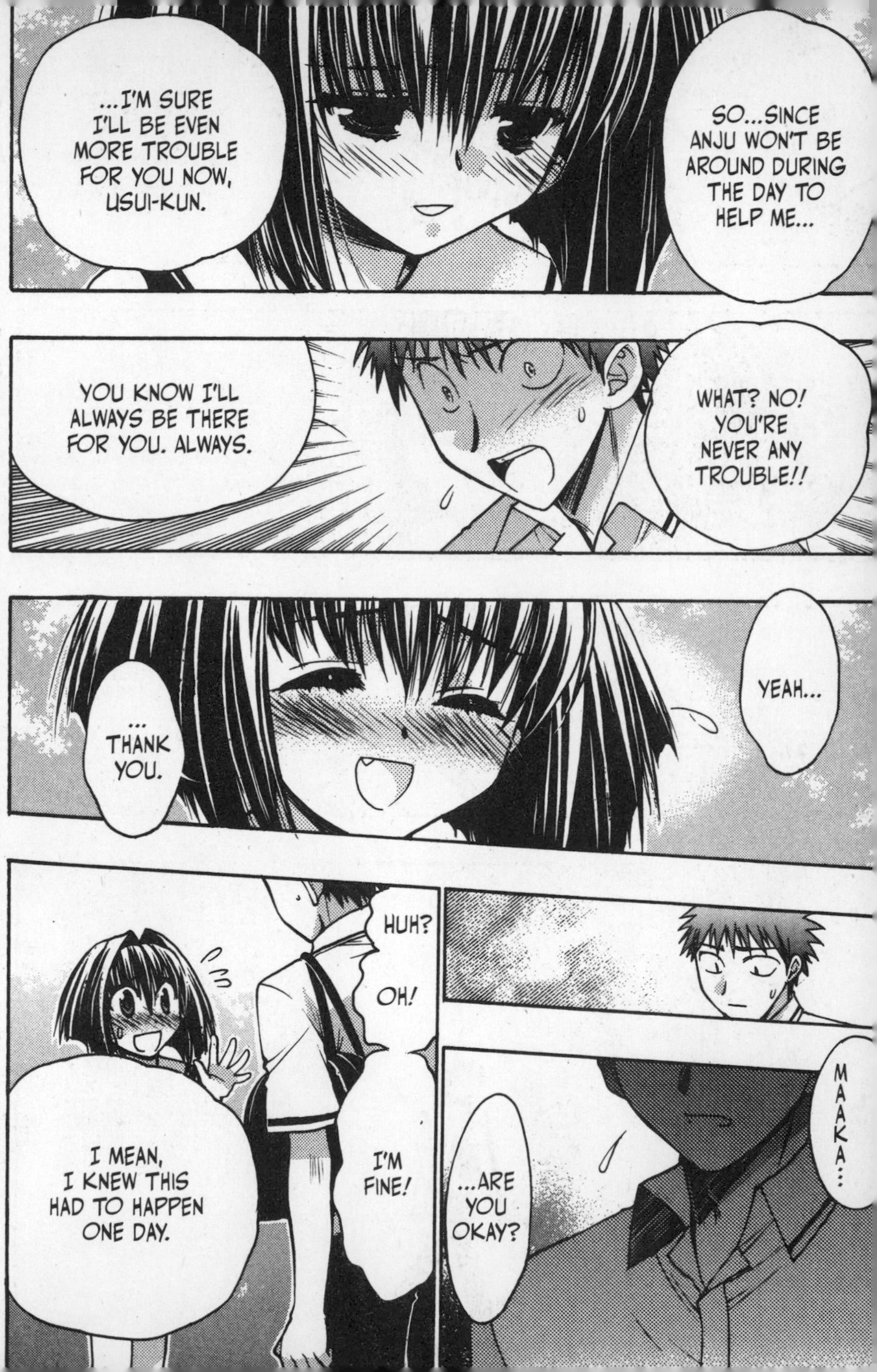
SO...SINCE ANJU WON'T BE AROUND DURING THE DAY TO HELP ME...
...I'M SURE I'LL BE EVEN MORE TROUBLE FOR YOU NOW, USUI-KUN.
WHAT? NO! YOU'RE NEVER ANY TROUBLE!!
YOU KNOW I'LL ALWAYS BE THERE FOR YOU. ALWAYS.
YEAH...
...THANK YOU.
MAAKA...
...ARE YOU OKAY?
HUH?
OH!
I'M FINE!
I MEAN, I KNEW THIS HAD TO HAPPEN ONE DAY.

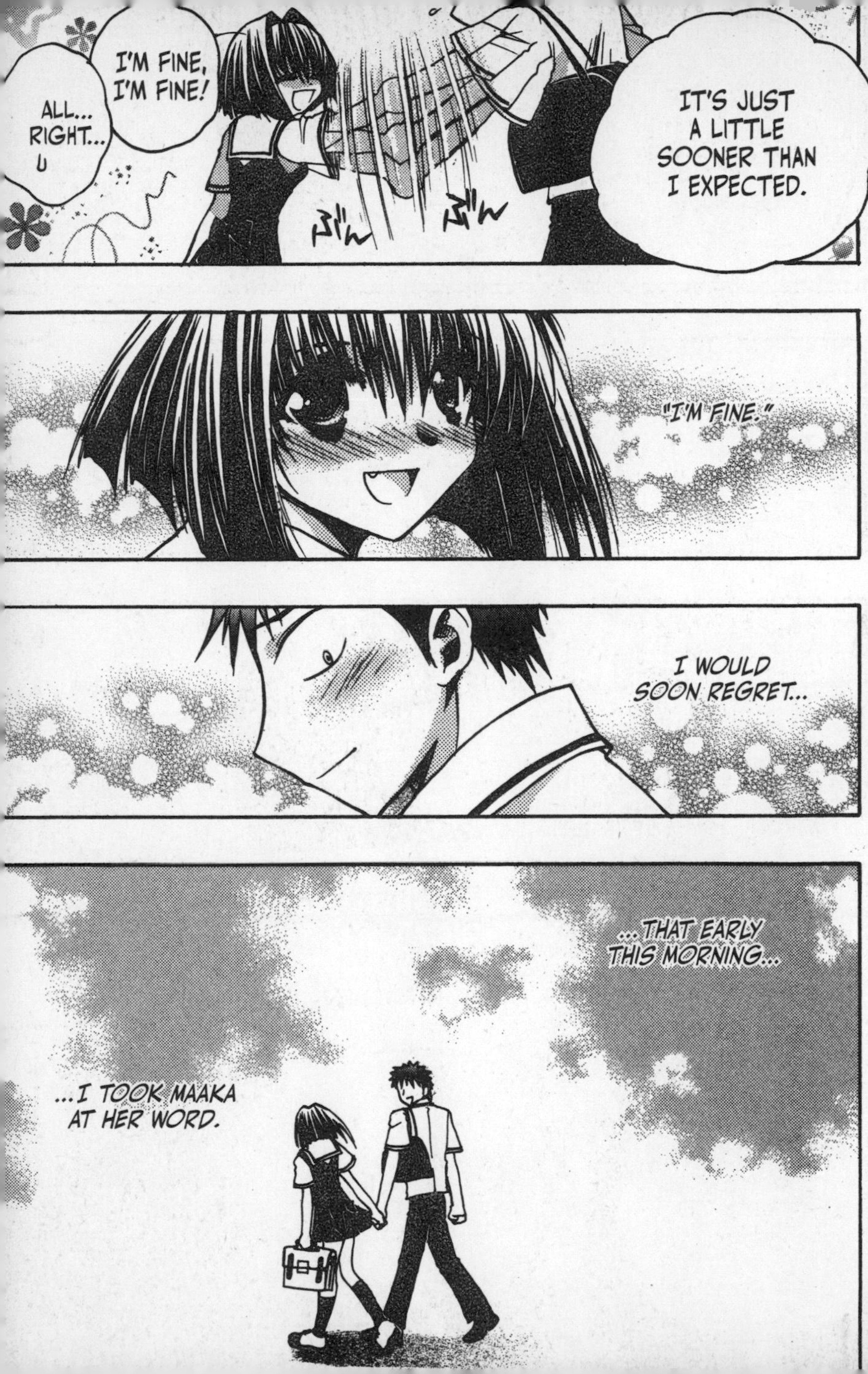
IT'S JUST A LITTLE SOONER THAN I EXPECTED.
ぶん
ぶん
I'M FINE, I'M FINE!
ALL... RIGHT...
"I'M FINE."
I WOULD SOON REGRET...
...THAT EARLY THIS MORNING...
...I TOOK MAAKA AT HER WORD.

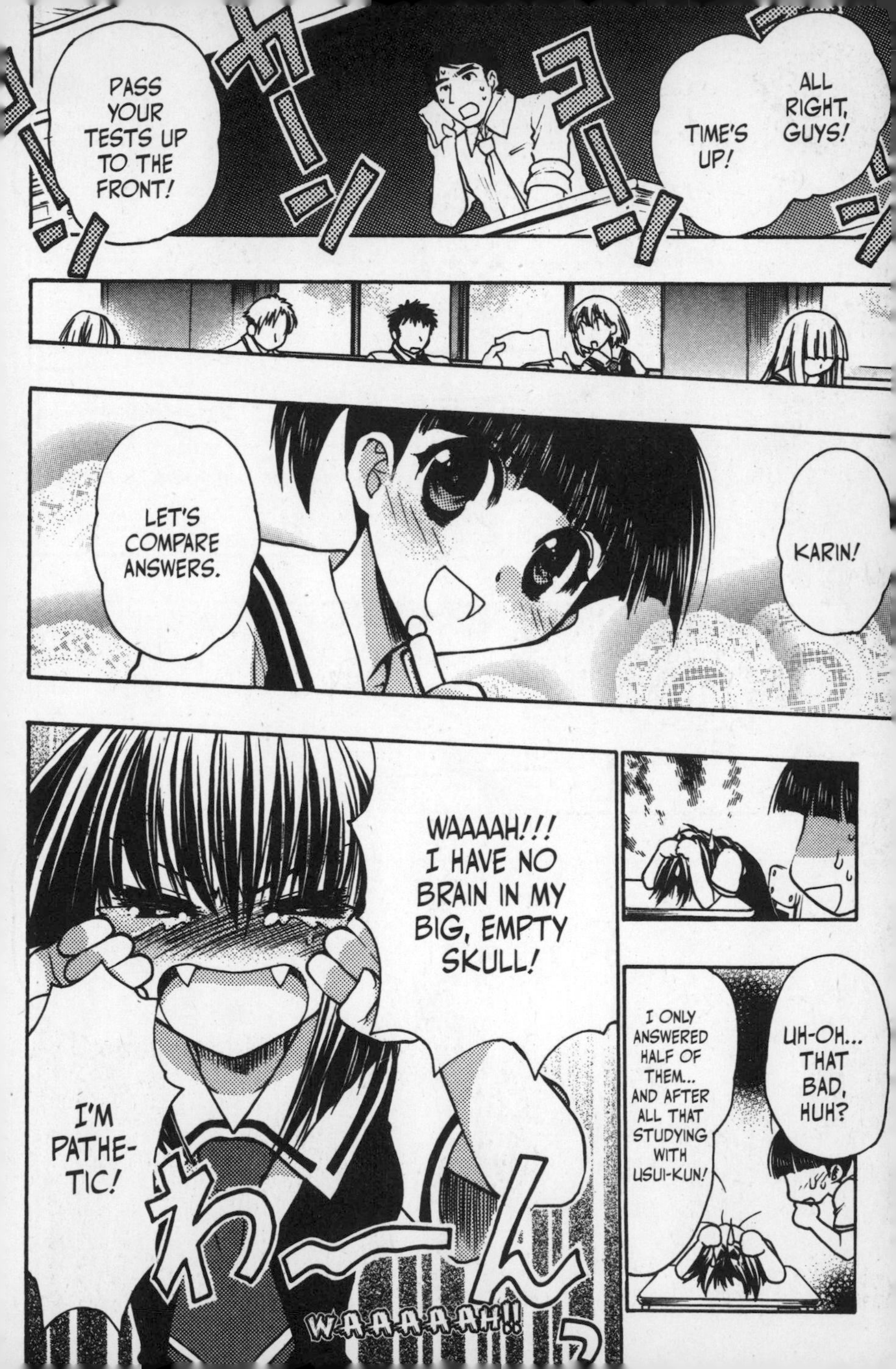

ALL RIGHT, GUYS!
TIME'S UP!
PASS YOUR TESTS UP TO THE FRONT!
KARIN!
LET'S COMPARE ANSWERS.
UH-OH... THAT BAD, HUH?
I ONLY ANSWERED HALF OF THEM... AND AFTER ALL THAT STUDYING WITH USUI-KUN!
WAAAAH!!! I HAVE NO BRAIN IN MY BIG, EMPTY SKULL!
I'M PATHE-TIC!
わ～ん
WAAAAAAH!!

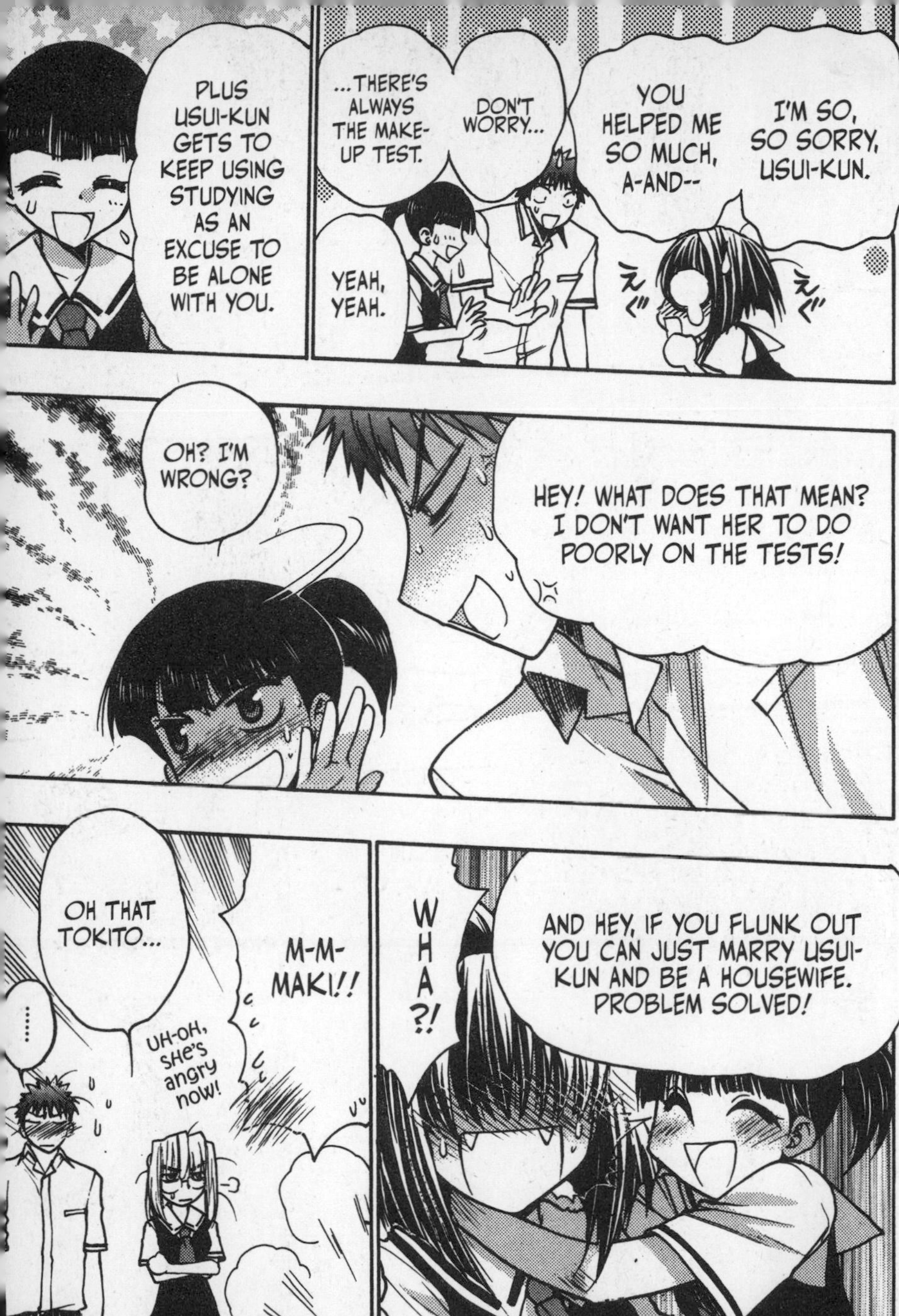
I'M SO, SO SORRY, USUI-KUN.
YOU HELPED ME SO MUCH, A-AND--
えぐ
えぐ
DON'T WORRY...
...THERE'S ALWAYS THE MAKE-UP TEST.
YEAH, YEAH.
PLUS USUI-KUN GETS TO KEEP USING STUDYING AS AN EXCUSE TO BE ALONE WITH YOU.
HEY! WHAT DOES THAT MEAN? I DON'T WANT HER TO DO POORLY ON THE TESTS!
OH? I'M WRONG?
AND HEY, IF YOU FLUNK OUT YOU CAN JUST MARRY USUI-KUN AND BE A HOUSEWIFE. PROBLEM SOLVED!
WHA?!
M-M-MAKI!!
UH-OH, SHE's angry now!
OH THAT TOKITO...
......

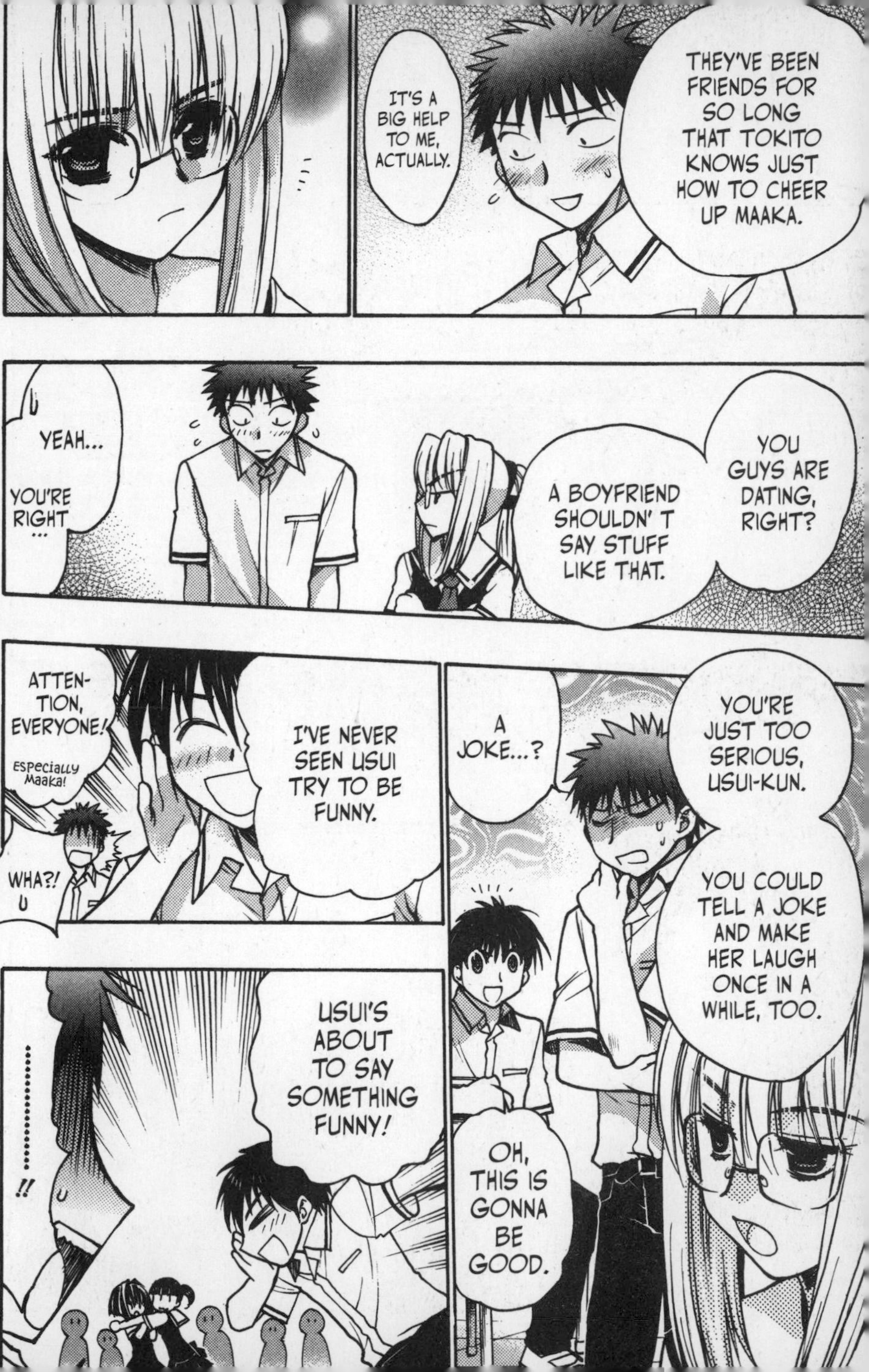
THEY'VE BEEN FRIENDS FOR SO LONG THAT TOKITO KNOWS JUST HOW TO CHEER UP MAAKA.
IT'S A BIG HELP TO ME, ACTUALLY.
YOU GUYS ARE DATING, RIGHT?
A BOYFRIEND SHOULDN' T SAY STUFF LIKE THAT.
YEAH...
YOU'RE RIGHT...
YOU'RE JUST TOO SERIOUS, USUI-KUN.
YOU COULD TELL A JOKE AND MAKE HER LAUGH ONCE IN A WHILE, TOO.
A JOKE...?
OH, THIS IS GONNA BE GOOD.
I'VE NEVER SEEN USUI TRY TO BE FUNNY.
ATTENTION, EVERYONE!
Especially Maaka!
WHA?!
USUI'S ABOUT TO SAY SOMETHING FUNNY!
..........!!

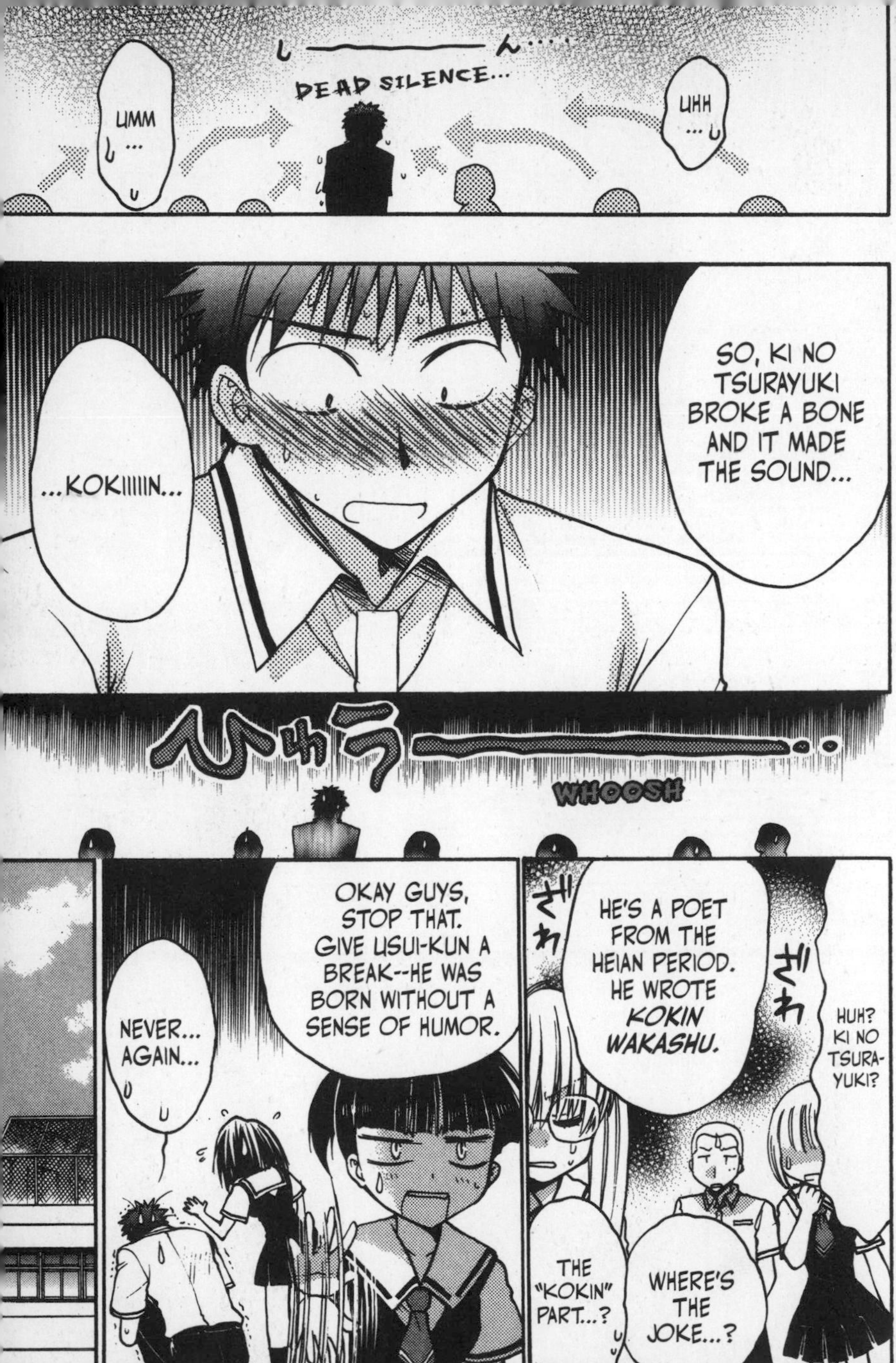
し―――ん…
DEAD SILENCE...
UHH ...
UMM ...
SO, KI NO TSURAYUKI BROKE A BONE AND IT MADE THE SOUND...
...KOKIIIIIN...
ひゅう―――
WHOOSH
ざわ
ざわ
HUH? KI NO TSURA-YUKI?
HE'S A POET FROM THE HEIAN PERIOD. HE WROTE KOKIN WAKASHU.
WHERE'S THE JOKE...?
THE "KOKIN" PART...?
OKAY GUYS, STOP THAT. GIVE USUI-KUN A BREAK--HE WAS BORN WITHOUT A SENSE OF HUMOR.
NEVER... AGAIN...

Thanks for the bad pun, Ruu Itsuki!

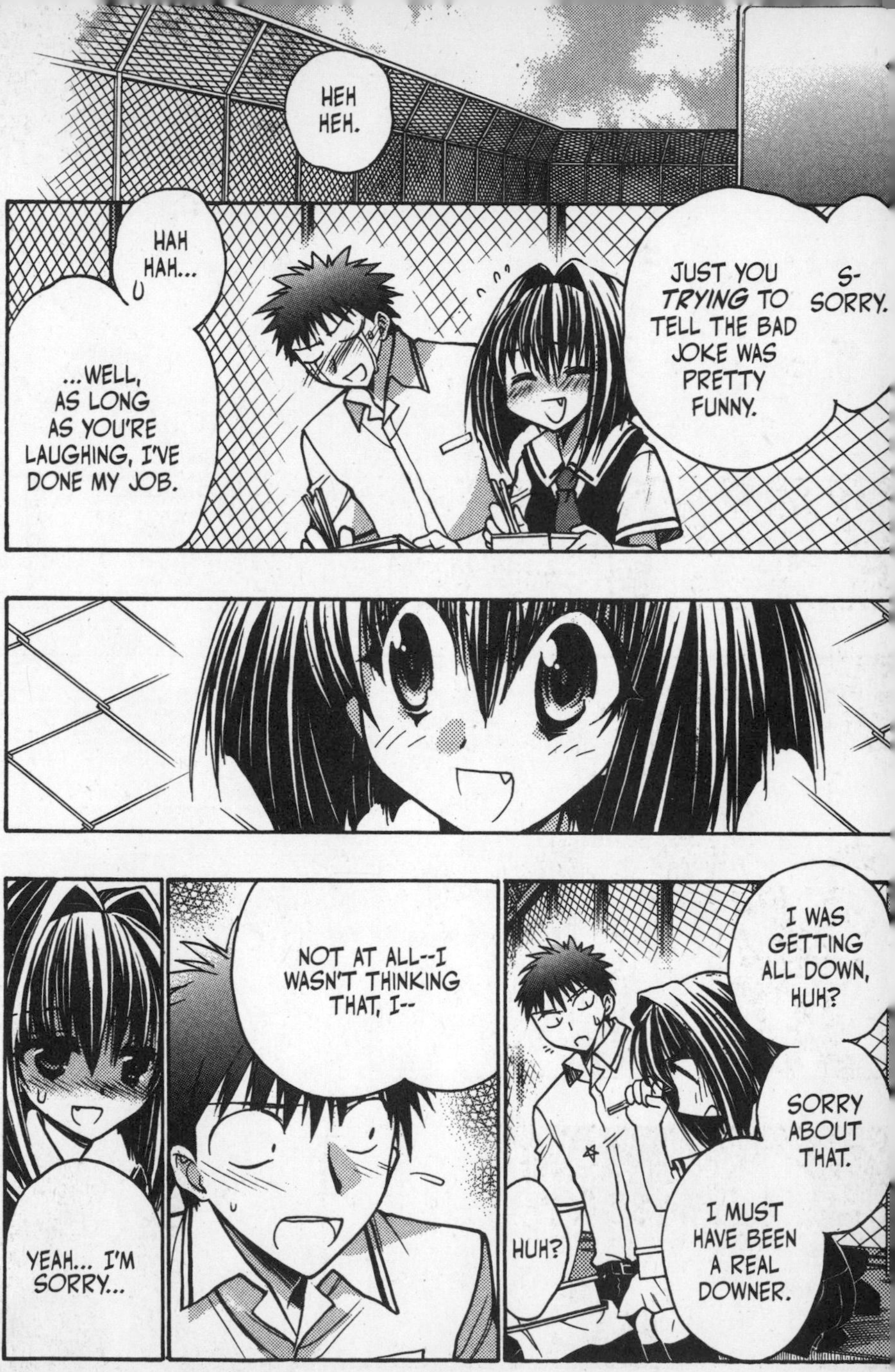
HEH HEH.
S-SORRY.
JUST YOU TRYING TO TELL THE BAD JOKE WAS PRETTY FUNNY.
HAH HAH...
...WELL, AS LONG AS YOU'RE LAUGHING, I'VE DONE MY JOB.
I WAS GETTING ALL DOWN, HUH?
SORRY ABOUT THAT.
I MUST HAVE BEEN A REAL DOWNER.
HUH?
NOT AT ALL--I WASN'T THINKING THAT, I--
YEAH... I'M SORRY...

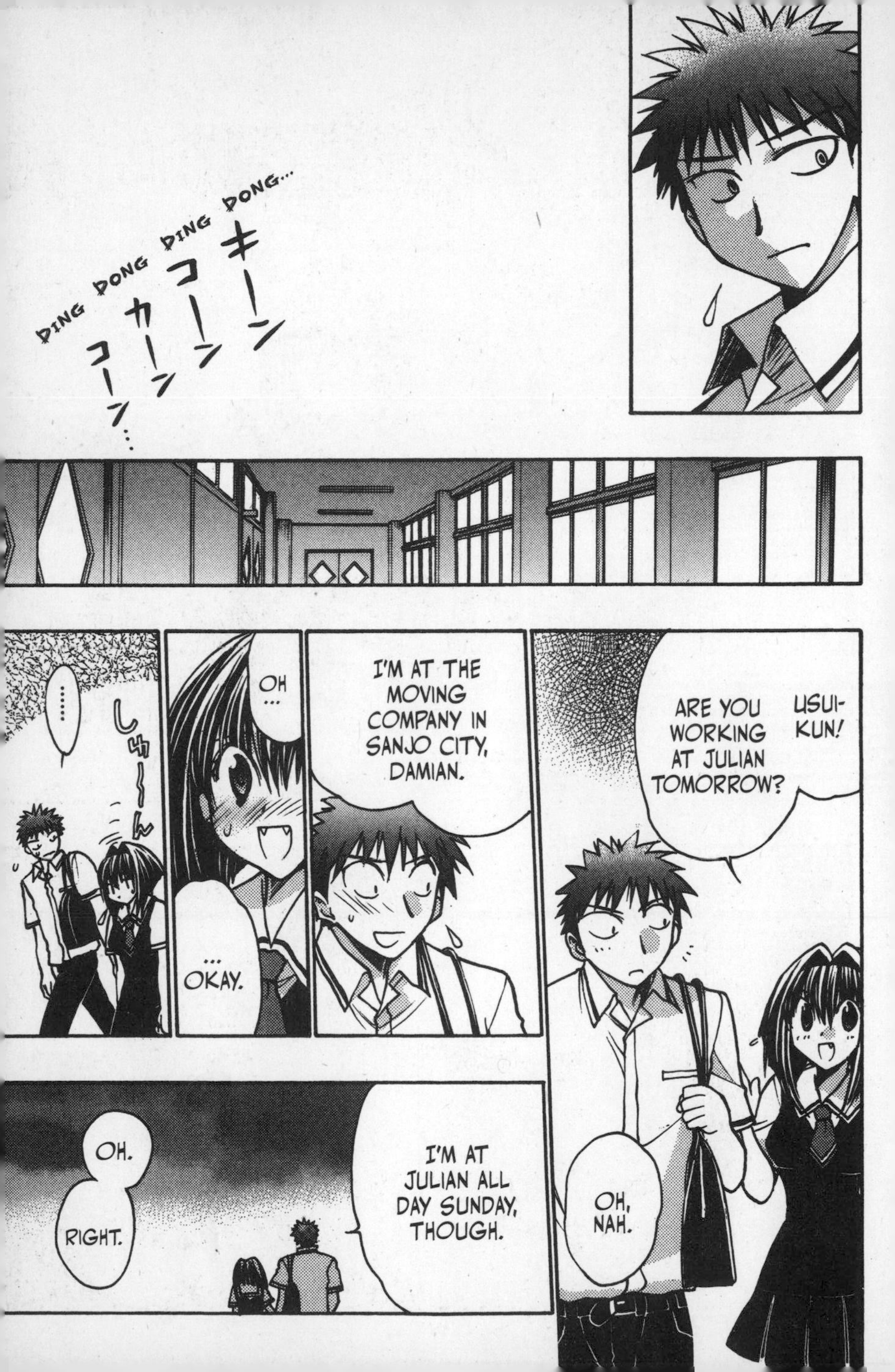
DING DONG DING DONG...
キーン
コーン
カーン
コーン…
USUI-KUN!
ARE YOU WORKING AT JULIAN TOMORROW?
OH, NAH.
I'M AT THE MOVING COMPANY IN SANJO CITY, DAMIAN.
OH ...
... OKAY.
......
しゅ~ん
I'M AT JULIAN ALL DAY SUNDAY, THOUGH.
OH.
RIGHT.

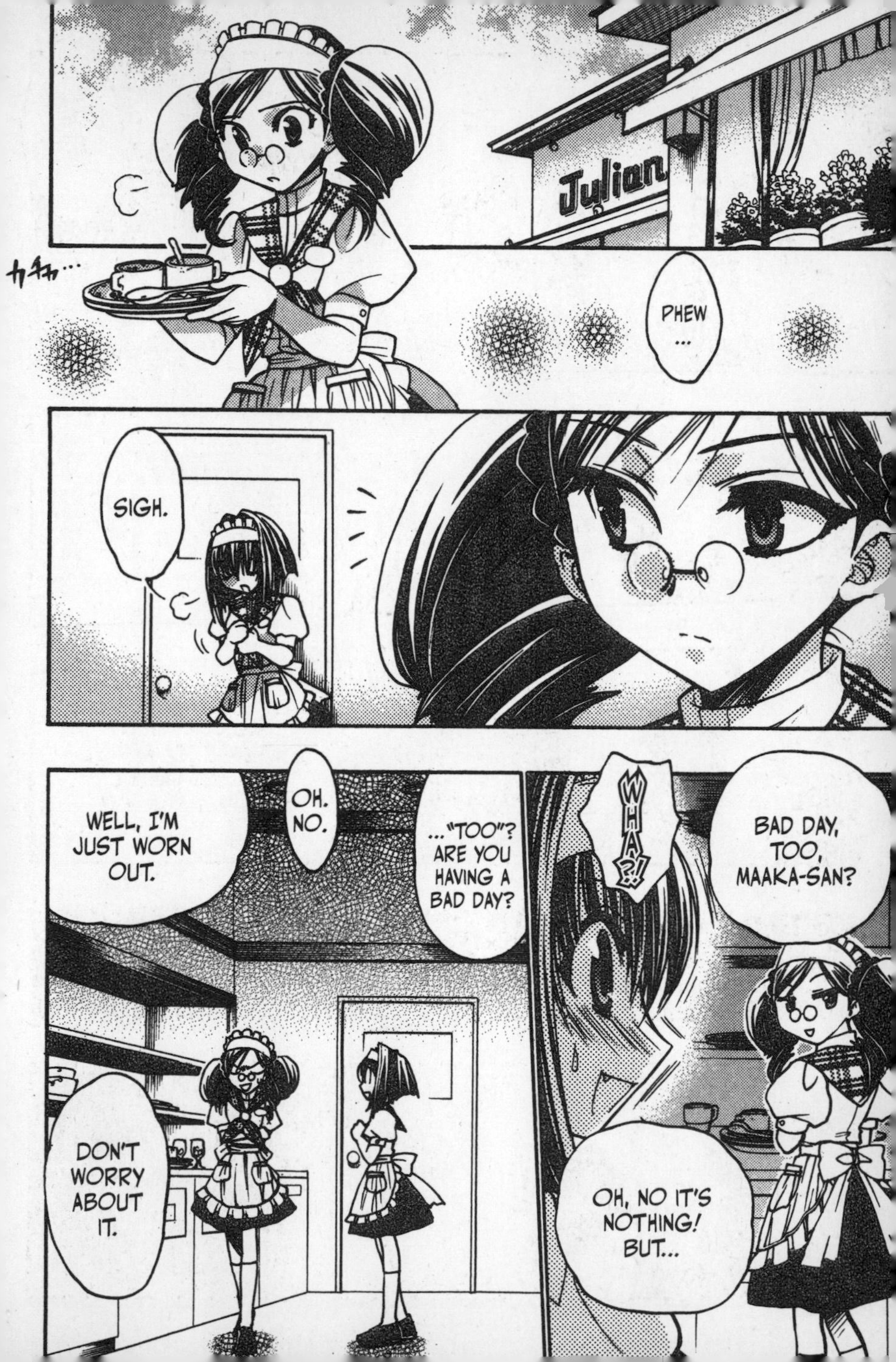
Julian
カチャ…
PHEW ...
SIGH.
BAD DAY, TOO, MAAKA-SAN?
WHA?!
..."TOO"? ARE YOU HAVING A BAD DAY?
OH. NO.
WELL, I'M JUST WORN OUT.
OH, NO IT'S NOTHING! BUT...
DON'T WORRY ABOUT IT.

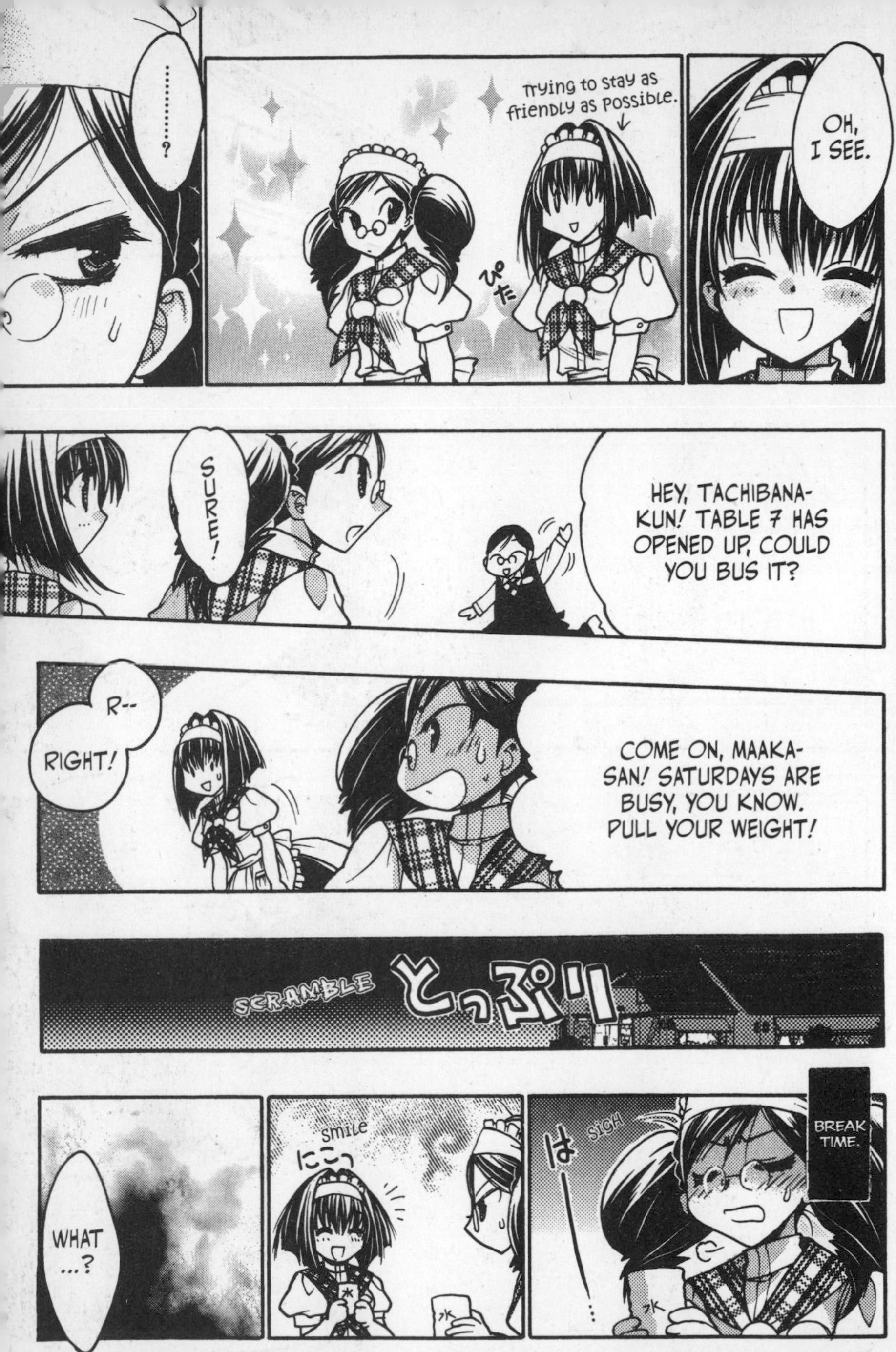
OH, I SEE.
Trying to stay as friendly as possible.
ぴた
......?
HEY, TACHIBANA-KUN! TABLE 7 HAS OPENED UP, COULD YOU BUS IT?
SURE!
COME ON, MAAKA-SAN! SATURDAYS ARE BUSY, YOU KNOW. PULL YOUR WEIGHT!
R-- RIGHT!
SCRAMBLE
とっぷり
BREAK TIME.
SIGH
は--...
水
SMILE
にこっ
水
水
WHAT ...?

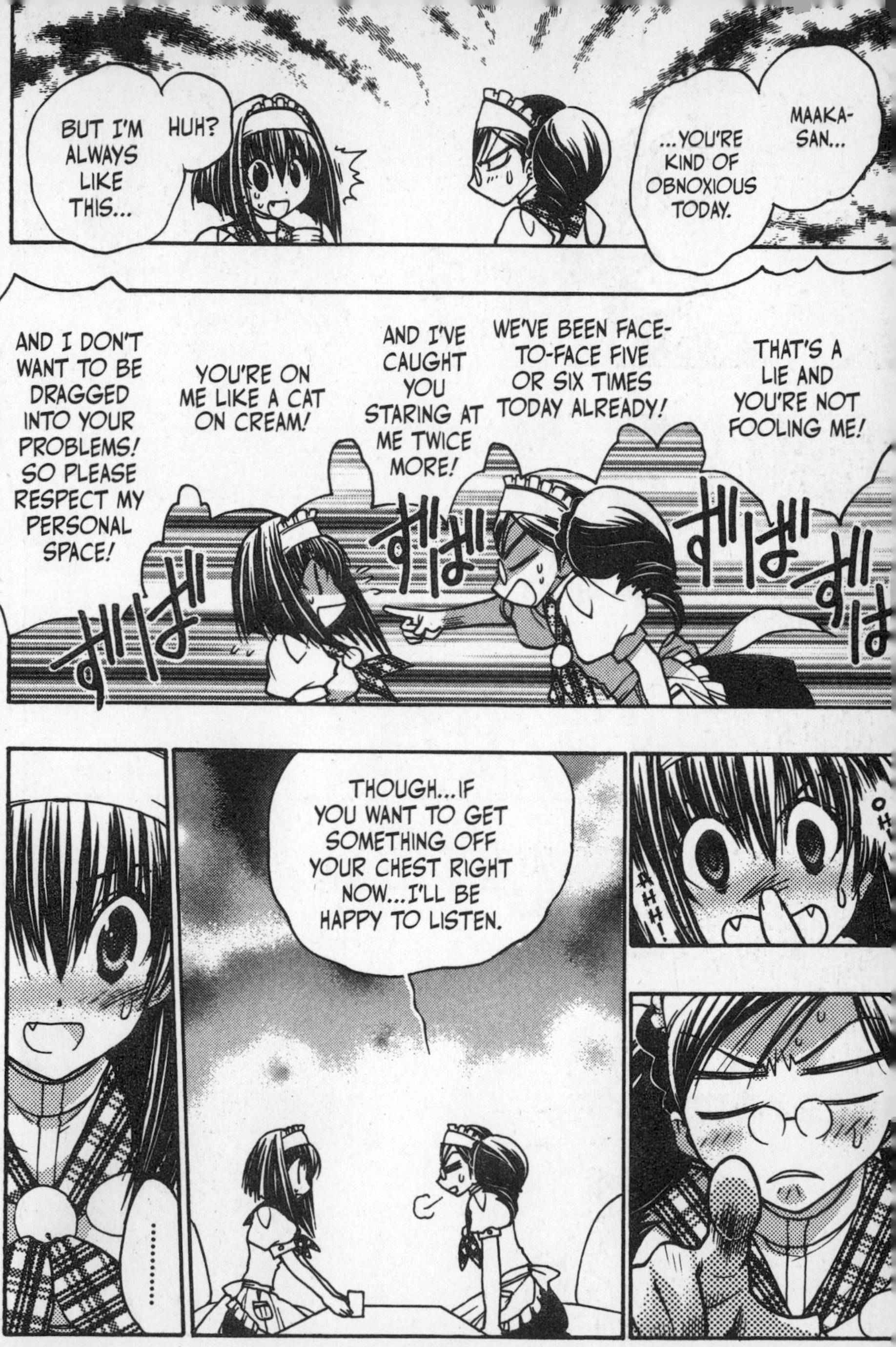
MAAKA-SAN...
...YOU'RE KIND OF OBNOXIOUS TODAY.
HUH?
BUT I'M ALWAYS LIKE THIS...
THAT'S A LIE AND YOU'RE NOT FOOLING ME!
WE'VE BEEN FACE-TO-FACE FIVE OR SIX TIMES TODAY ALREADY!
AND I'VE CAUGHT YOU STARING AT ME TWICE MORE!
YOU'RE ON ME LIKE A CAT ON CREAM!
AND I DON'T WANT TO BE DRAGGED INTO YOUR PROBLEMS! SO PLEASE RESPECT MY PERSONAL SPACE!
OH!
AHH!
THOUGH...IF YOU WANT TO GET SOMETHING OFF YOUR CHEST RIGHT NOW...I'LL BE HAPPY TO LISTEN.
....

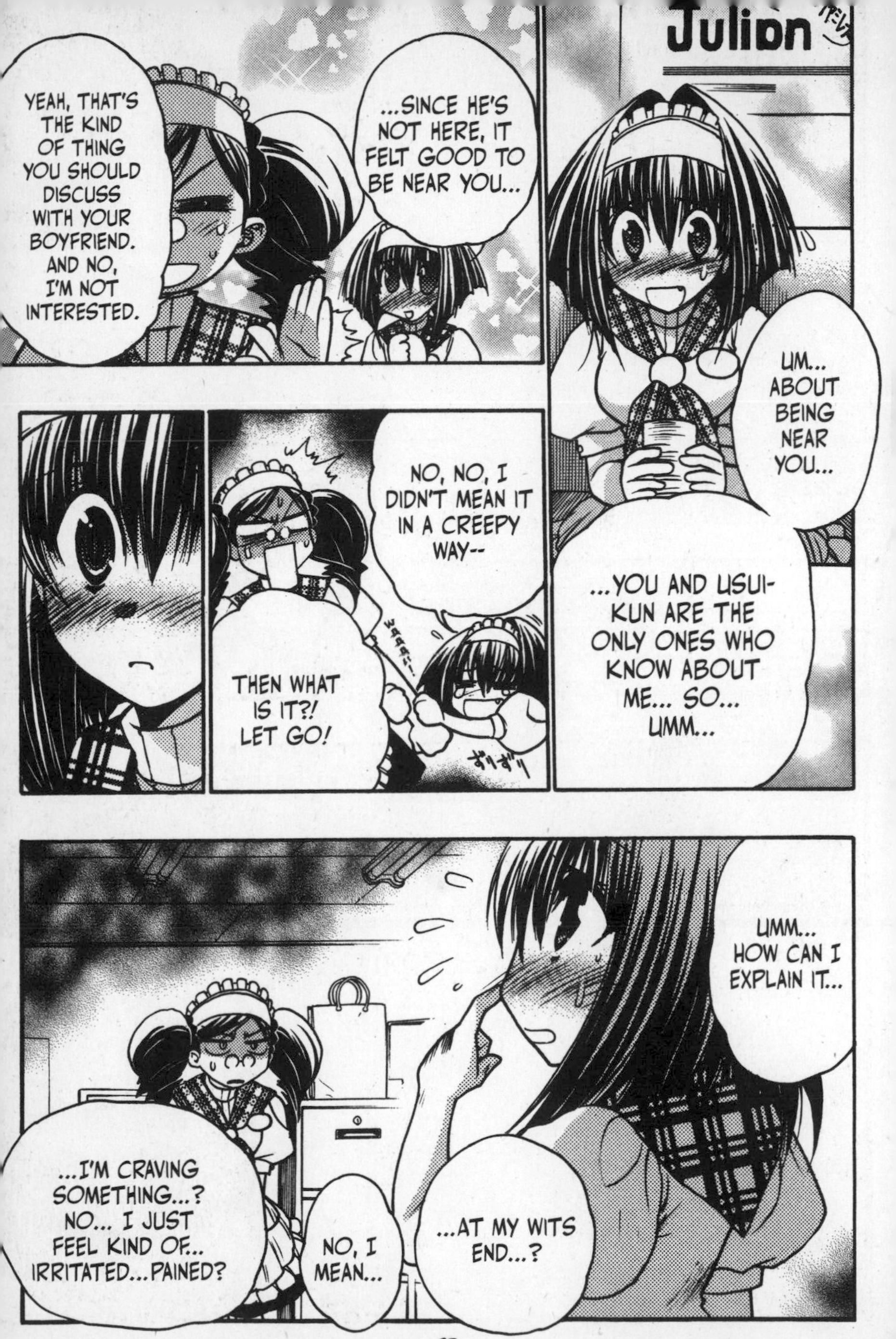
Julion
UM... ABOUT BEING NEAR YOU...
...YOU AND USUI-KUN ARE THE ONLY ONES WHO KNOW ABOUT ME... SO... UMM...
...SINCE HE'S NOT HERE, IT FELT GOOD TO BE NEAR YOU...
YEAH, THAT'S THE KIND OF THING YOU SHOULD DISCUSS WITH YOUR BOYFRIEND. AND NO, I'M NOT INTERESTED.
NO, NO, I DIDN'T MEAN IT IN A CREEPY WAY--
THEN WHAT IS IT?! LET GO!
UMM... HOW CAN I EXPLAIN IT...
...AT MY WITS END...?
NO, I MEAN...
...I'M CRAVING SOMETHING...? NO... I JUST FEEL KIND OF... IRRITATED...PAINED?

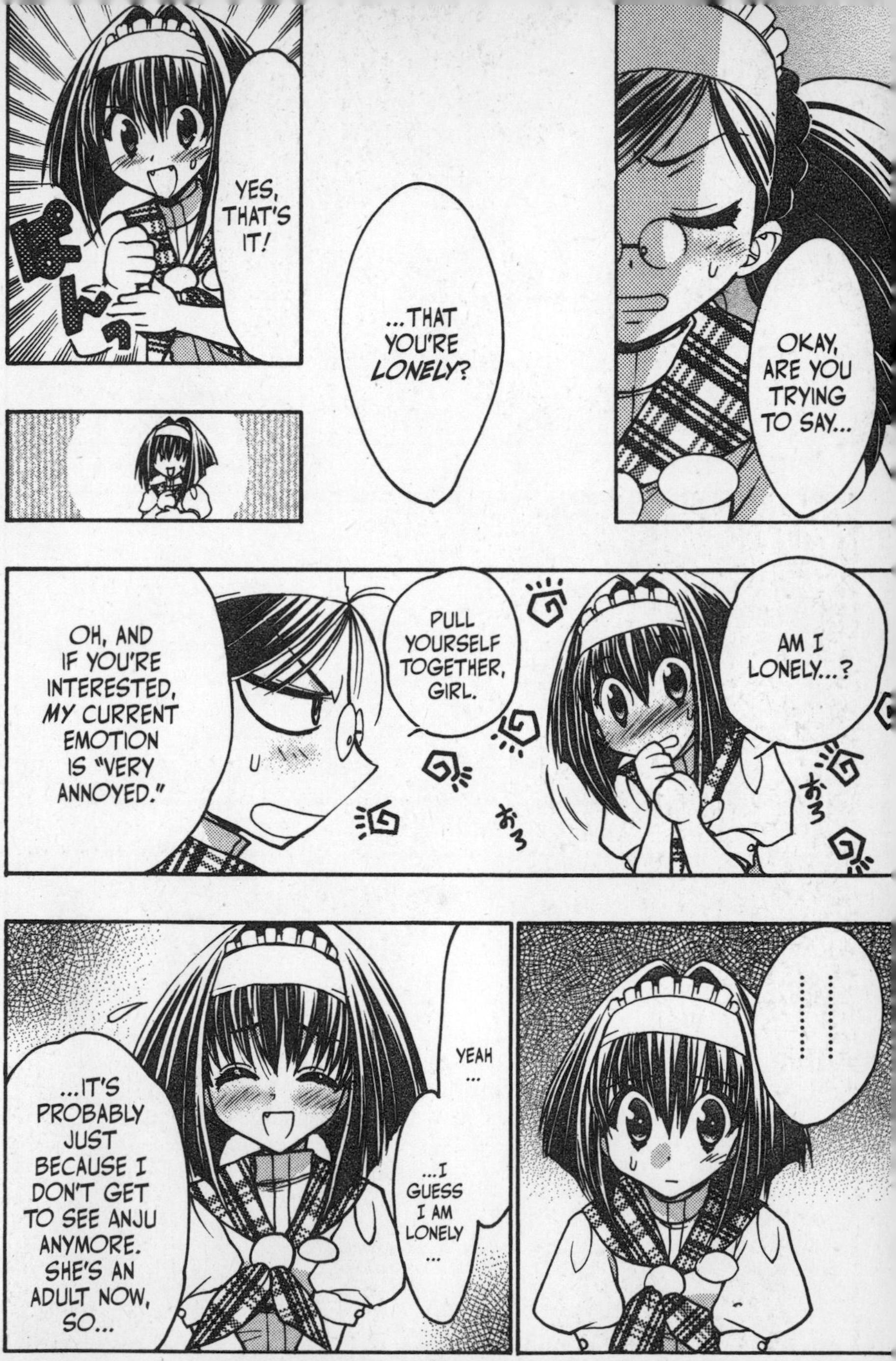
OKAY, ARE YOU TRYING TO SAY...
...THAT YOU'RE *LONELY*?
YES, THAT'S IT!
AM I LONELY...?
おろ
おろ
PULL YOURSELF TOGETHER, GIRL.
OH, AND IF YOU'RE INTERESTED, *MY* CURRENT EMOTION IS "VERY ANNOYED."
......!!
YEAH ...
...I GUESS I AM LONELY ...
...IT'S PROBABLY JUST BECAUSE I DON'T GET TO SEE ANJU ANYMORE. SHE'S AN ADULT NOW, SO...

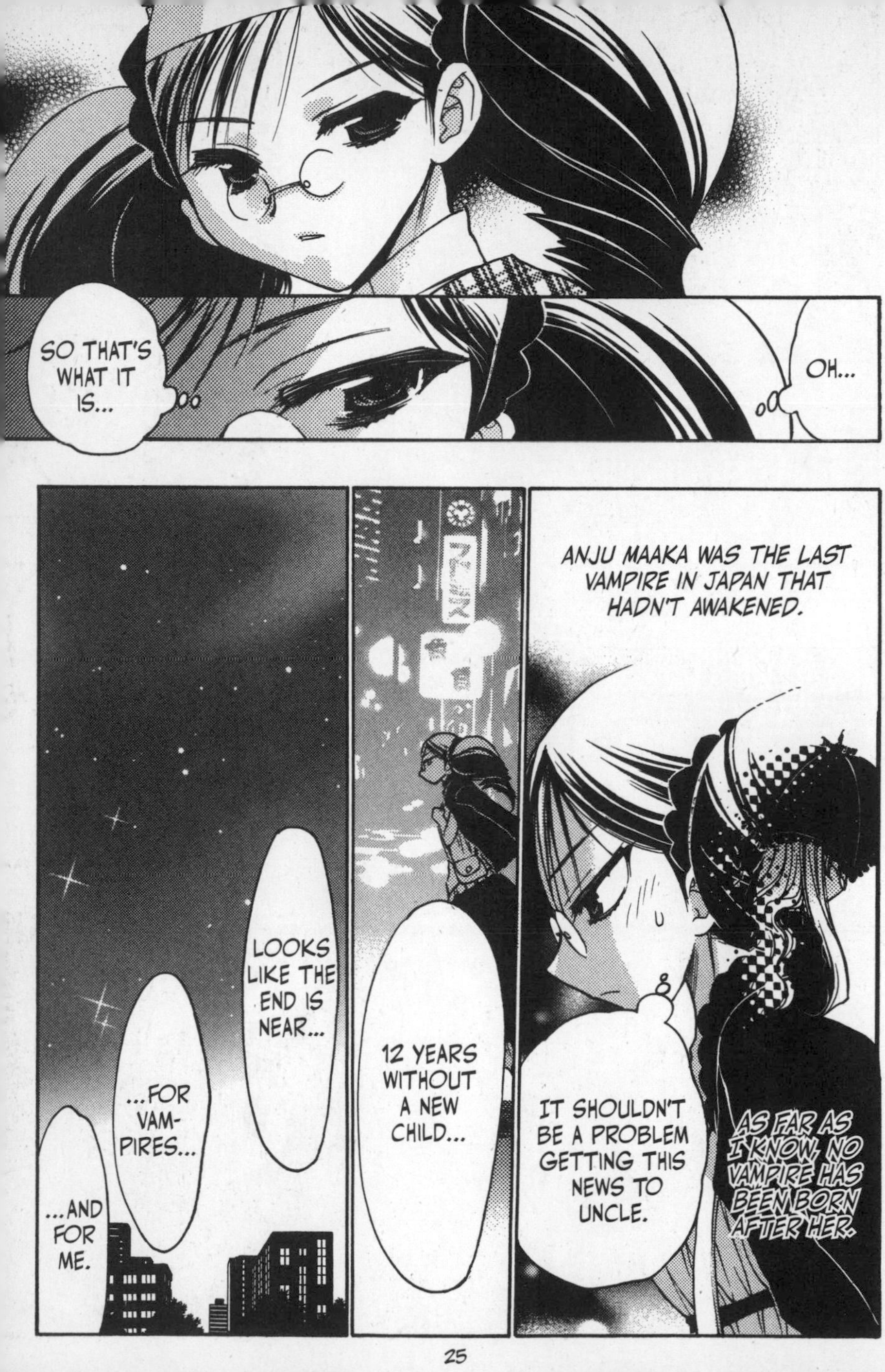
OH...
SO THAT'S WHAT IT IS...
ANJU MAAKA WAS THE LAST VAMPIRE IN JAPAN THAT HADN'T AWAKENED.
AS FAR AS I KNOW, NO VAMPIRE HAS BEEN BORN AFTER HER.
IT SHOULDN'T BE A PROBLEM GETTING THIS NEWS TO UNCLE.
12 YEARS WITHOUT A NEW CHILD...
LOOKS LIKE THE END IS NEAR...
...FOR VAMPIRES...
...AND FOR ME.

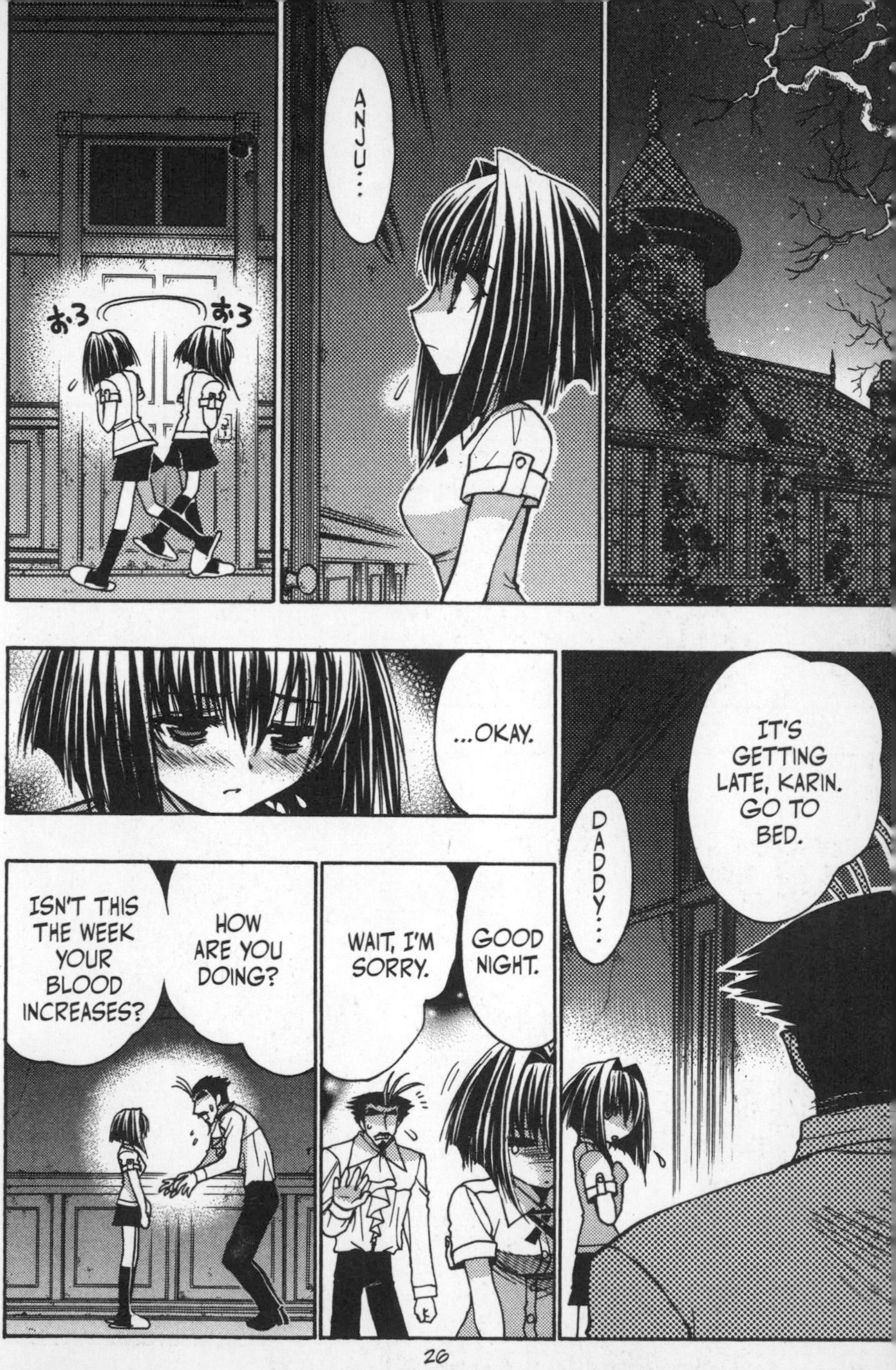
ANJU...
おろ おろ
IT'S GETTING LATE, KARIN. GO TO BED.
DADDY...
...OKAY.
GOOD NIGHT.
WAIT, I'M SORRY.
HOW ARE YOU DOING?
ISN'T THIS THE WEEK YOUR BLOOD INCREASES?

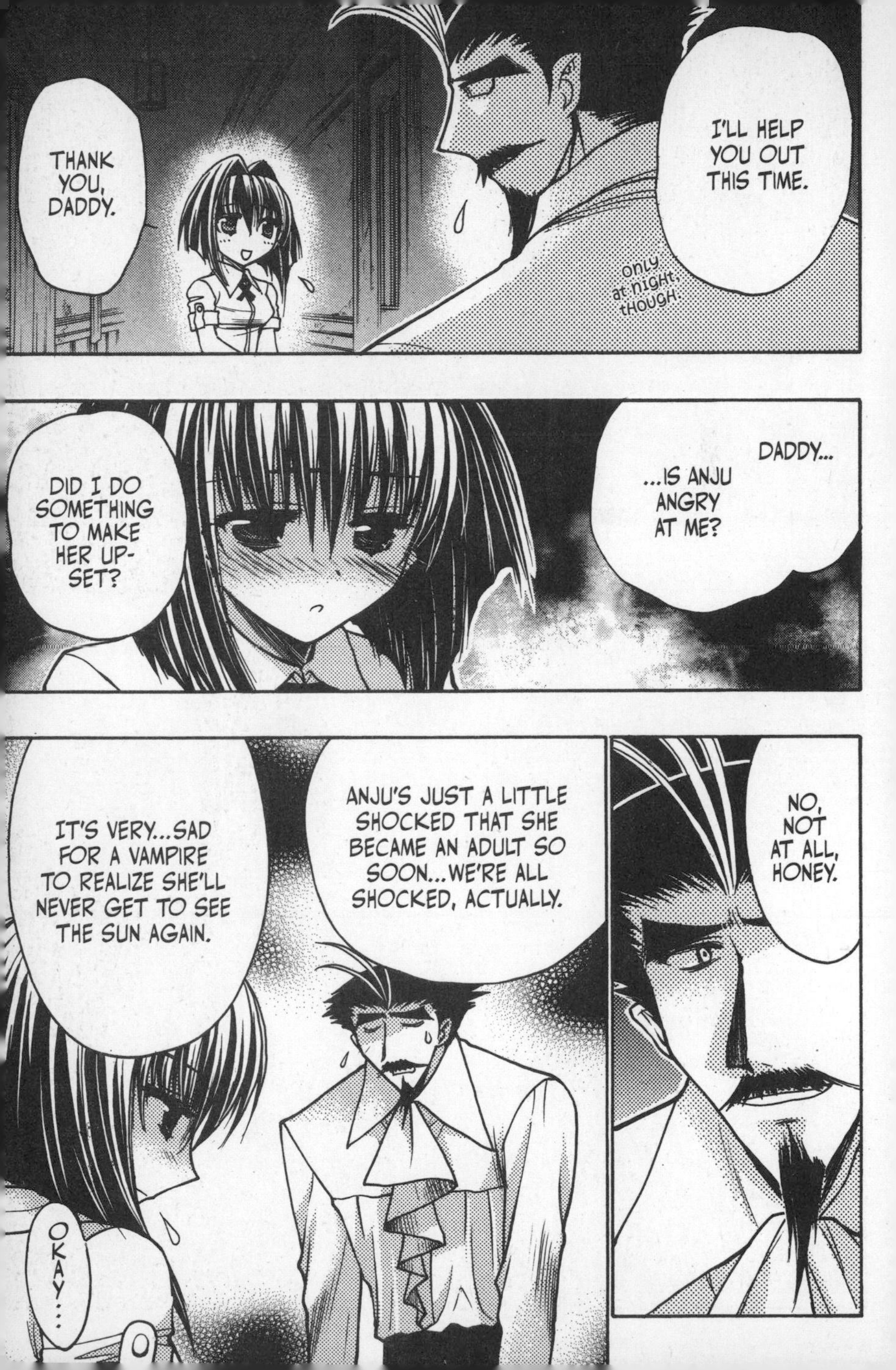

I'LL HELP YOU OUT THIS TIME.
Only at night, though.
THANK YOU, DADDY.
DADDY...
...IS ANJU ANGRY AT ME?
DID I DO SOMETHING TO MAKE HER UP-SET?
NO, NOT AT ALL, HONEY.
ANJU'S JUST A LITTLE SHOCKED THAT SHE BECAME AN ADULT SO SOON...WE'RE ALL SHOCKED, ACTUALLY.
IT'S VERY...SAD FOR A VAMPIRE TO REALIZE SHE'LL NEVER GET TO SEE THE SUN AGAIN.
OKAY...

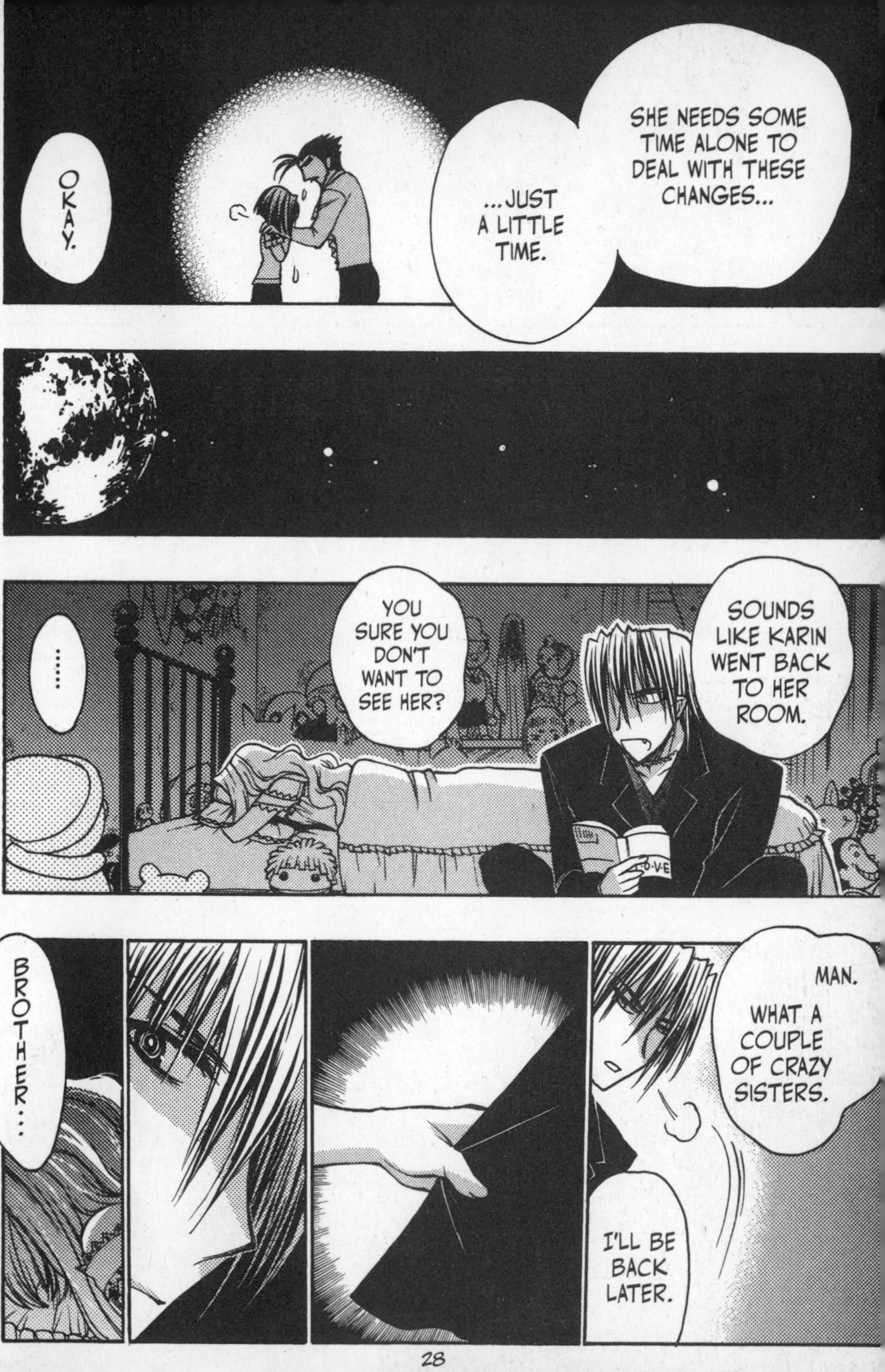
SHE NEEDS SOME TIME ALONE TO DEAL WITH THESE CHANGES...
...JUST A LITTLE TIME.
OKAY.
SOUNDS LIKE KARIN WENT BACK TO HER ROOM.
YOU SURE YOU DON'T WANT TO SEE HER?
......
MAN.
WHAT A COUPLE OF CRAZY SISTERS.
I'LL BE BACK LATER.
BROTHER...

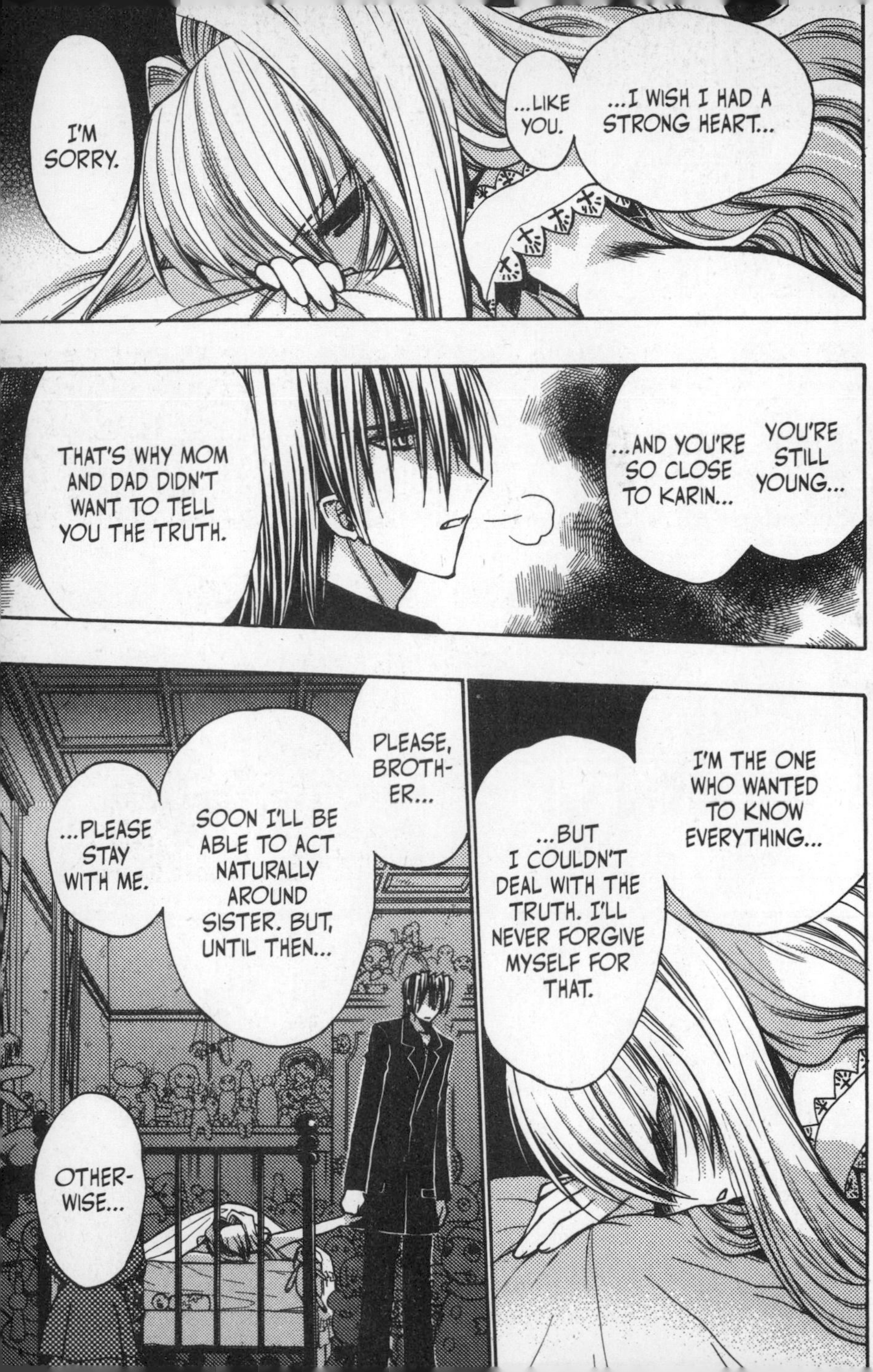
...I WISH I HAD A STRONG HEART...
...LIKE YOU.
I'M SORRY.
YOU'RE STILL YOUNG...
...AND YOU'RE SO CLOSE TO KARIN...
THAT'S WHY MOM AND DAD DIDN'T WANT TO TELL YOU THE TRUTH.
I'M THE ONE WHO WANTED TO KNOW EVERYTHING...
...BUT I COULDN'T DEAL WITH THE TRUTH. I'LL NEVER FORGIVE MYSELF FOR THAT.
PLEASE, BROTHER...
SOON I'LL BE ABLE TO ACT NATURALLY AROUND SISTER. BUT, UNTIL THEN...
...PLEASE STAY WITH ME.
OTHERWISE...

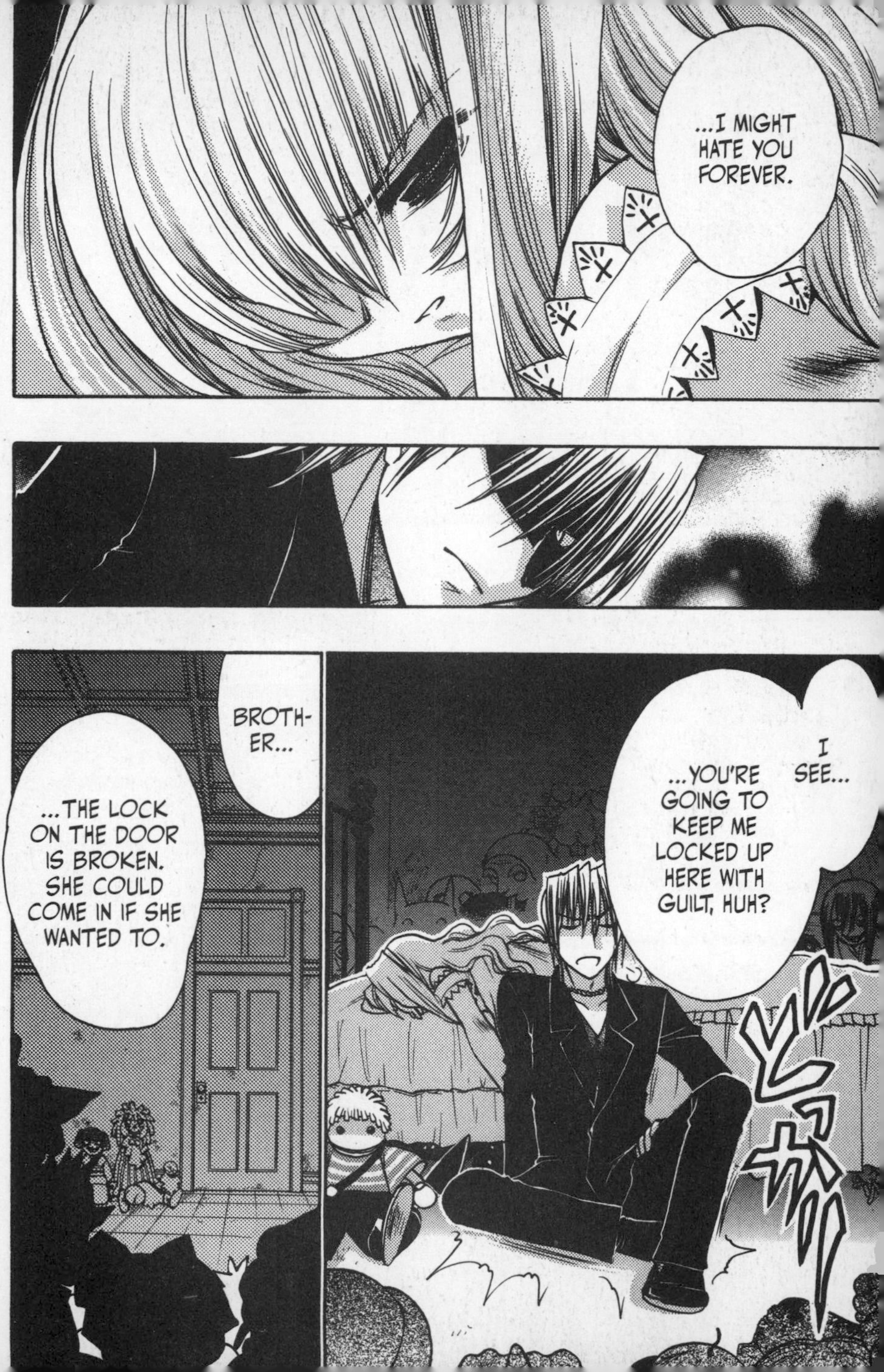
...I MIGHT HATE YOU FOREVER.
I SEE...
...YOU'RE GOING TO KEEP ME LOCKED UP HERE WITH GUILT, HUH?
BROTH-ER...
...THE LOCK ON THE DOOR IS BROKEN. SHE COULD COME IN IF SHE WANTED TO.

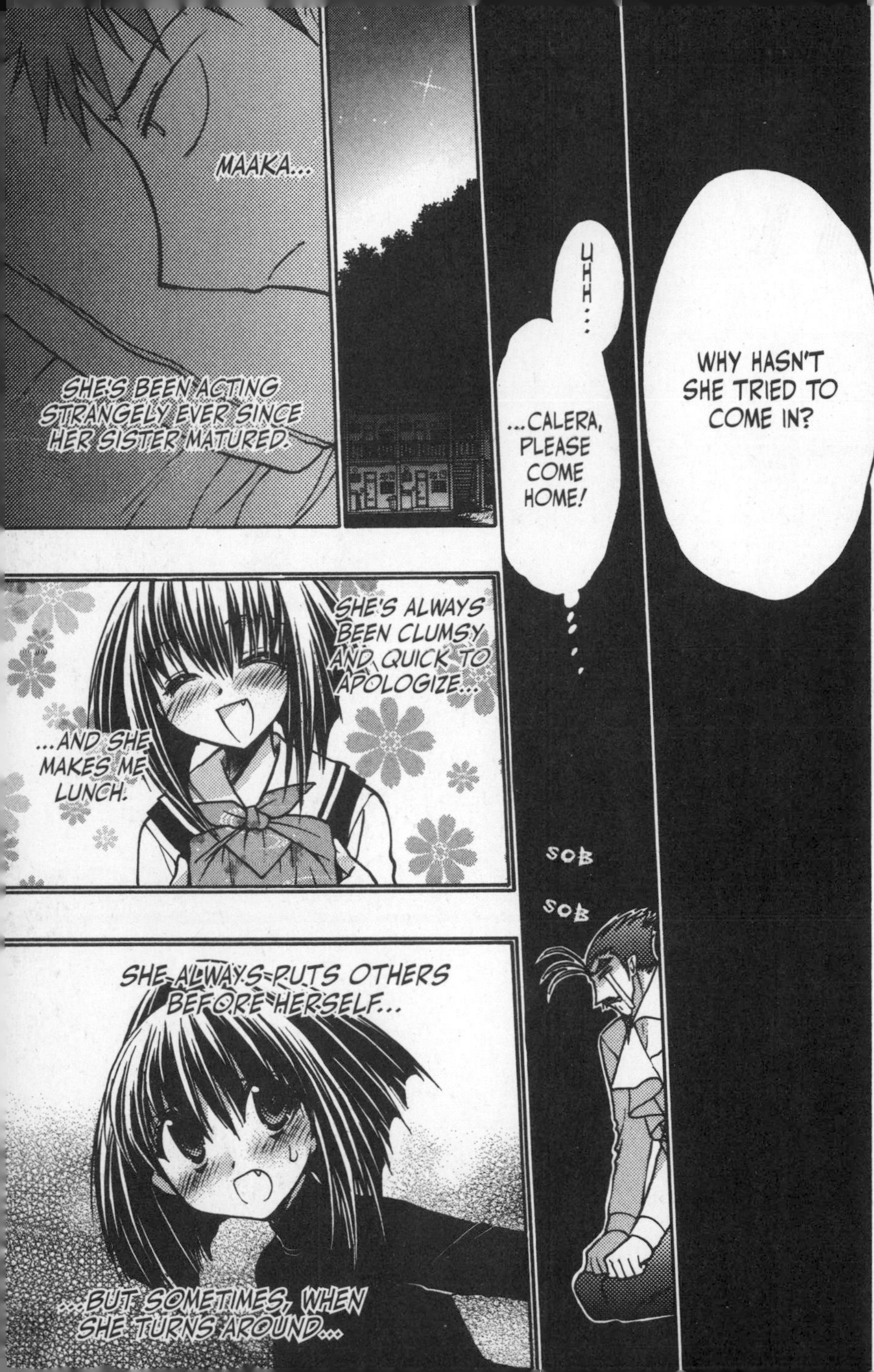
WHY HASN'T SHE TRIED TO COME IN?
UHH...
...CALERA, PLEASE COME HOME!
SOB
SOB
MAAKA...
SHE'S BEEN ACTING STRANGELY EVER SINCE HER SISTER MATURED.
SHE'S ALWAYS BEEN CLUMSY AND QUICK TO APOLOGIZE...
...AND SHE MAKES ME LUNCH.
SHE ALWAYS PUTS OTHERS BEFORE HERSELF...
...BUT SOMETIMES, WHEN SHE TURNS AROUND...

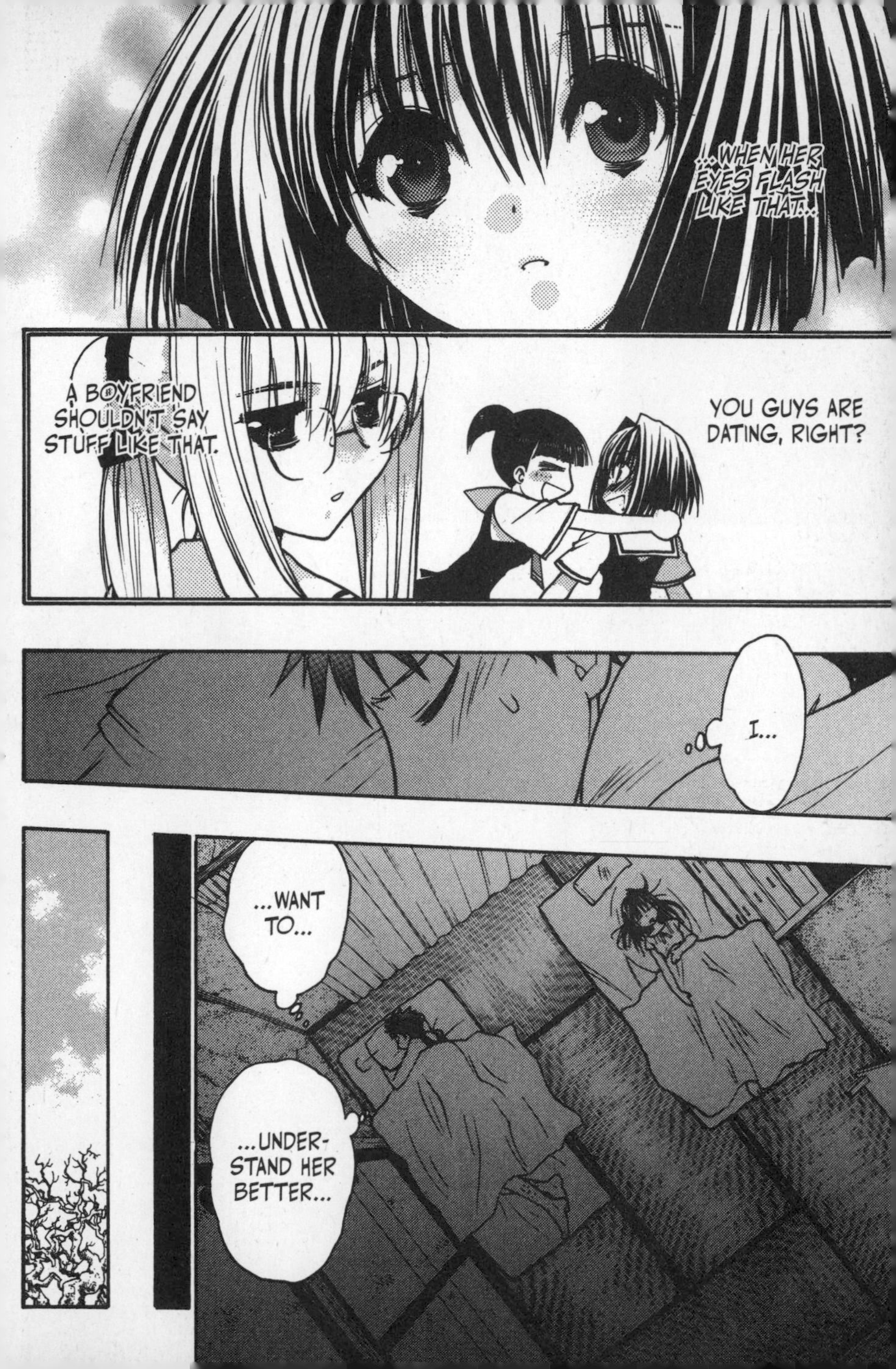
...WHEN HER EYES FLASH LIKE THAT...
YOU GUYS ARE DATING, RIGHT?
A BOYFRIEND SHOULDN'T SAY STUFF LIKE THAT.
I...
...WANT TO...
...UNDER-STAND HER BETTER...

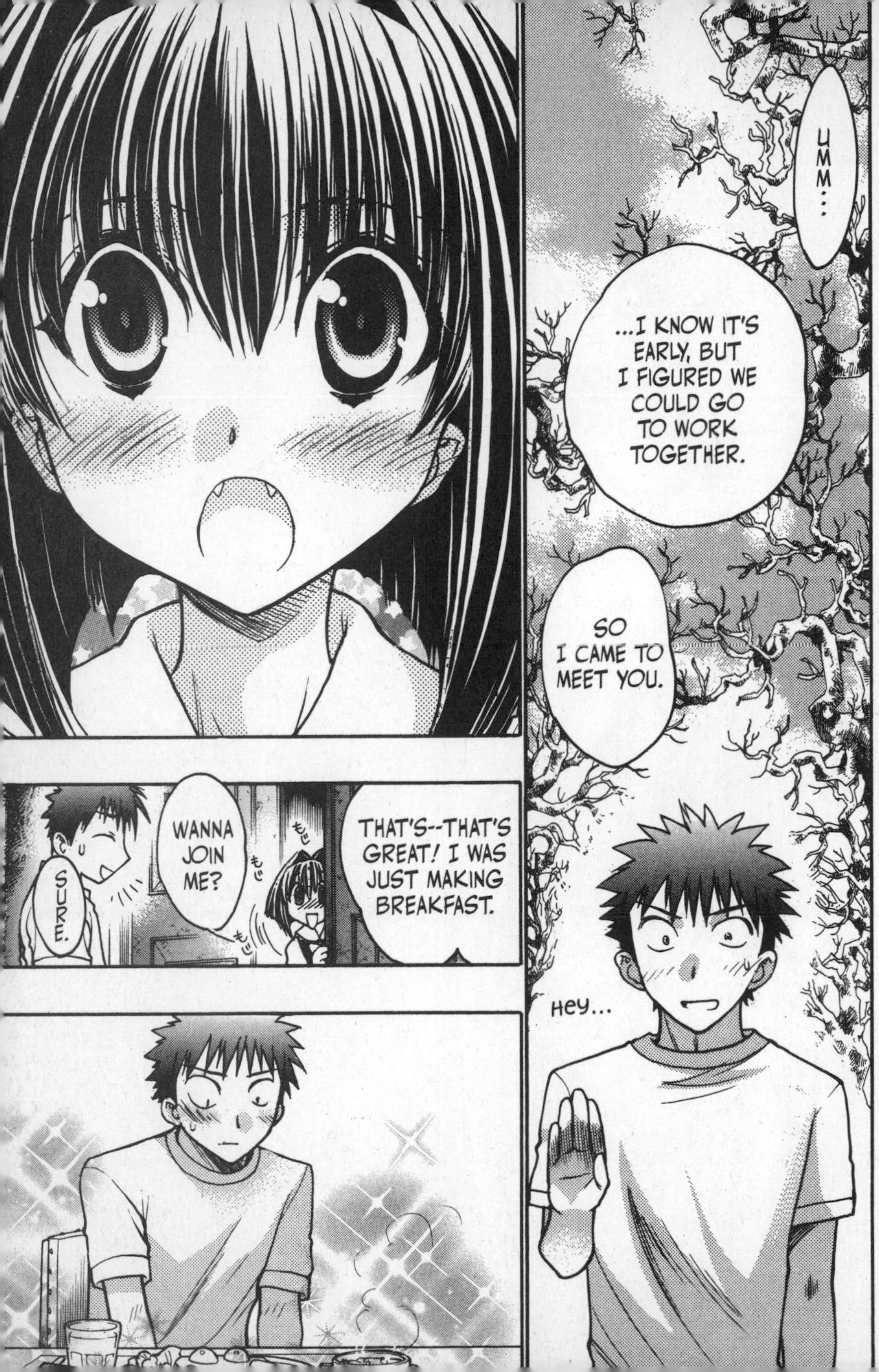
UMM...
...I KNOW IT'S EARLY, BUT I FIGURED WE COULD GO TO WORK TOGETHER.
SO I CAME TO MEET YOU.
Hey...
THAT'S--THAT'S GREAT! I WAS JUST MAKING BREAKFAST.
もじ もじ
WANNA JOIN ME?
SURE.

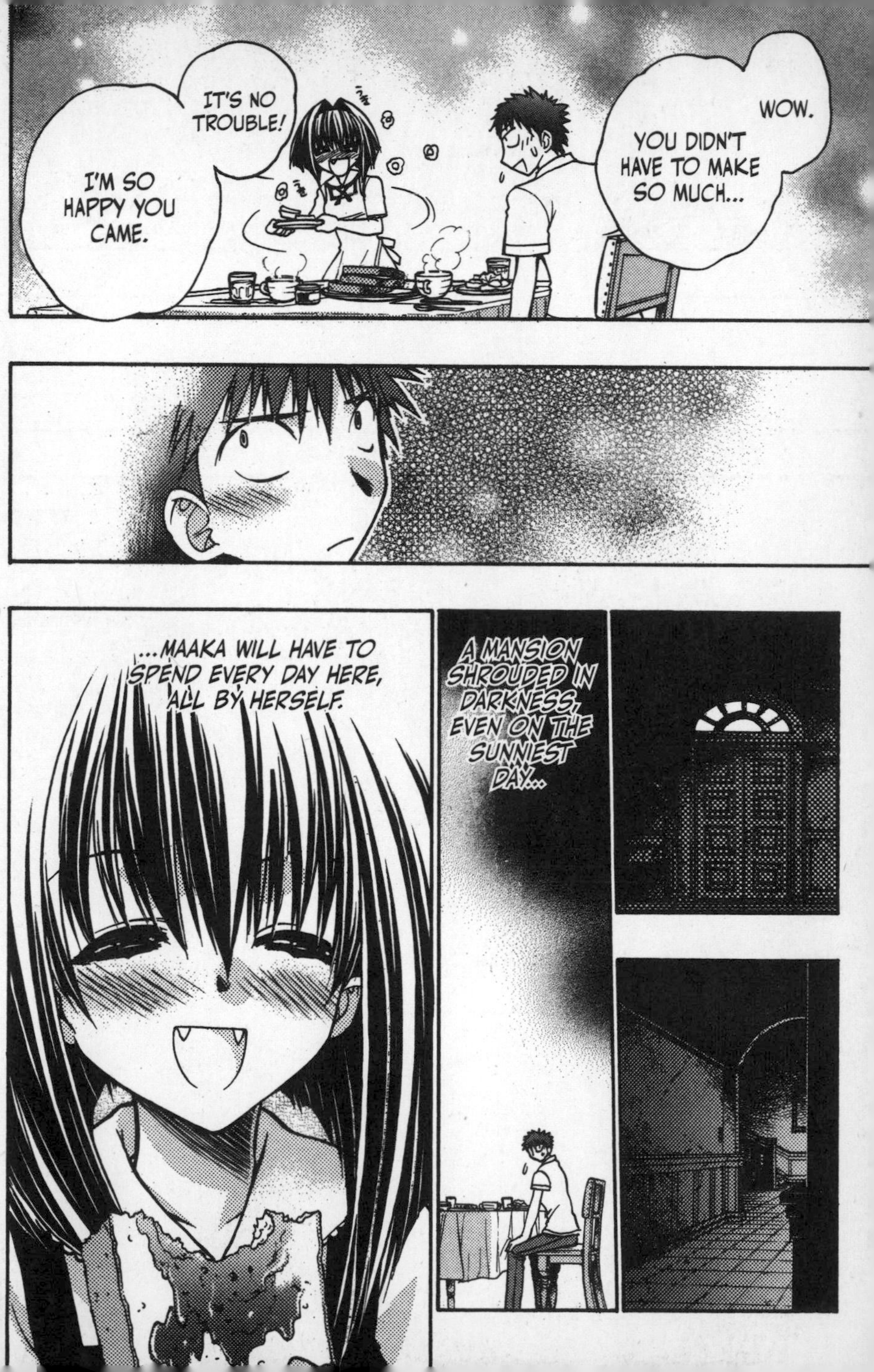
WOW.
YOU DIDN'T HAVE TO MAKE SO MUCH...
IT'S NO TROUBLE!
I'M SO HAPPY YOU CAME.
A MANSION SHROUDED IN DARKNESS, EVEN ON THE SUNNIEST DAY...
...MAAKA WILL HAVE TO SPEND EVERY DAY HERE, ALL BY HERSELF.

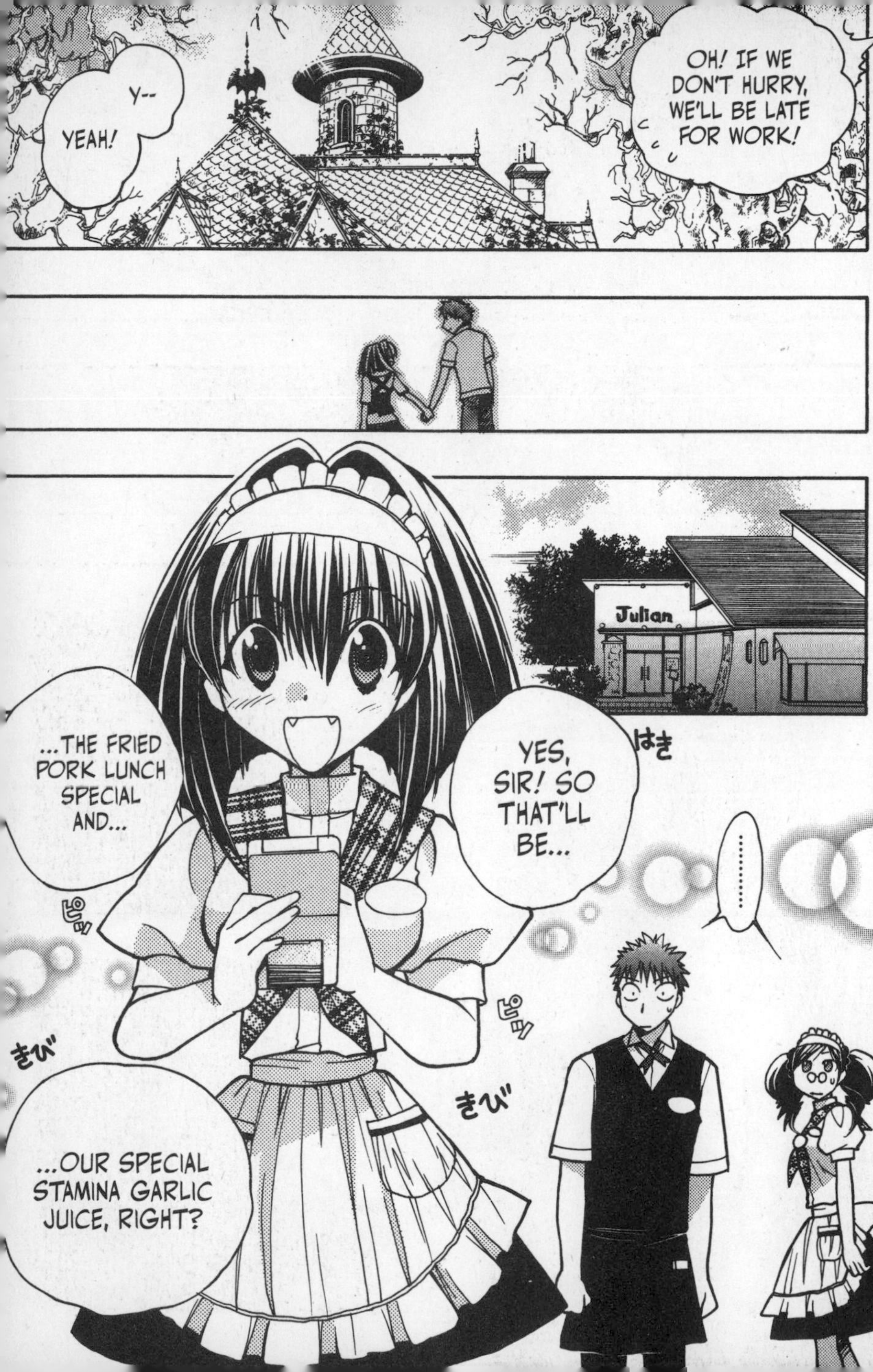
OH! IF WE DON'T HURRY, WE'LL BE LATE FOR WORK!
Y-- YEAH!
Julian
はき
YES, SIR! SO THAT'LL BE...
...THE FRIED PORK LUNCH SPECIAL AND...
ピッ
ピッ
......
きび
きび
...OUR SPECIAL STAMINA GARLIC JUICE, RIGHT?

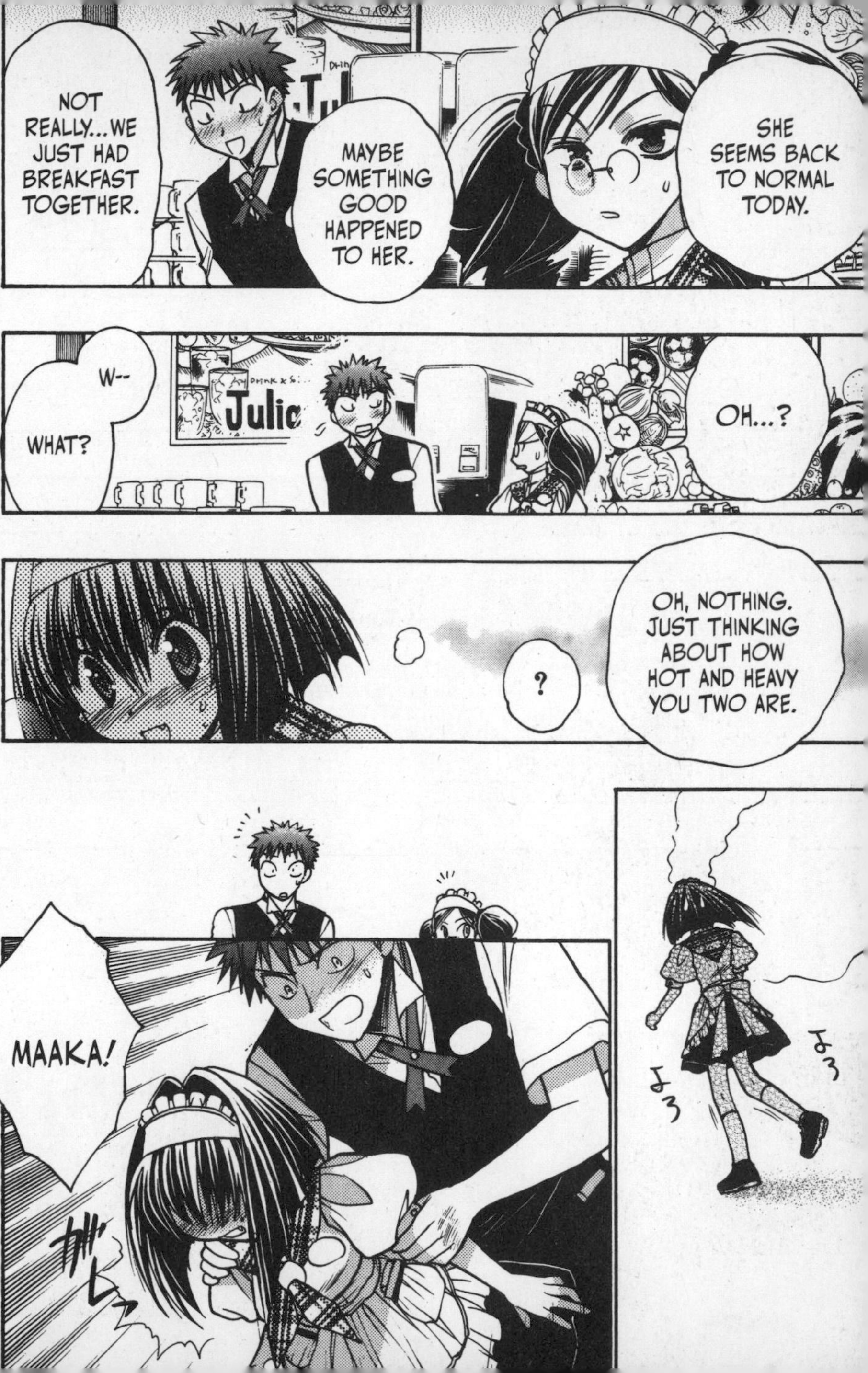
SHE SEEMS BACK TO NORMAL TODAY.
MAYBE SOMETHING GOOD HAPPENED TO HER.
NOT REALLY...WE JUST HAD BREAKFAST TOGETHER.
OH...?
W-- WHAT?
OH, NOTHING. JUST THINKING ABOUT HOW HOT AND HEAVY YOU TWO ARE.
?
よろ
よろ
MAAKA!

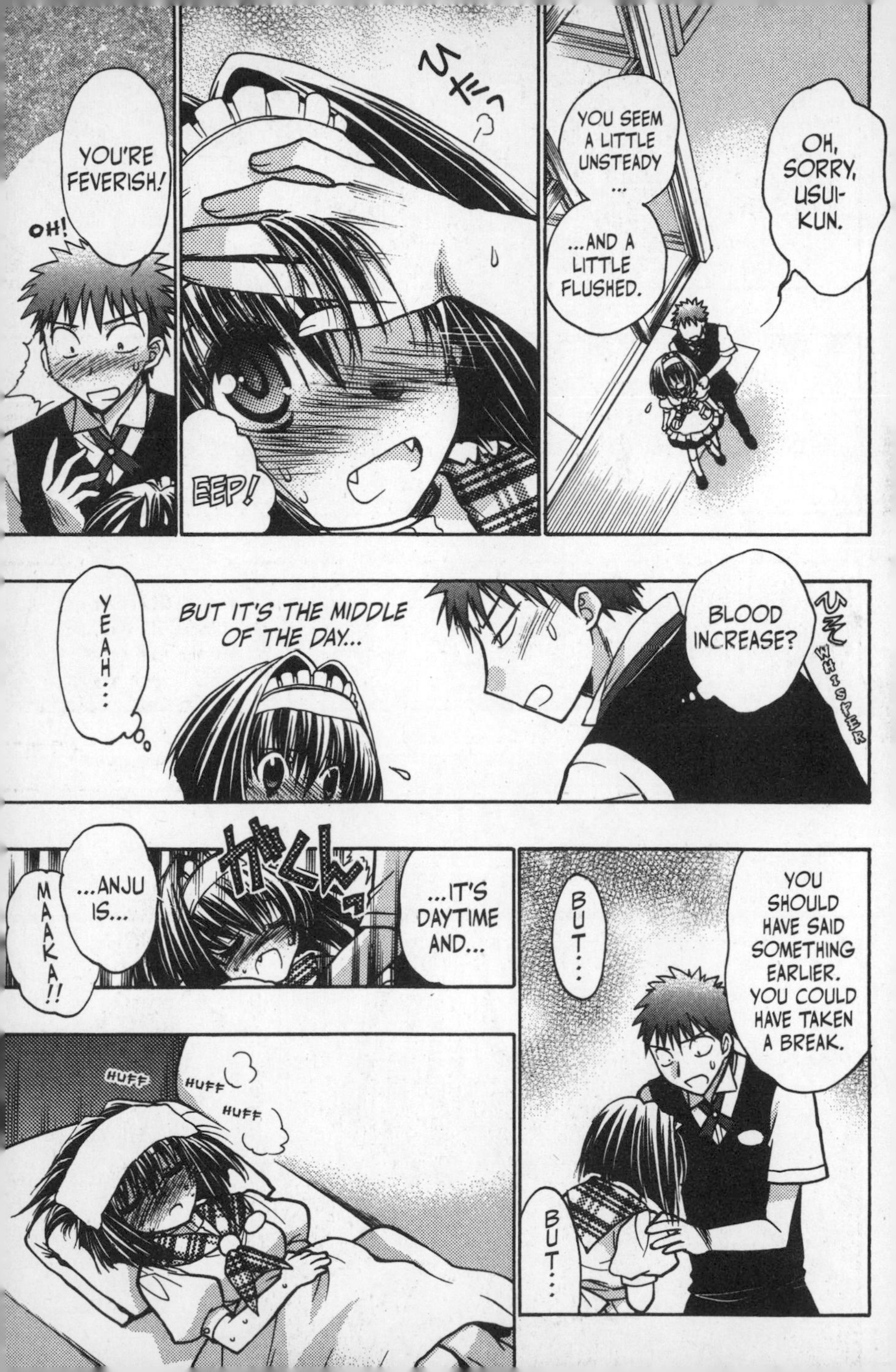

OH, SORRY, USUI-KUN.
YOU SEEM A LITTLE UNSTEADY...
...AND A LITTLE FLUSHED.
EEP!
YOU'RE FEVERISH!
OH!
BLOOD INCREASE?
WHISPER
BUT IT'S THE MIDDLE OF THE DAY...
YEAH...
YOU SHOULD HAVE SAID SOMETHING EARLIER. YOU COULD HAVE TAKEN A BREAK.
BUT...
BUT...
...IT'S DAYTIME AND...
...ANJU IS...
MAAKA!!
HUFF
HUFF
HUFF

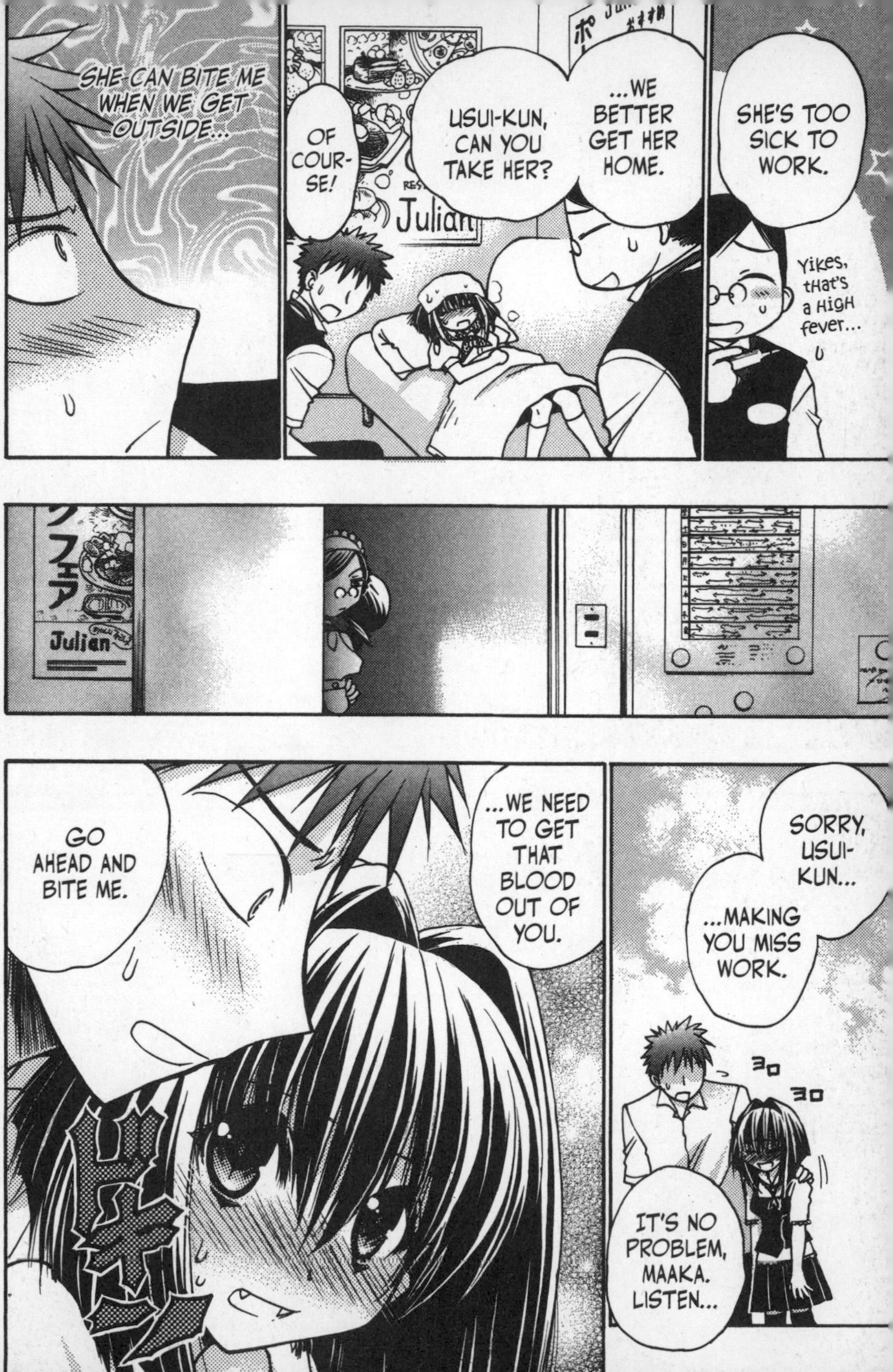
SHE'S TOO SICK TO WORK.
Yikes, that's a HIGH fever...
...WE BETTER GET HER HOME.
USUI-KUN, CAN YOU TAKE HER?
OF COURSE!
Julian
SHE CAN BITE ME WHEN WE GET OUTSIDE...
フェア
Julian
SORRY, USUI-KUN...
...MAKING YOU MISS WORK.
ヨロ
ヨロ
IT'S NO PROBLEM, MAAKA. LISTEN...
...WE NEED TO GET THAT BLOOD OUT OF YOU.
GO AHEAD AND BITE ME.

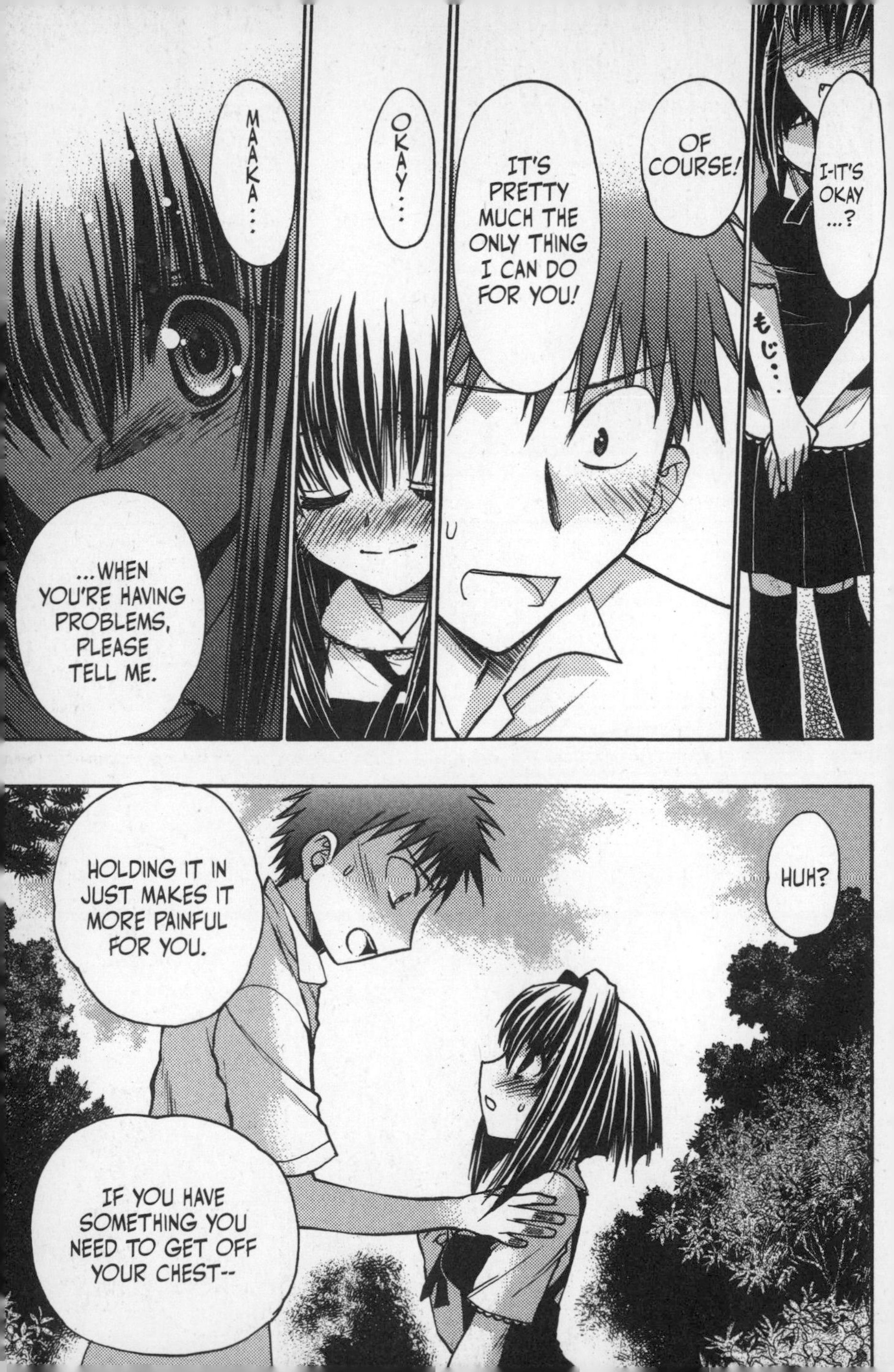
I-IT'S OKAY ...?
もじ...
OF COURSE!
IT'S PRETTY MUCH THE ONLY THING I CAN DO FOR YOU!
OKAY...
MAAKA...
...WHEN YOU'RE HAVING PROBLEMS, PLEASE TELL ME.
HUH?
HOLDING IT IN JUST MAKES IT MORE PAINFUL FOR YOU.
IF YOU HAVE SOMETHING YOU NEED TO GET OFF YOUR CHEST--

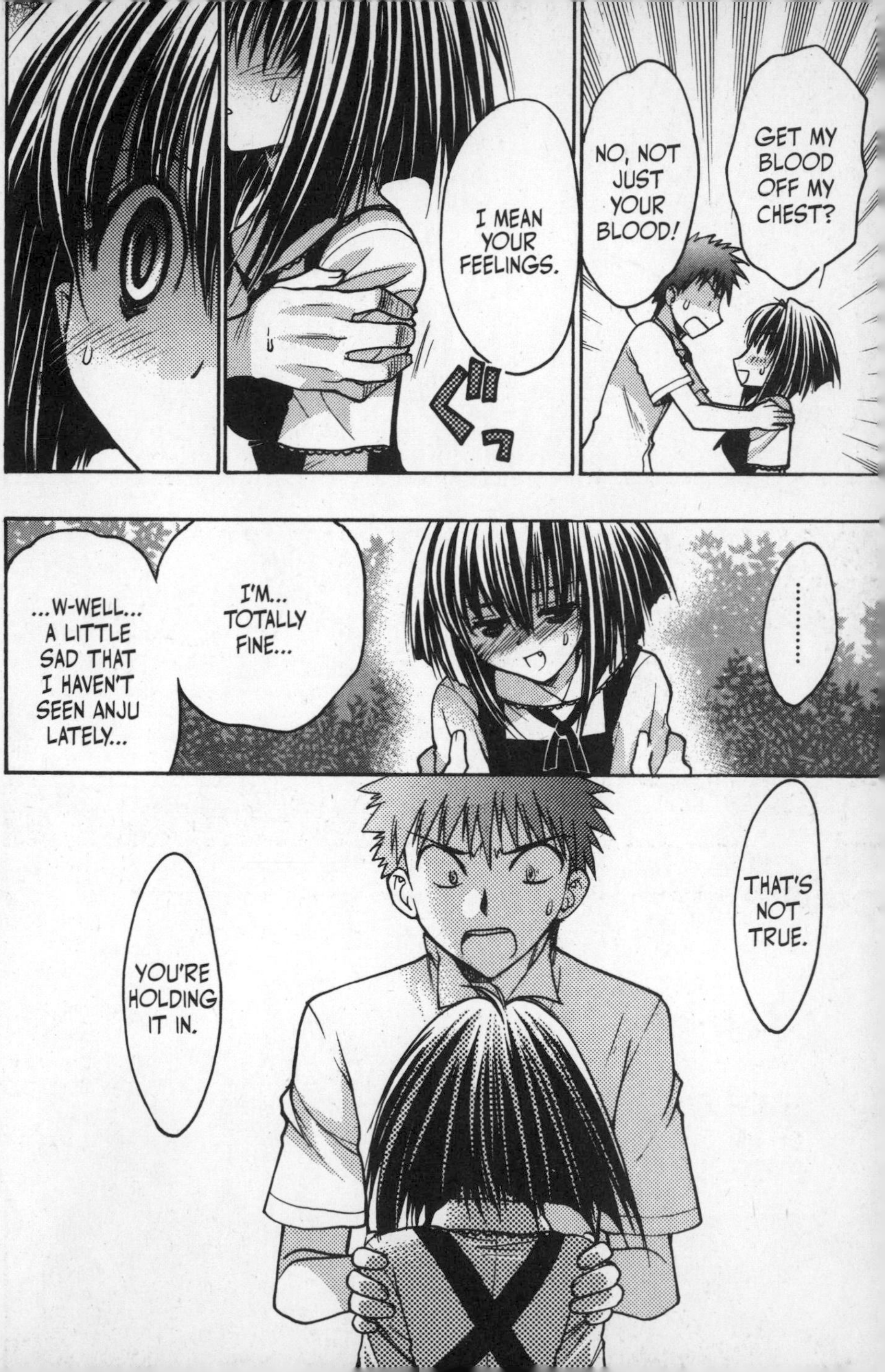
GET MY BLOOD OFF MY CHEST?
NO, NOT JUST YOUR BLOOD!
I MEAN YOUR FEELINGS.
ぐっ
......
I'M... TOTALLY FINE...
...W-WELL... A LITTLE SAD THAT I HAVEN'T SEEN ANJU LATELY...
THAT'S NOT TRUE.
YOU'RE HOLDING IT IN.

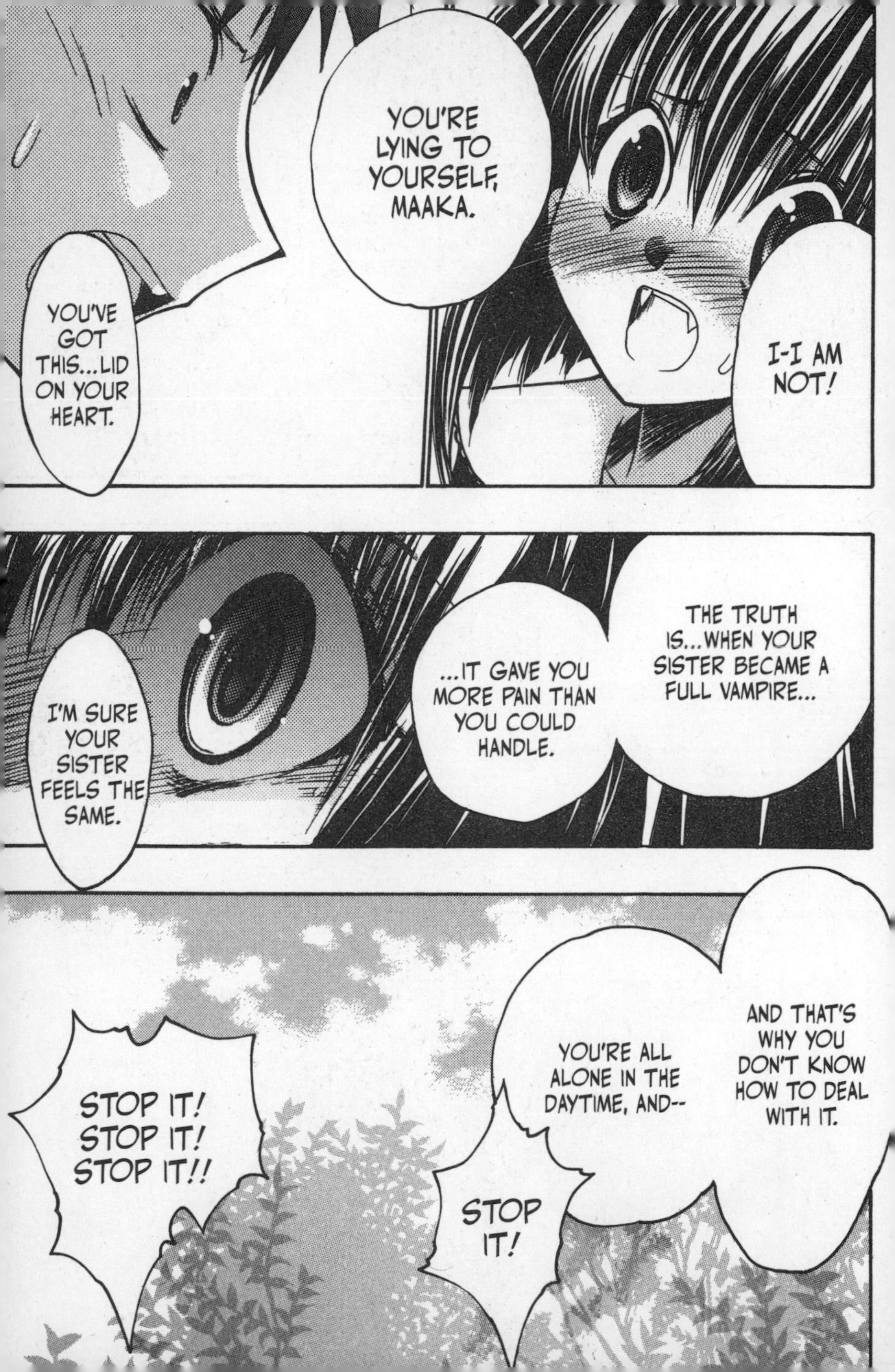
YOU'RE LYING TO YOURSELF, MAAKA.
I-I AM NOT!
YOU'VE GOT THIS...LID ON YOUR HEART.
THE TRUTH IS...WHEN YOUR SISTER BECAME A FULL VAMPIRE...
...IT GAVE YOU MORE PAIN THAN YOU COULD HANDLE.
I'M SURE YOUR SISTER FEELS THE SAME.
AND THAT'S WHY YOU DON'T KNOW HOW TO DEAL WITH IT.
YOU'RE ALL ALONE IN THE DAYTIME, AND--
STOP IT!
STOP IT! STOP IT! STOP IT!!

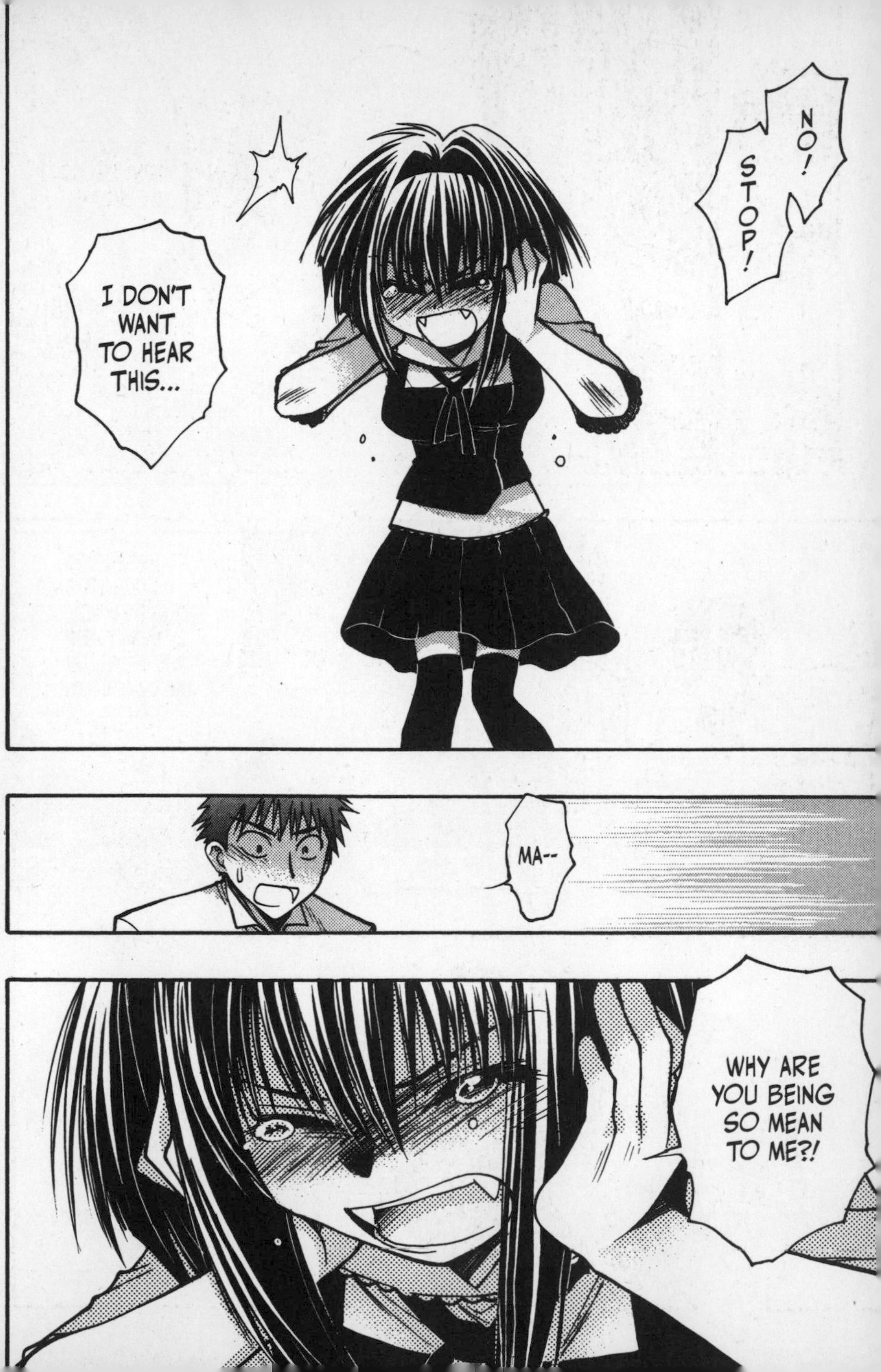
NO! STOP!
I DON'T WANT TO HEAR THIS...
MA--
WHY ARE YOU BEING SO MEAN TO ME?!

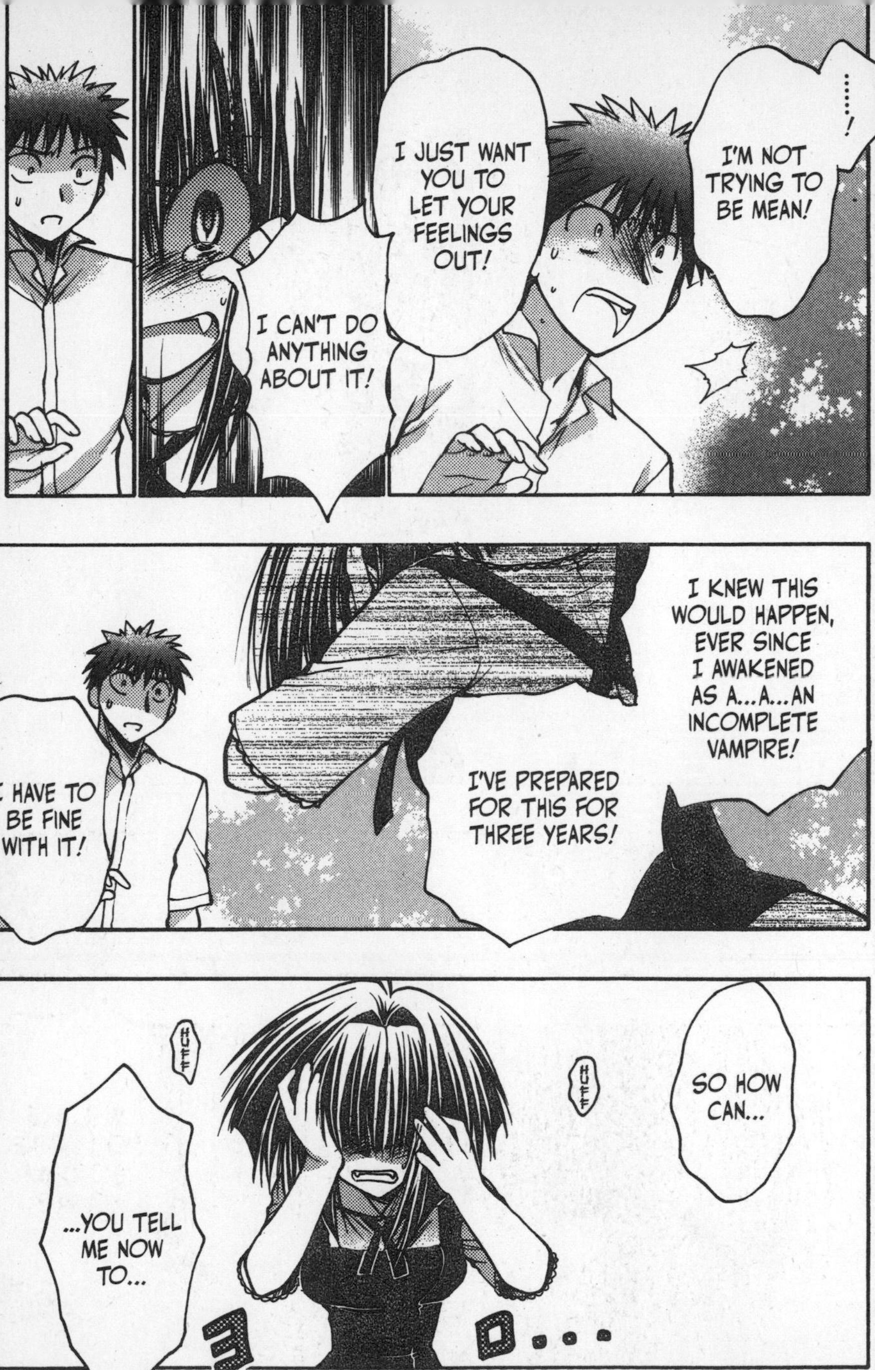
......!
I'M NOT TRYING TO BE MEAN!
I JUST WANT YOU TO LET YOUR FEELINGS OUT!
I CAN'T DO ANYTHING ABOUT IT!
I KNEW THIS WOULD HAPPEN, EVER SINCE I AWAKENED AS A...A...AN INCOMPLETE VAMPIRE!
I'VE PREPARED FOR THIS FOR THREE YEARS!
I HAVE TO BE FINE WITH IT!
SO HOW CAN...
HUFF
HUFF
...YOU TELL ME NOW TO...
D...

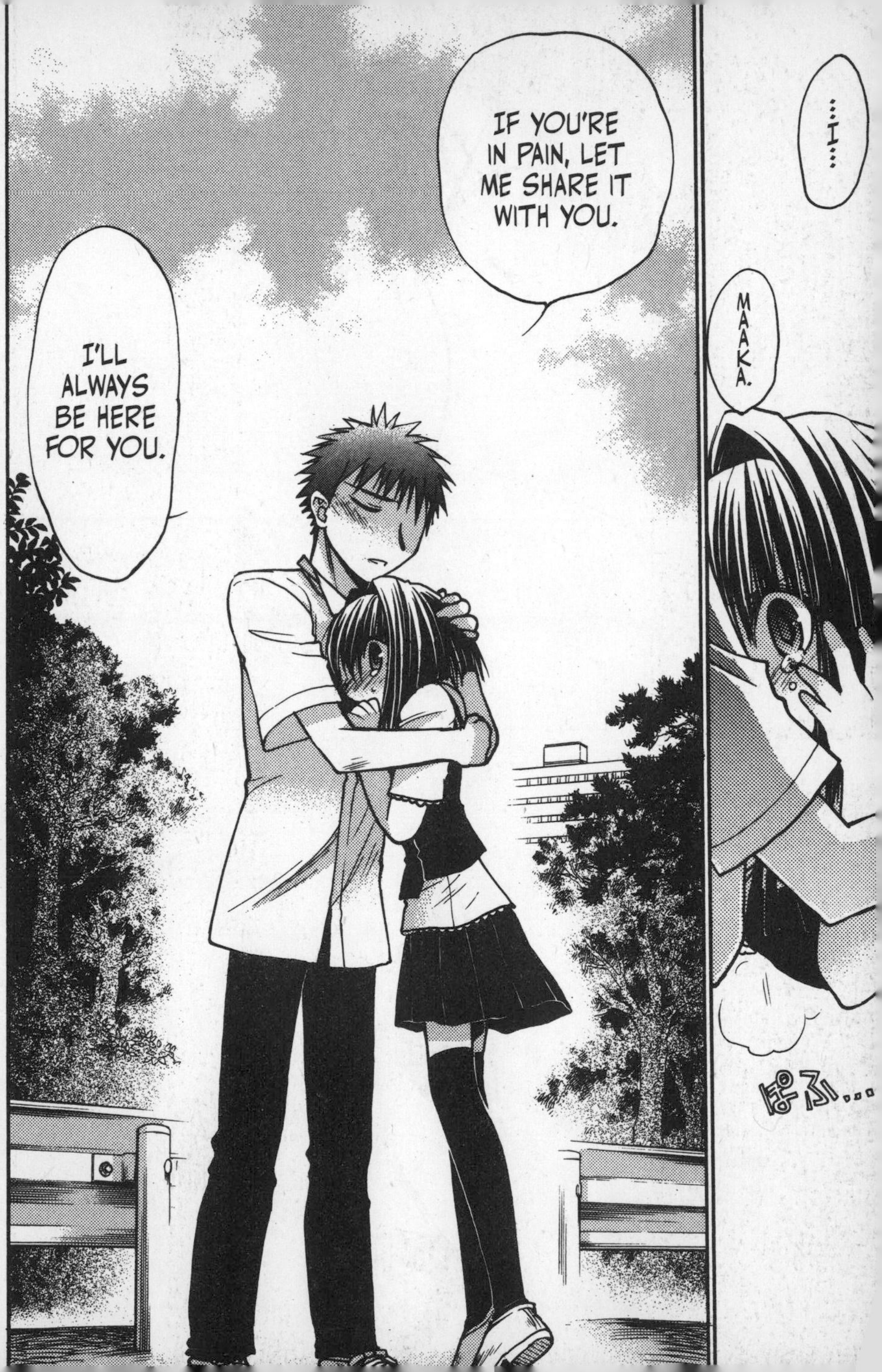
...I...
MAAKA.
ぽふ...
IF YOU'RE IN PAIN, LET ME SHARE IT WITH YOU.
I'LL ALWAYS BE HERE FOR YOU.

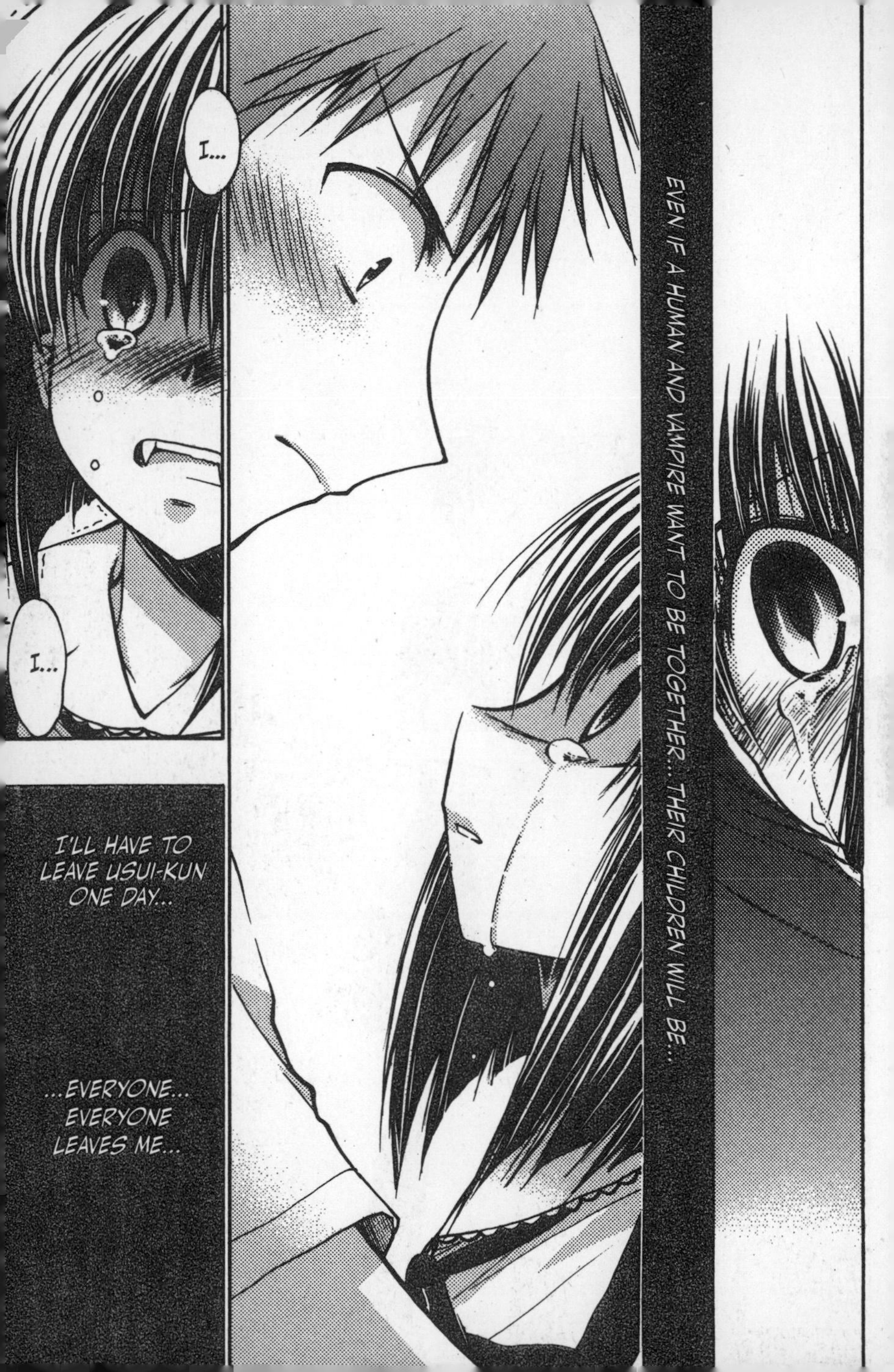
EVEN IF A HUMAN AND VAMPIRE WANT TO BE TOGETHER... THEIR CHILDREN WILL BE...
I...
I...
I'LL HAVE TO LEAVE USUI-KUN ONE DAY...
...EVERYONE... EVERYONE LEAVES ME...

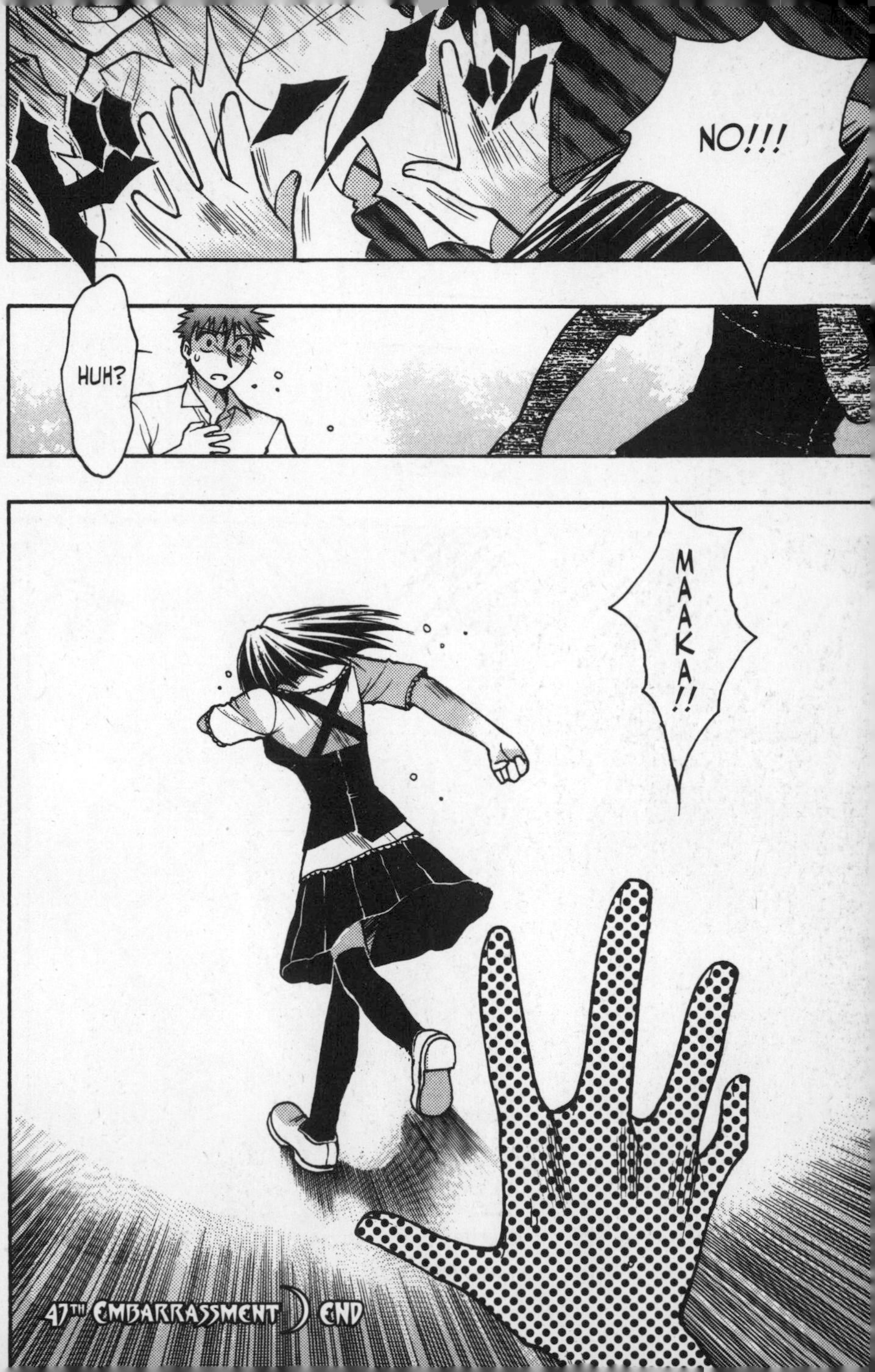
NO!!!
HUH?
MAAKA!!
47TH EMBARRASSMENT END

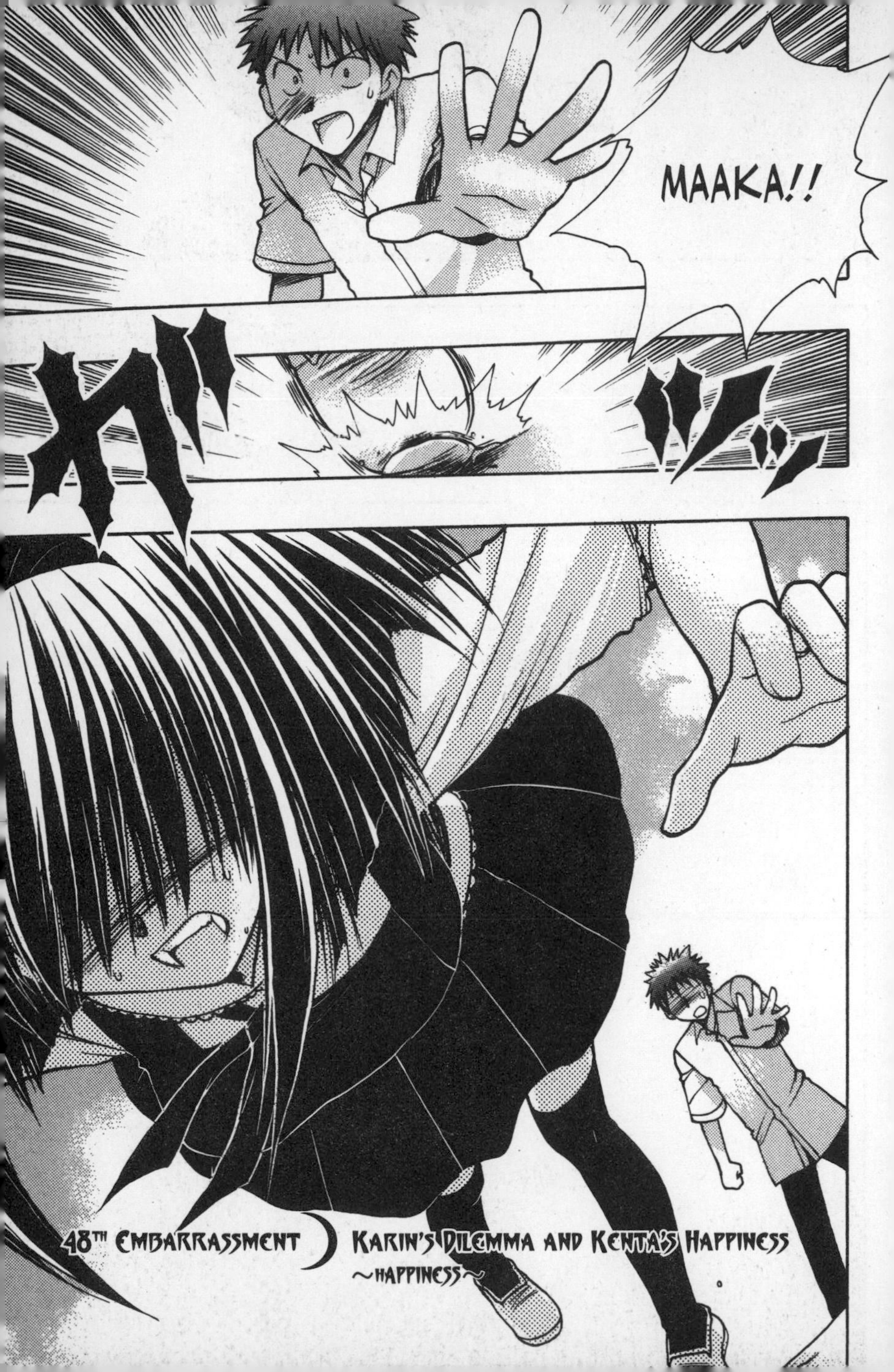
MAAKA!!
48th Embarrassment
Karin's Dilemma and Kenta's Happiness
~happiness~

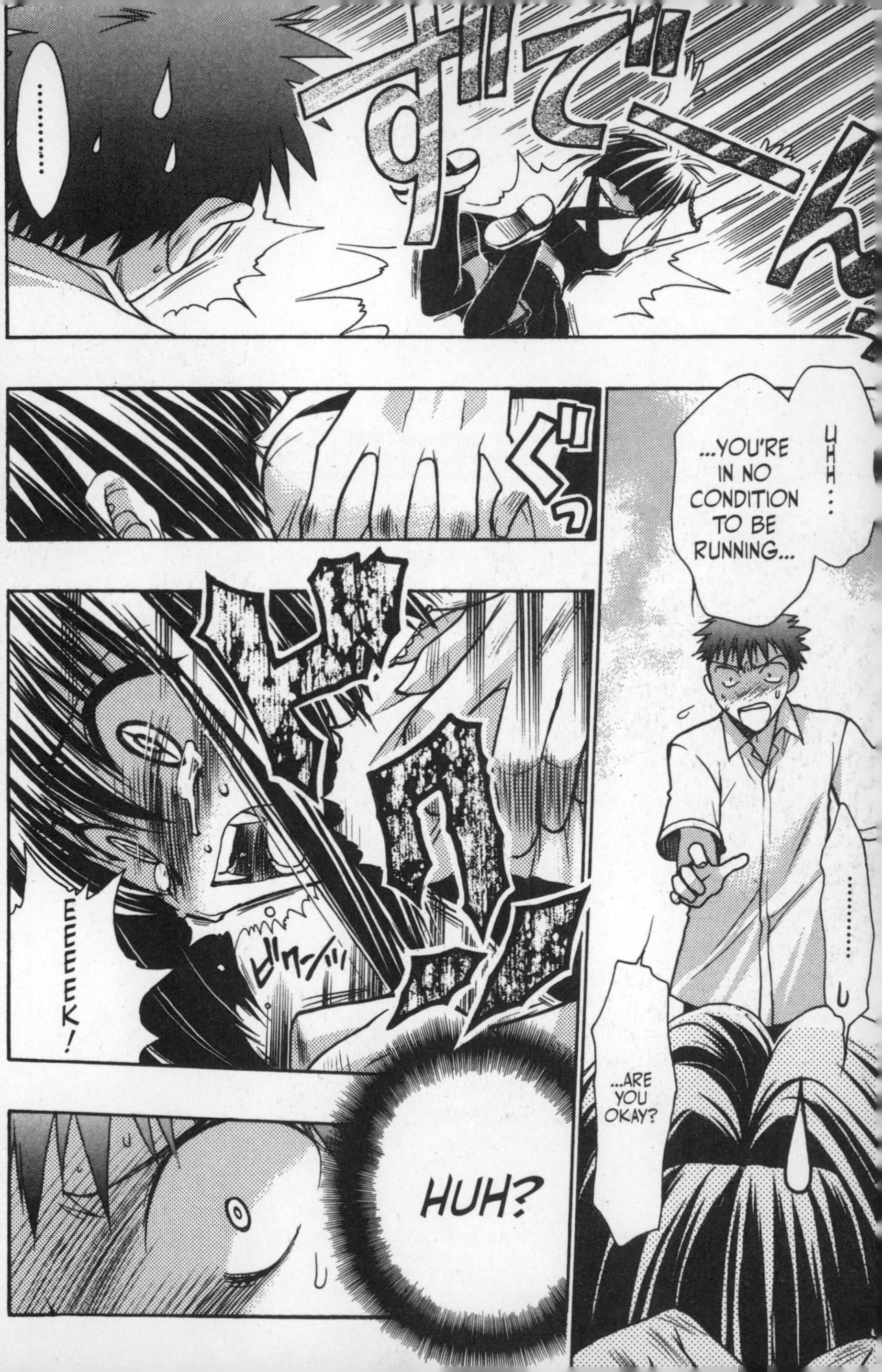
......
UHH...
...YOU'RE IN NO CONDITION TO BE RUNNING...
......
...ARE YOU OKAY?
EEEEEK!
HUH?

48TH EMBARRASSMENT KARIN'S DILEMMA AND KENTA'S HAPPINESS
~ HAPPINESS ~

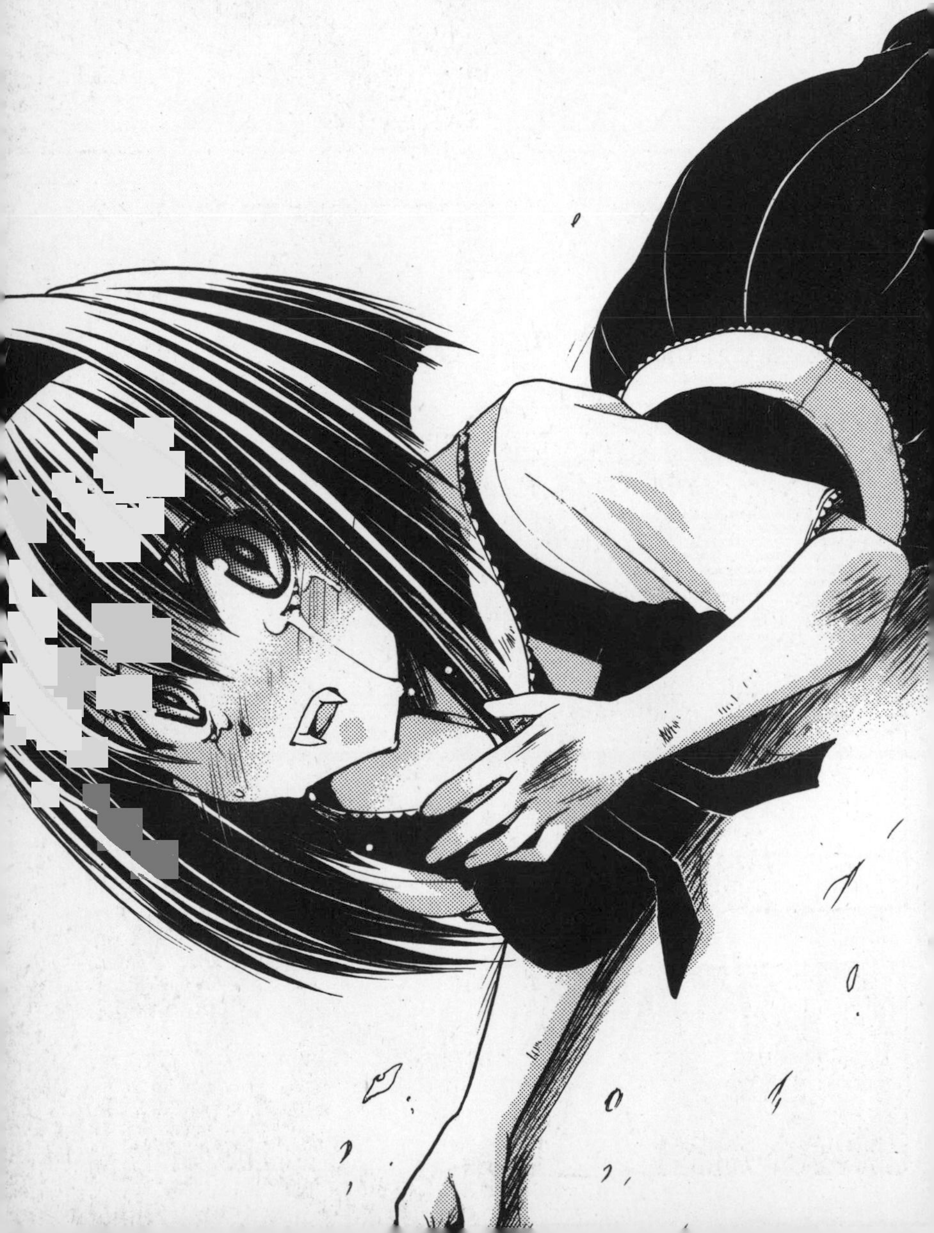

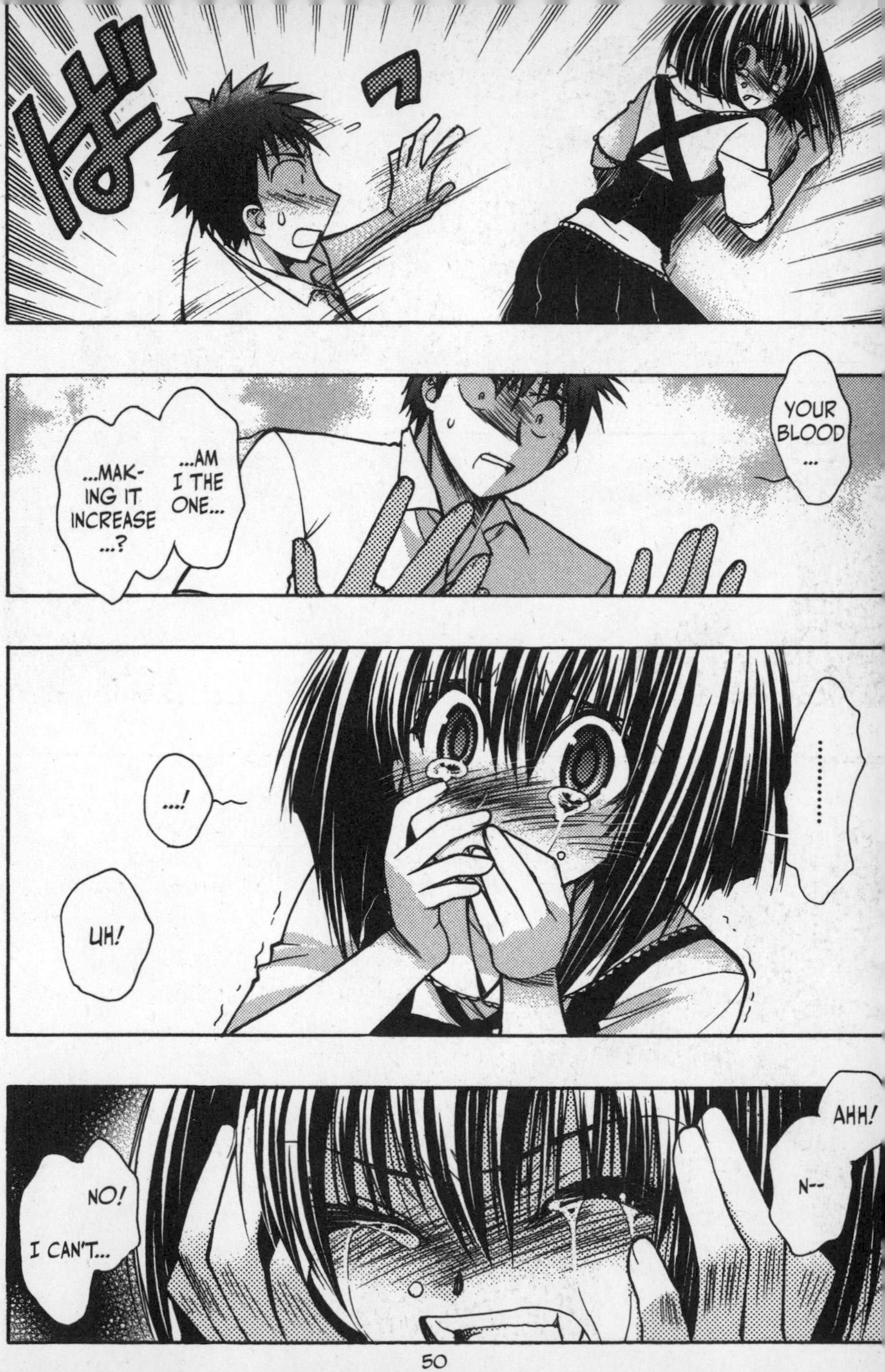
ばっ
YOUR BLOOD ...
...AM I THE ONE...
...MAK-ING IT INCREASE ...?
....
...!
UH!
AHH!
N--
NO!
I CAN'T...

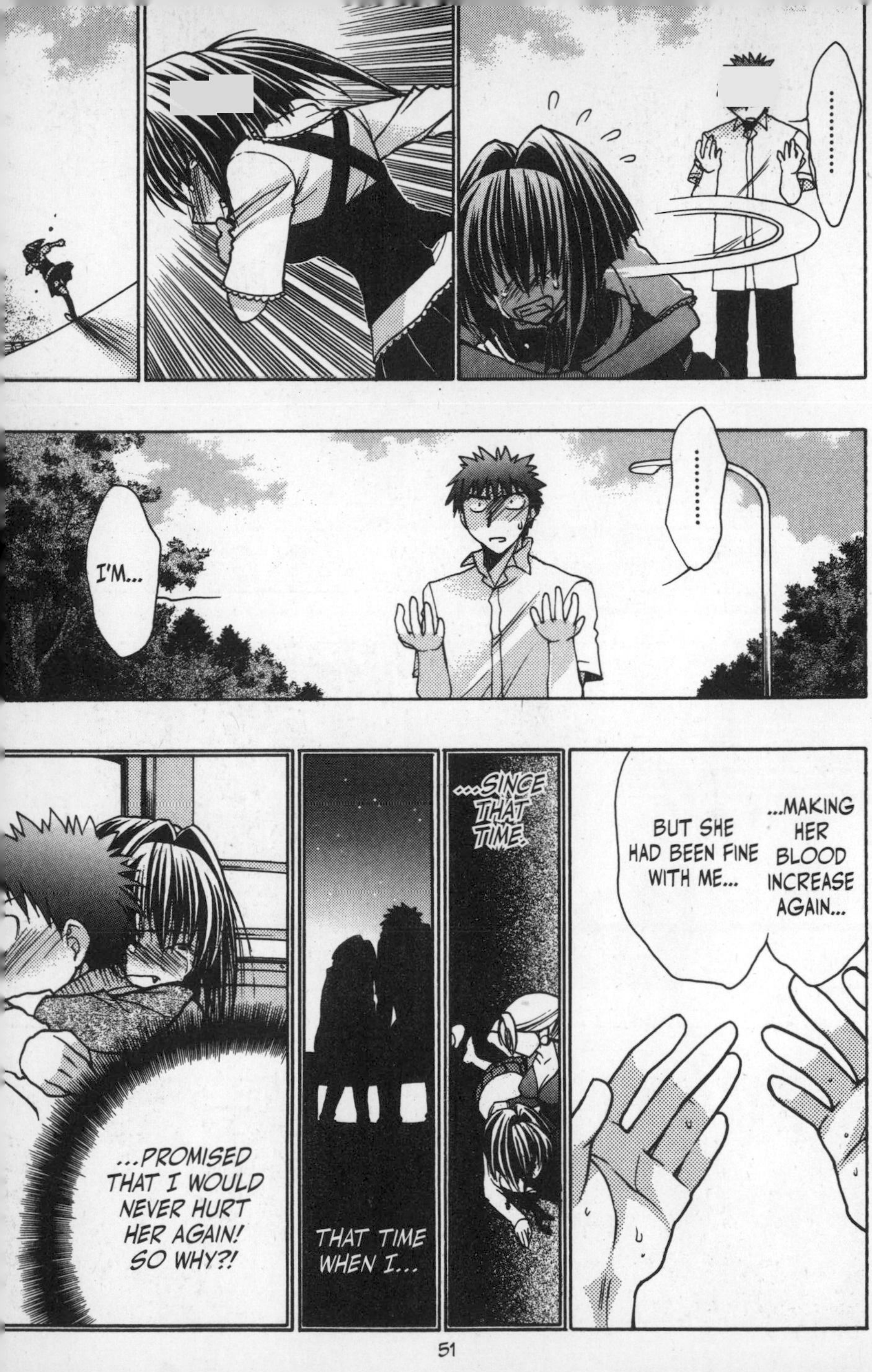
……
……
I'M...
...MAKING HER BLOOD INCREASE AGAIN...
BUT SHE HAD BEEN FINE WITH ME...
...SINCE THAT TIME.
THAT TIME WHEN I...
...PROMISED THAT I WOULD NEVER HURT HER AGAIN! SO WHY?!

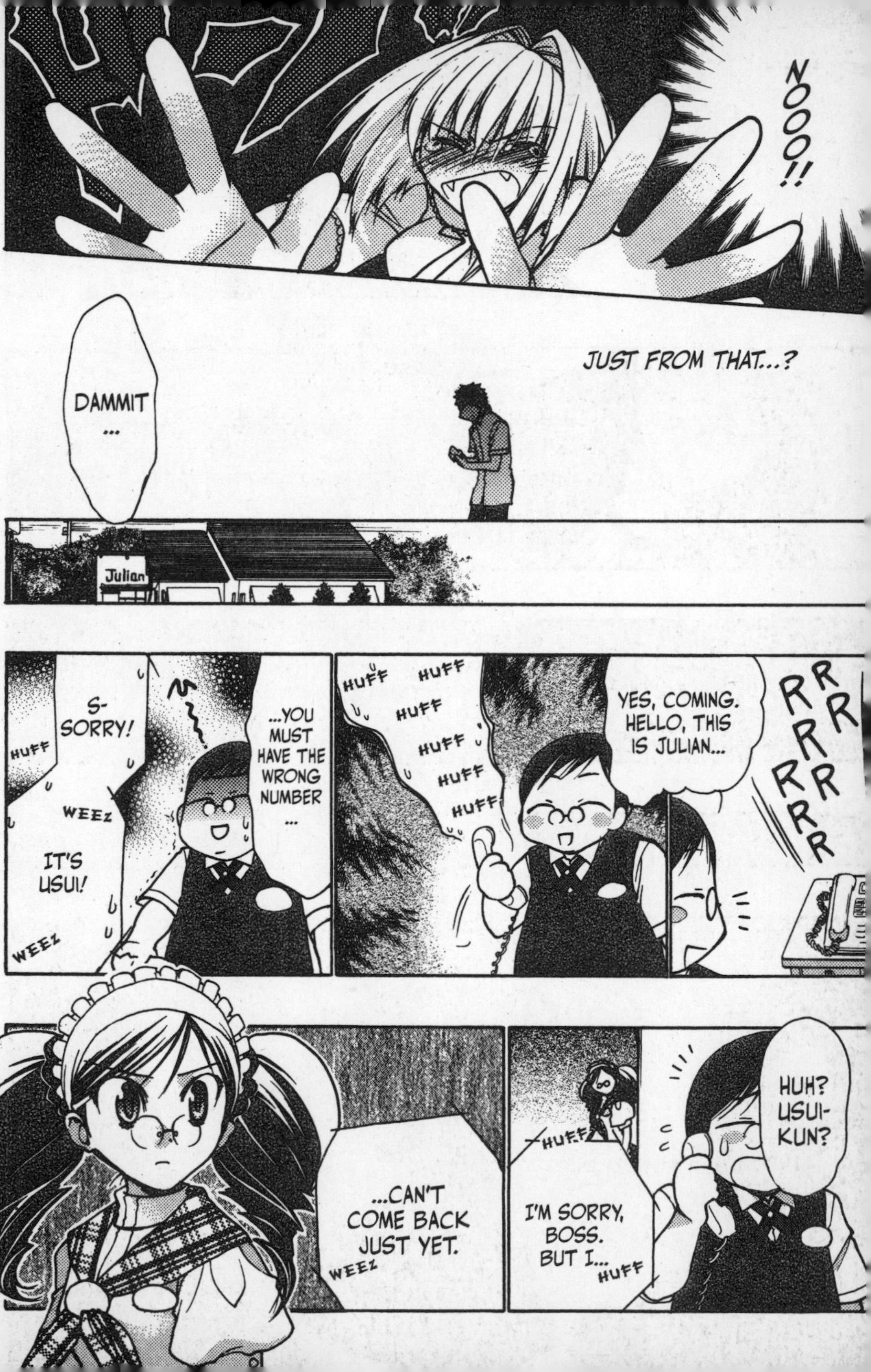
NOOOO!!
JUST FROM THAT...?
DAMMIT ...
Julian
RRRRRRRRR
YES, COMING. HELLO, THIS IS JULIAN...
HUFF HUFF HUFF HUFF HUFF HUFF
...YOU MUST HAVE THE WRONG NUMBER ...
S-SORRY!
HUFF
WEEZ
IT'S USUI!
WEEZ
HUH? USUI-KUN?
HUFF
I'M SORRY, BOSS. BUT I...
HUFF
...CAN'T COME BACK JUST YET.
WEEZ

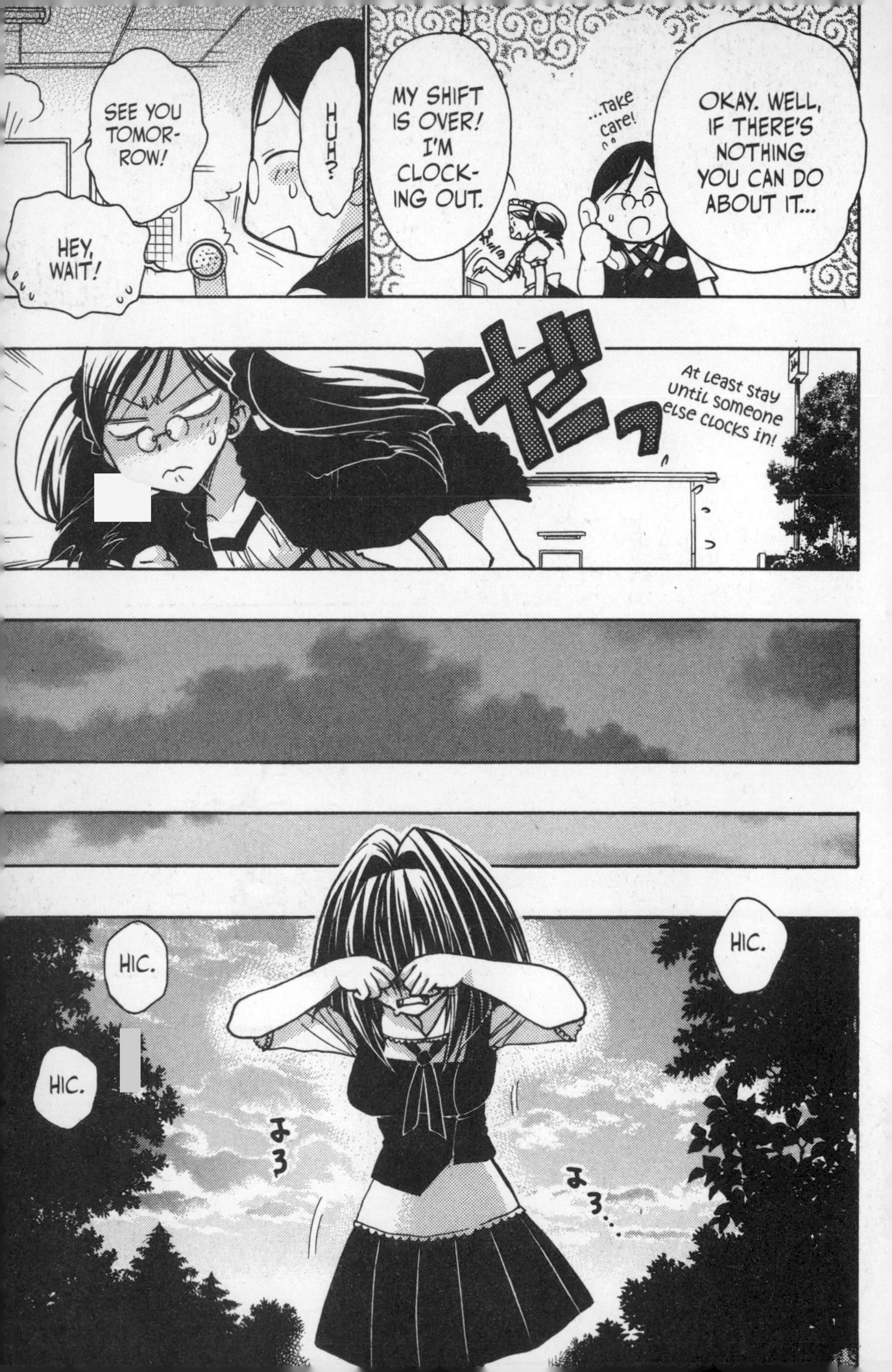
OKAY. WELL, IF THERE'S NOTHING YOU CAN DO ABOUT IT...
...Take care!
MY SHIFT IS OVER! I'M CLOCKING OUT.
HUH?
SEE YOU TOMORROW!
HEY, WAIT!
At least stay until someone else clocks in!
HIC.
HIC.
HIC.
よろ
よろ...

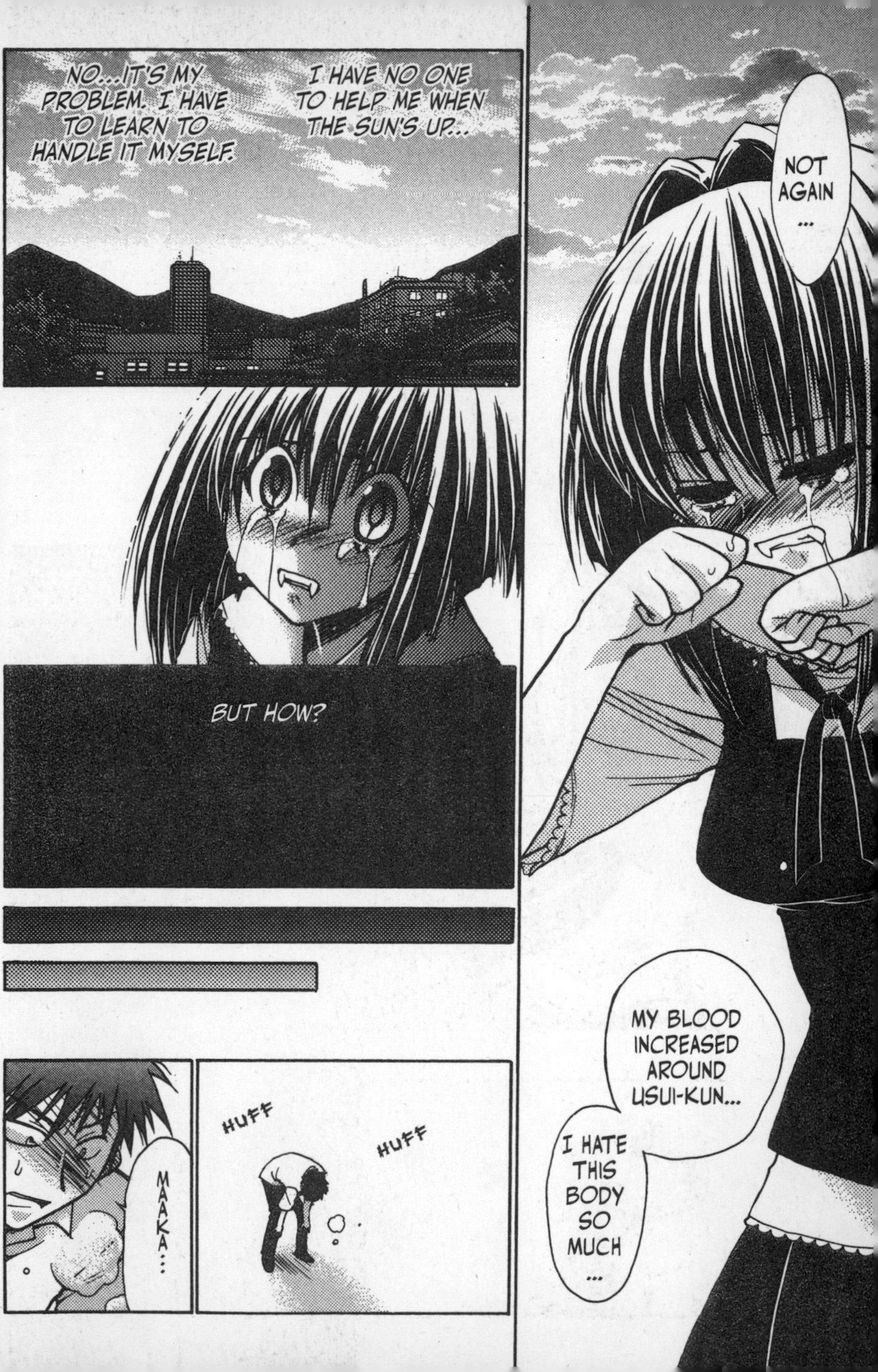
NOT AGAIN ...
MY BLOOD INCREASED AROUND USUI-KUN...
I HATE THIS BODY SO MUCH ...
I HAVE NO ONE TO HELP ME WHEN THE SUN'S UP...
NO...IT'S MY PROBLEM. I HAVE TO LEARN TO HANDLE IT MYSELF.
BUT HOW?
HUFF
HUFF
MAAKA...

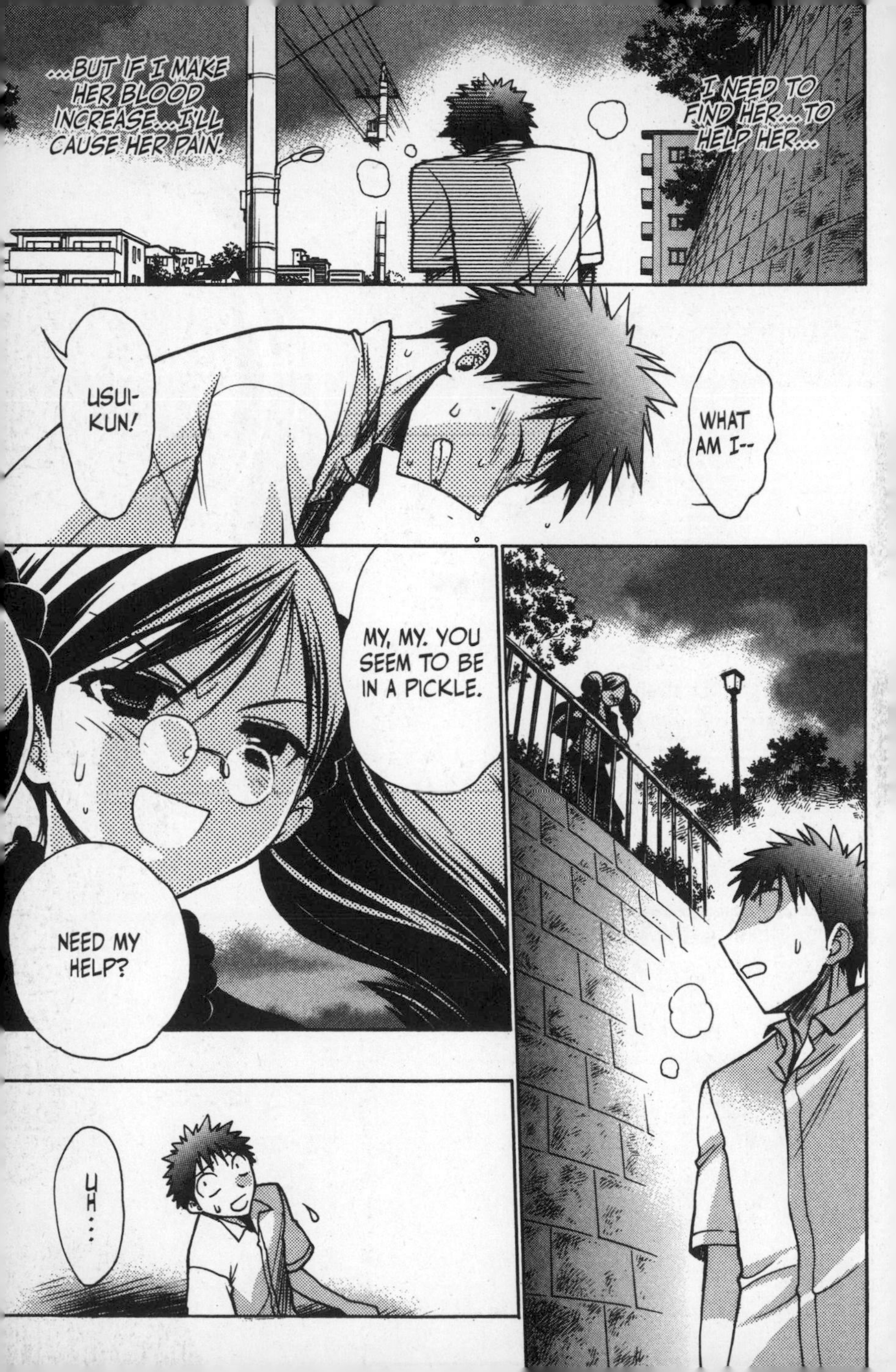
I NEED TO FIND HER... TO HELP HER...
...BUT IF I MAKE HER BLOOD INCREASE...I'LL CAUSE HER PAIN.
WHAT AM I--
USUI-KUN!
MY, MY. YOU SEEM TO BE IN A PICKLE.
NEED MY HELP?
UH...

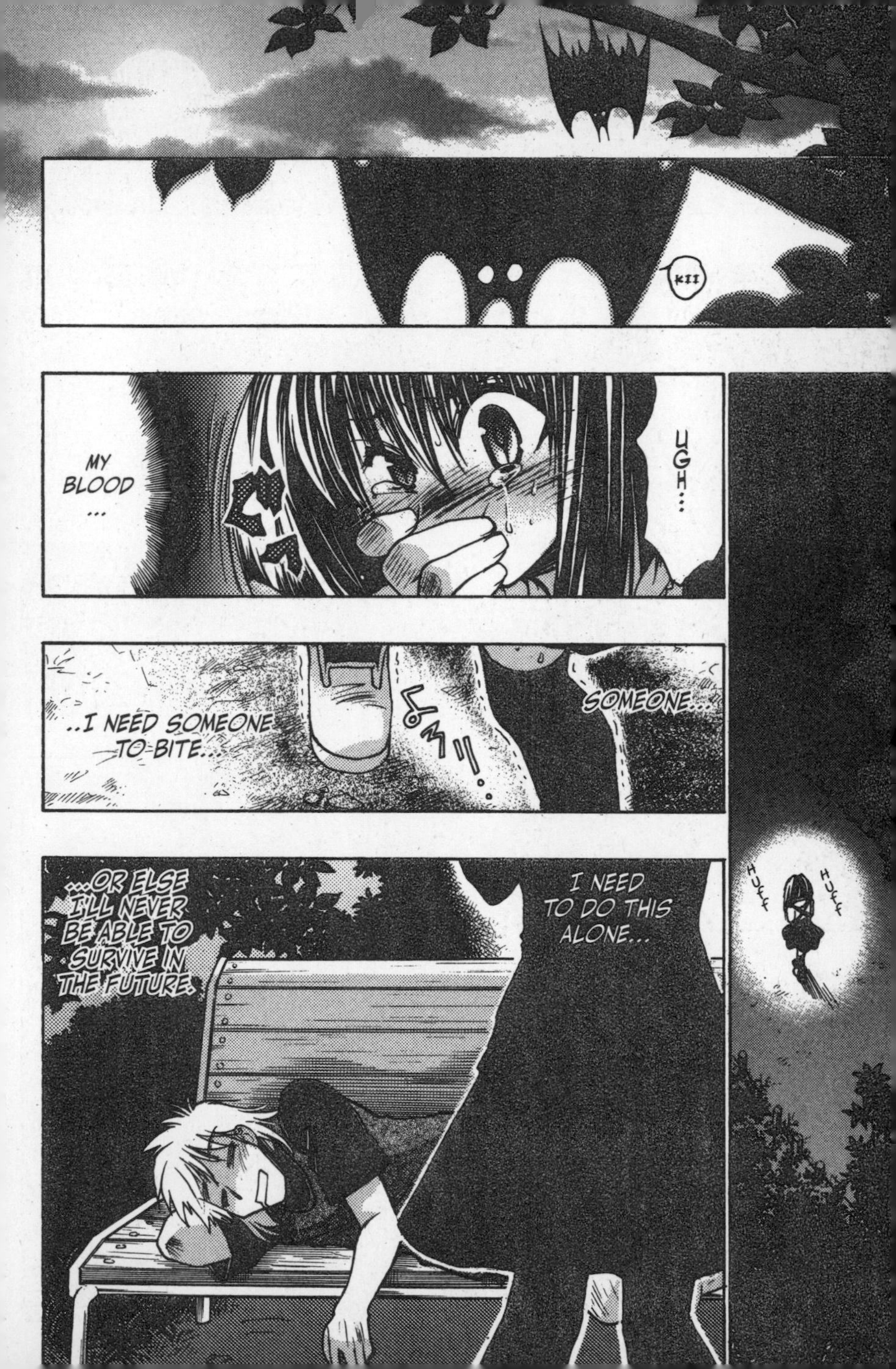
KII
UGH...
MY BLOOD ...
SOMEONE...
...I NEED SOMEONE TO BITE...
HUFF HUFF
I NEED TO DO THIS ALONE...
...OR ELSE I'LL NEVER BE ABLE TO SURVIVE IN THE FUTURE.

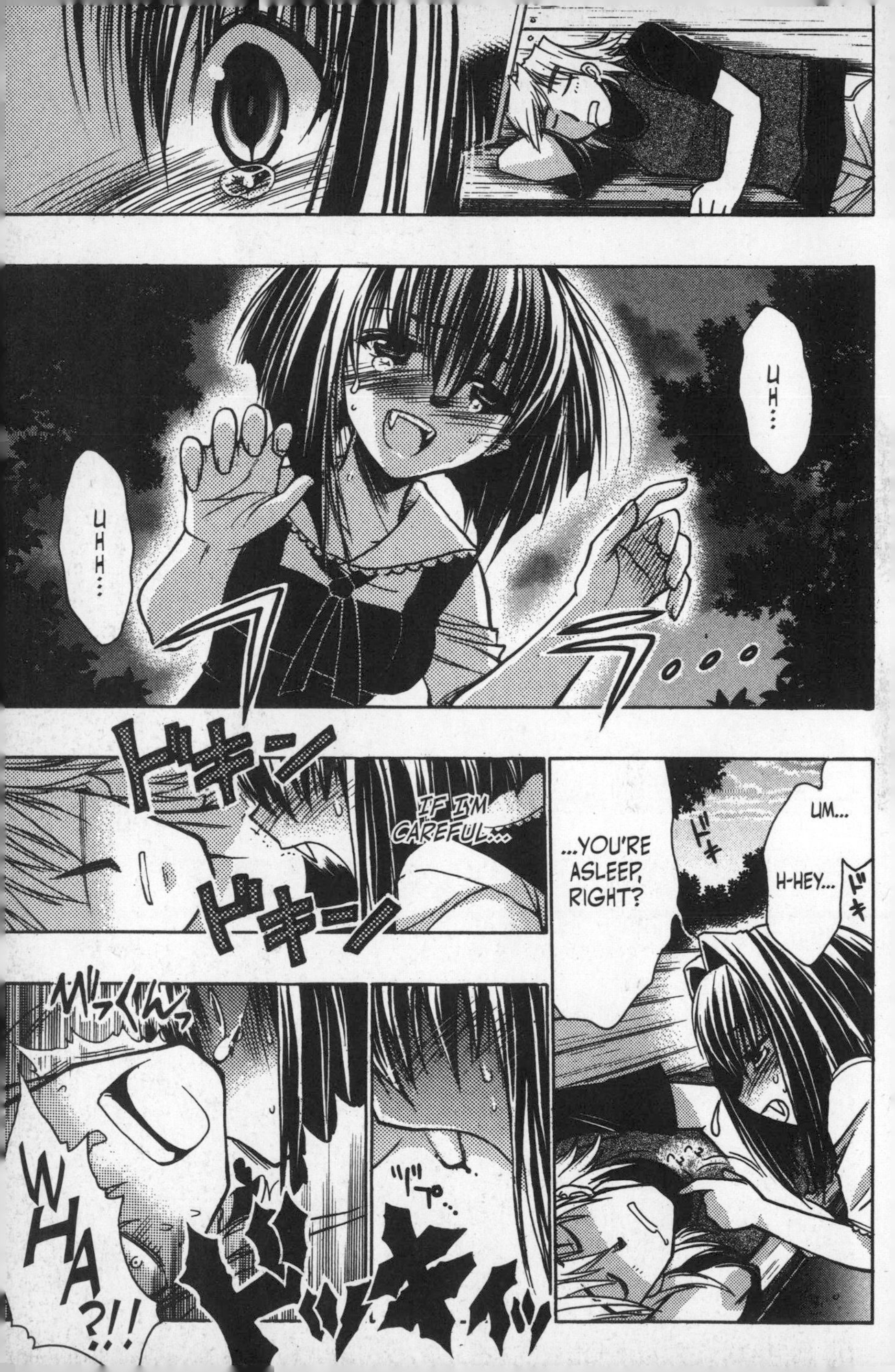
UH...
UHH...
....
UM...
H-HEY...
ドキ
ドキ
...YOU'RE ASLEEP, RIGHT?
ドキーン
ドキーン
IF I'M CAREFUL...
WHA?!!

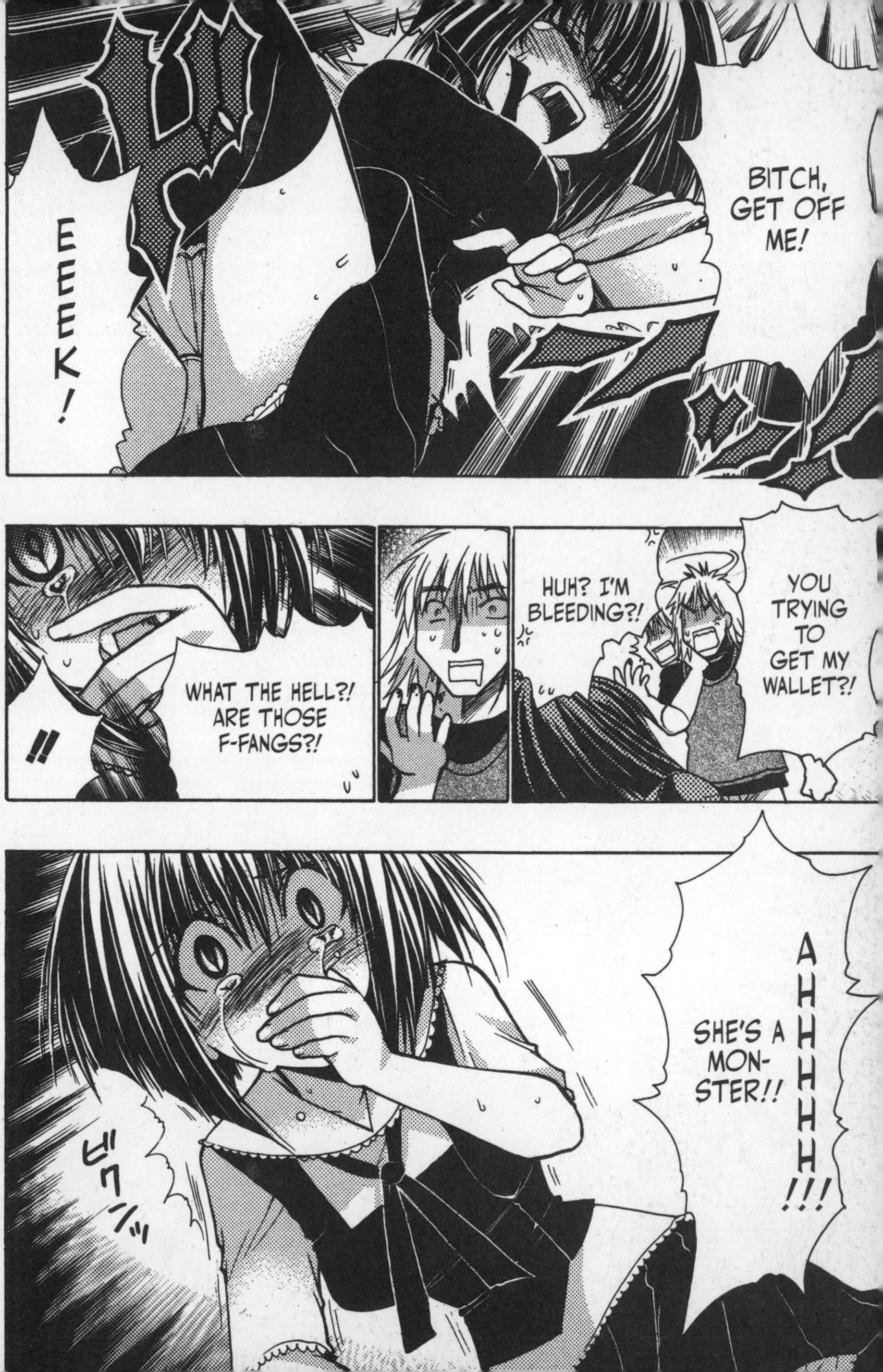
BITCH, GET OFF ME!
EEEEK!
YOU TRYING TO GET MY WALLET?!
HUH? I'M BLEEDING?!
WHAT THE HELL?! ARE THOSE F-FANGS?!
!!
AHHHHHH!!!
SHE'S A MON-STER!!
ビクンッ

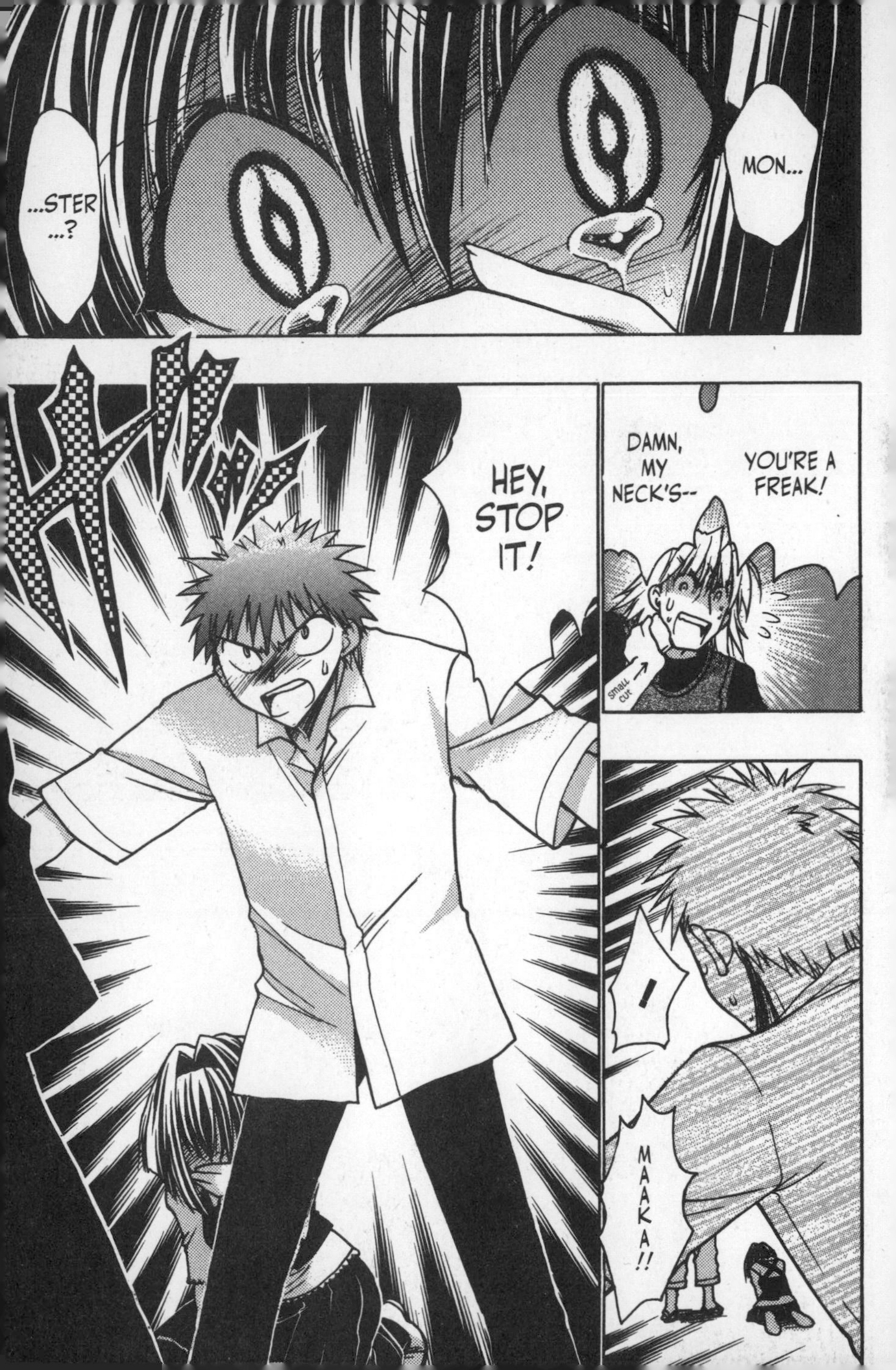
MON...
...STER ...?
YOU'RE A FREAK!
DAMN, MY NECK'S--
SMALL CUT
HEY, STOP IT!
!
MAAKA!!

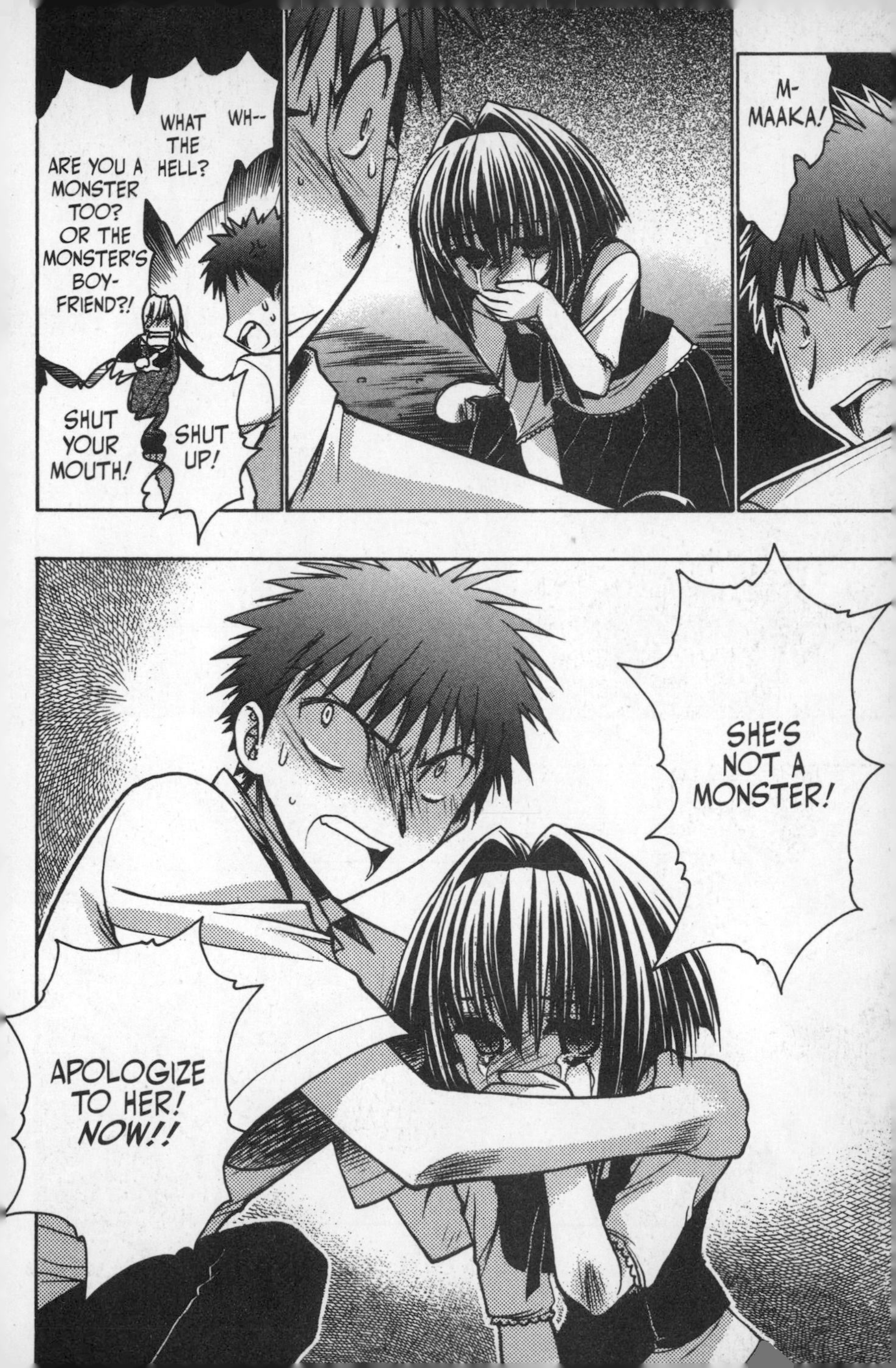
M- MAAKA!
WH--
WHAT THE HELL?
ARE YOU A MONSTER TOO? OR THE MONSTER'S BOY-FRIEND?!
SHUT UP!
SHUT YOUR MOUTH!
SHE'S NOT A MONSTER!
APOLOGIZE TO HER! NOW!!

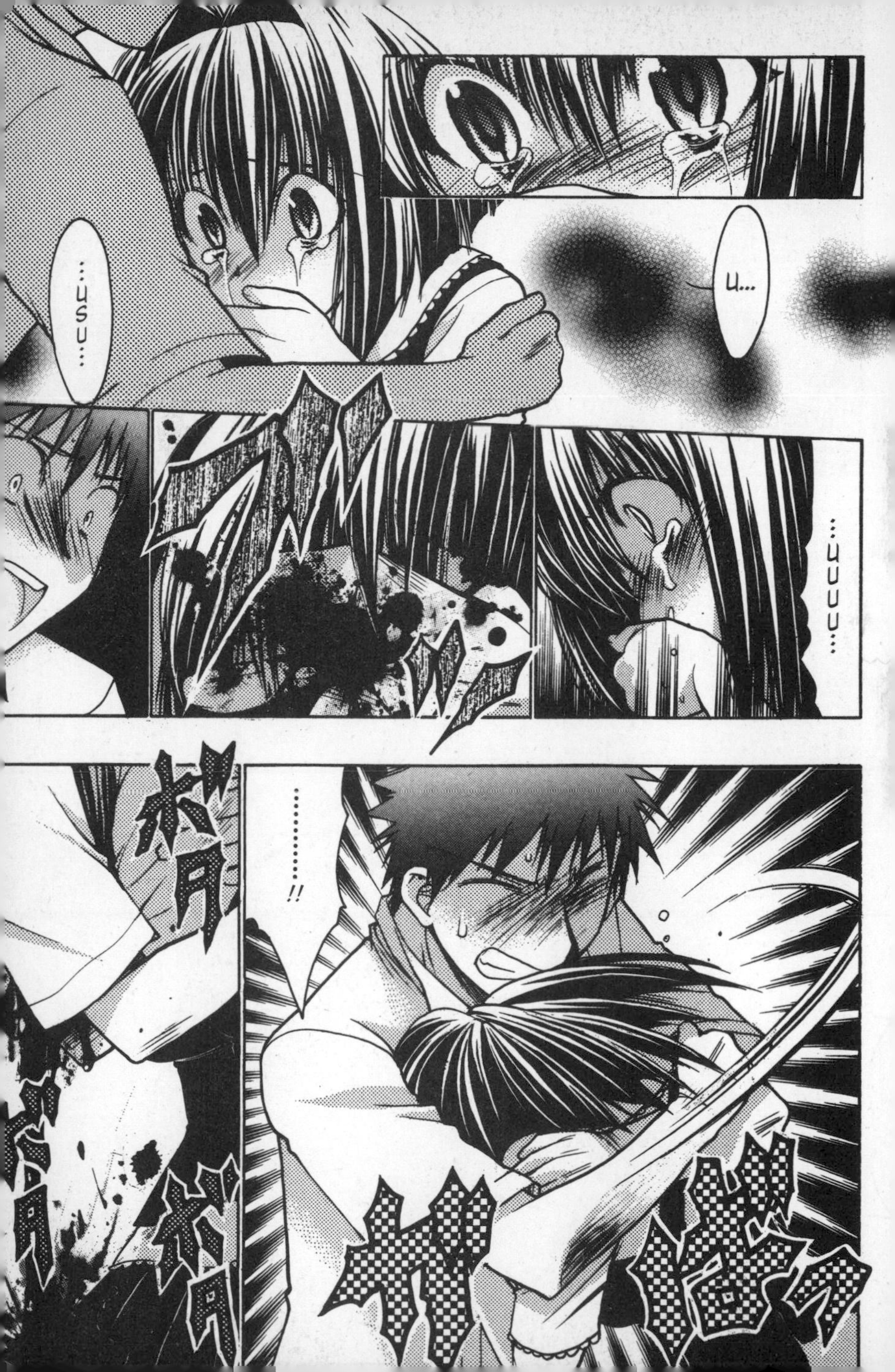
U...
...USU...
...UUUU...
......!!

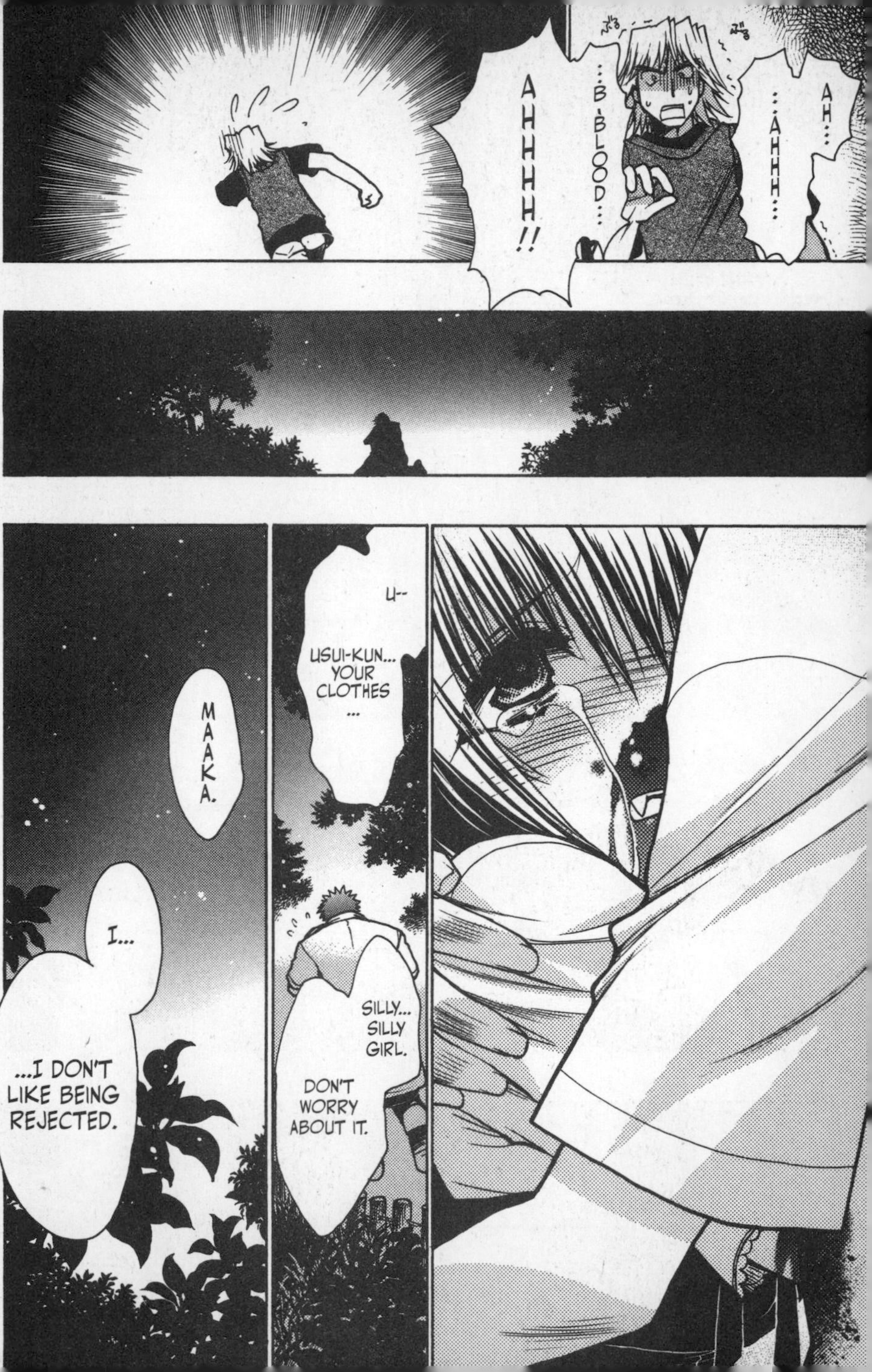
AH...
...AHHH...
...B-BLOOD...
AHHHH!!
U--
USUI-KUN... YOUR CLOTHES ...
SILLY... SILLY GIRL.
DON'T WORRY ABOUT IT.
MAAKA.
I...
...I DON'T LIKE BEING REJECTED.

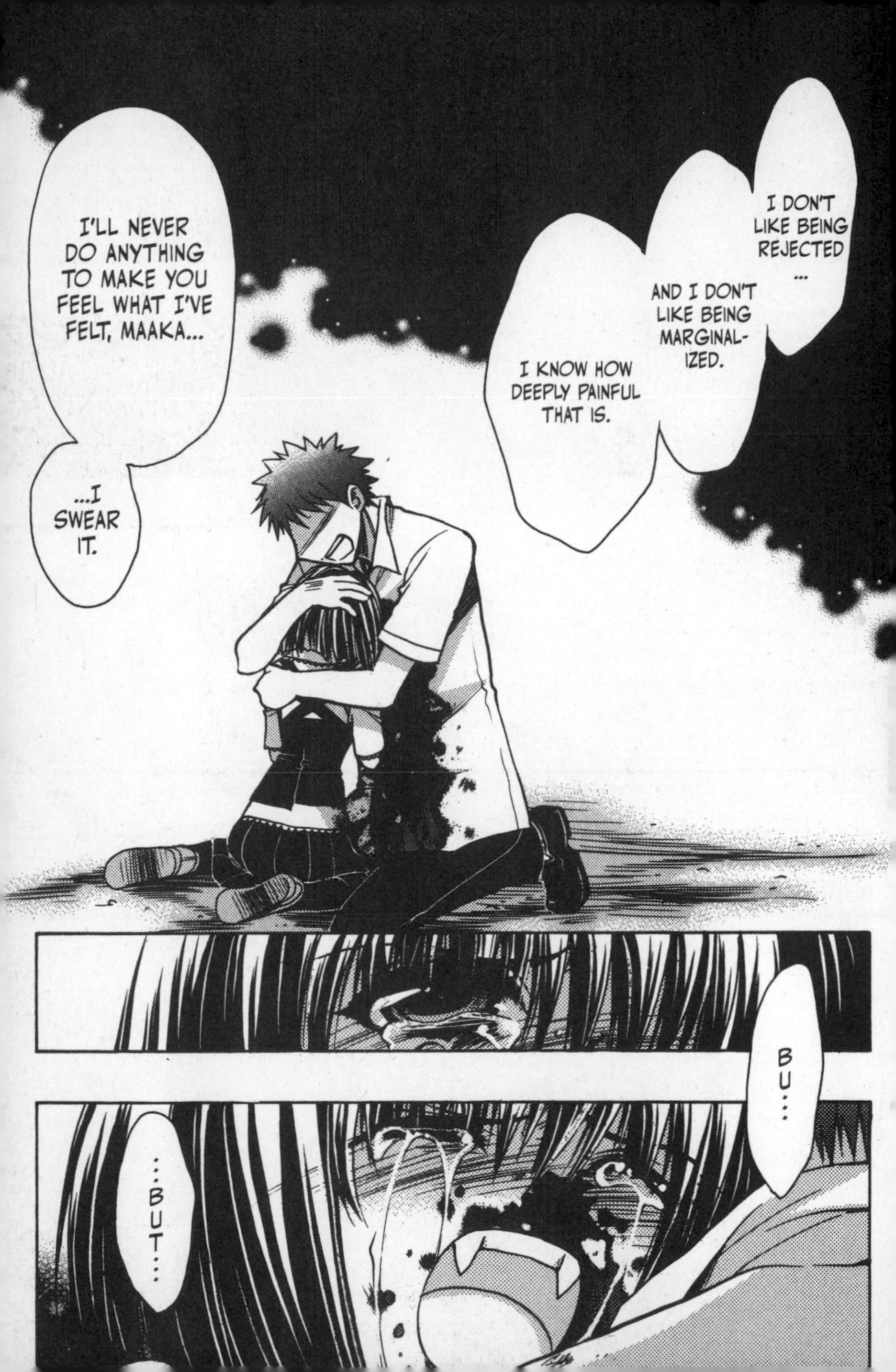
I DON'T LIKE BEING REJECTED ...
AND I DON'T LIKE BEING MARGINAL-IZED.
I KNOW HOW DEEPLY PAINFUL THAT IS.
I'LL NEVER DO ANYTHING TO MAKE YOU FEEL WHAT I'VE FELT, MAAKA...
...I SWEAR IT.
BU...
...BUT...

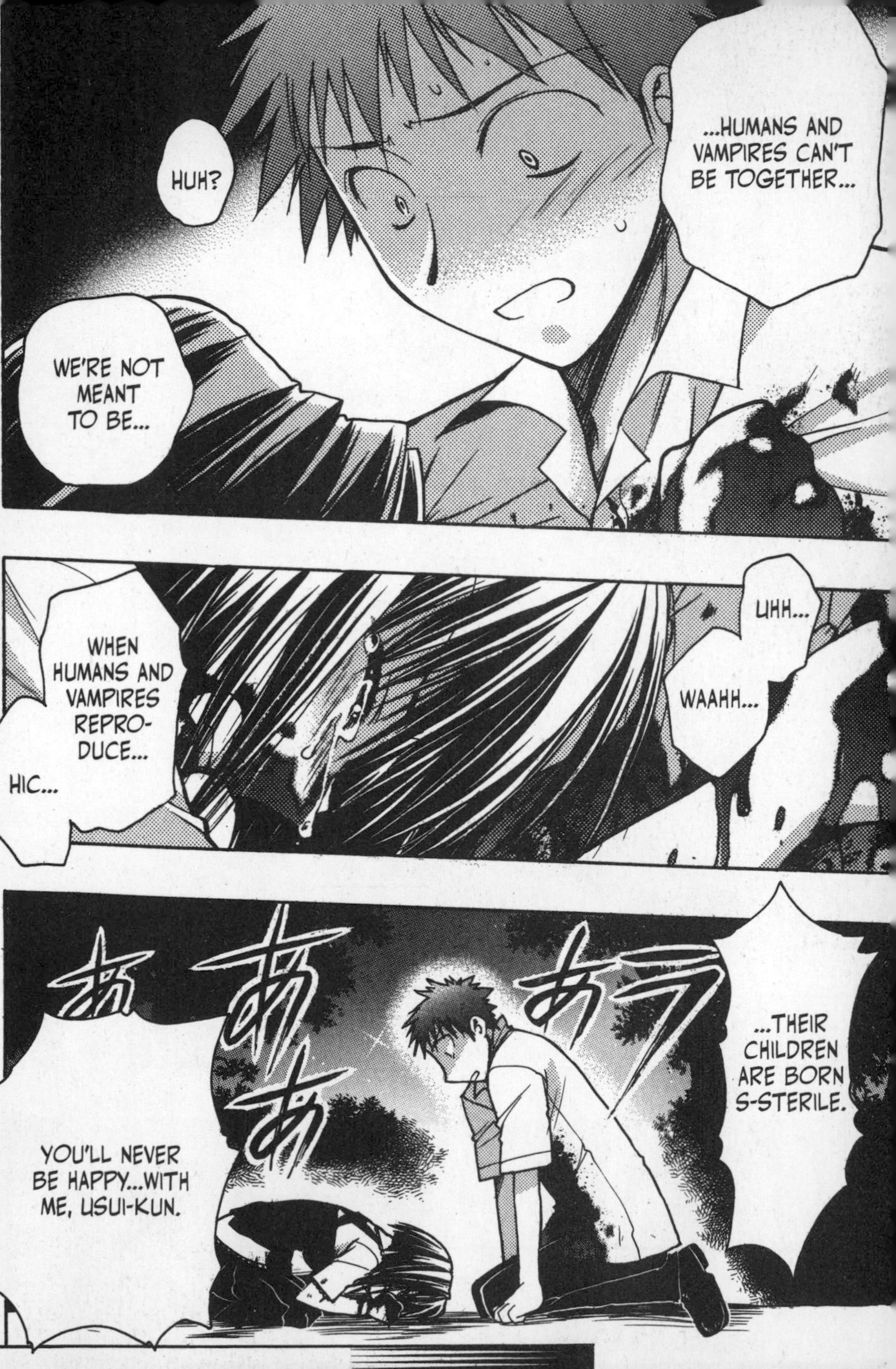
...HUMANS AND VAMPIRES CAN'T BE TOGETHER...
HUH?
WE'RE NOT MEANT TO BE...
UHH...
WAAHH...
WHEN HUMANS AND VAMPIRES REPRO-DUCE...
HIC...
...THEIR CHILDREN ARE BORN S-STERILE.
あ あ あ あ
YOU'LL NEVER BE HAPPY...WITH ME, USUI-KUN.

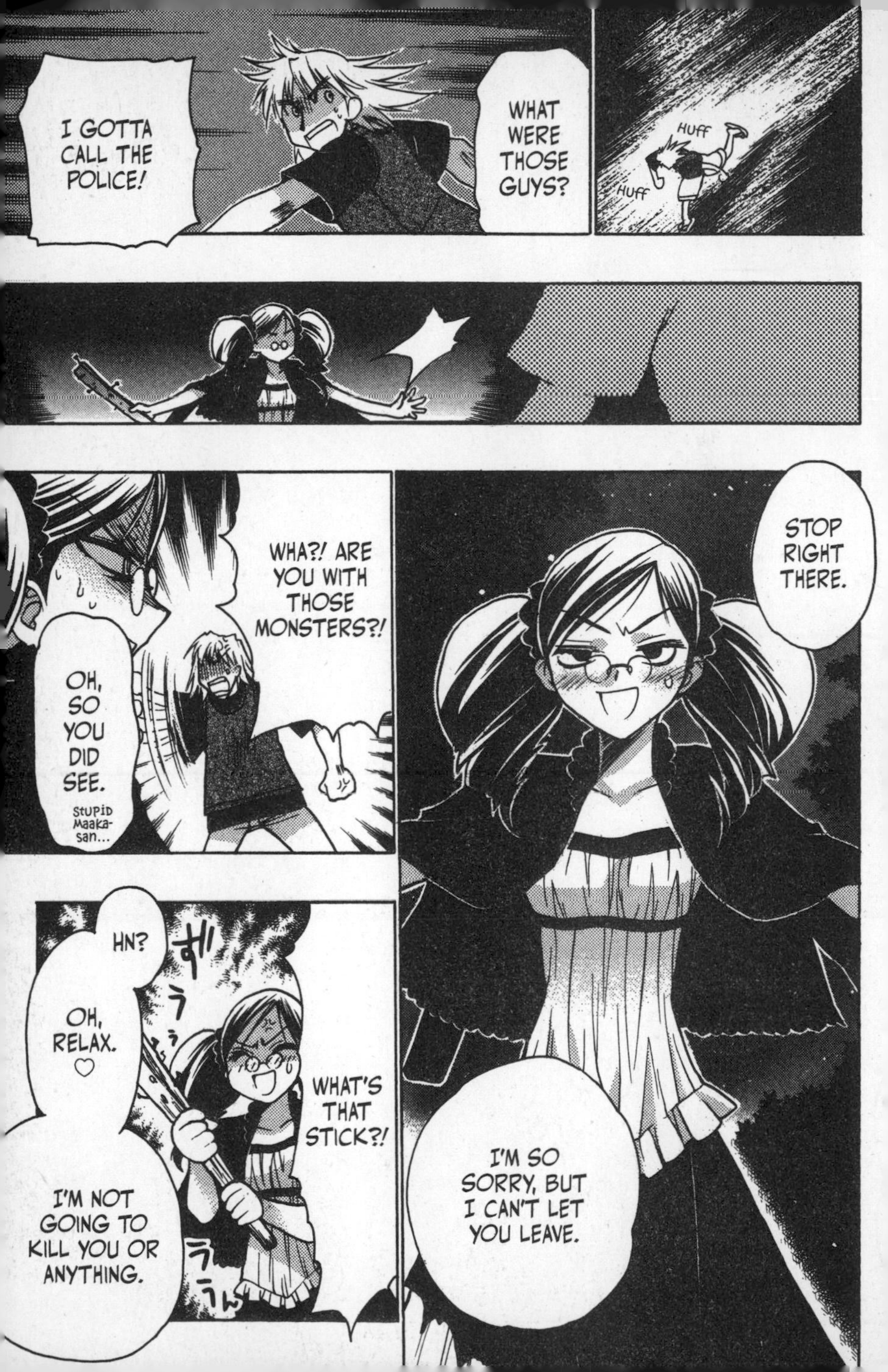
Huff
Huff
WHAT WERE THOSE GUYS?
I GOTTA CALL THE POLICE!
STOP RIGHT THERE.
I'M SO SORRY, BUT I CAN'T LET YOU LEAVE.
WHA?! ARE YOU WITH THOSE MONSTERS?!
OH, SO YOU DID SEE.
Stupid Maaka-san...
WHAT'S THAT STICK?!
HN?
OH, RELAX. ♡
I'M NOT GOING TO KILL YOU OR ANYTHING.

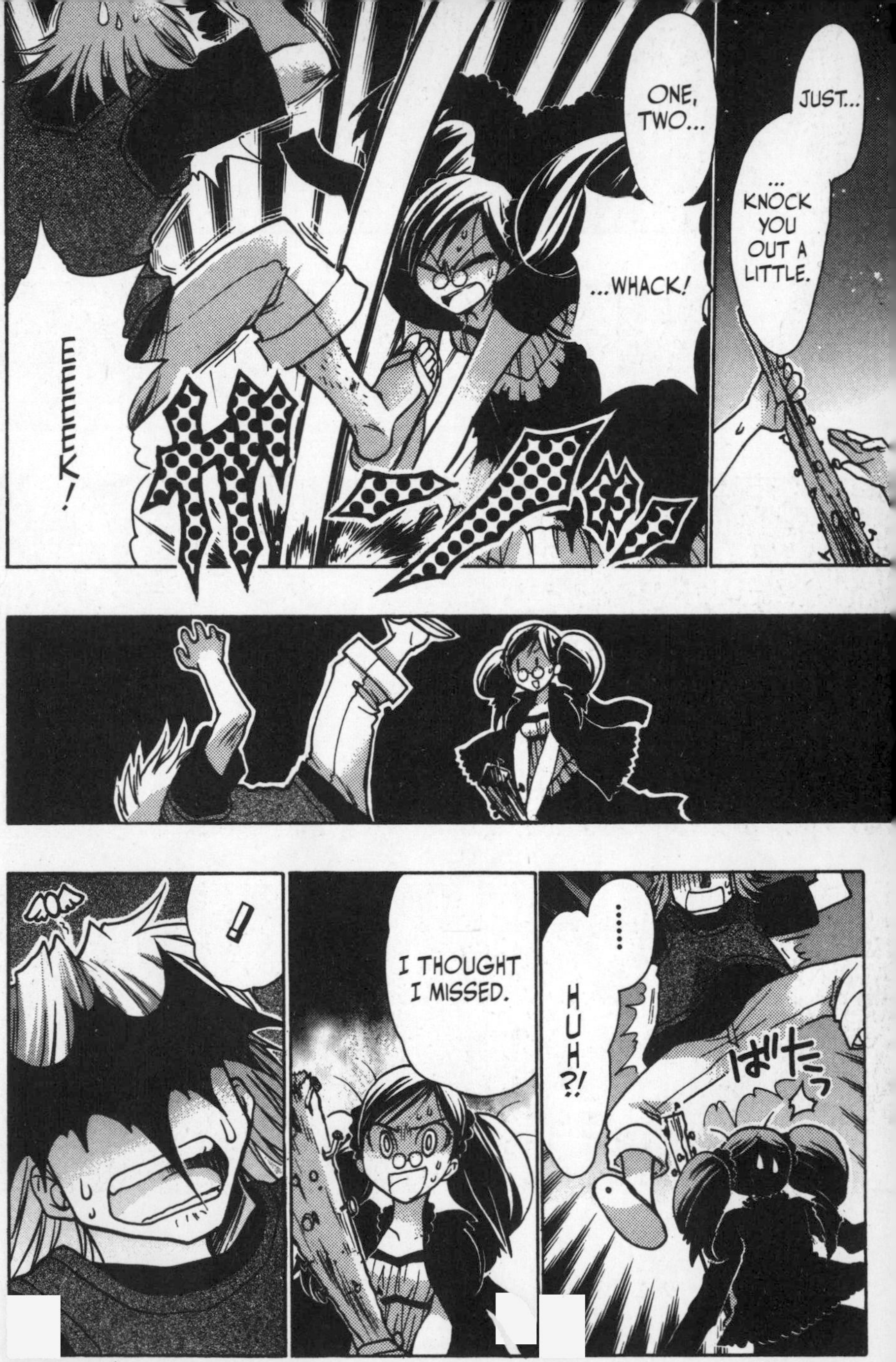
JUST...
...KNOCK YOU OUT A LITTLE.
ONE, TWO...
...WHACK!
EEEEEEK!
......
HUH?!
ぱたっ
I THOUGHT I MISSED.
!

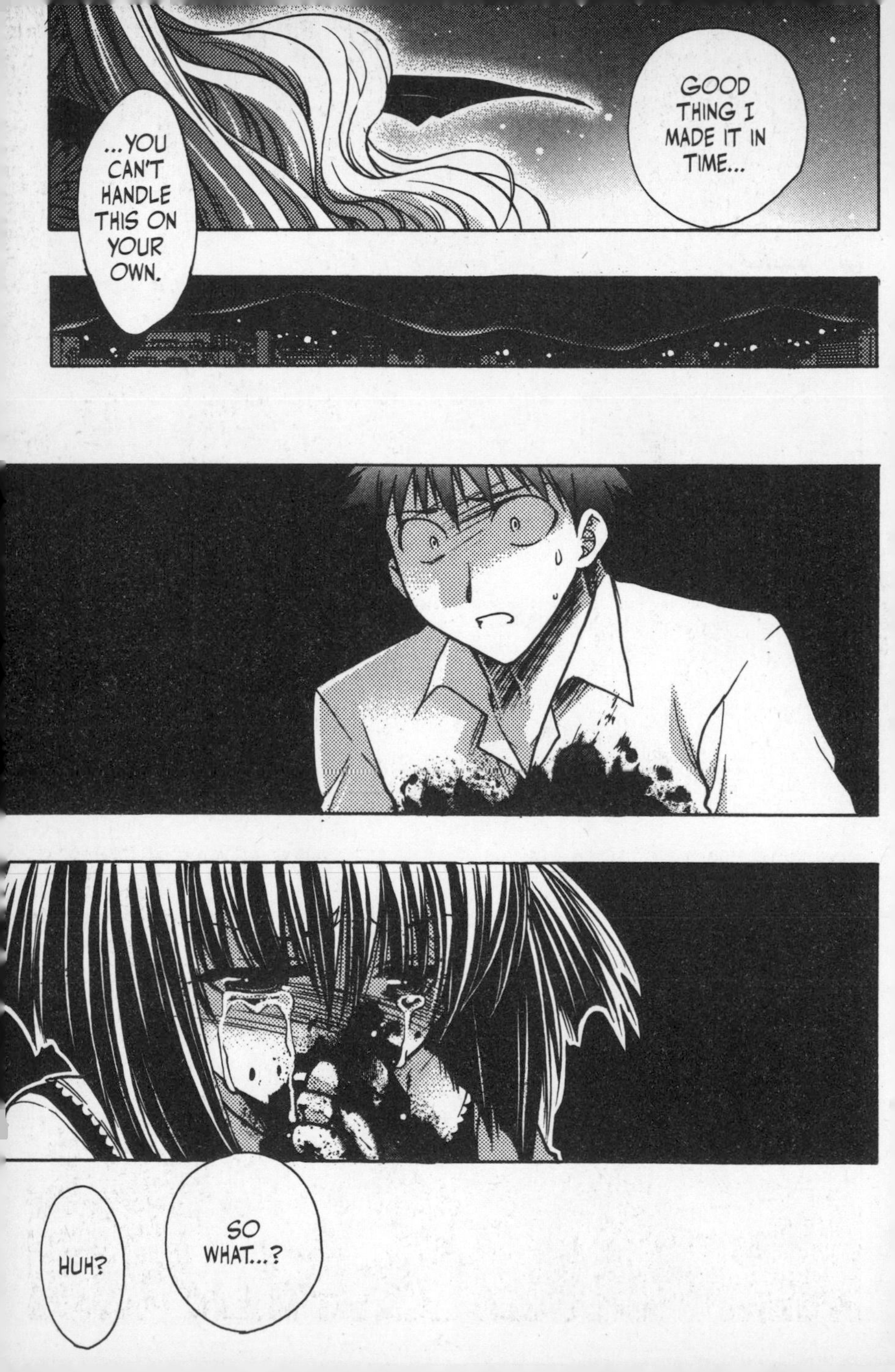
GOOD THING I MADE IT IN TIME...
...YOU CAN'T HANDLE THIS ON YOUR OWN.
SO WHAT...?
HUH?

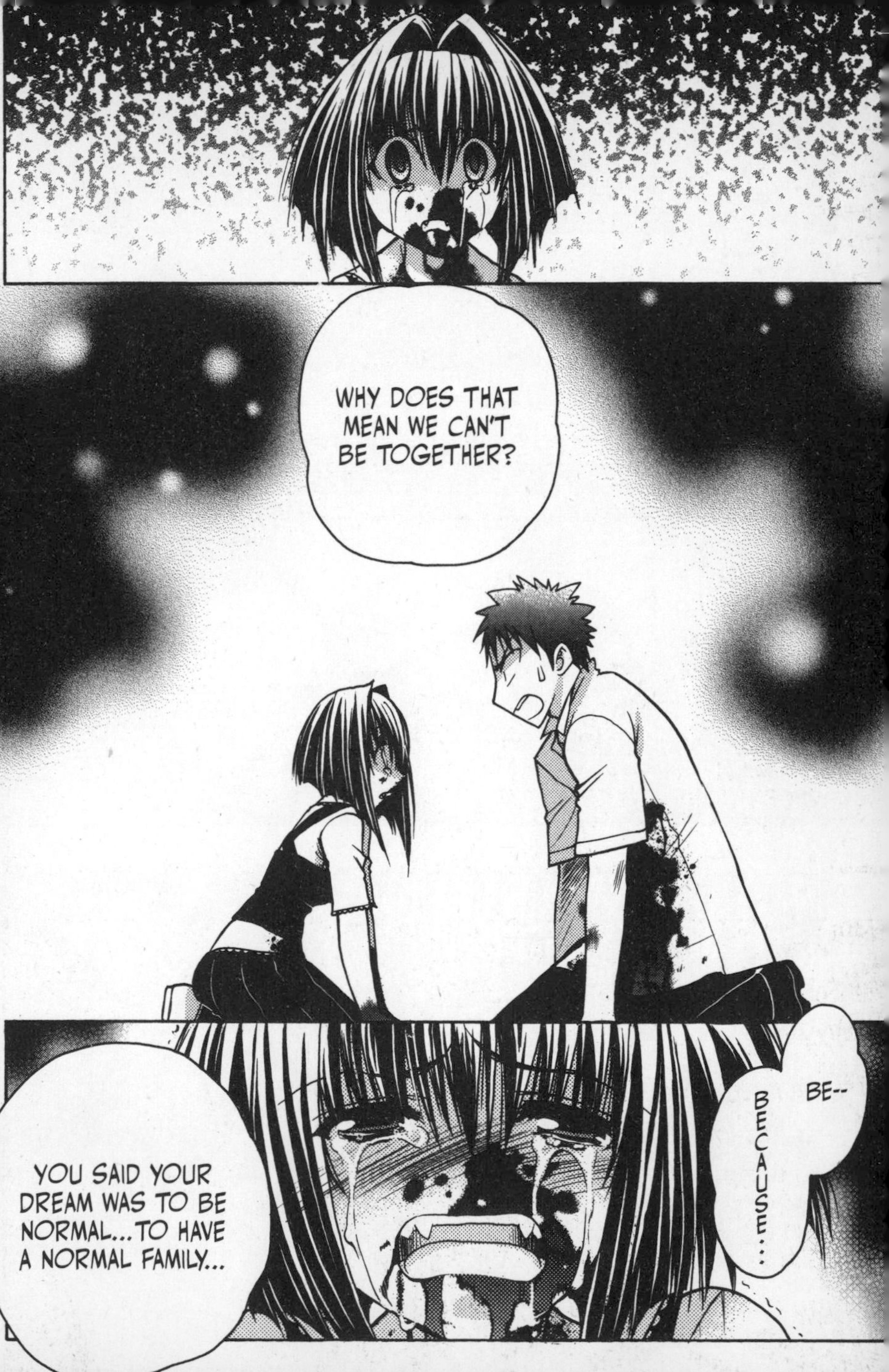
WHY DOES THAT MEAN WE CAN'T BE TOGETHER?
BE-- BECAUSE...
YOU SAID YOUR DREAM WAS TO BE NORMAL... TO HAVE A NORMAL FAMILY...

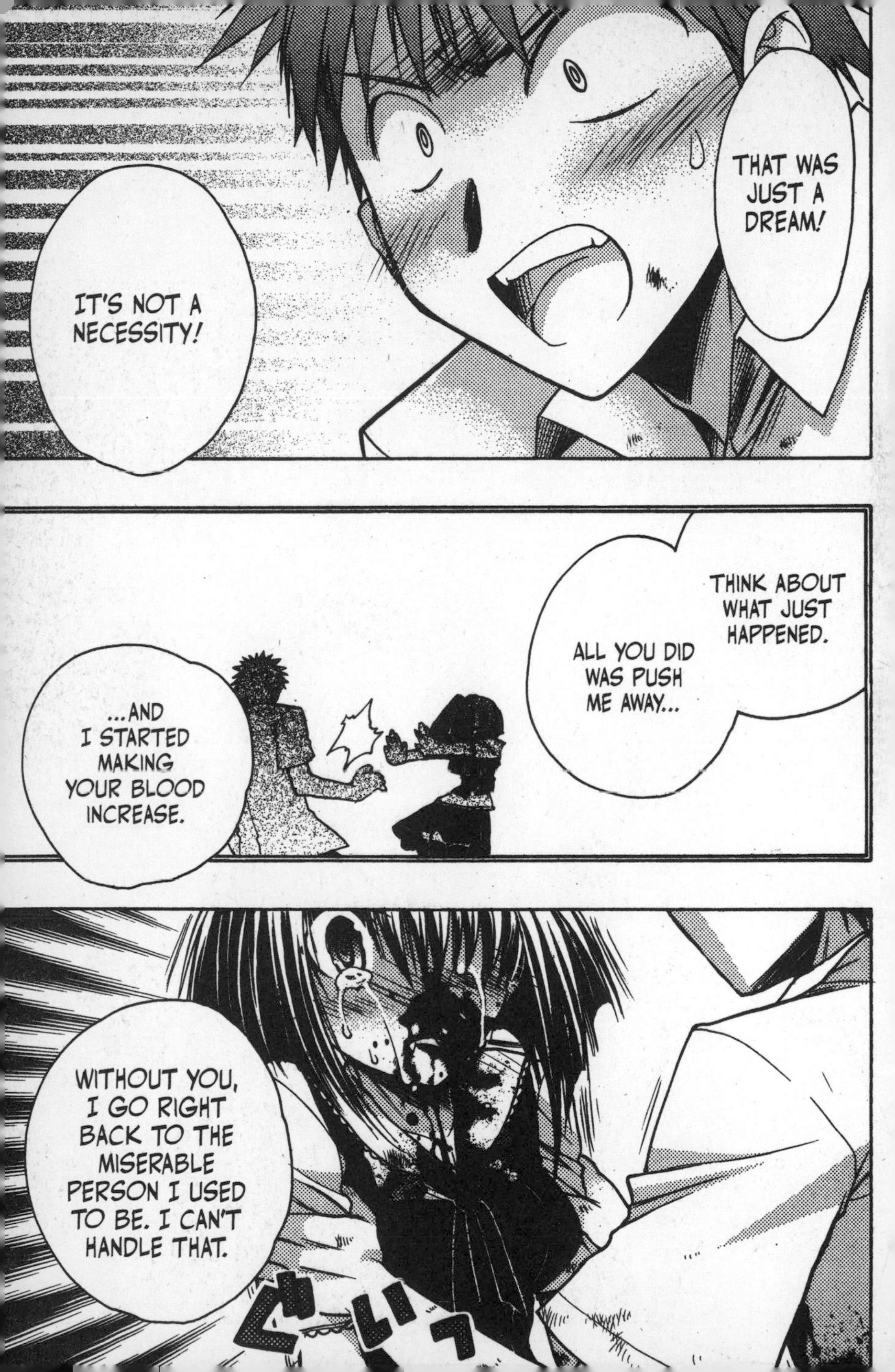
THAT WAS JUST A DREAM!
IT'S NOT A NECESSITY!
THINK ABOUT WHAT JUST HAPPENED.
ALL YOU DID WAS PUSH ME AWAY...
...AND I STARTED MAKING YOUR BLOOD INCREASE.
WITHOUT YOU, I GO RIGHT BACK TO THE MISERABLE PERSON I USED TO BE. I CAN'T HANDLE THAT.

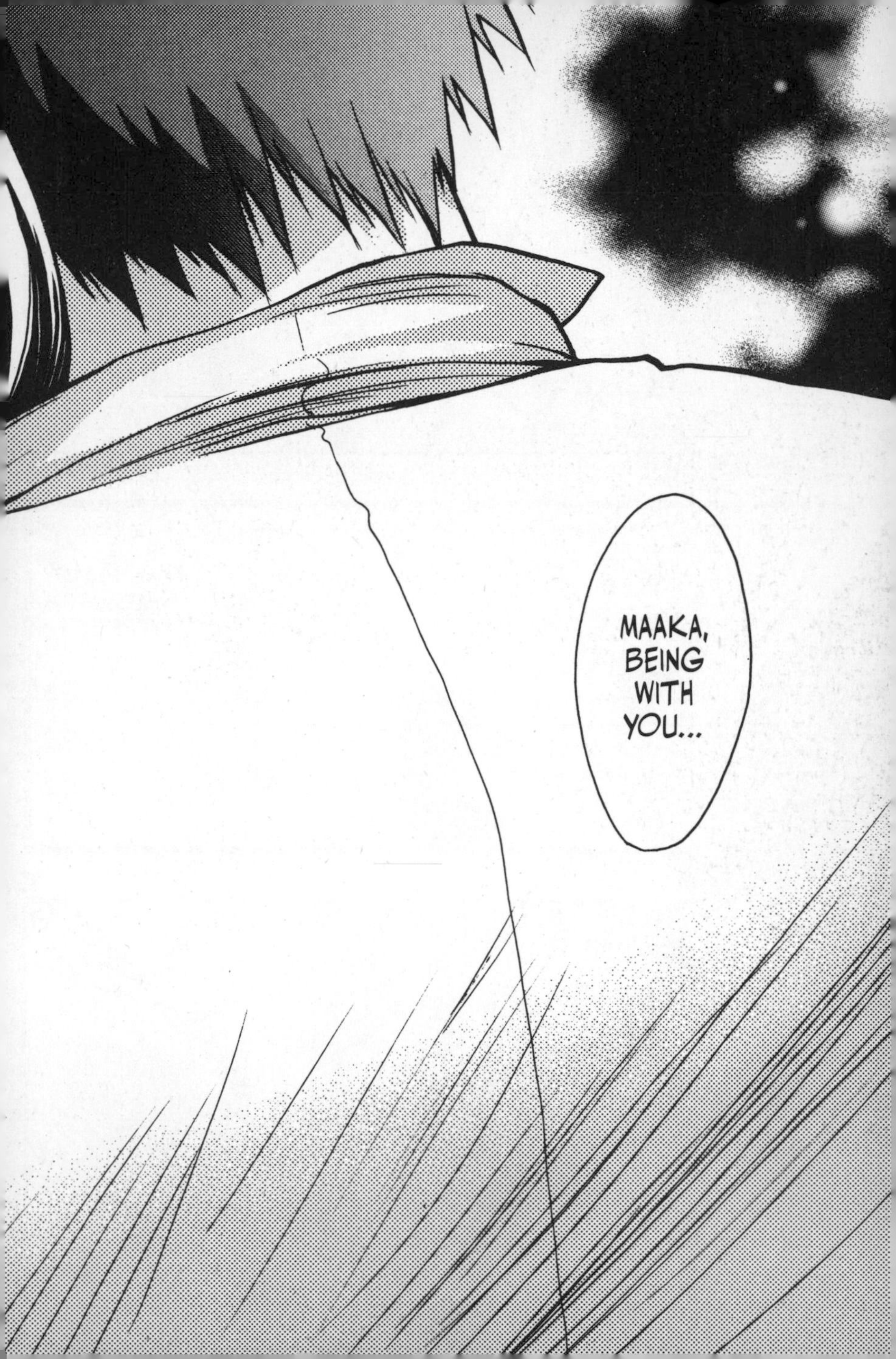
MAAKA, BEING WITH YOU...

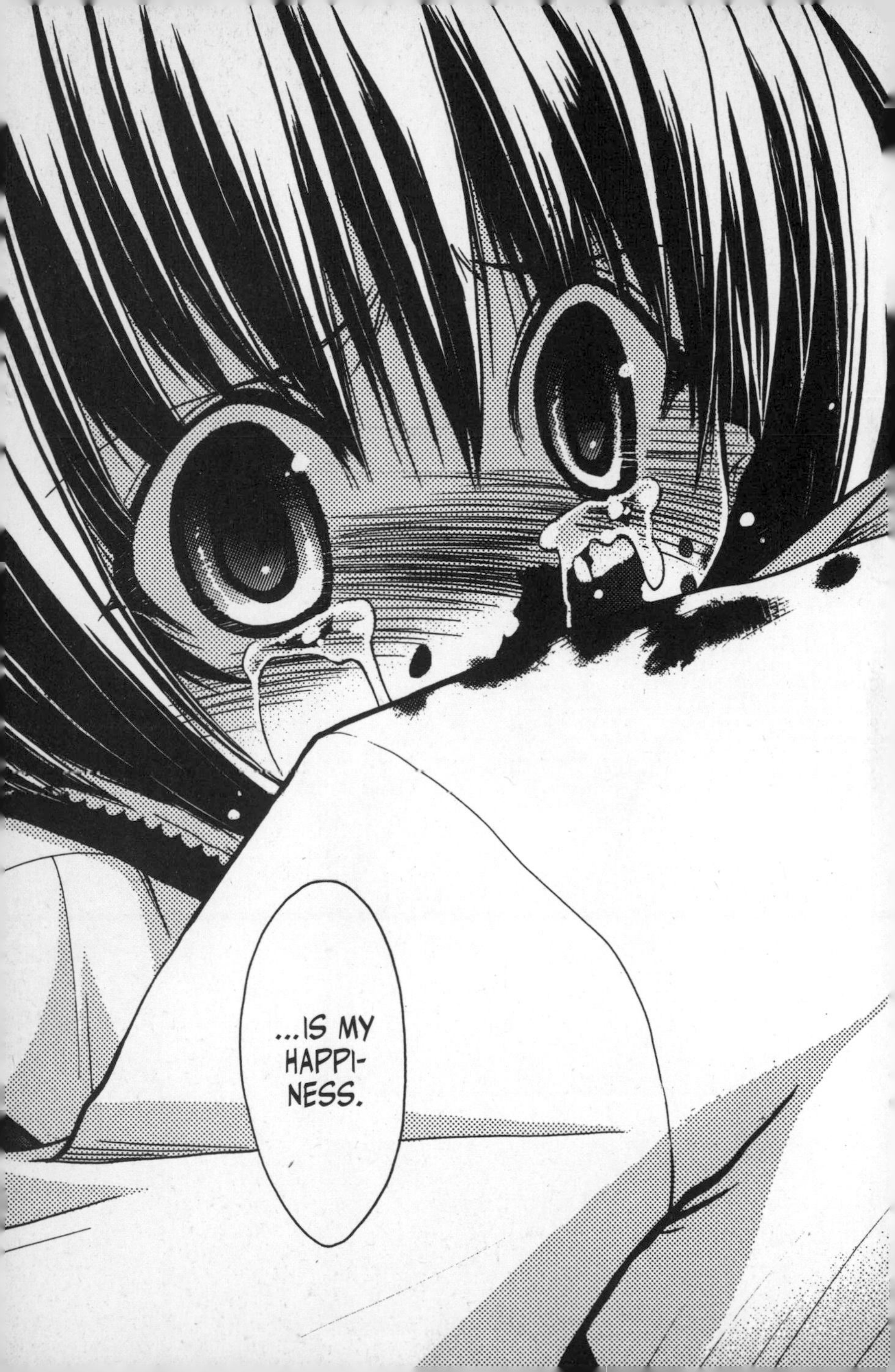
...IS MY HAPPI- NESS.

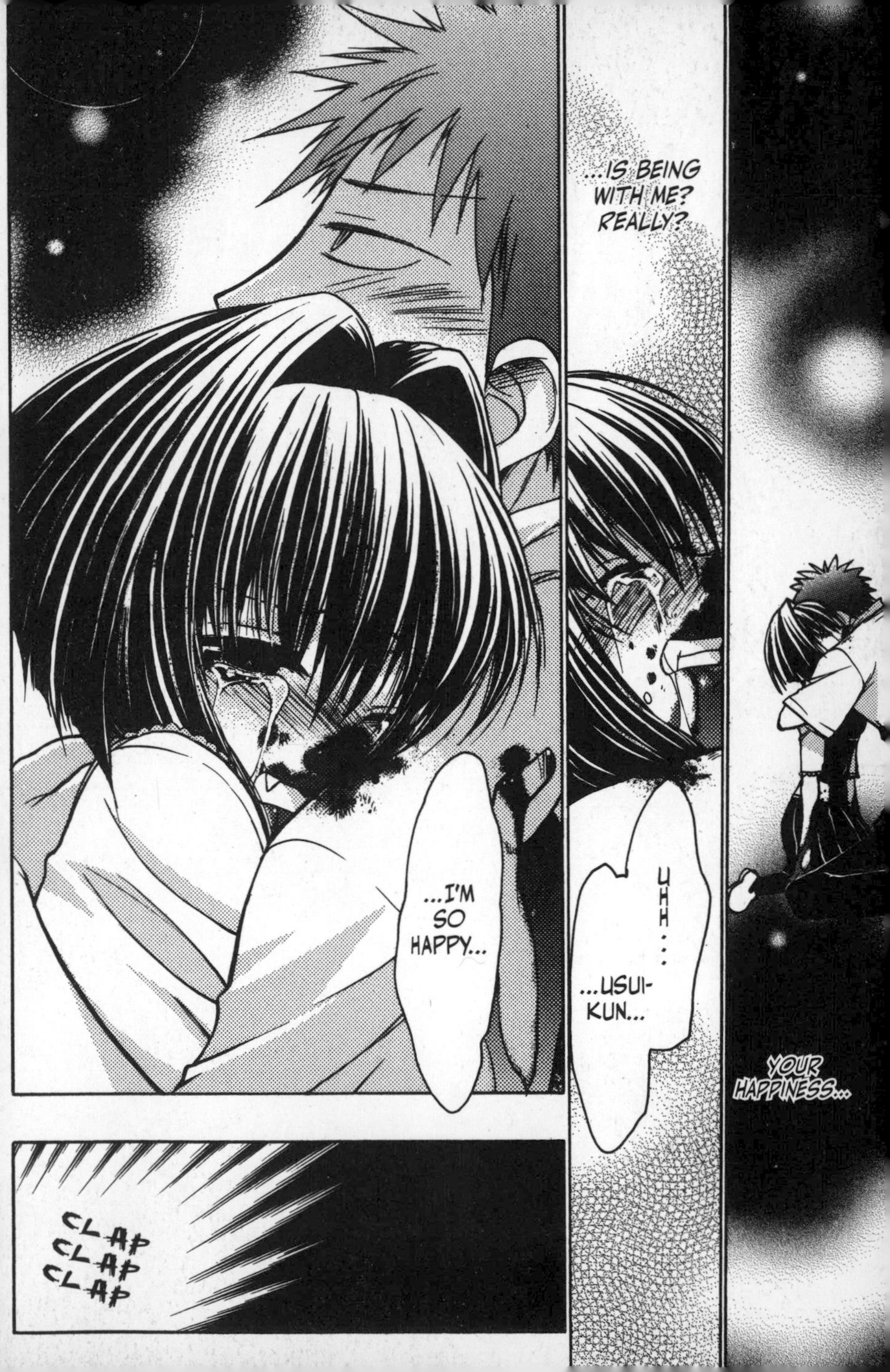
YOUR HAPPINESS...
...IS BEING WITH ME? REALLY?
UHH...
...USUI-KUN...
...I'M SO HAPPY...
CLAP CLAP CLAP

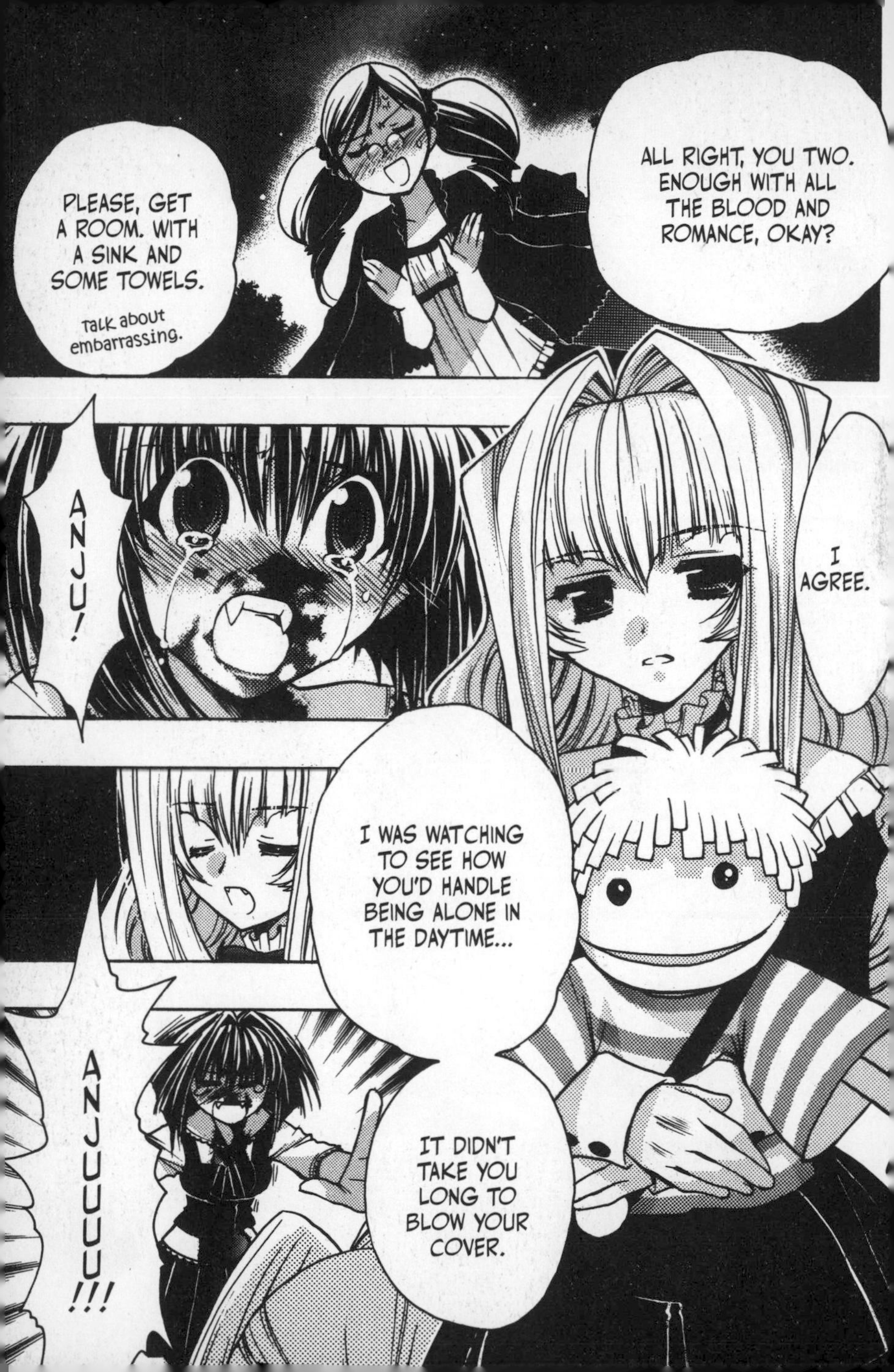
ALL RIGHT, YOU TWO. ENOUGH WITH ALL THE BLOOD AND ROMANCE, OKAY?
PLEASE, GET A ROOM. WITH A SINK AND SOME TOWELS.
Talk about embarrassing.
I AGREE.
ANJU!
I WAS WATCHING TO SEE HOW YOU'D HANDLE BEING ALONE IN THE DAYTIME...
IT DIDN'T TAKE YOU LONG TO BLOW YOUR COVER.
ANJUUUU!!!

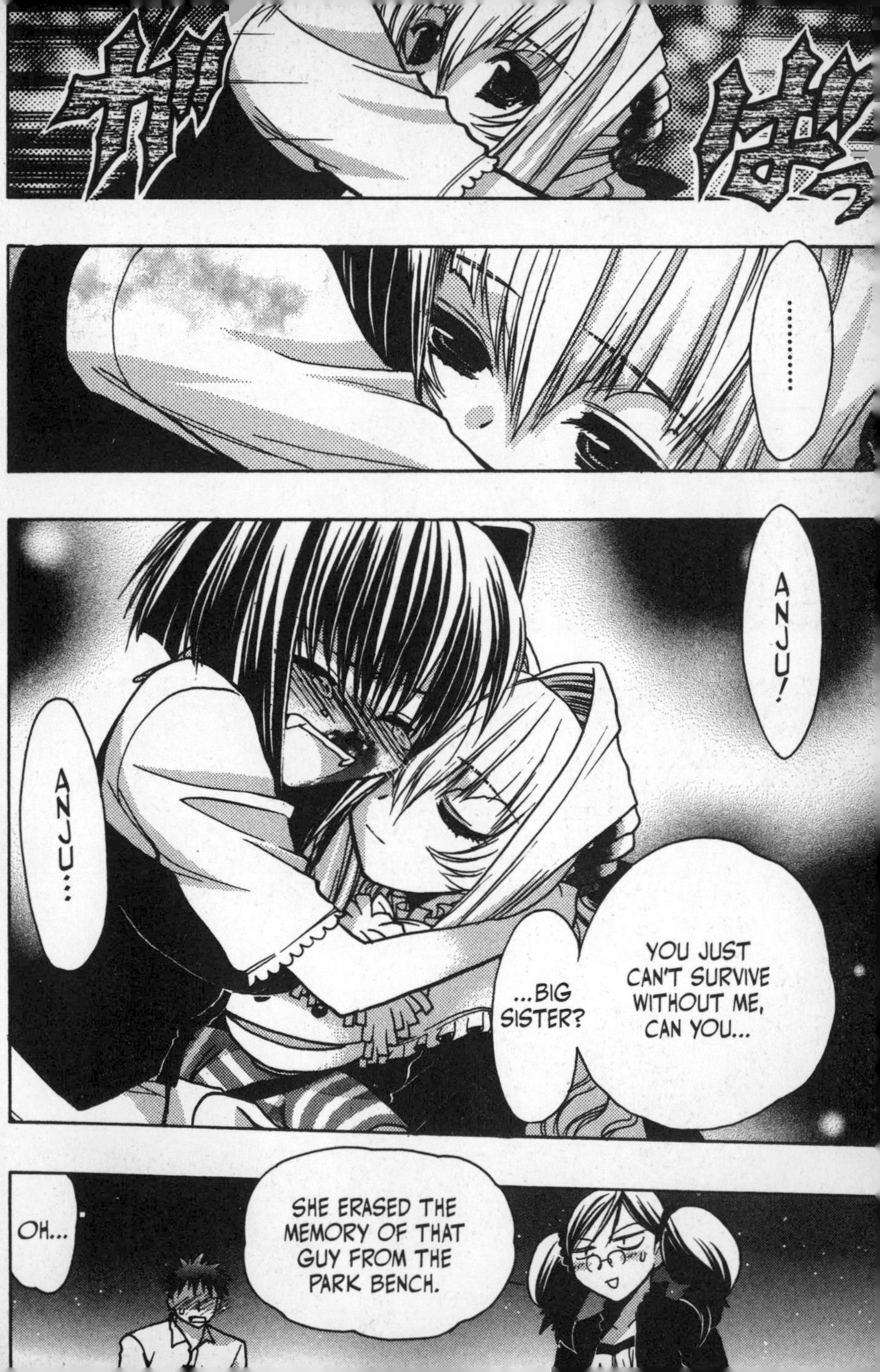

......
ANJU!
ANJU...
YOU JUST CAN'T SURVIVE WITHOUT ME, CAN YOU...
...BIG SISTER?
SHE ERASED THE MEMORY OF THAT GUY FROM THE PARK BENCH.
OH...

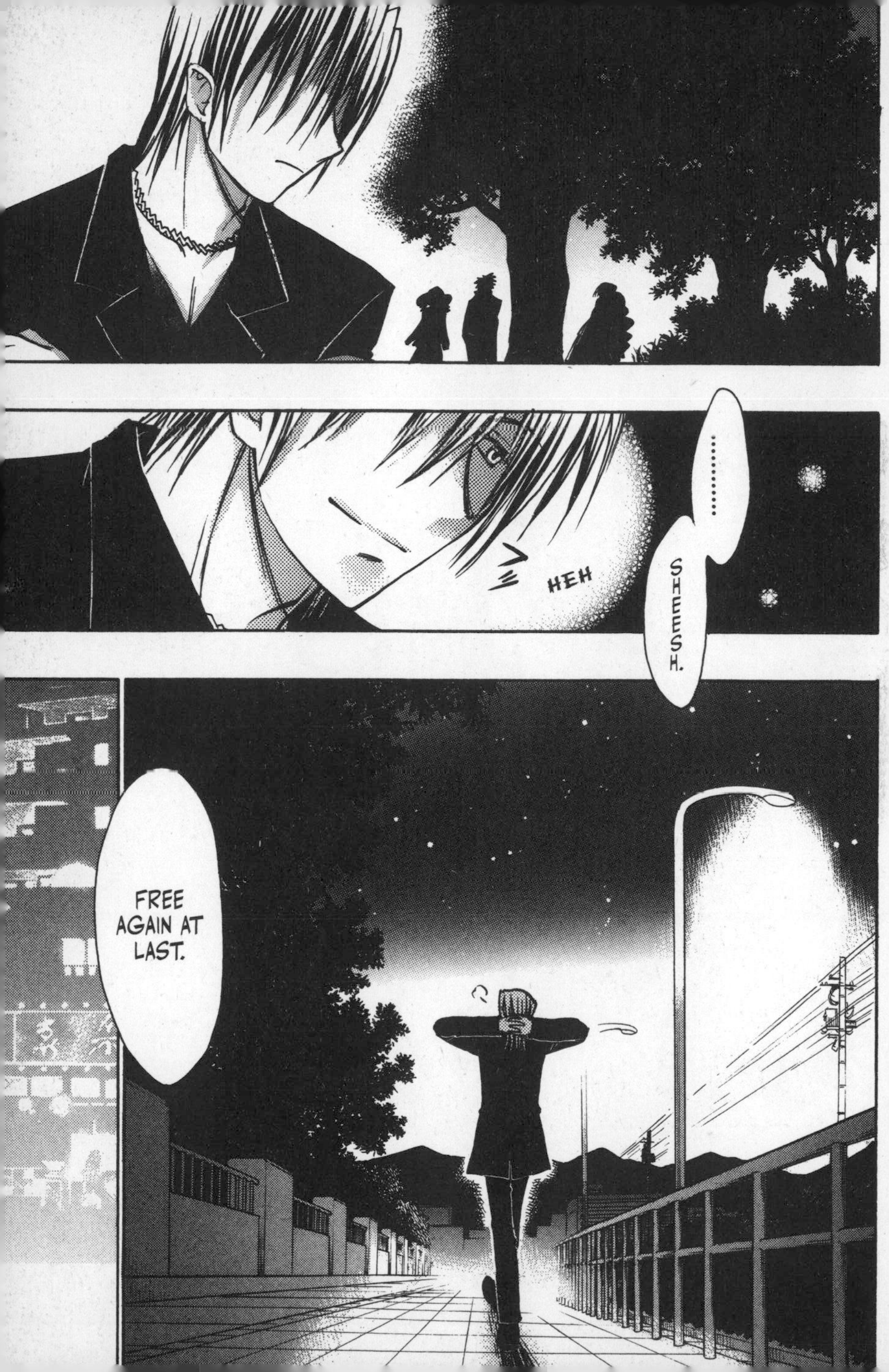
......
SHEESH.
HEH
FREE AGAIN AT LAST.

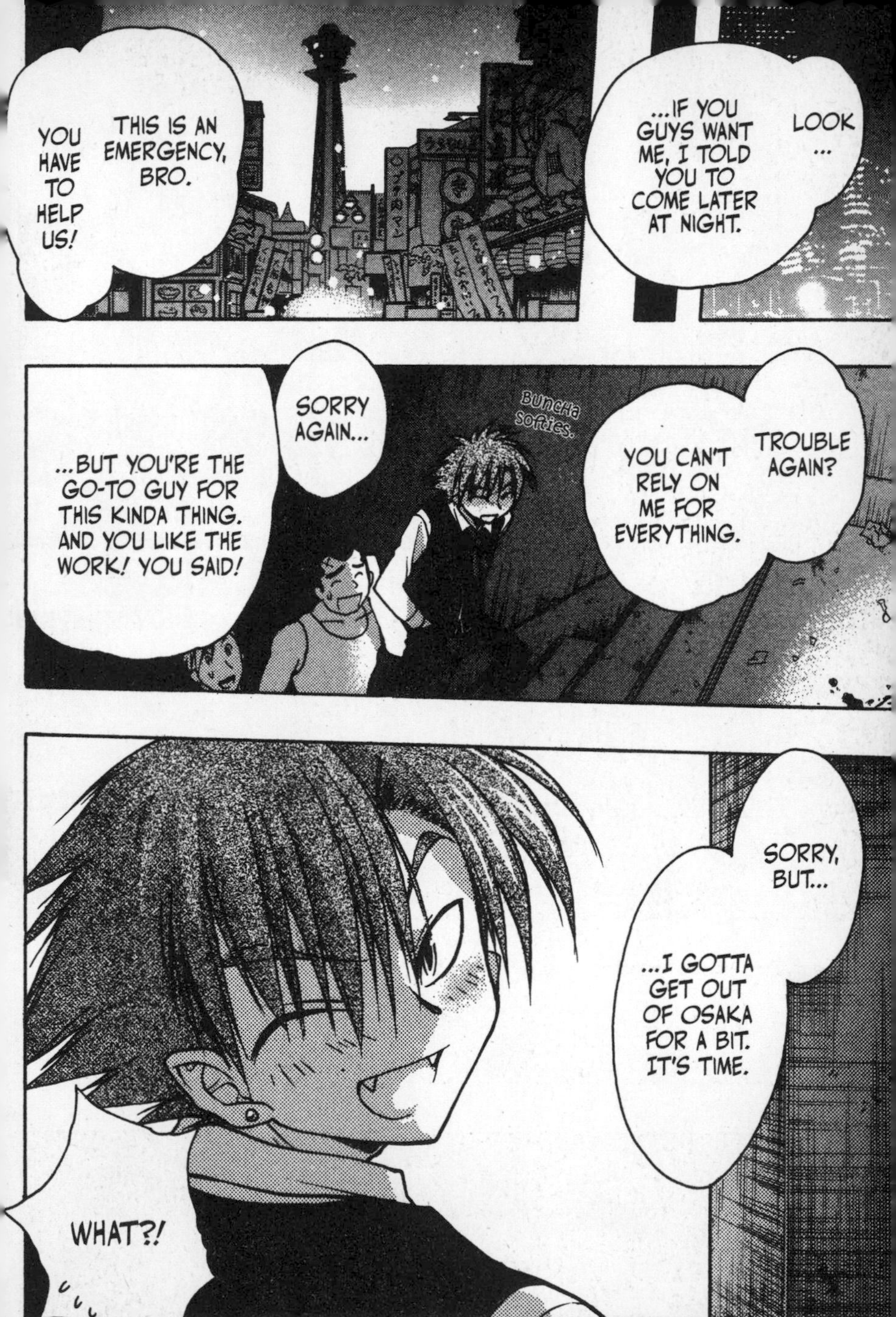
LOOK ...
...IF YOU GUYS WANT ME, I TOLD YOU TO COME LATER AT NIGHT.
THIS IS AN EMERGENCY, BRO.
YOU HAVE TO HELP US!
TROUBLE AGAIN?
YOU CAN'T RELY ON ME FOR EVERYTHING.
BUNCHA SOFTIES.
SORRY AGAIN...
...BUT YOU'RE THE GO-TO GUY FOR THIS KINDA THING. AND YOU LIKE THE WORK! YOU SAID!
SORRY, BUT...
...I GOTTA GET OUT OF OSAKA FOR A BIT. IT'S TIME.
WHAT?!

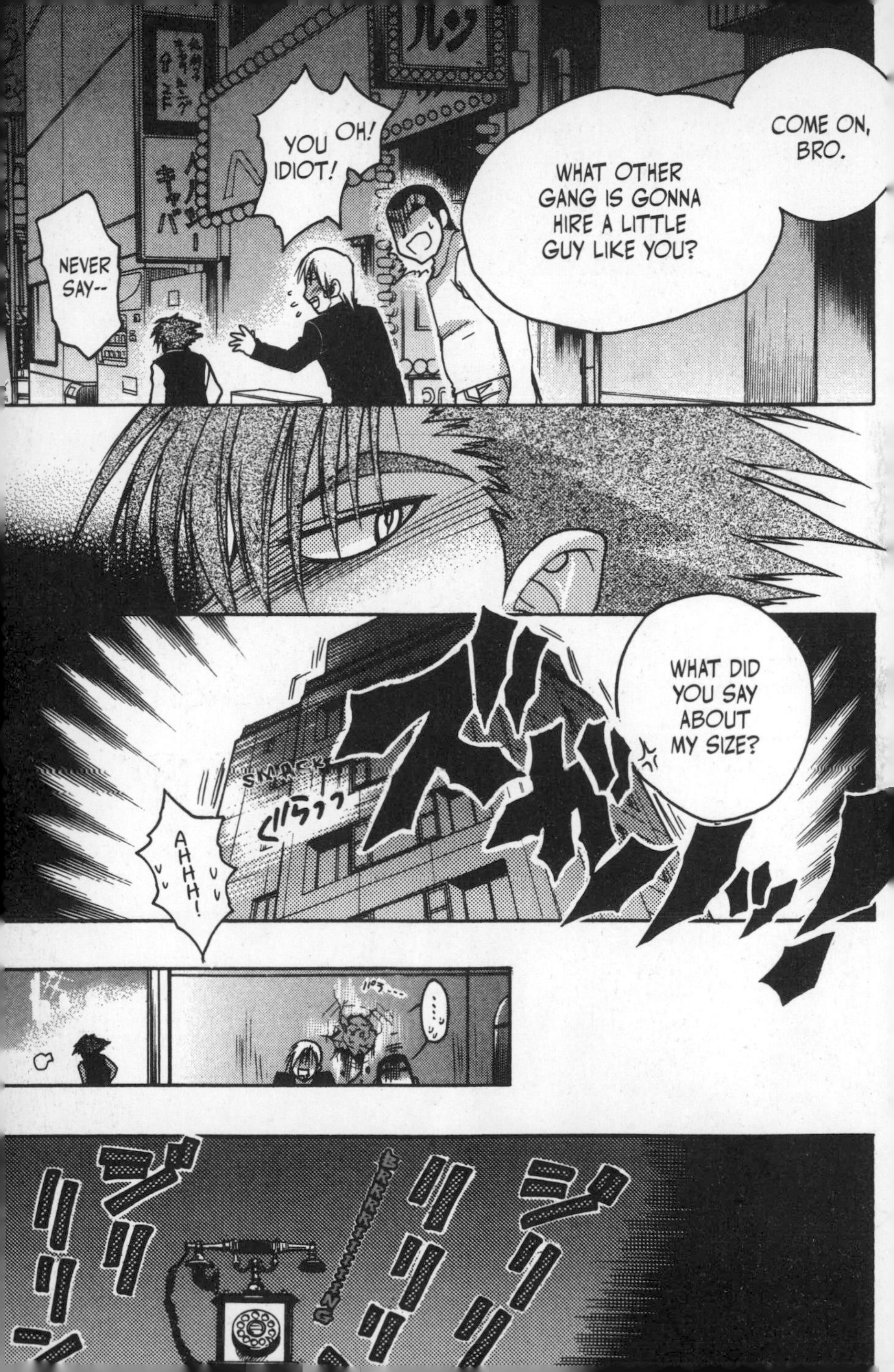
COME ON, BRO.
WHAT OTHER GANG IS GONNA HIRE A LITTLE GUY LIKE YOU?
OH! YOU IDIOT!
NEVER SAY--
WHAT DID YOU SAY ABOUT MY SIZE?
SMACK
AHHHH!

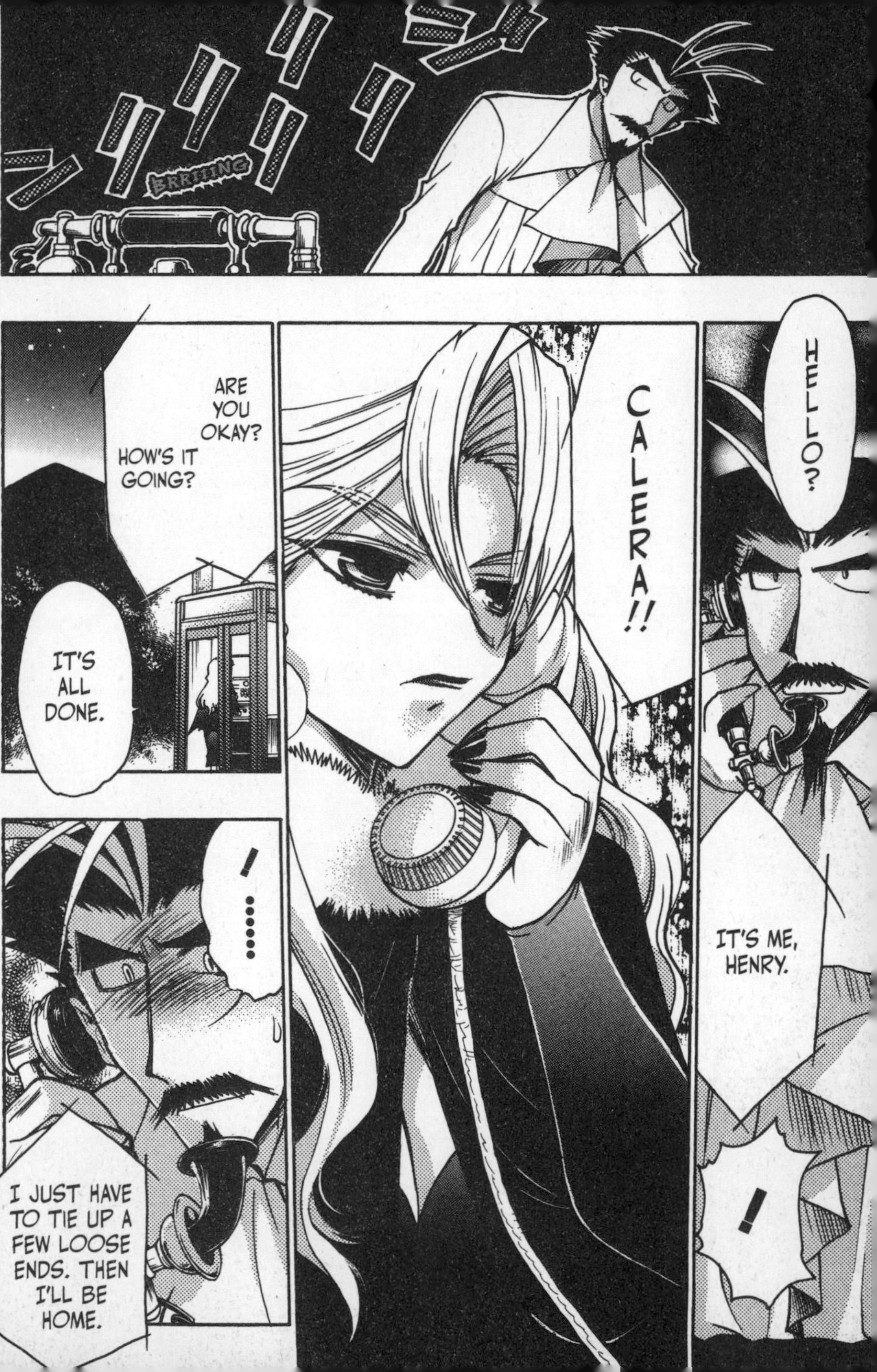
BRRIIING
HELLO?
IT'S ME, HENRY.
!
CALERA!!
ARE YOU OKAY?
HOW'S IT GOING?
IT'S ALL DONE.
!......
I JUST HAVE TO TIE UP A FEW LOOSE ENDS. THEN I'LL BE HOME.

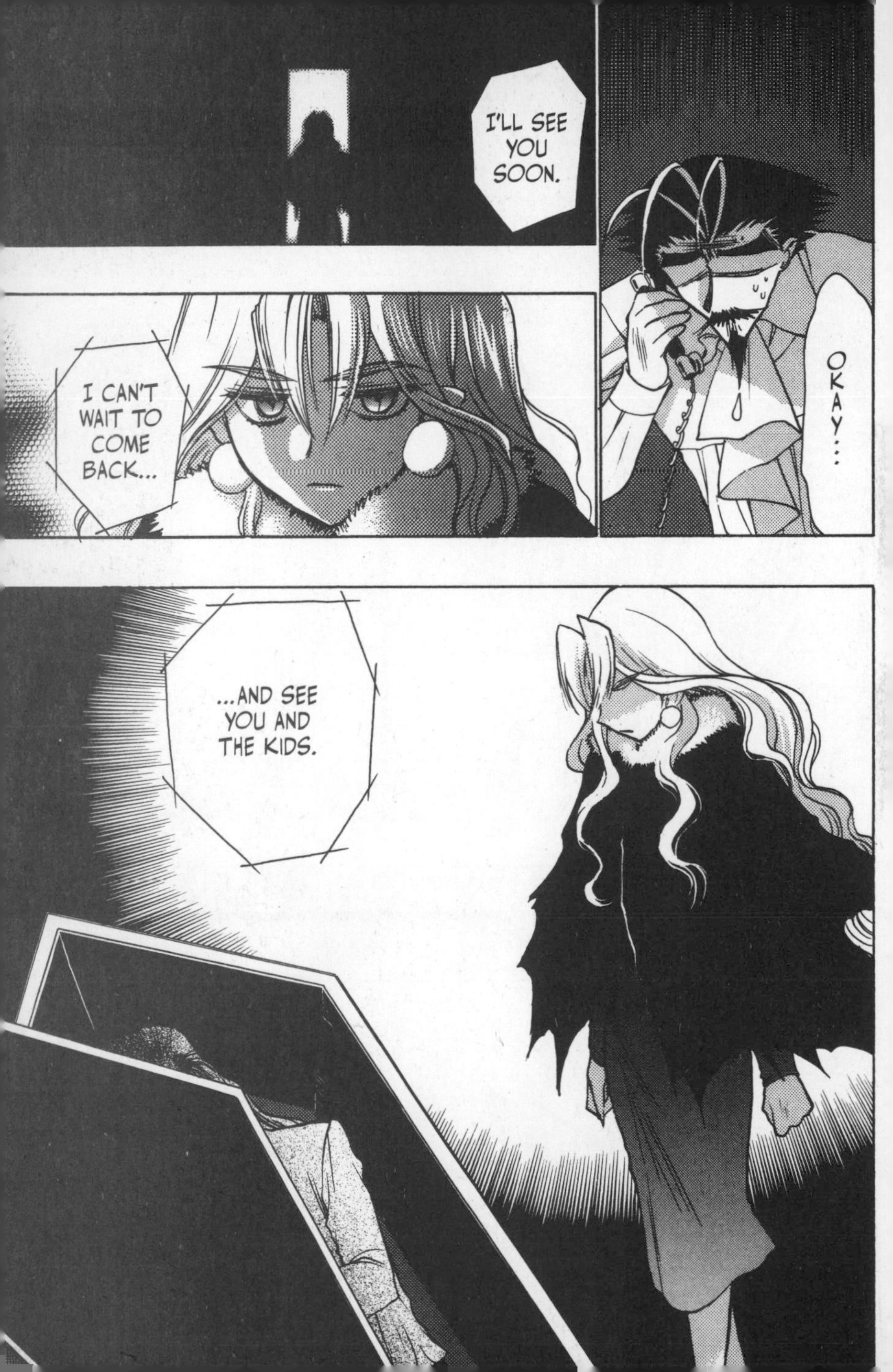

I'LL SEE YOU SOON.
OKAY...
I CAN'T WAIT TO COME BACK...
...AND SEE YOU AND THE KIDS.

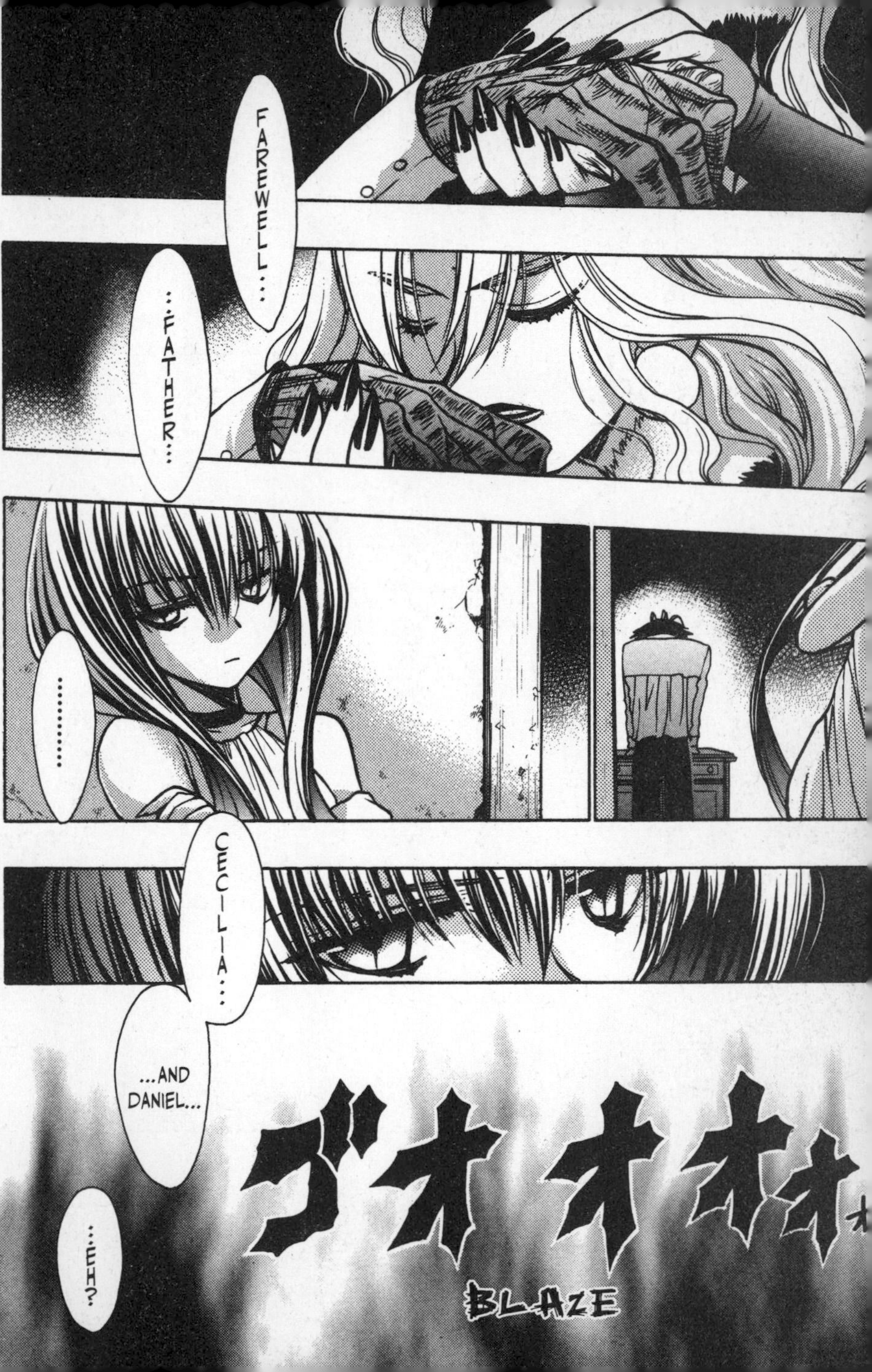
FAREWELL...
...FATHER...
....
CECILIA...
...AND DANIEL...
...EH?
ゴオオオオ
BLAZE

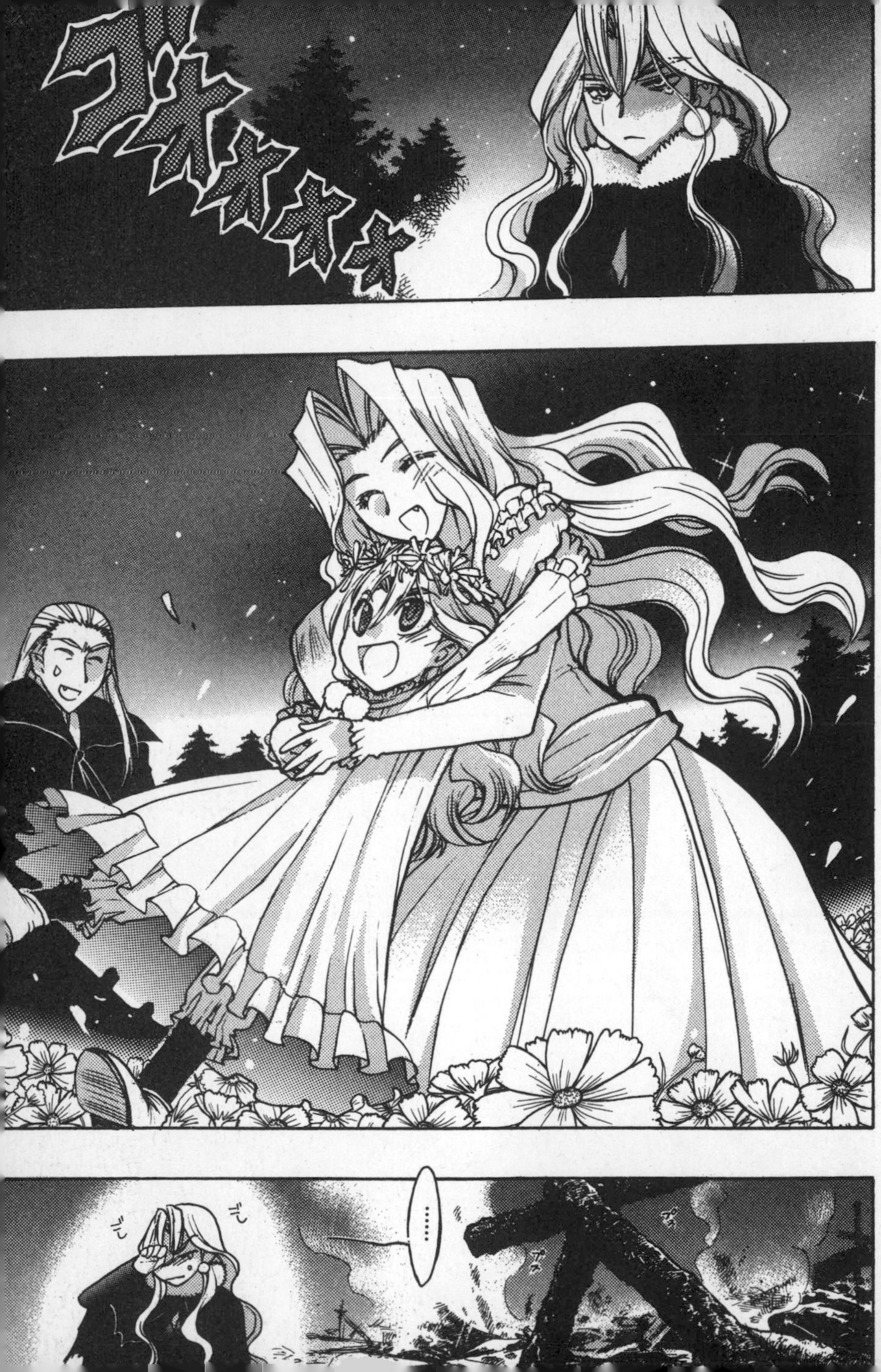
ゴオオオオ
……
プス

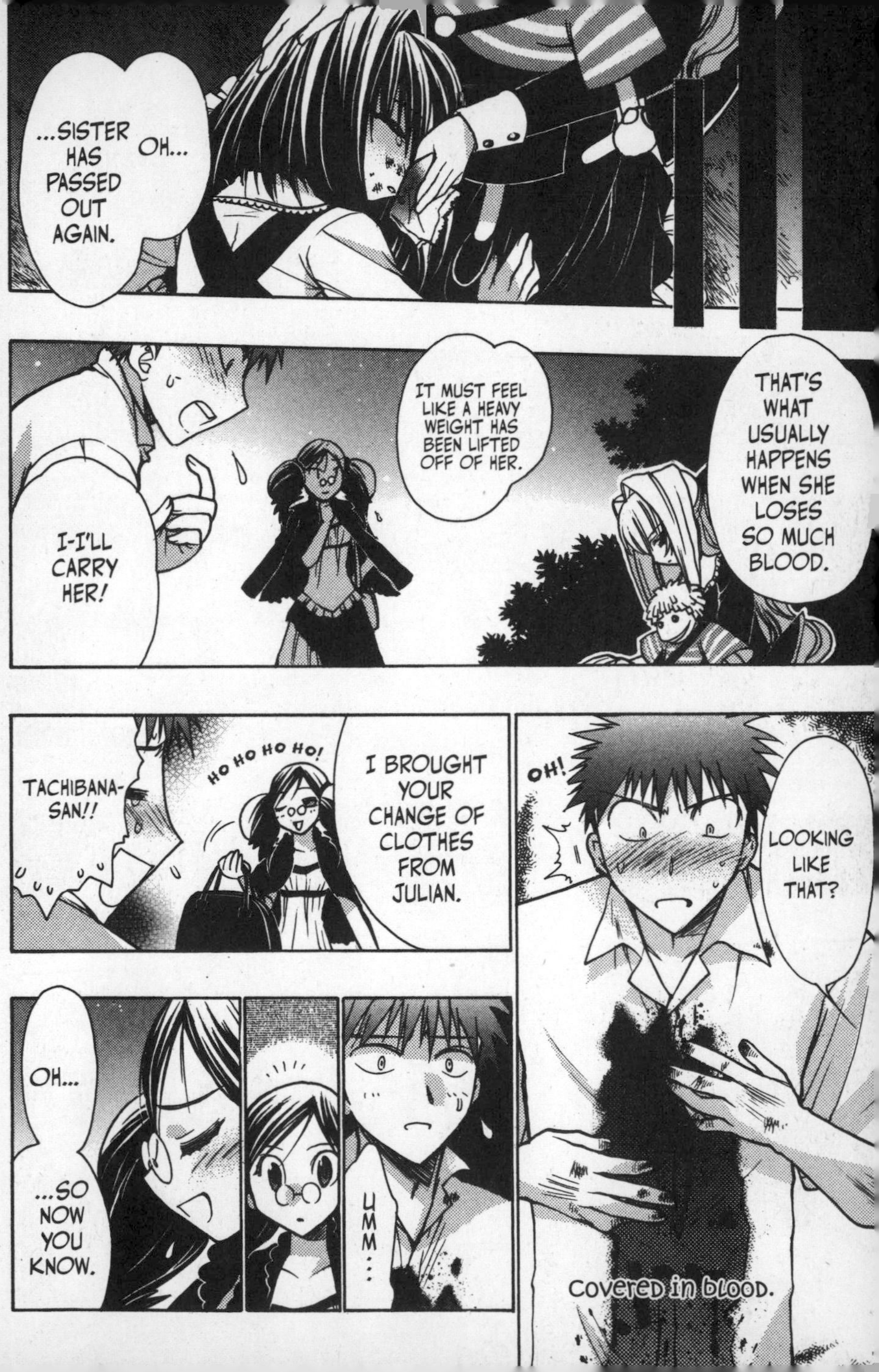
OH...
...SISTER HAS PASSED OUT AGAIN.
THAT'S WHAT USUALLY HAPPENS WHEN SHE LOSES SO MUCH BLOOD.
IT MUST FEEL LIKE A HEAVY WEIGHT HAS BEEN LIFTED OFF OF HER.
I-I'LL CARRY HER!
LOOKING LIKE THAT?
OH!
Covered in blood.
I BROUGHT YOUR CHANGE OF CLOTHES FROM JULIAN.
HO HO HO HO!
TACHIBANA-SAN!!
UMM...
OH...
...SO NOW YOU KNOW.

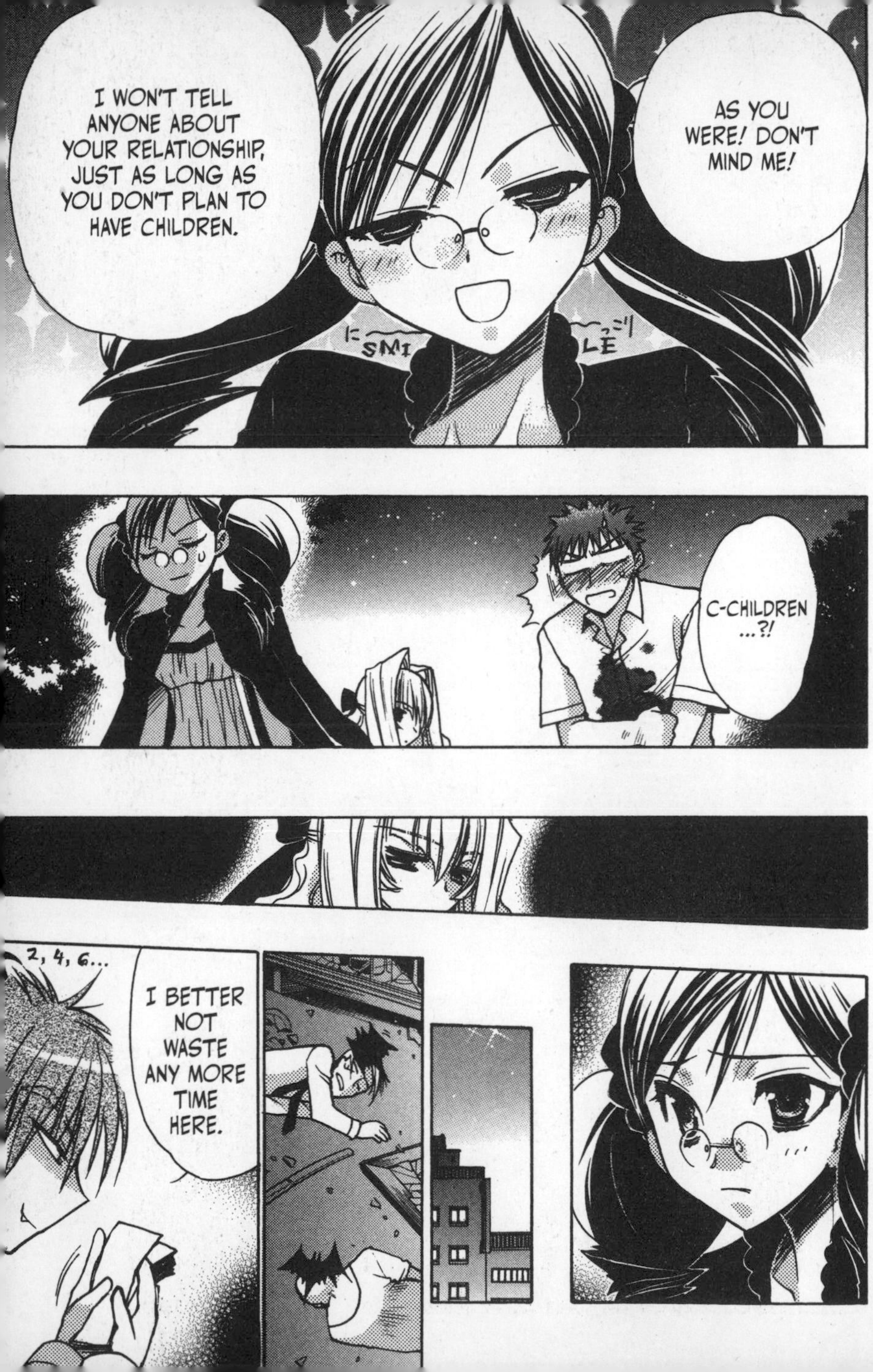
AS YOU WERE! DON'T MIND ME!
I WON'T TELL ANYONE ABOUT YOUR RELATIONSHIP, JUST AS LONG AS YOU DON'T PLAN TO HAVE CHILDREN.
SMILE
C-CHILDREN ...?!
...
I BETTER NOT WASTE ANY MORE TIME HERE.
2, 4, 6...

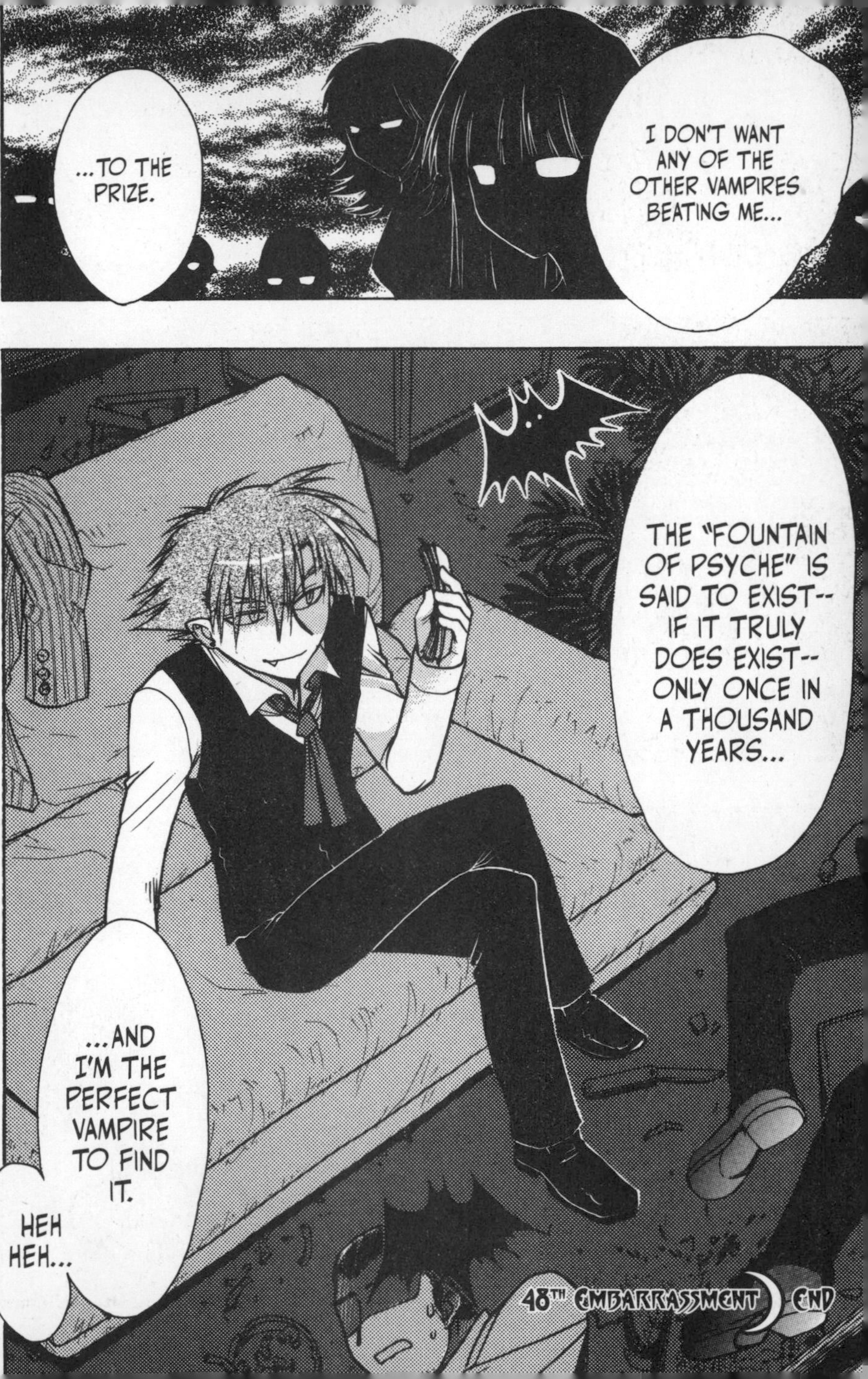
I DON'T WANT ANY OF THE OTHER VAMPIRES BEATING ME...
...TO THE PRIZE.
THE "FOUNTAIN OF PSYCHE" IS SAID TO EXIST-- IF IT TRULY DOES EXIST-- ONLY ONCE IN A THOUSAND YEARS...
...AND I'M THE PERFECT VAMPIRE TO FIND IT.
HEH HEH...
48TH EMBARRASSMENT END

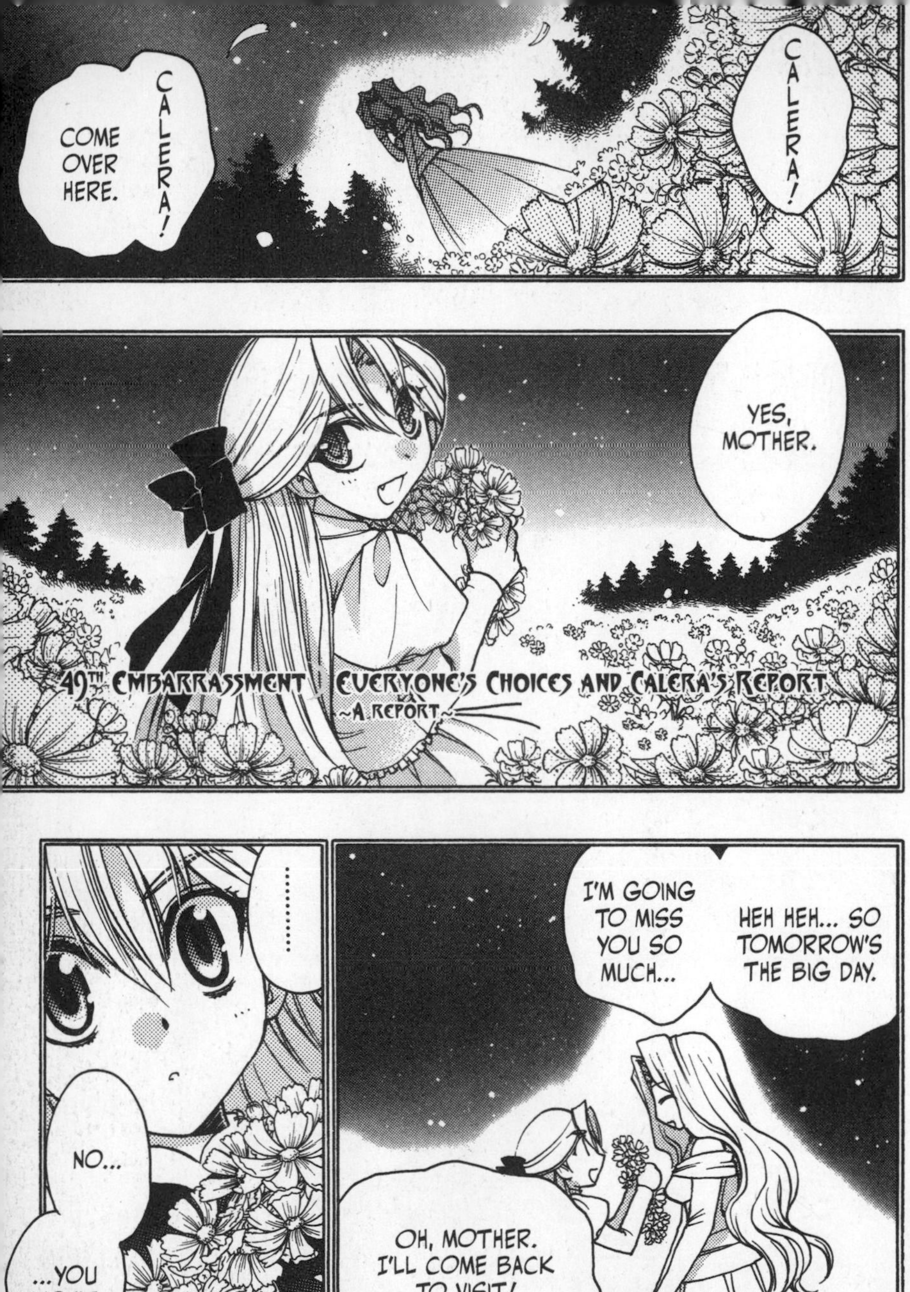
CALERA!
CALERA! COME OVER HERE.
YES, MOTHER.
49TH EMBARRASSMENT EVERYONE'S CHOICES AND CALERA'S REPORT
~A REPORT~
HEH HEH... SO TOMORROW'S THE BIG DAY.
I'M GOING TO MISS YOU SO MUCH...
OH, MOTHER. I'LL COME BACK TO VISIT!
......
NO...
...YOU WON'T.

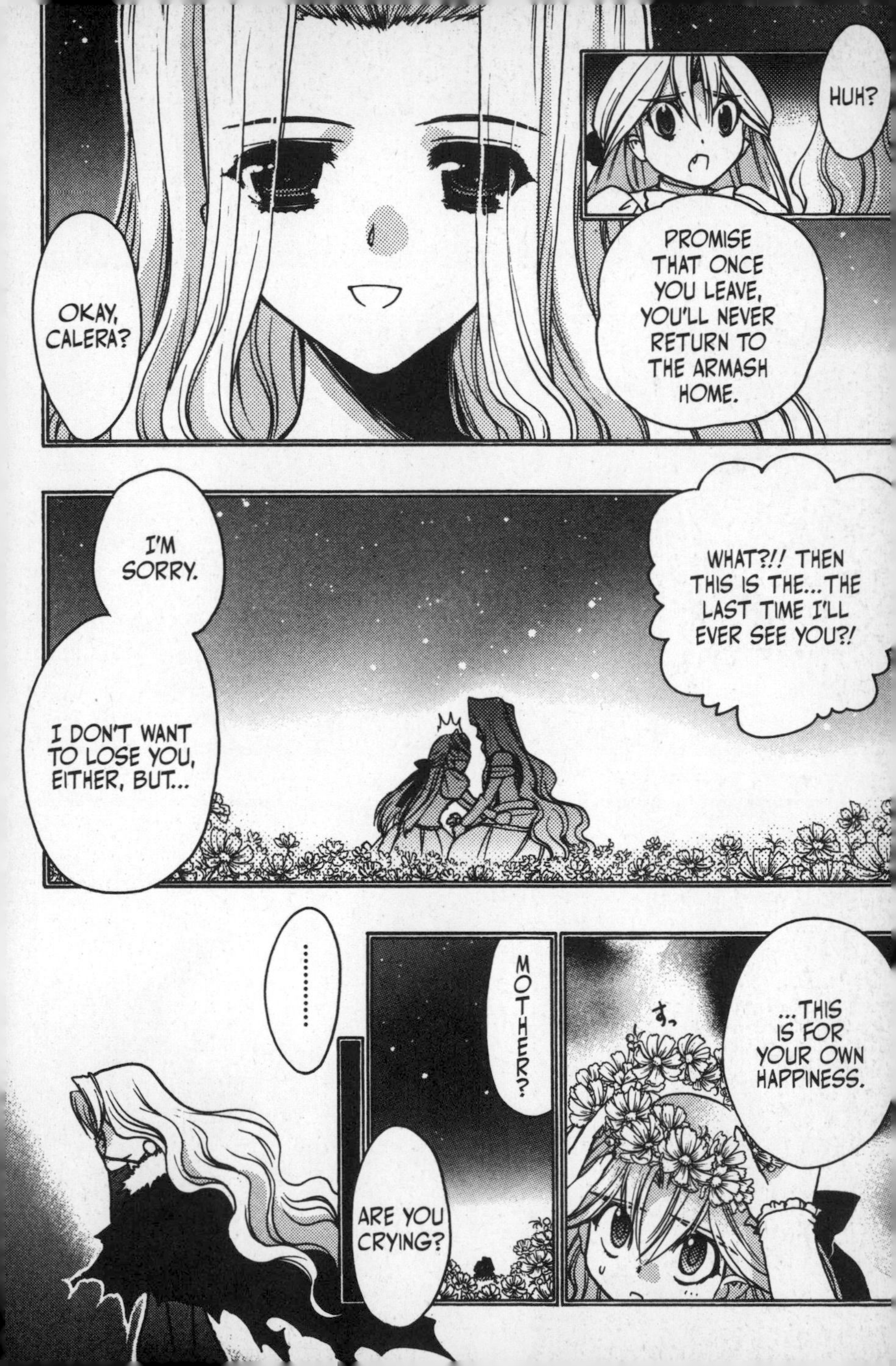

PROMISE THAT ONCE YOU LEAVE, YOU'LL NEVER RETURN TO THE ARMASH HOME.
OKAY, CALERA?
HUH?
WHAT?!! THEN THIS IS THE...THE LAST TIME I'LL EVER SEE YOU?!
I'M SORRY.
I DON'T WANT TO LOSE YOU, EITHER, BUT...
...THIS IS FOR YOUR OWN HAPPINESS.
すっ
MOTHER?
ARE YOU CRYING?
....

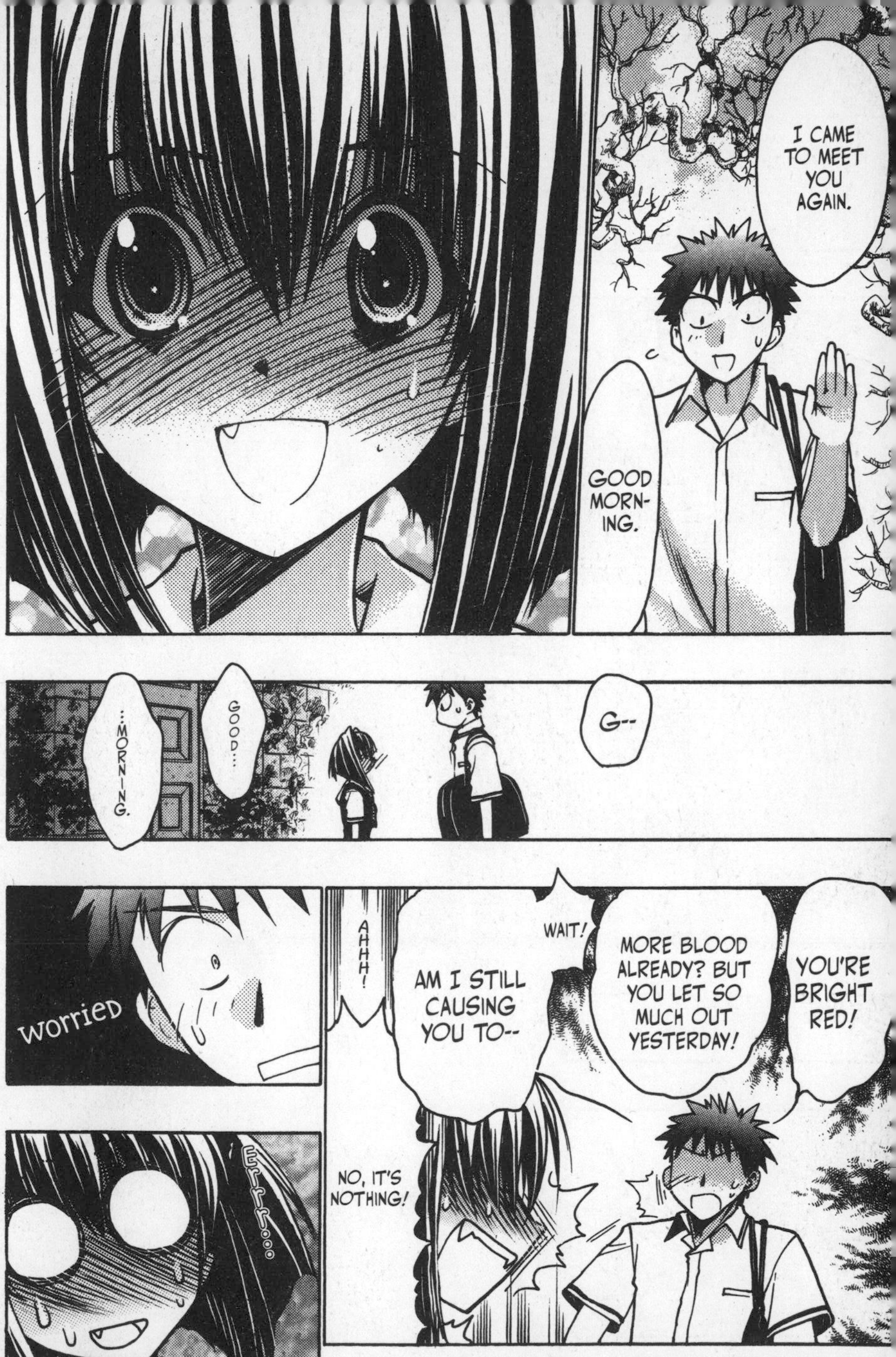
I CAME TO MEET YOU AGAIN.
GOOD MORN-ING.
G--
GOOD...
...MORNING.
YOU'RE BRIGHT RED!
MORE BLOOD ALREADY? BUT YOU LET SO MUCH OUT YESTERDAY!
WAIT!
AM I STILL CAUSING YOU TO--
AHHH!
NO, IT'S NOTHING!
worried
Errr...

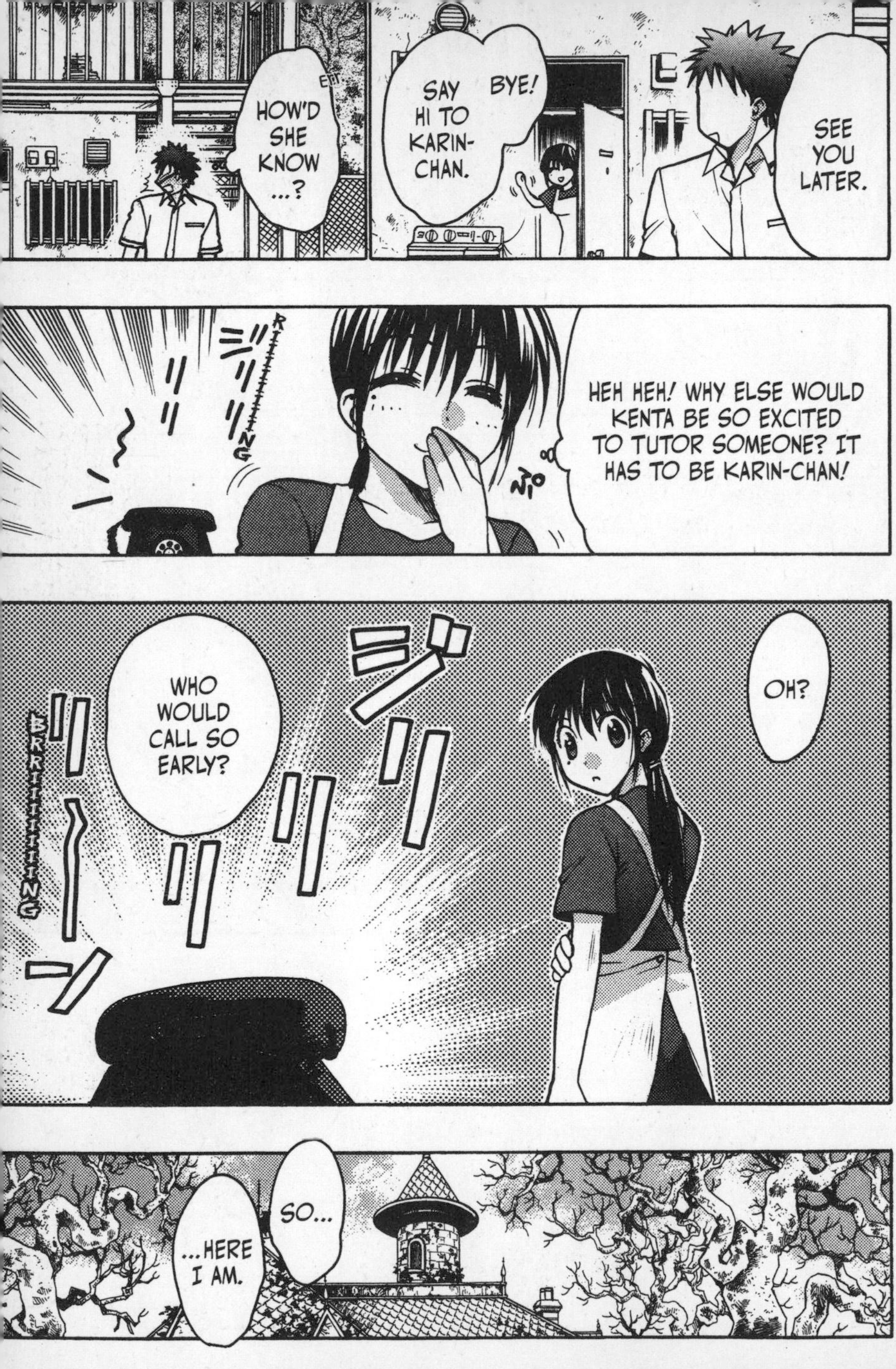
SEE YOU LATER.
BYE!
SAY HI TO KARIN-CHAN.
HOW'D SHE KNOW ...?
HEH HEH! WHY ELSE WOULD KENTA BE SO EXCITED TO TUTOR SOMEONE? IT HAS TO BE KARIN-CHAN!
RIIIIIIIIING
OH?
WHO WOULD CALL SO EARLY?
BRRIIIIIIING
SO...
...HERE I AM.

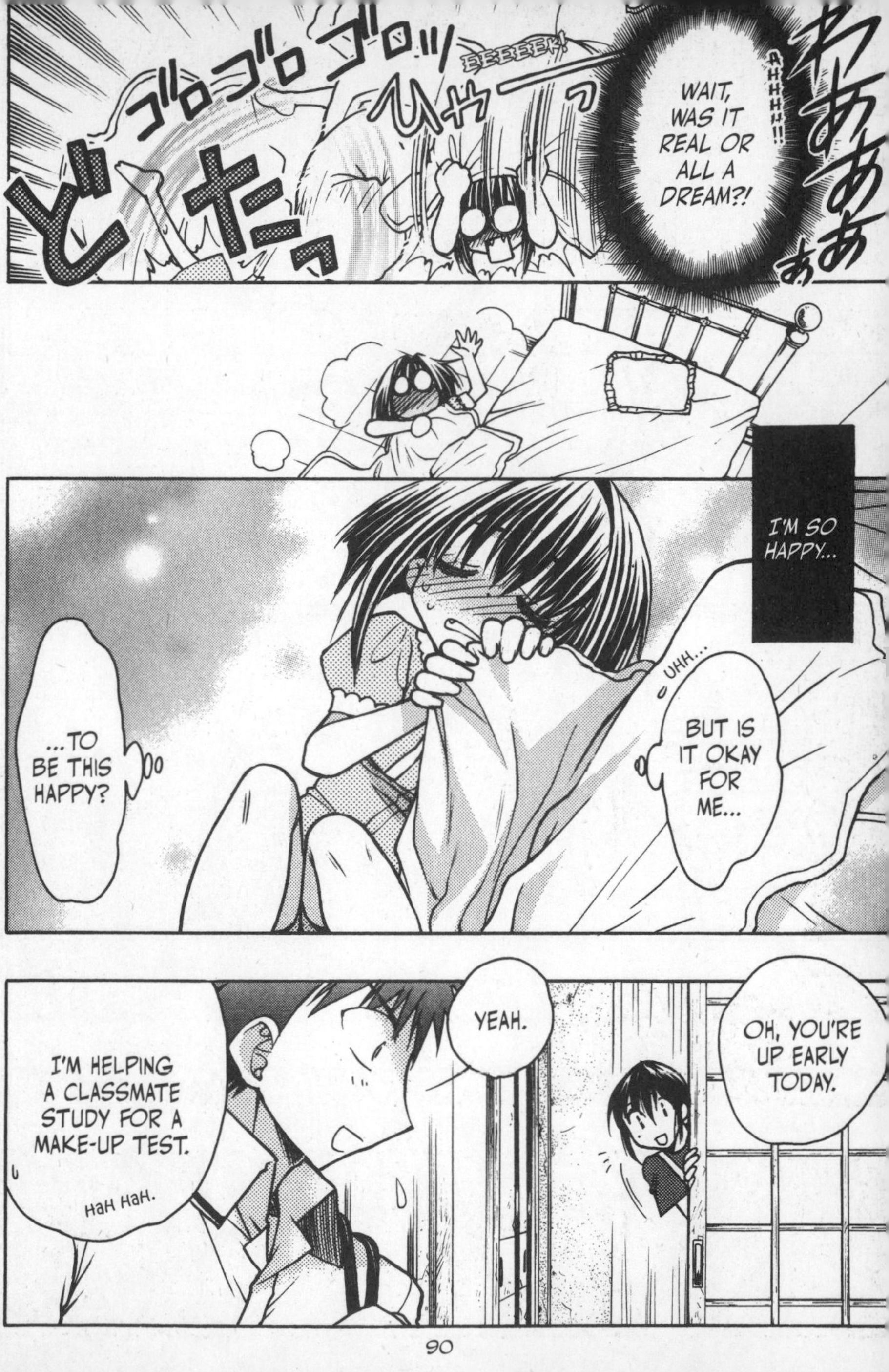
AHHHH!!
WAIT, WAS IT REAL OR ALL A DREAM?!
EEEEEEK!
I'M SO HAPPY...
UHH...
BUT IS IT OKAY FOR ME...
...TO BE THIS HAPPY?
OH, YOU'RE UP EARLY TODAY.
YEAH.
I'M HELPING A CLASSMATE STUDY FOR A MAKE-UP TEST.
HAH HAH.

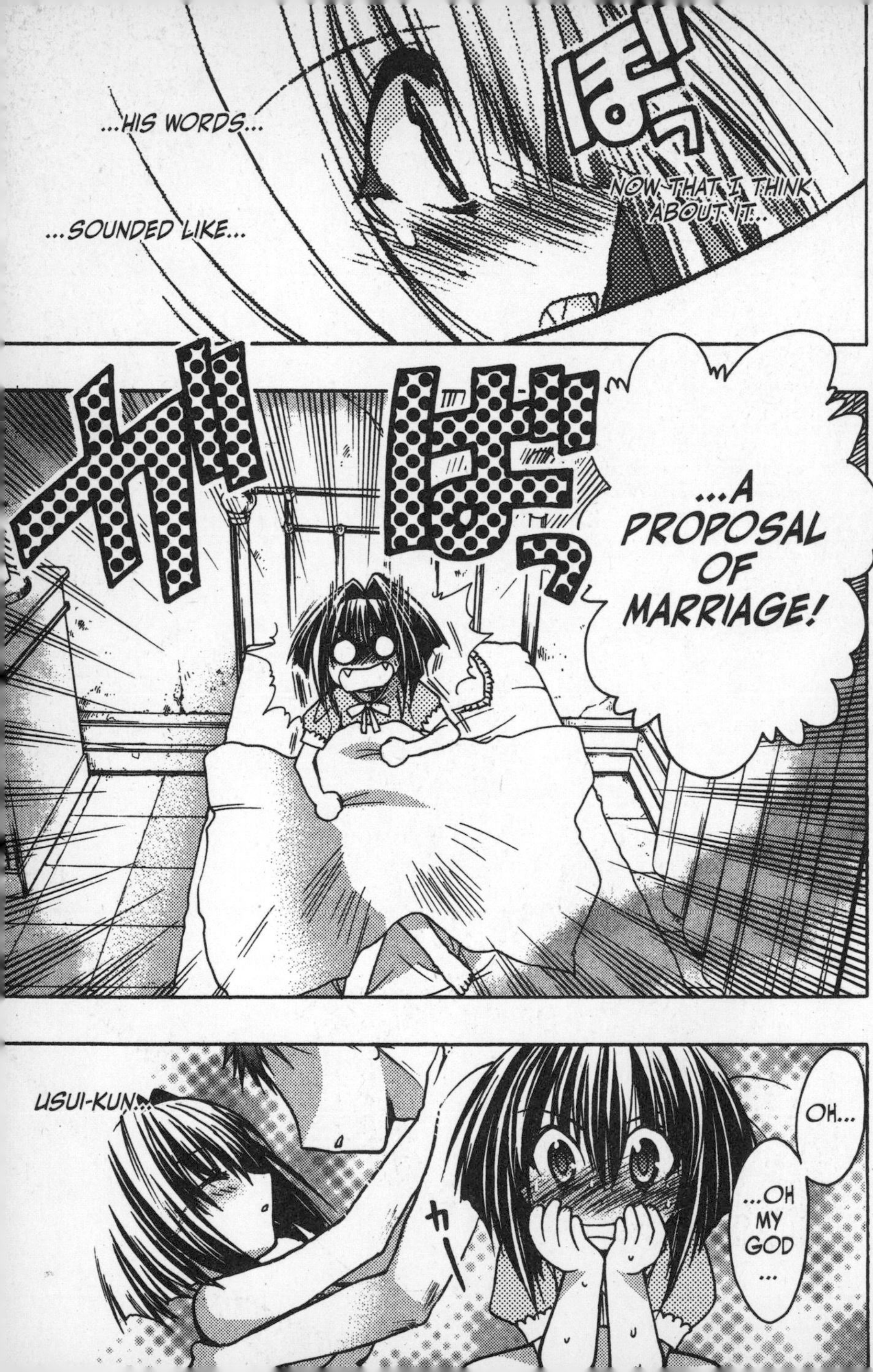
NOW THAT I THINK ABOUT IT...
...HIS WORDS...
...SOUNDED LIKE...
...A PROPOSAL OF MARRIAGE!
OH...
...OH MY GOD ...
USUI-KUN...

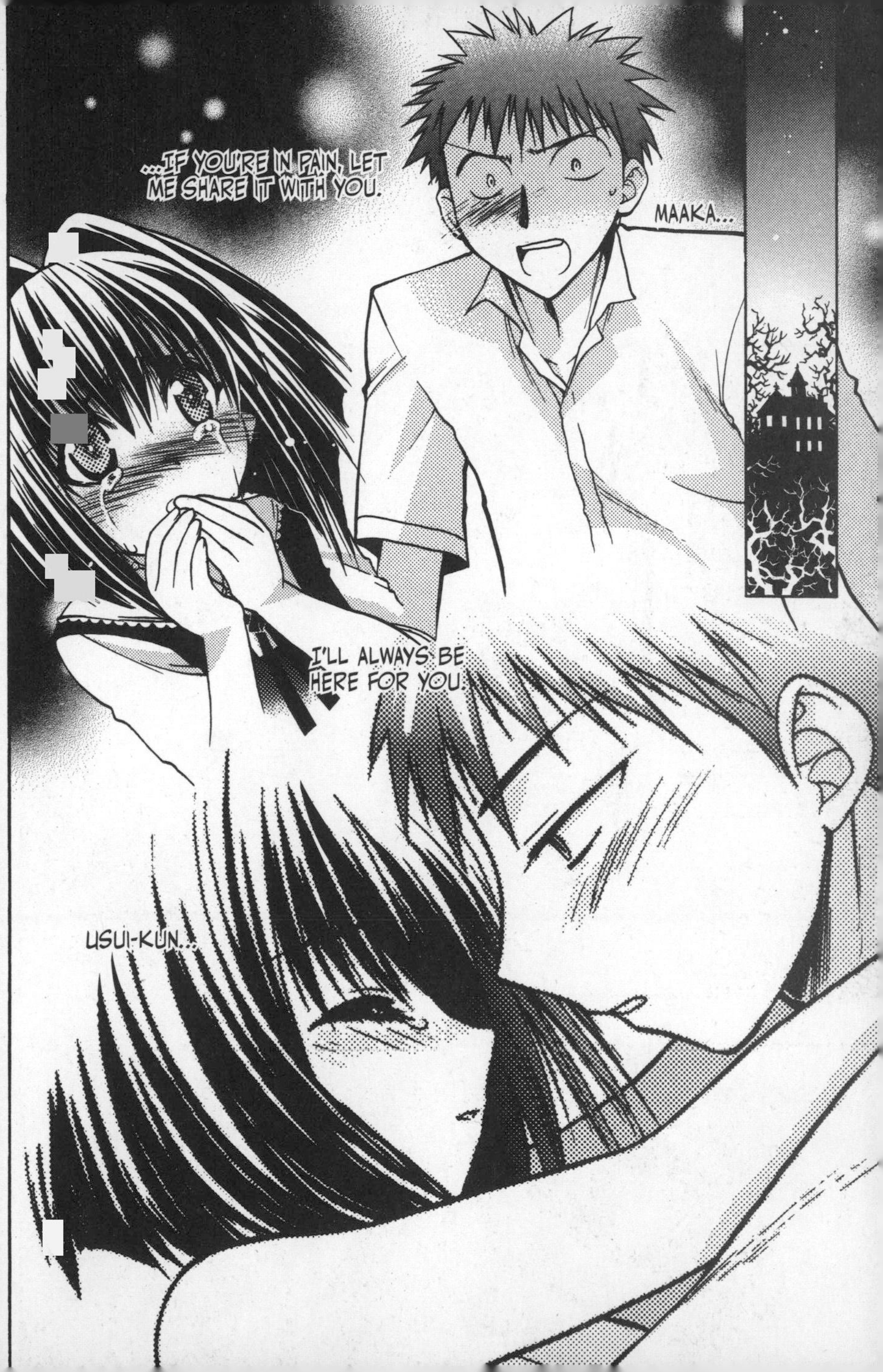
MAAKA...
...IF YOU'RE IN PAIN, LET ME SHARE IT WITH YOU.
I'LL ALWAYS BE HERE FOR YOU.
USUI-KUN...

49th Embarrassment) Everyone's Choices and Calera's Report

~A Report~

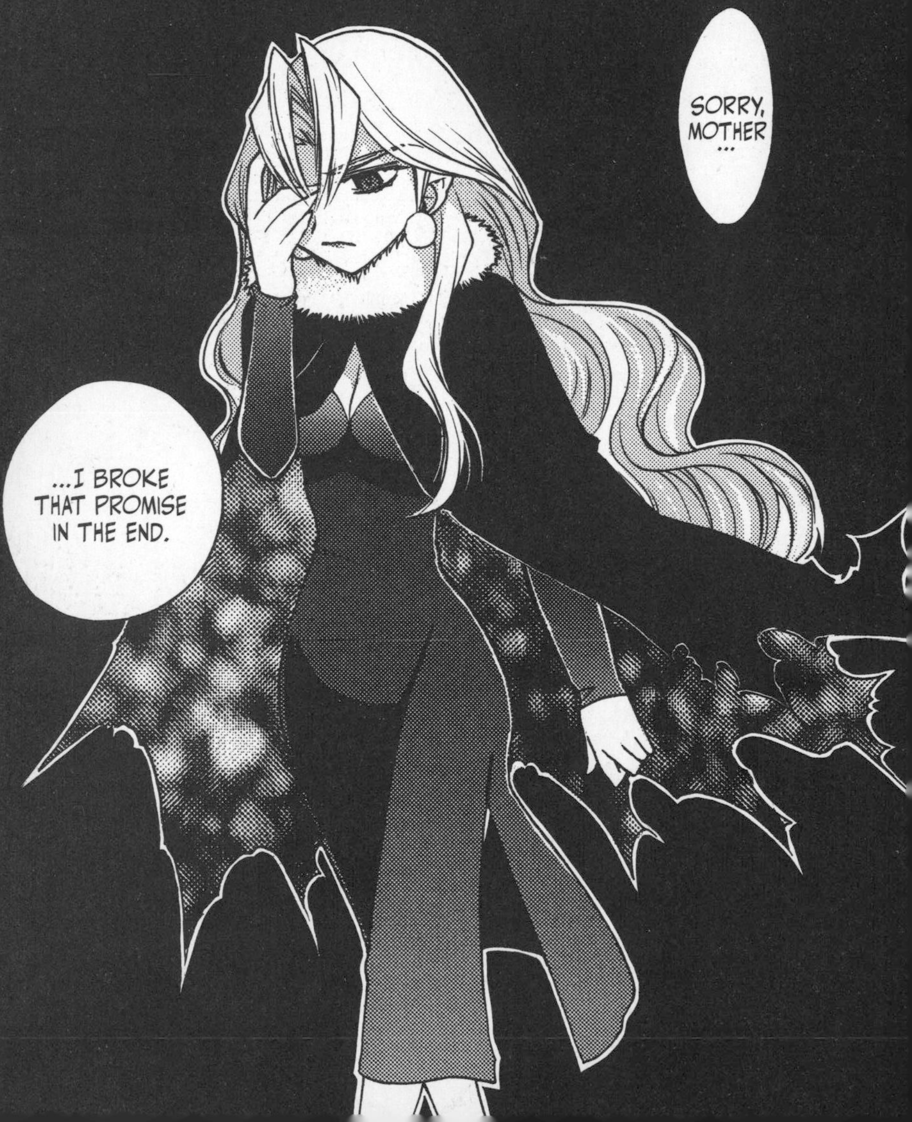

SORRY, MOTHER ...
...I BROKE THAT PROMISE IN THE END.

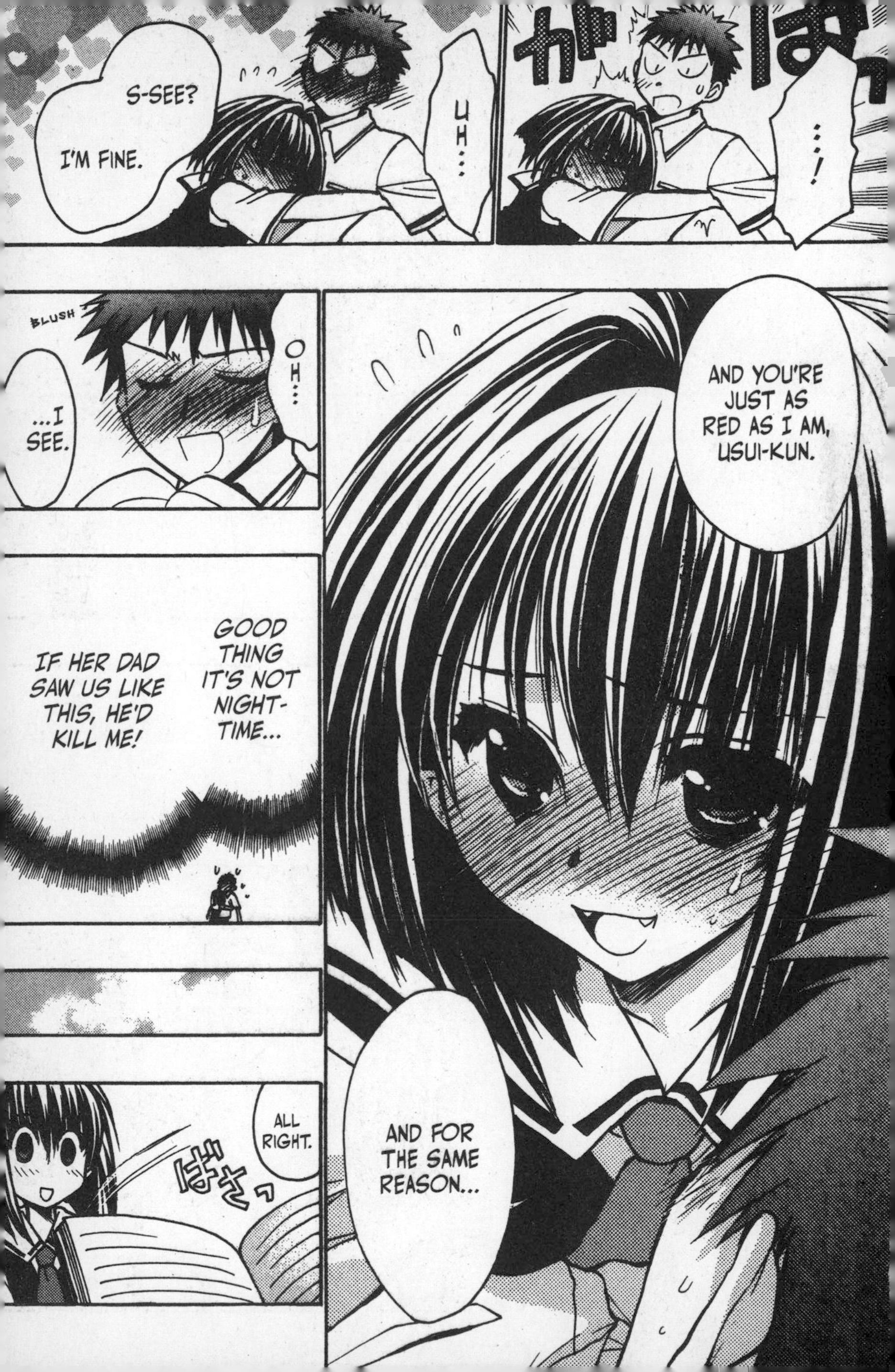
UH...
S-SEE?
I'M FINE.
...!
OH...
...I SEE.
BLUSH
AND YOU'RE JUST AS RED AS I AM, USUI-KUN.
AND FOR THE SAME REASON...
GOOD THING IT'S NOT NIGHT-TIME...
IF HER DAD SAW US LIKE THIS, HE'D KILL ME!
ALL RIGHT.

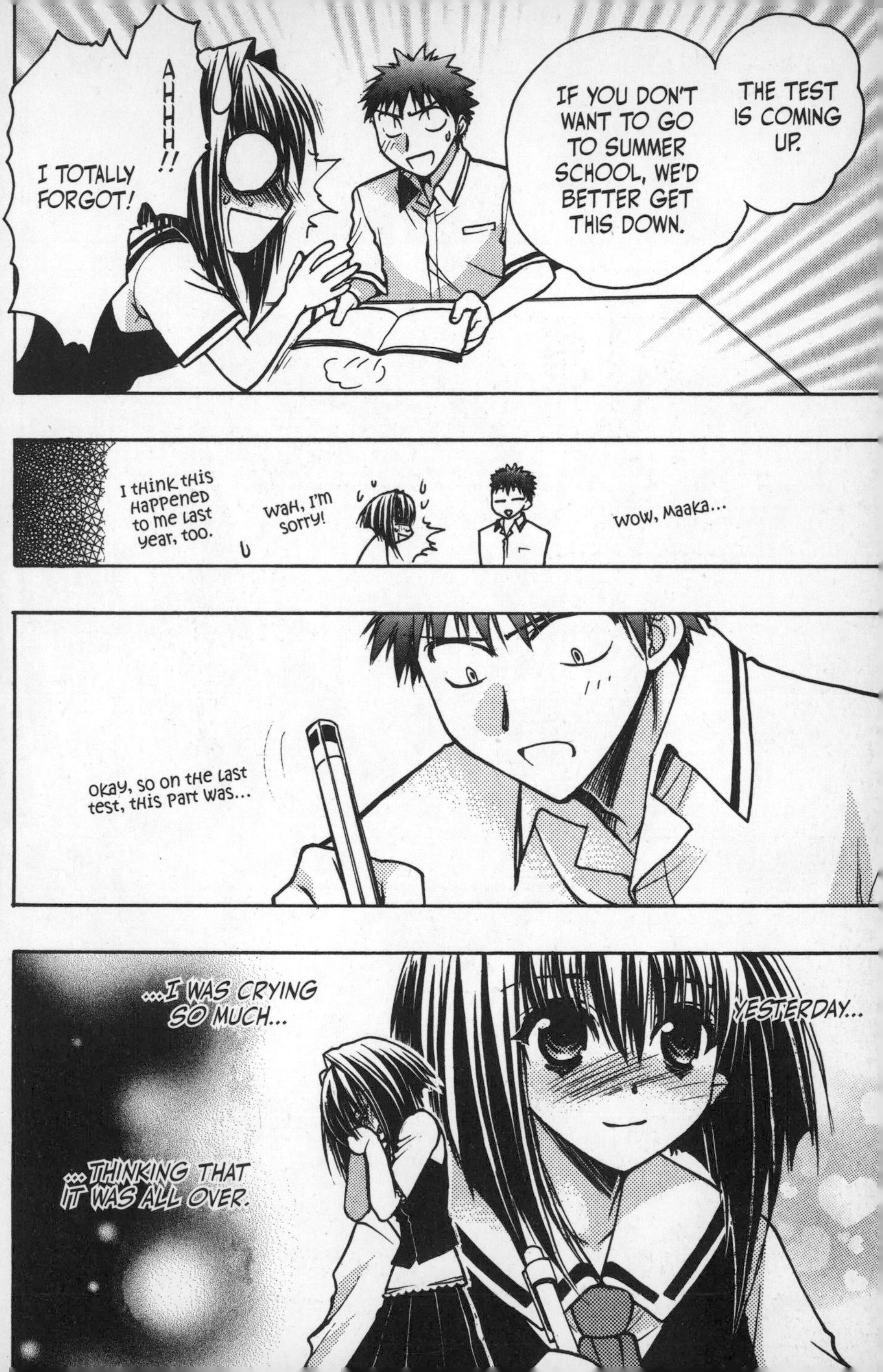
THE TEST IS COMING UP.
IF YOU DON'T WANT TO GO TO SUMMER SCHOOL, WE'D BETTER GET THIS DOWN.
AHHH!!
I TOTALLY FORGOT!
WOW, MAAKA...
WAH, I'M SORRY!
I THINK THIS HAPPENED TO ME LAST YEAR, TOO.
OKAY, SO ON THE LAST TEST, THIS PART WAS...
YESTERDAY...
...I WAS CRYING SO MUCH...
...THINKING THAT IT WAS ALL OVER.

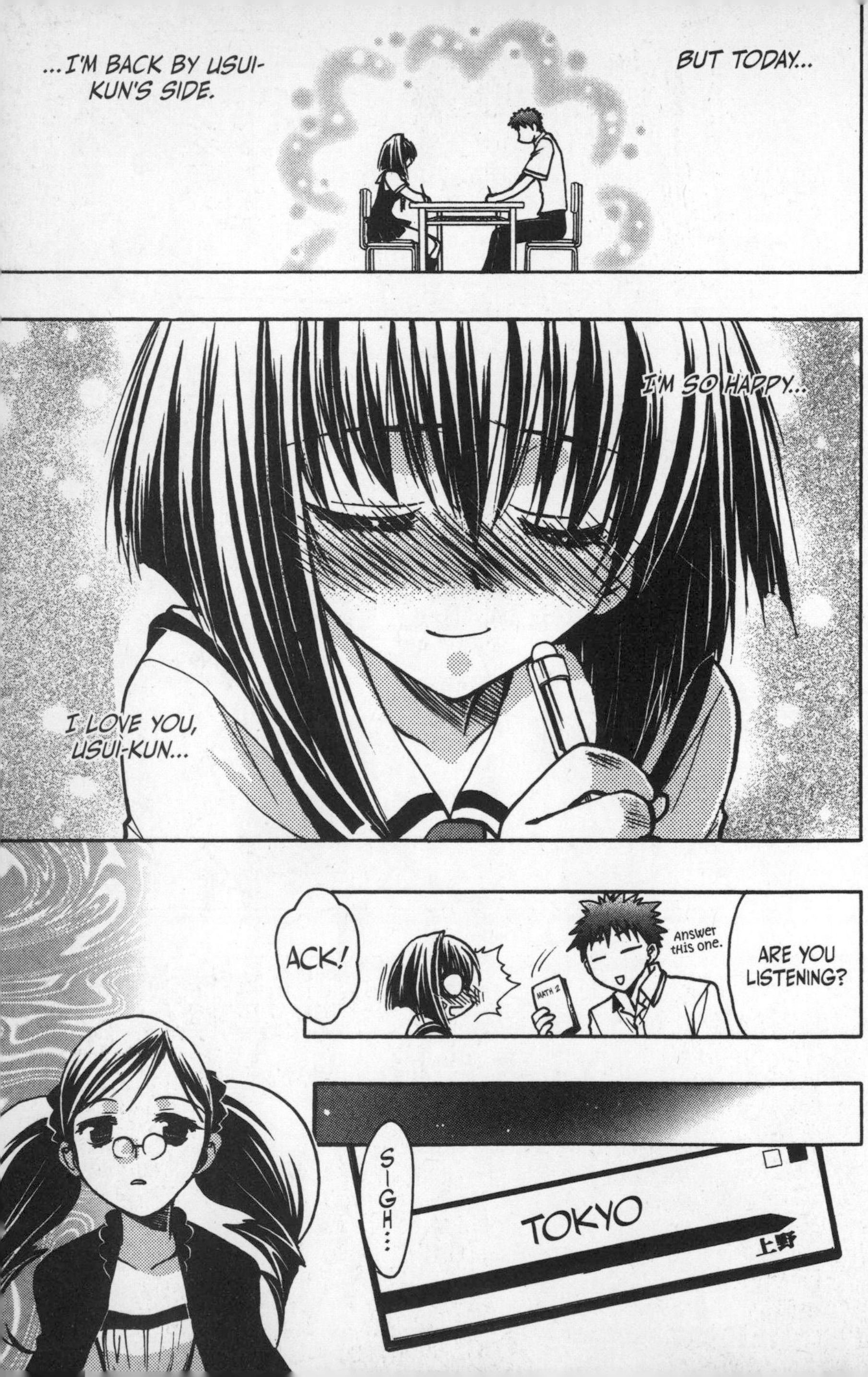
BUT TODAY...
...I'M BACK BY USUI-KUN'S SIDE.
I'M SO HAPPY...
I LOVE YOU, USUI-KUN...
ARE YOU LISTENING?
Answer this one.
MATH 2
ACK!
TOKYO
上野
SIGH...

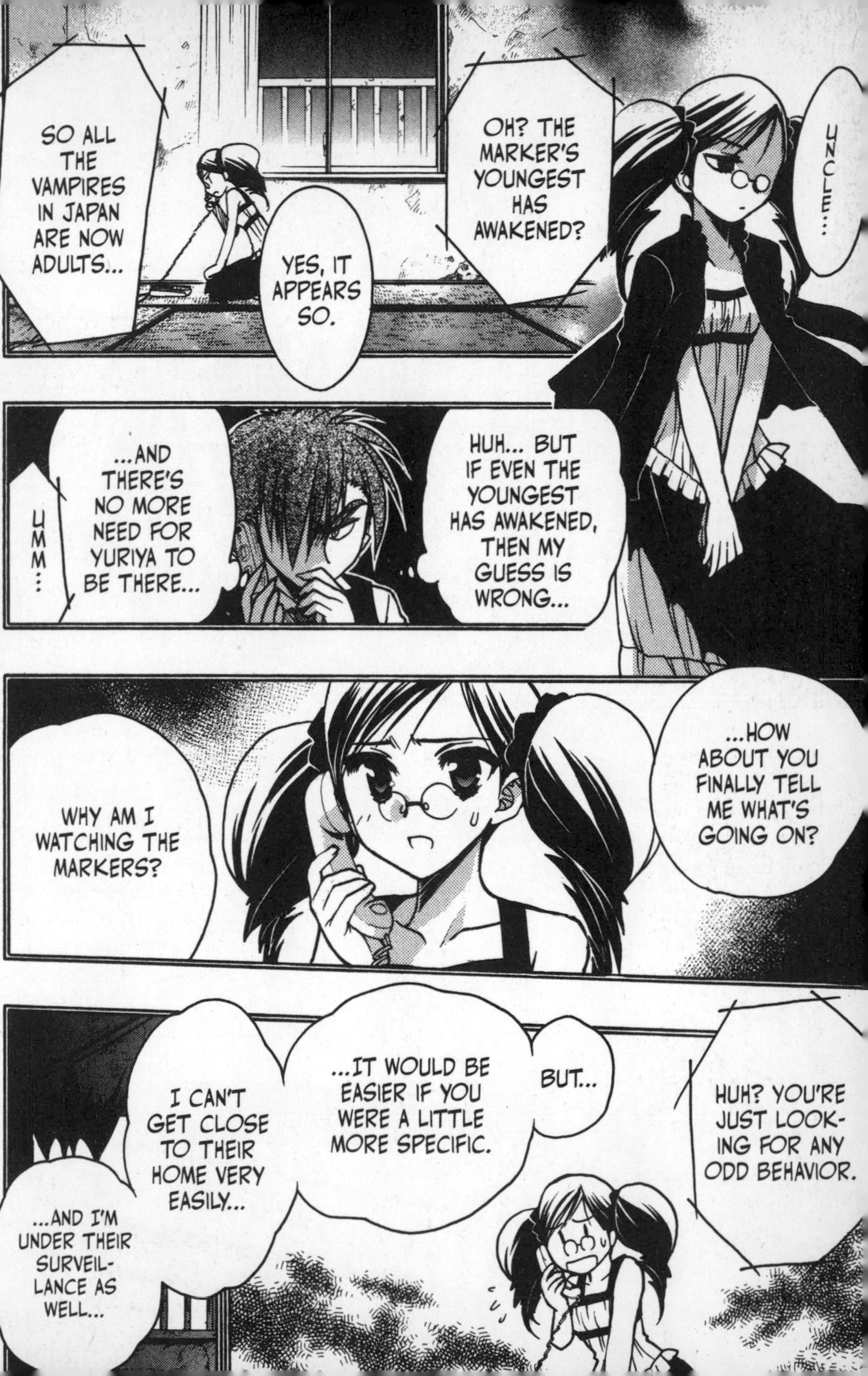
UNCLE...
OH? THE MARKER'S YOUNGEST HAS AWAKENED?
YES, IT APPEARS SO.
SO ALL THE VAMPIRES IN JAPAN ARE NOW ADULTS...
HUH... BUT IF EVEN THE YOUNGEST HAS AWAKENED, THEN MY GUESS IS WRONG...
...AND THERE'S NO MORE NEED FOR YURIYA TO BE THERE...
UMM...
...HOW ABOUT YOU FINALLY TELL ME WHAT'S GOING ON?
WHY AM I WATCHING THE MARKERS?
HUH? YOU'RE JUST LOOKING FOR ANY ODD BEHAVIOR.
BUT...
...IT WOULD BE EASIER IF YOU WERE A LITTLE MORE SPECIFIC.
I CAN'T GET CLOSE TO THEIR HOME VERY EASILY...
...AND I'M UNDER THEIR SURVEILLANCE AS WELL...

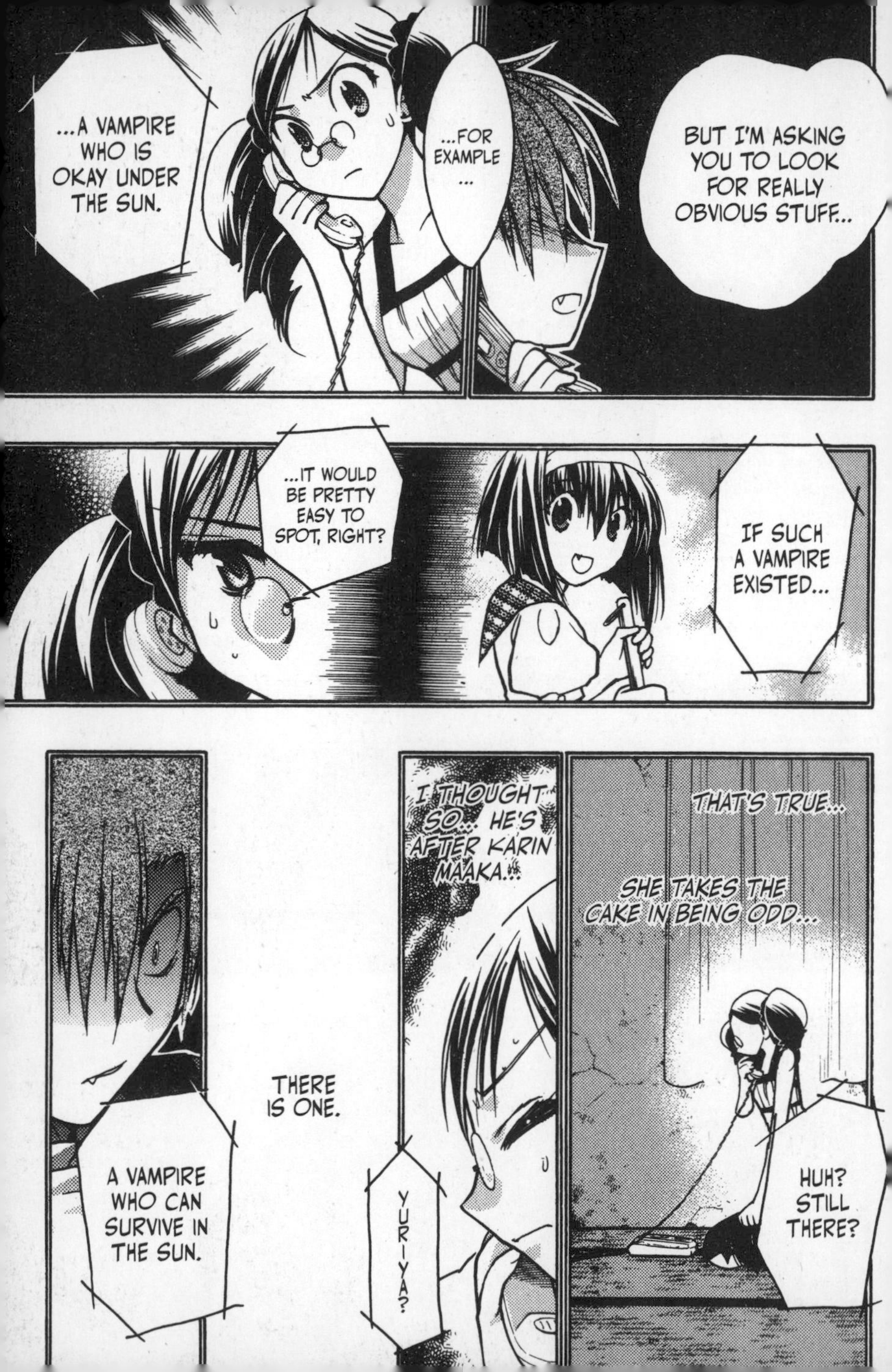
BUT I'M ASKING YOU TO LOOK FOR REALLY OBVIOUS STUFF...
...FOR EXAMPLE ...
...A VAMPIRE WHO IS OKAY UNDER THE SUN.
IF SUCH A VAMPIRE EXISTED...
...IT WOULD BE PRETTY EASY TO SPOT, RIGHT?
THAT'S TRUE...
SHE TAKES THE CAKE IN BEING ODD...
HUH? STILL THERE?
I THOUGHT SO... HE'S AFTER KARIN MAAKA...
YURIYA?
THERE IS ONE.
A VAMPIRE WHO CAN SURVIVE IN THE SUN.

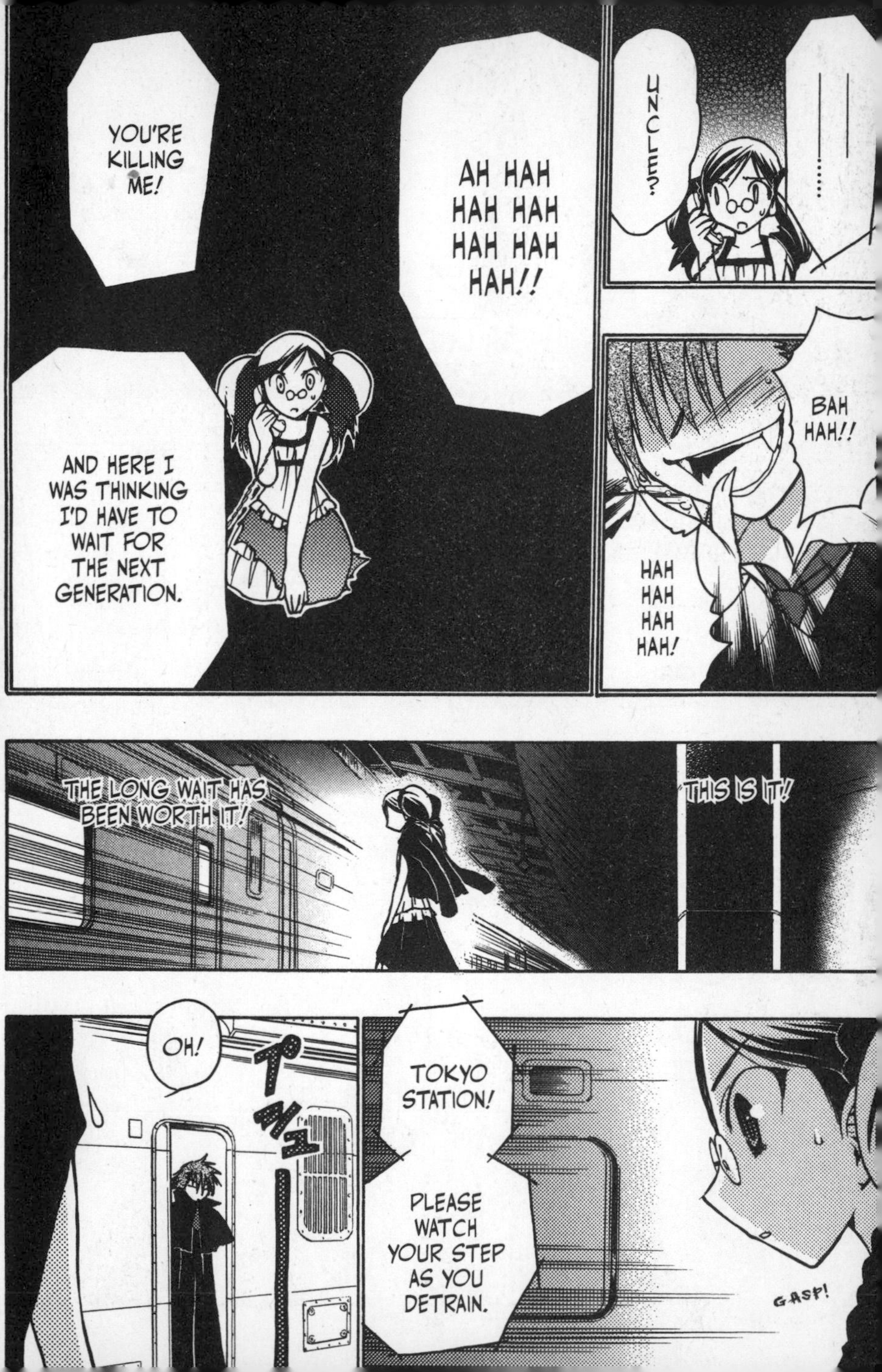
......
UNCLE?
BAH HAH!!
HAH HAH HAH HAH!
AH HAH HAH HAH HAH HAH HAH!!
YOU'RE KILLING ME!
AND HERE I WAS THINKING I'D HAVE TO WAIT FOR THE NEXT GENERATION.
THIS IS IT!
THE LONG WAIT HAS BEEN WORTH IT!
GASP!
TOKYO STATION!
PLEASE WATCH YOUR STEP AS YOU DETRAIN.
OH!

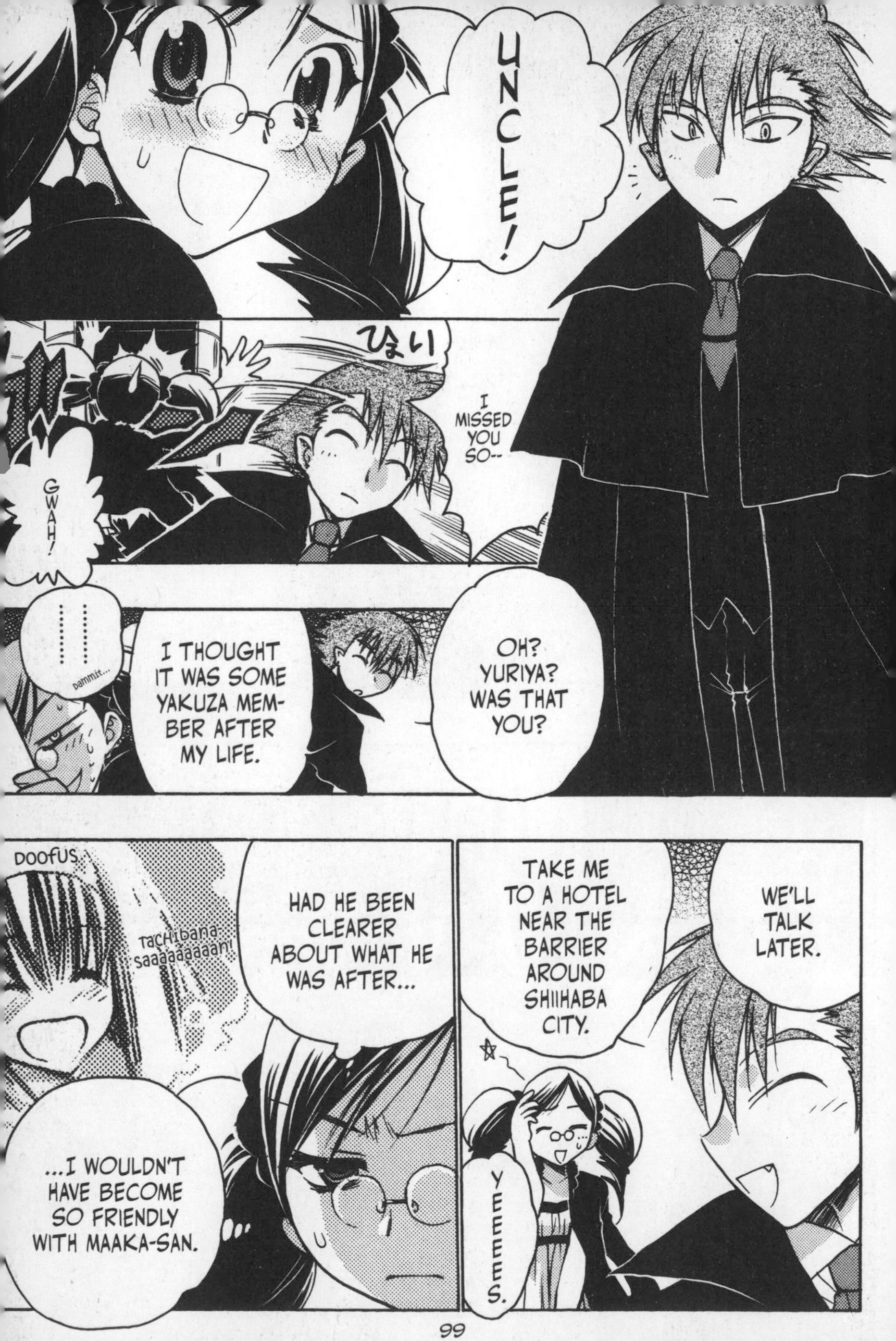
UNCLE!
ひょい
I MISSED YOU SO--
GWAH!
OH? YURIYA? WAS THAT YOU?
I THOUGHT IT WAS SOME YAKUZA MEMBER AFTER MY LIFE.
......
Dammit...
WE'LL TALK LATER.
TAKE ME TO A HOTEL NEAR THE BARRIER AROUND SHIIHABA CITY.
YEEEES.
HAD HE BEEN CLEARER ABOUT WHAT HE WAS AFTER...
...I WOULDN'T HAVE BECOME SO FRIENDLY WITH MAAKA-SAN.
TaChibana-saaaaaaaaan!
DOOfUS.

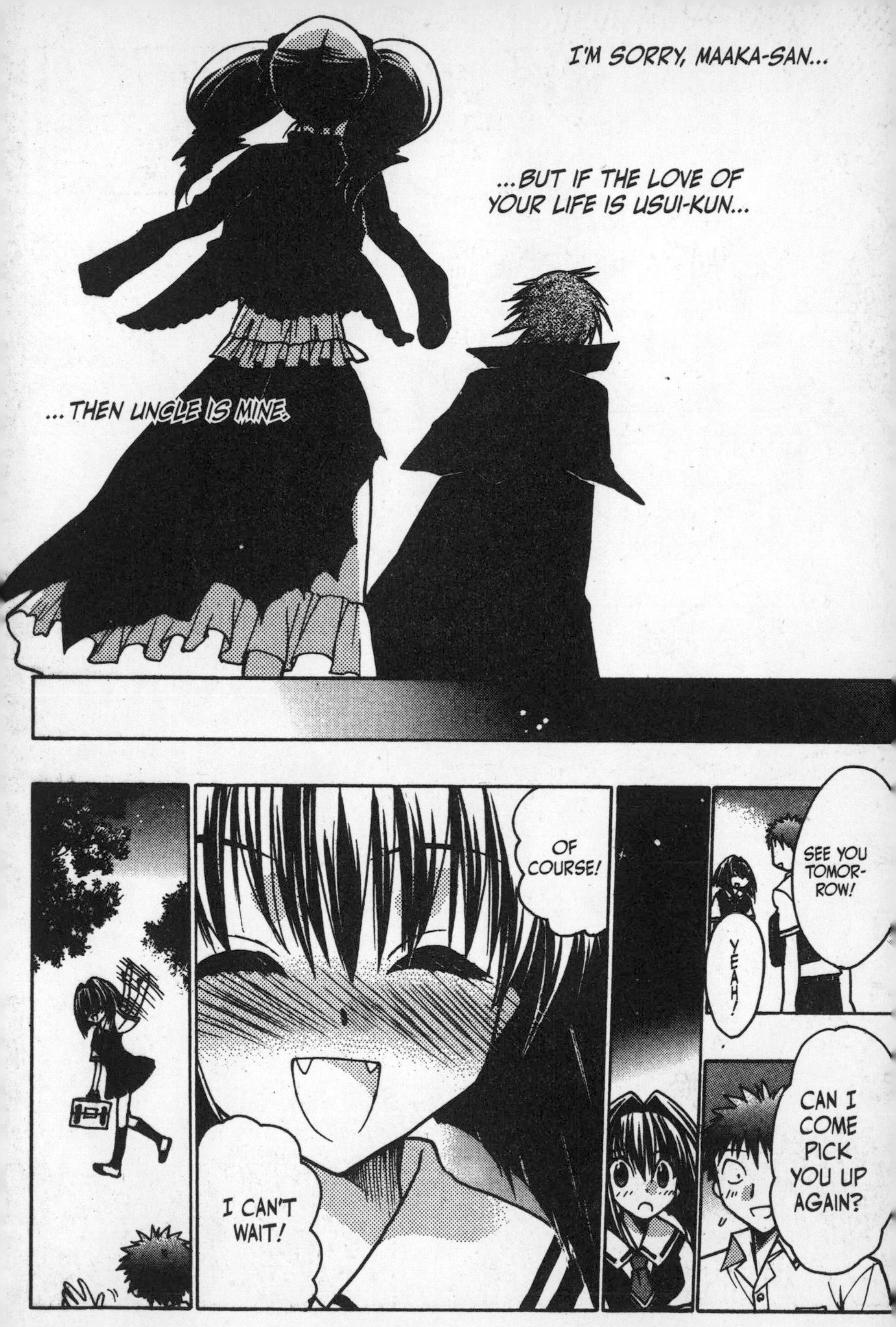
I'M SORRY, MAAKA-SAN...
...BUT IF THE LOVE OF YOUR LIFE IS USUI-KUN...
...THEN UNCLE IS MINE.
SEE YOU TOMORROW!
YEAH!
CAN I COME PICK YOU UP AGAIN?
OF COURSE!
I CAN'T WAIT!

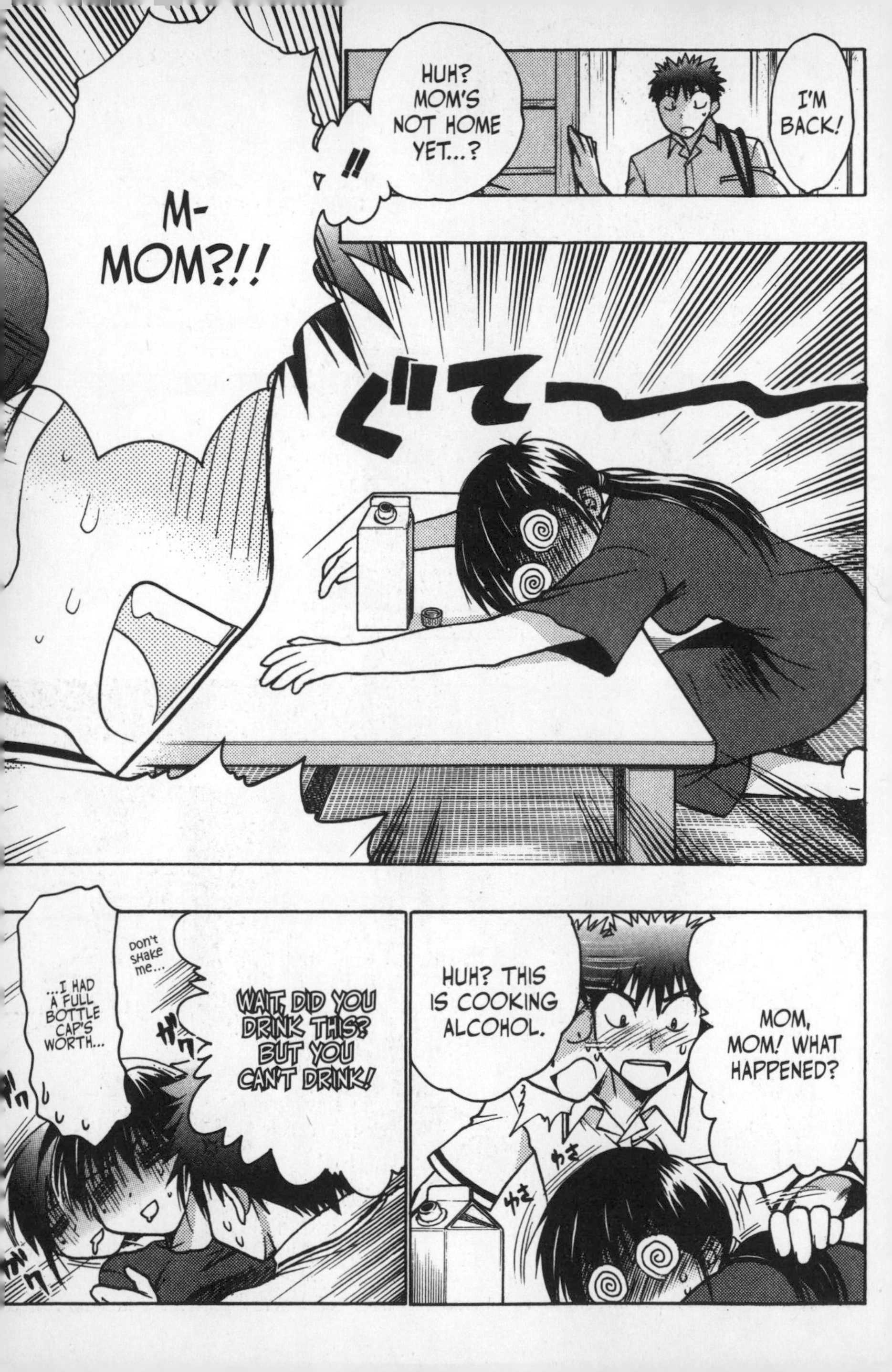
I'M BACK!
HUH? MOM'S NOT HOME YET...?
!!
M-MOM?!!
ぐて ー
MOM, MOM! WHAT HAPPENED?
HUH? THIS IS COOKING ALCOHOL.
WAIT, DID YOU DRINK THIS? BUT YOU CAN'T DRINK!
Don't shake me...
...I HAD A FULL BOTTLE CAP'S WORTH...

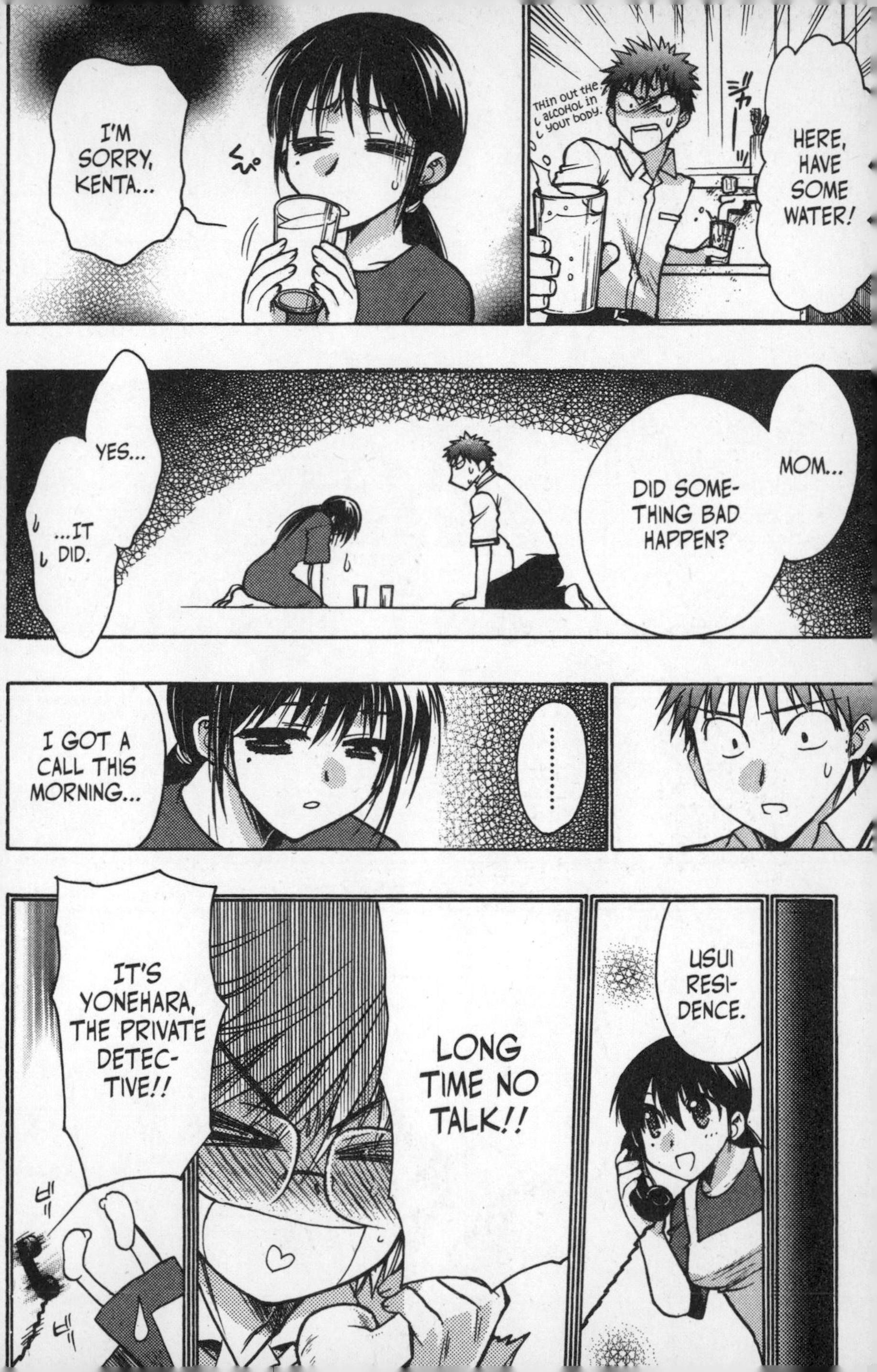
HERE, HAVE SOME WATER!
Thin out the alcohol in your body.
I'M SORRY, KENTA...
MOM...
DID SOME-THING BAD HAPPEN?
YES...
...IT DID.
......
I GOT A CALL THIS MORNING...
USUI RESI-DENCE.
LONG TIME NO TALK!!
IT'S YONEHARA, THE PRIVATE DETEC-TIVE!!

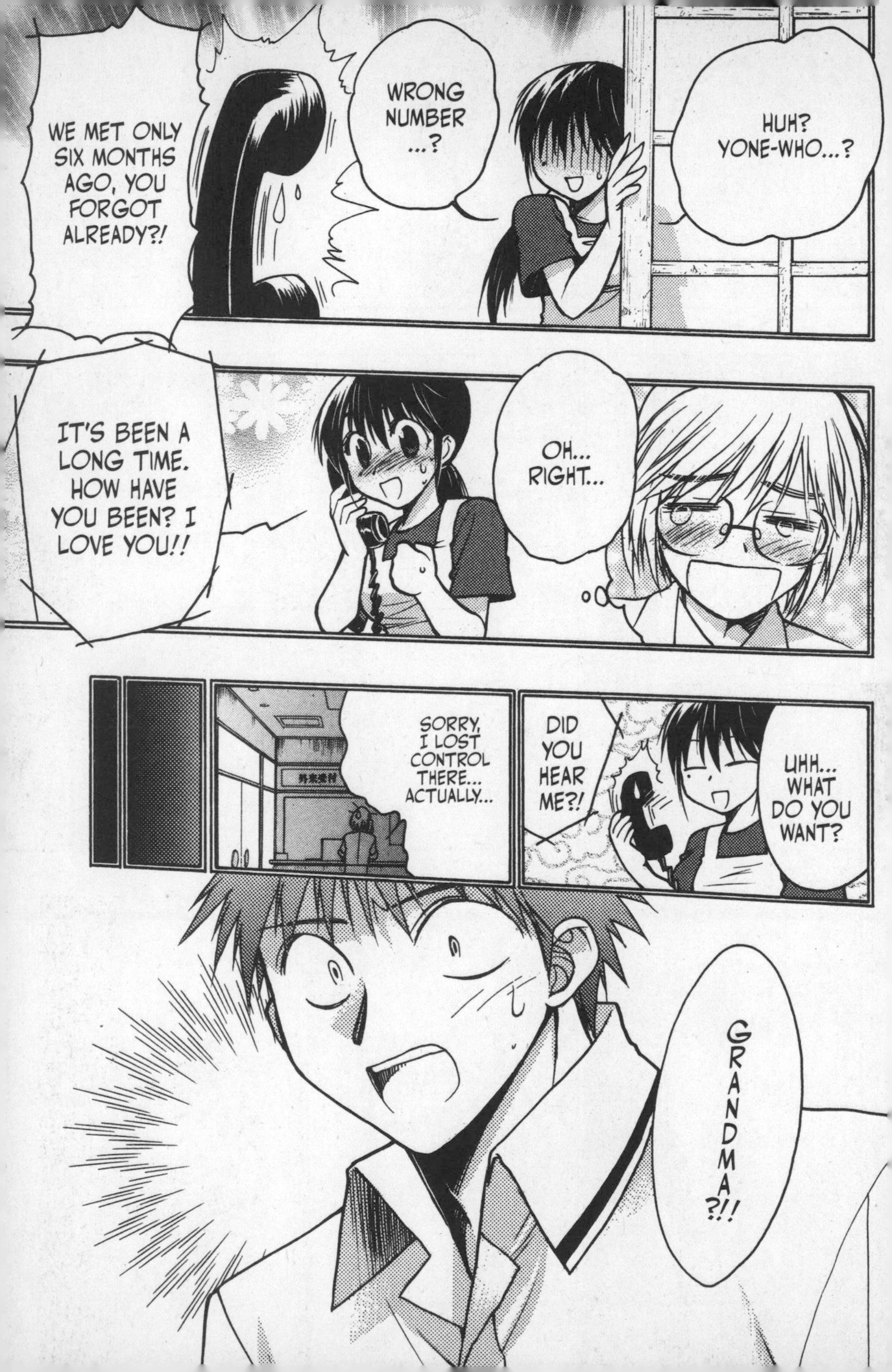
HUH? YONE-WHO...?
WRONG NUMBER ...?
WE MET ONLY SIX MONTHS AGO, YOU FORGOT ALREADY?!
OH... RIGHT...
IT'S BEEN A LONG TIME. HOW HAVE YOU BEEN? I LOVE YOU!!
UHH... WHAT DO YOU WANT?
DID YOU HEAR ME?!
SORRY, I LOST CONTROL THERE... ACTUALLY...
GRANDMA?!!

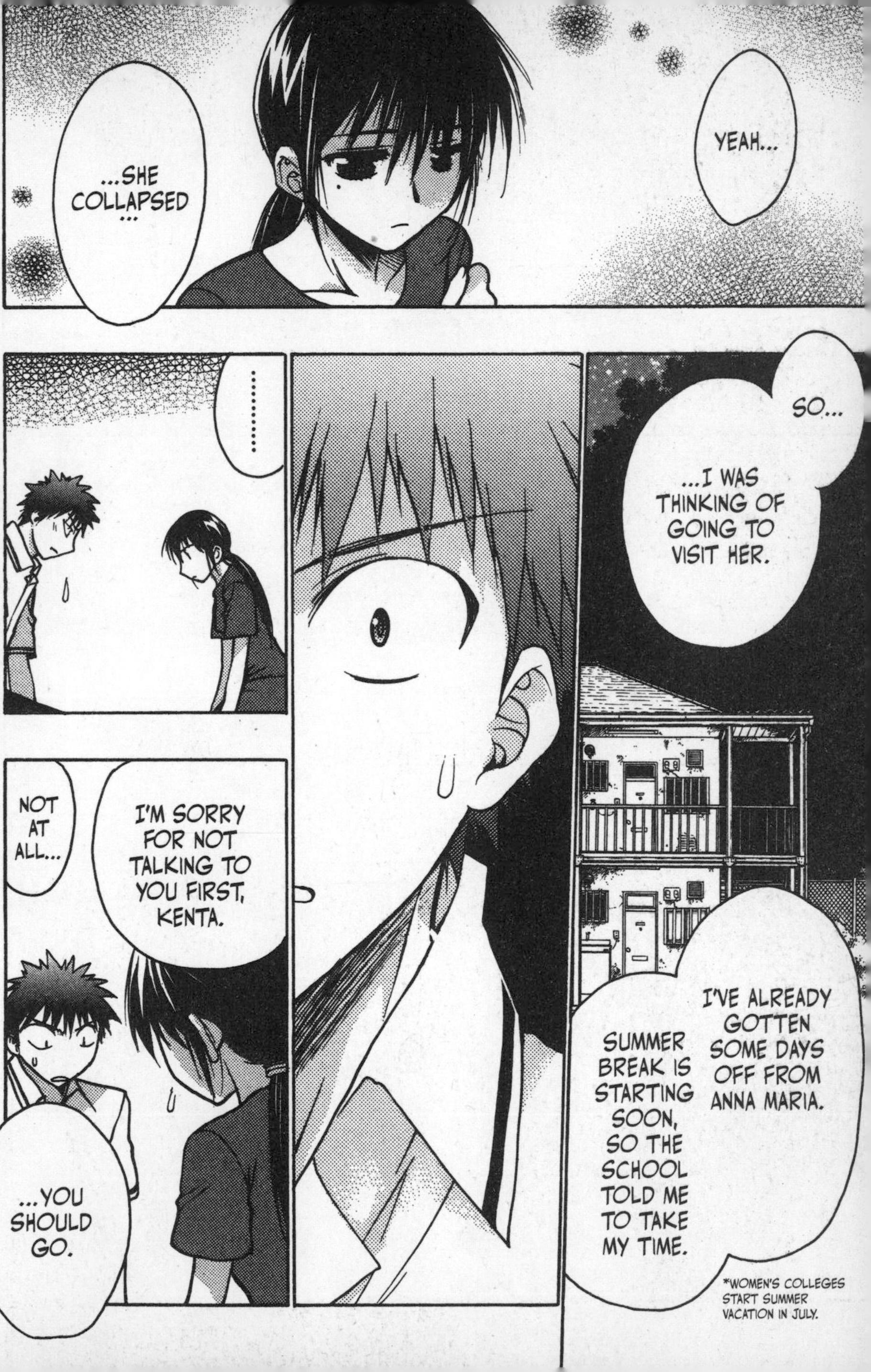
YEAH...
...SHE COLLAPSED...
SO...
...I WAS THINKING OF GOING TO VISIT HER.
I'VE ALREADY GOTTEN SOME DAYS OFF FROM ANNA MARIA.
SUMMER BREAK IS STARTING SOON, SO THE SCHOOL TOLD ME TO TAKE MY TIME.
*WOMEN'S COLLEGES START SUMMER VACATION IN JULY.
......
I'M SORRY FOR NOT TALKING TO YOU FIRST, KENTA.
NOT AT ALL...
...YOU SHOULD GO.

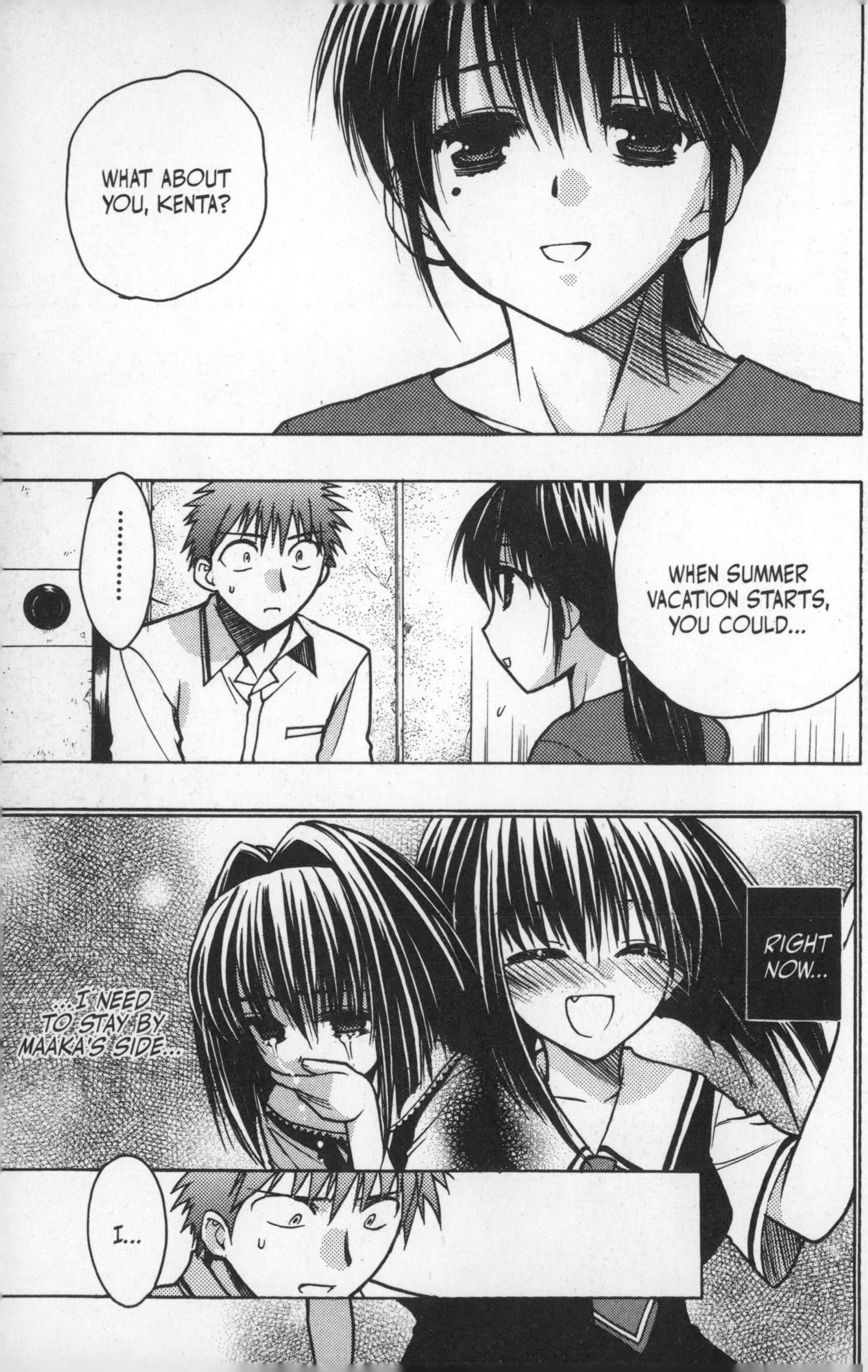
WHAT ABOUT YOU, KENTA?
WHEN SUMMER VACATION STARTS, YOU COULD...
....
RIGHT NOW...
...I NEED TO STAY BY MAAKA'S SIDE...
I...

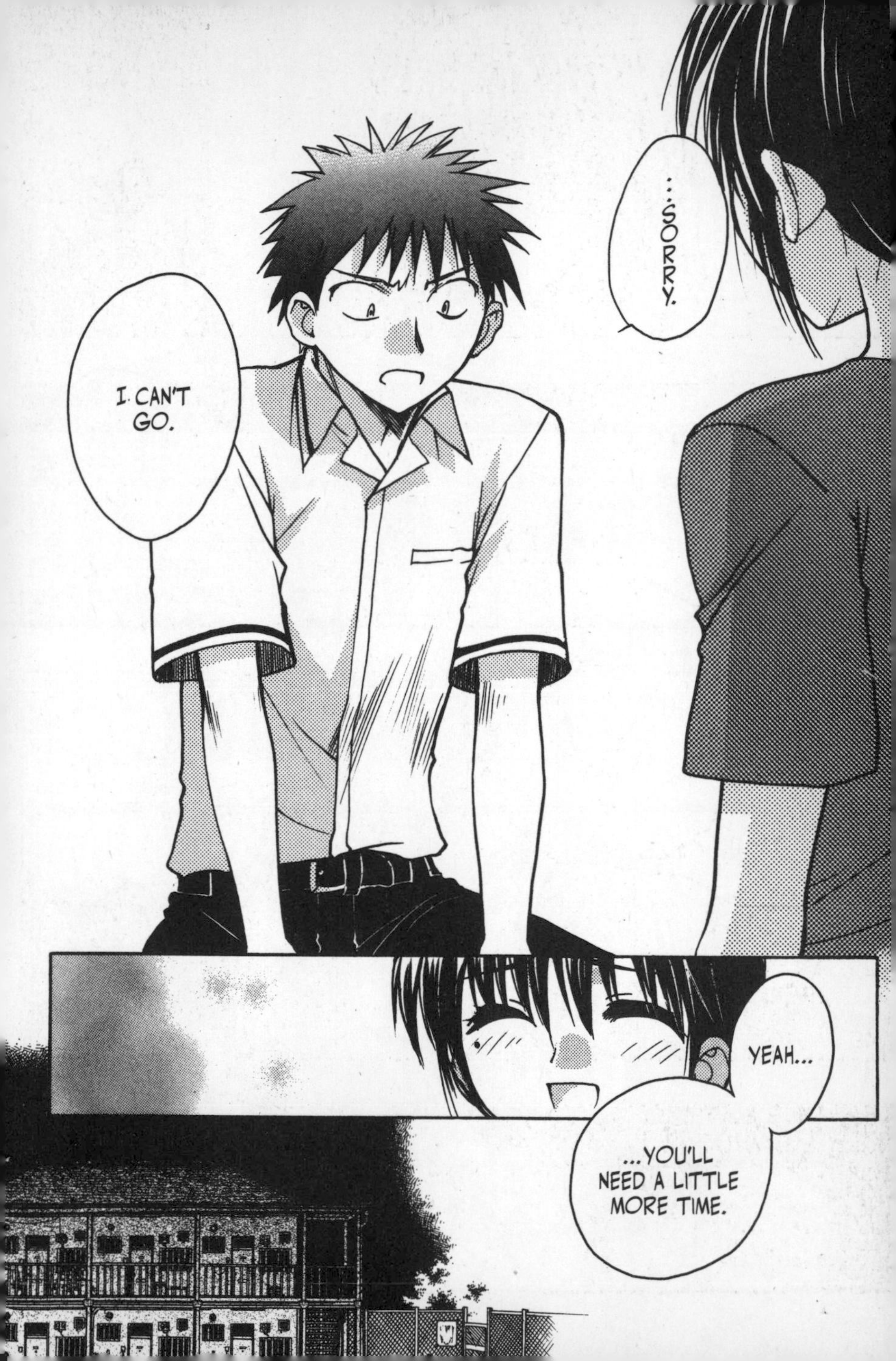
...SORRY.
I CAN'T GO.
YEAH...
...YOU'LL NEED A LITTLE MORE TIME.

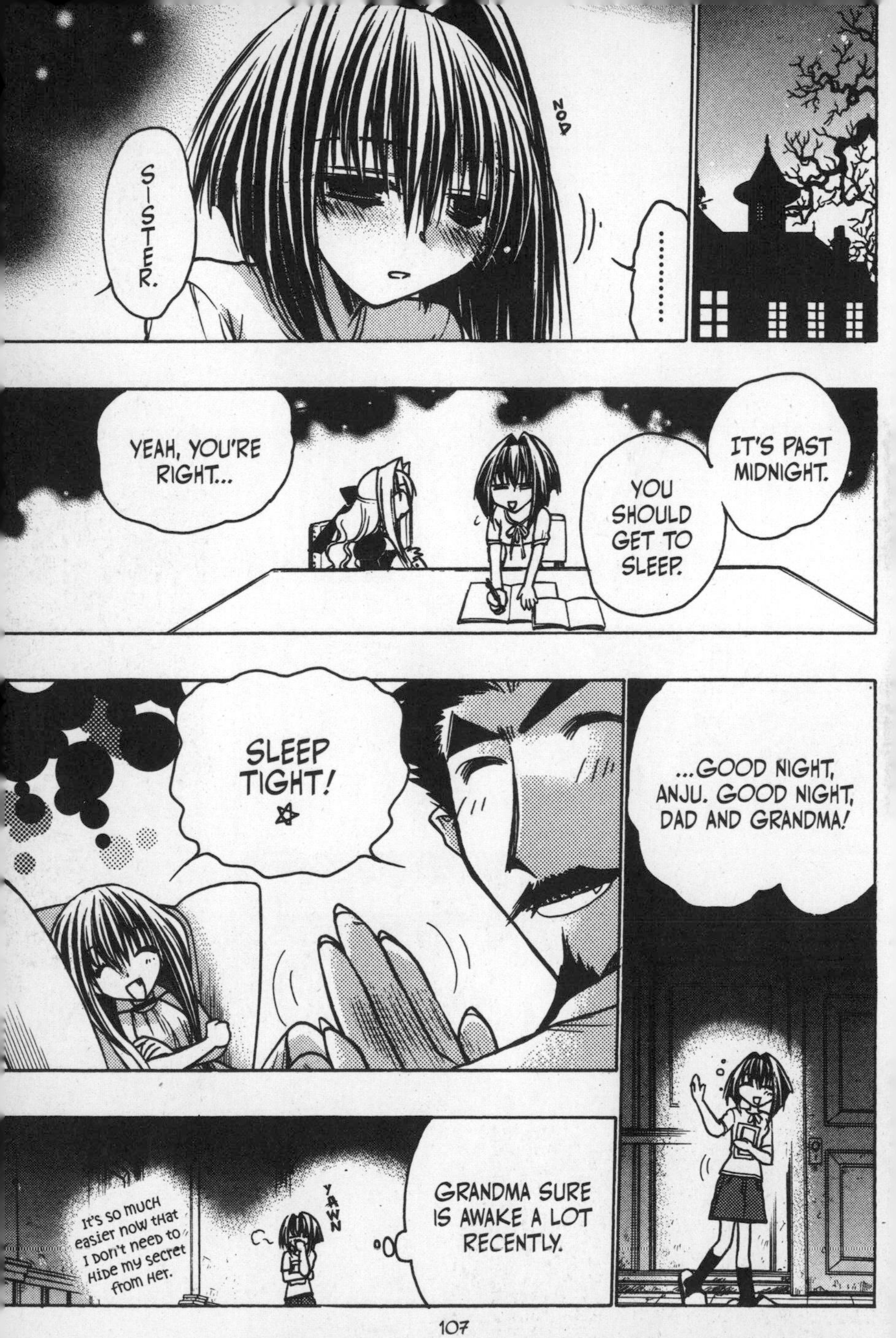
......
NOD
SISTER.
IT'S PAST MIDNIGHT.
YOU SHOULD GET TO SLEEP.
YEAH, YOU'RE RIGHT...
...GOOD NIGHT, ANJU. GOOD NIGHT, DAD AND GRANDMA!
SLEEP TIGHT!
GRANDMA SURE IS AWAKE A LOT RECENTLY.
YAWN
It's so much easier now that I don't need to hide my secret from her.

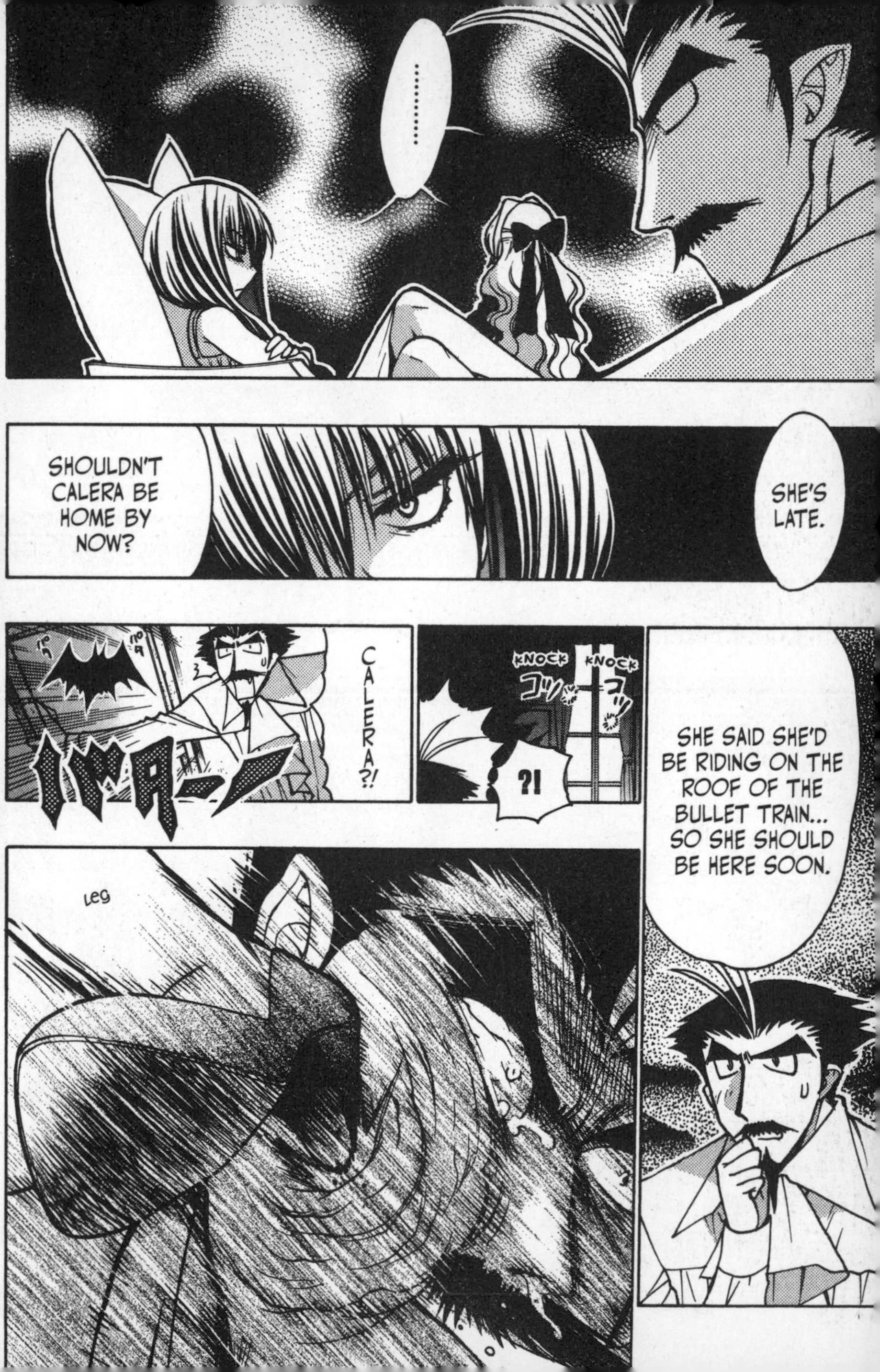
......
SHE'S LATE.
SHOULDN'T CALERA BE HOME BY NOW?
SHE SAID SHE'D BE RIDING ON THE ROOF OF THE BULLET TRAIN... SO SHE SHOULD BE HERE SOON.
KNOCK KNOCK
コツ コツ
?!
CALERA?!
leg

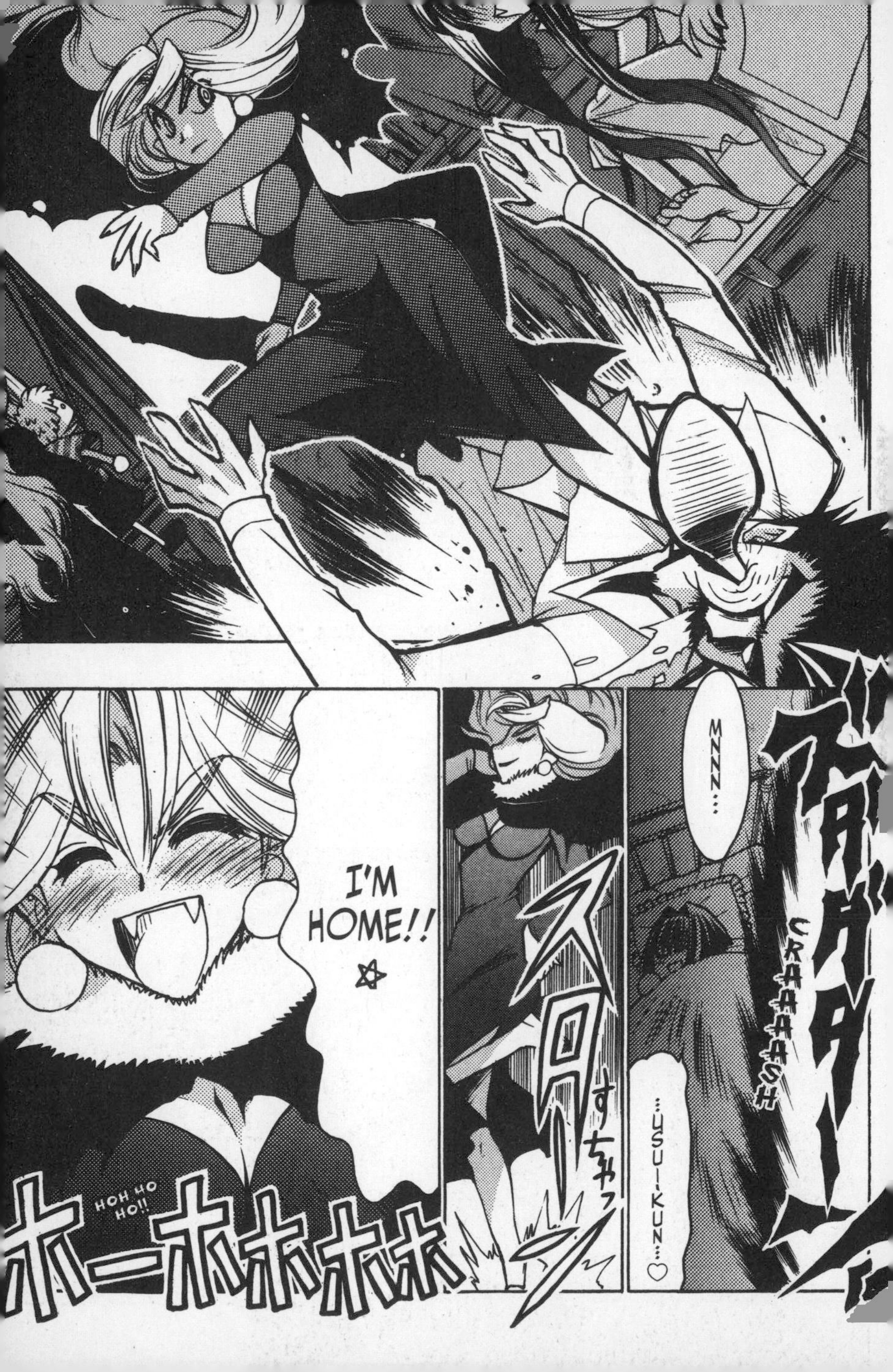
CRAAAAASH
MNNN...
...USUI-KUN...♡
すちゃっ
I'M HOME!!
HOH HO HO!!
ホーホホホホ

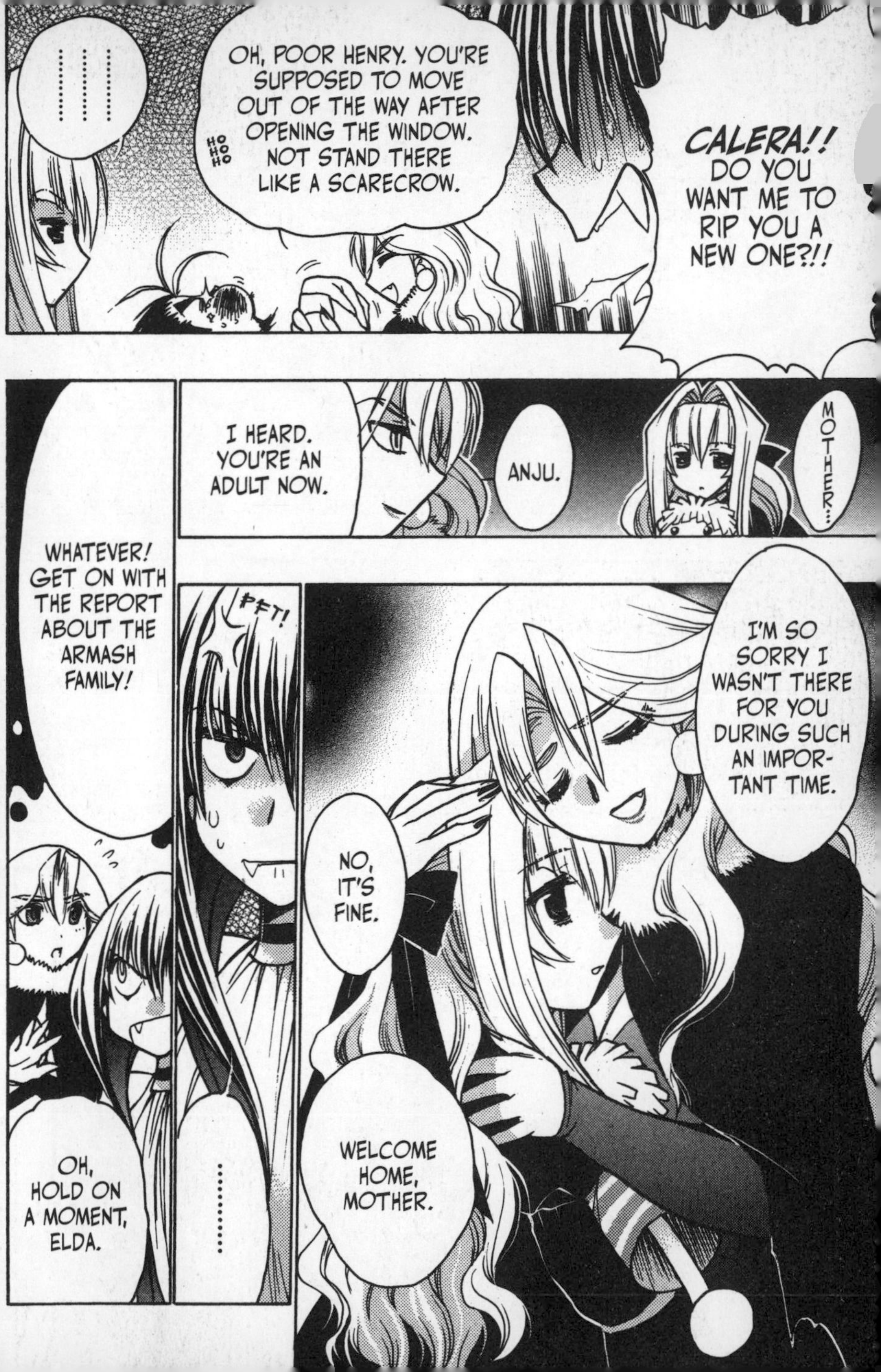
CALERA!! DO YOU WANT ME TO RIP YOU A NEW ONE?!!
OH, POOR HENRY. YOU'RE SUPPOSED TO MOVE OUT OF THE WAY AFTER OPENING THE WINDOW. NOT STAND THERE LIKE A SCARECROW.
HO HO HO
......
MOTHER...
ANJU.
I HEARD. YOU'RE AN ADULT NOW.
WHATEVER! GET ON WITH THE REPORT ABOUT THE ARMASH FAMILY!
I'M SO SORRY I WASN'T THERE FOR YOU DURING SUCH AN IMPOR-TANT TIME.
NO, IT'S FINE.
PFT!
WELCOME HOME, MOTHER.
......
OH, HOLD ON A MOMENT, ELDA.

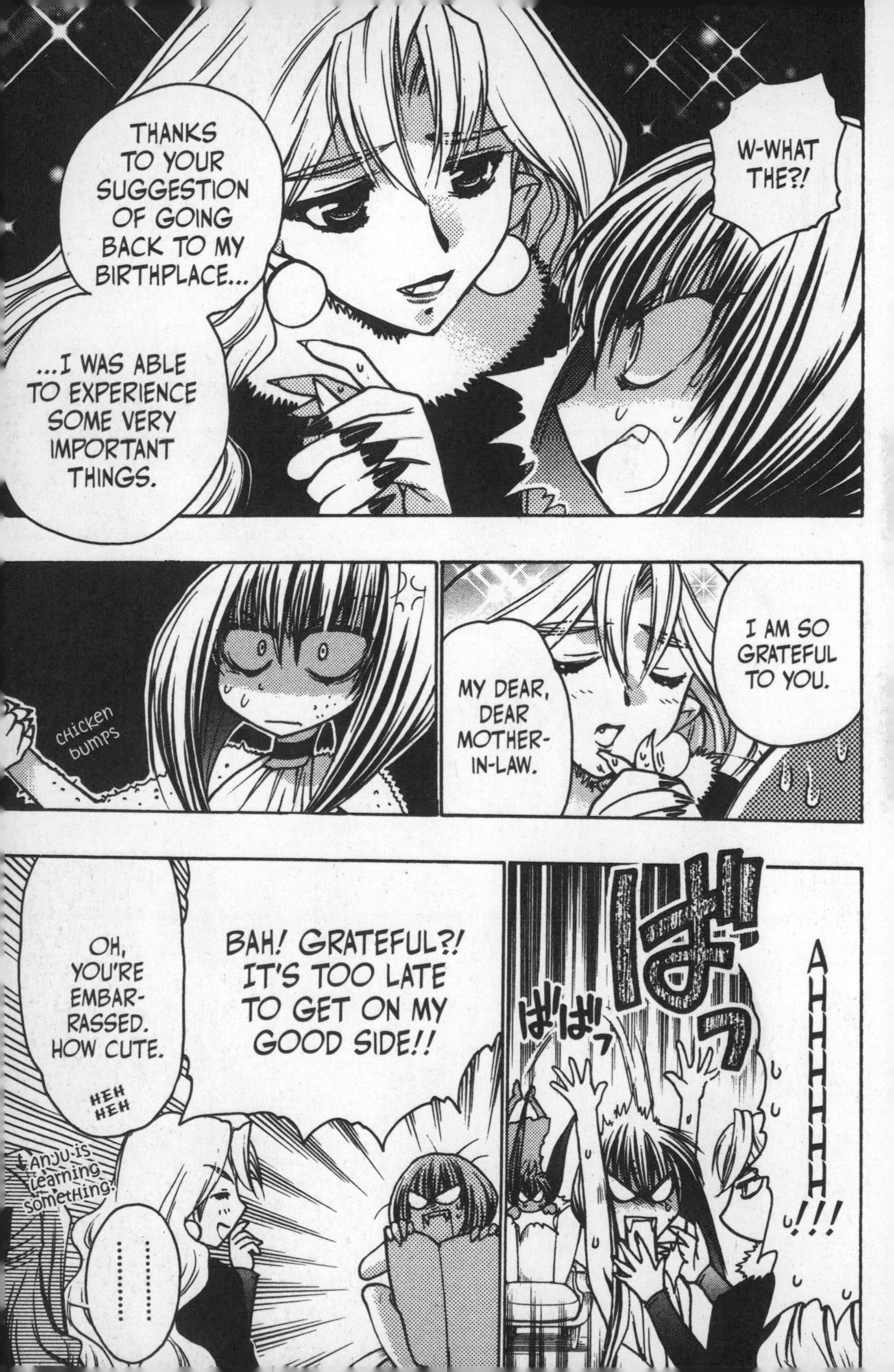

W-WHAT THE?!
THANKS TO YOUR SUGGESTION OF GOING BACK TO MY BIRTHPLACE...
...I WAS ABLE TO EXPERIENCE SOME VERY IMPORTANT THINGS.
I AM SO GRATEFUL TO YOU.
MY DEAR, DEAR MOTHER-IN-LAW.
CHICKEN BUMPS
ばっ
ばばっ
AHHHHHHH!!!
BAH! GRATEFUL?! IT'S TOO LATE TO GET ON MY GOOD SIDE!!
OH, YOU'RE EMBARRASSED. HOW CUTE.
HEH HEH
......
Anju is learning something.

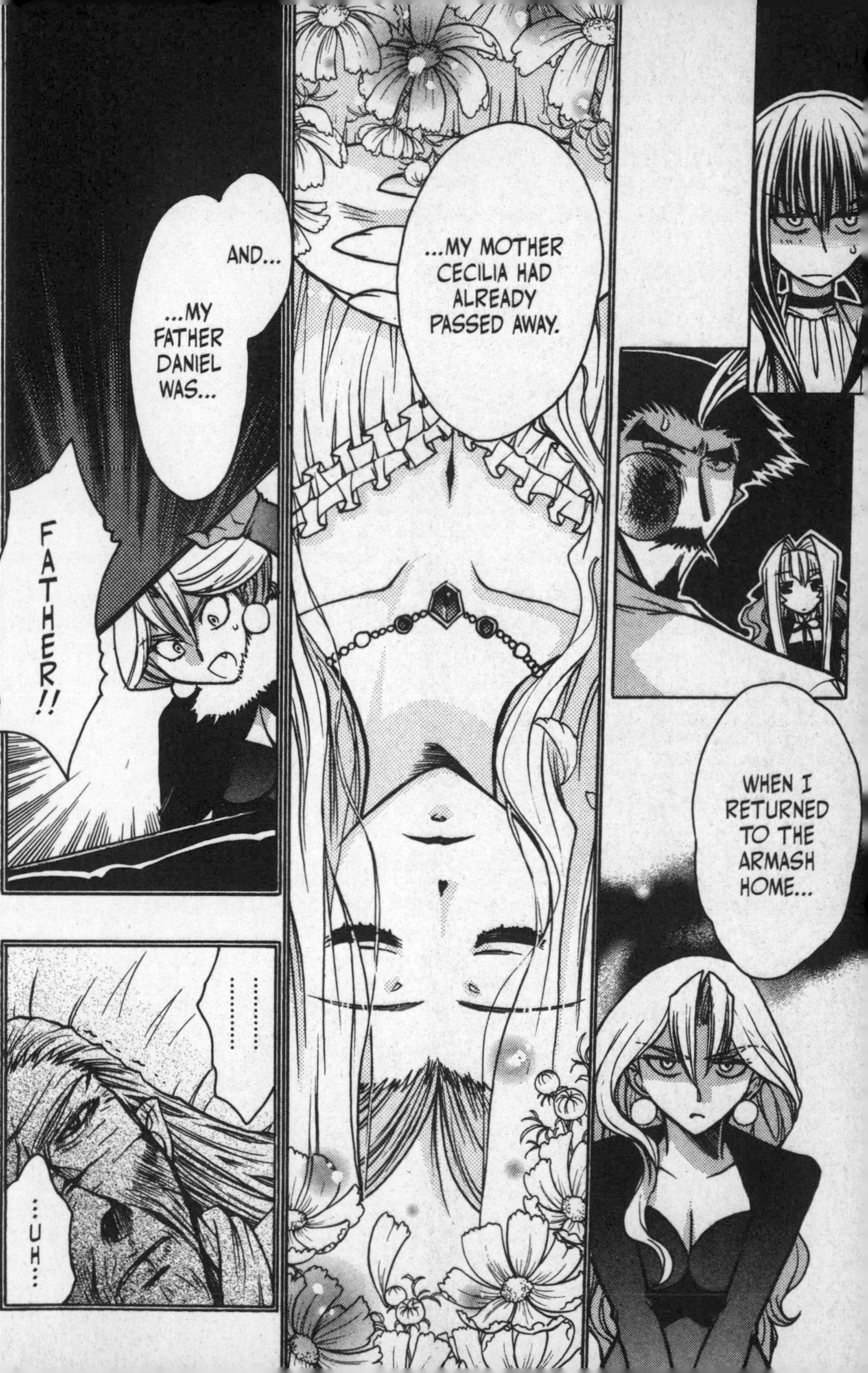
WHEN I RETURNED TO THE ARMASH HOME...
...MY MOTHER CECILIA HAD ALREADY PASSED AWAY.
AND...
...MY FATHER DANIEL WAS...
FATHER!!
......
...UH...

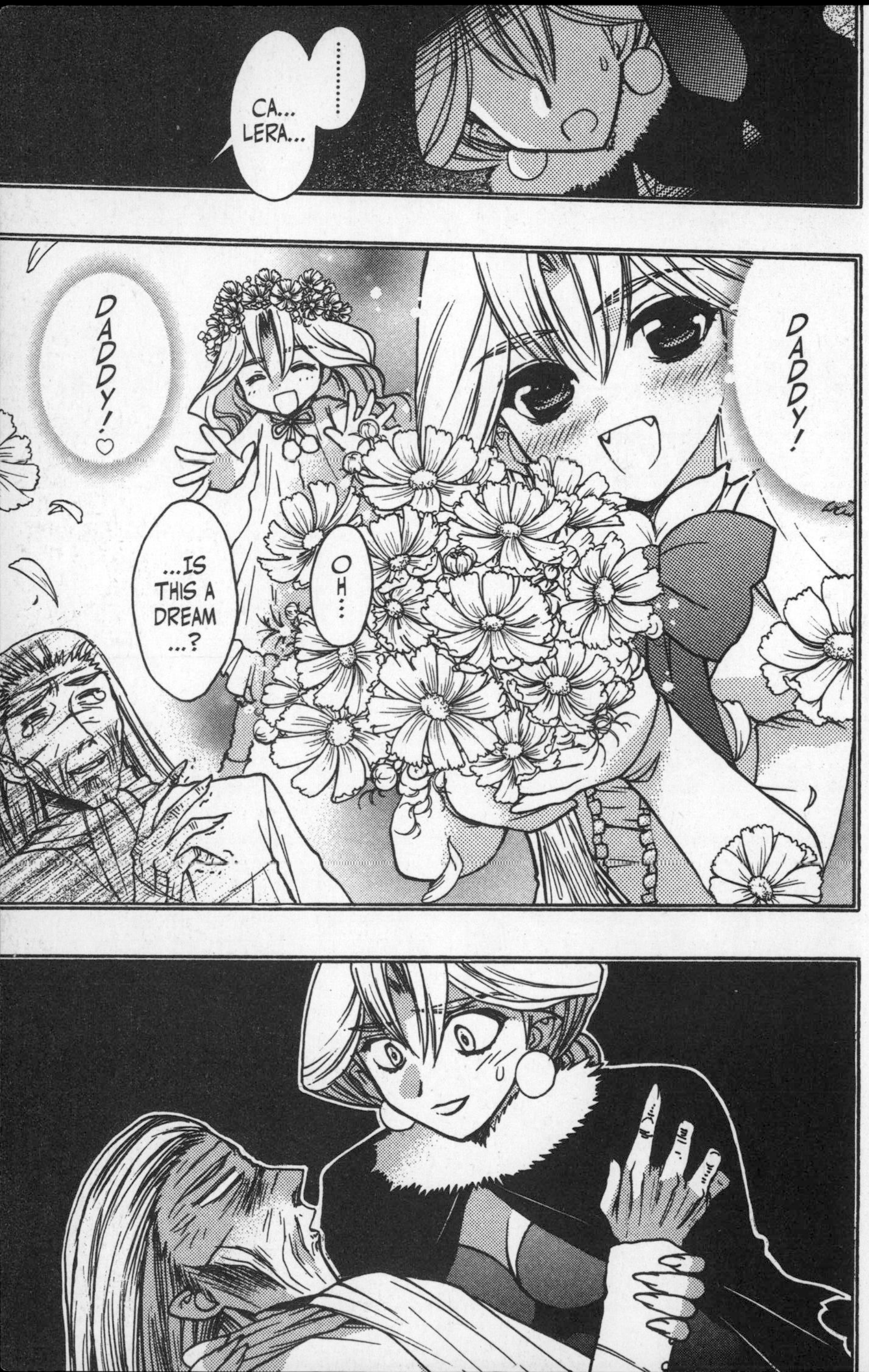
......
CA... LERA...
DADDY!
DADDY!♡
OH...
...IS THIS A DREAM ...?

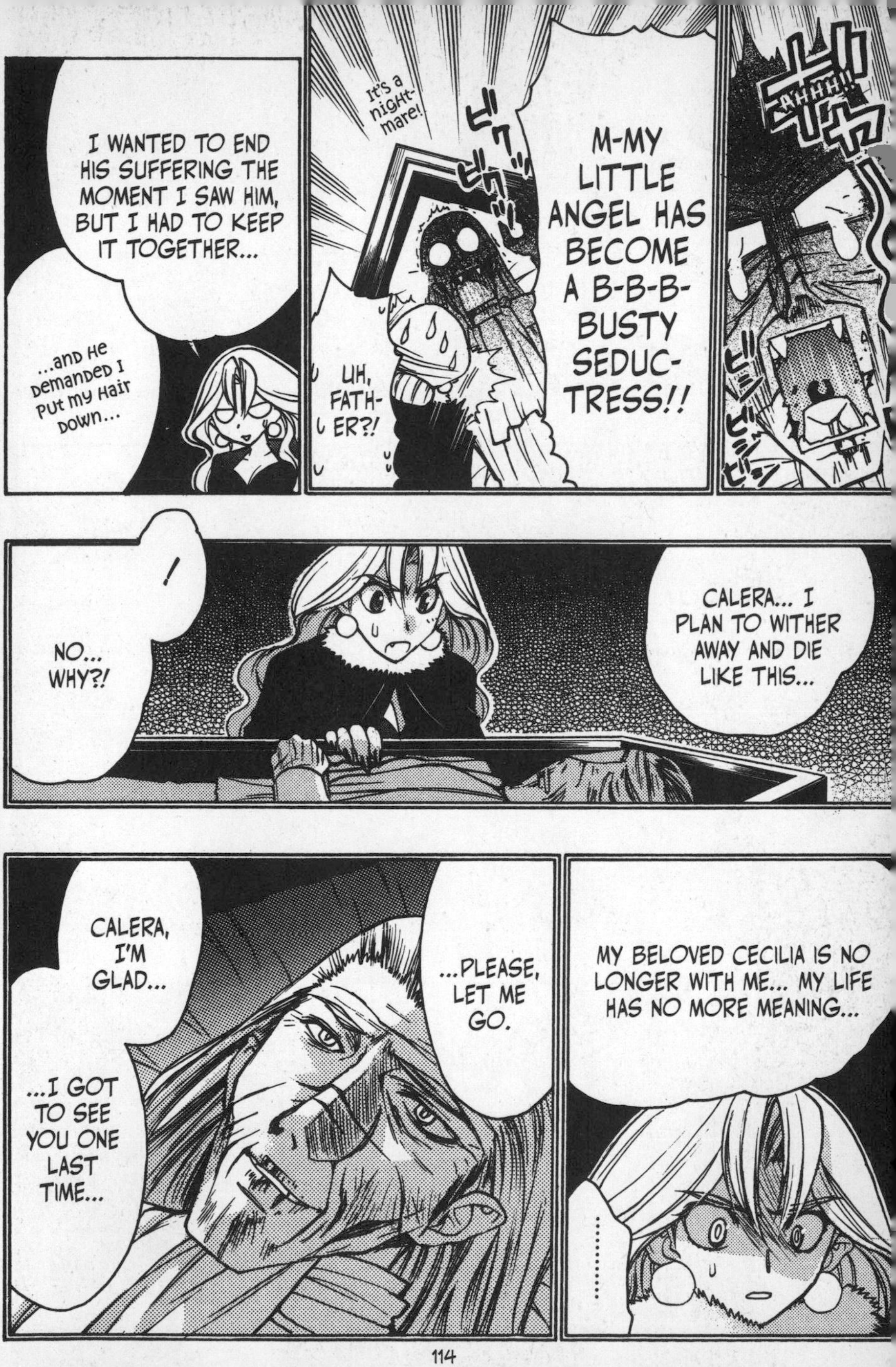
AHHHH!!
M-MY LITTLE ANGEL HAS BECOME A B-B-B-BUSTY SEDUC-TRESS!!
It's a night-mare!
UH, FATH-ER?!
I WANTED TO END HIS SUFFERING THE MOMENT I SAW HIM, BUT I HAD TO KEEP IT TOGETHER...
...and he demanded I put my hair down...
CALERA... I PLAN TO WITHER AWAY AND DIE LIKE THIS...
!
NO... WHY?!
MY BELOVED CECILIA IS NO LONGER WITH ME... MY LIFE HAS NO MORE MEANING...
......
...PLEASE, LET ME GO.
CALERA, I'M GLAD...
...I GOT TO SEE YOU ONE LAST TIME...

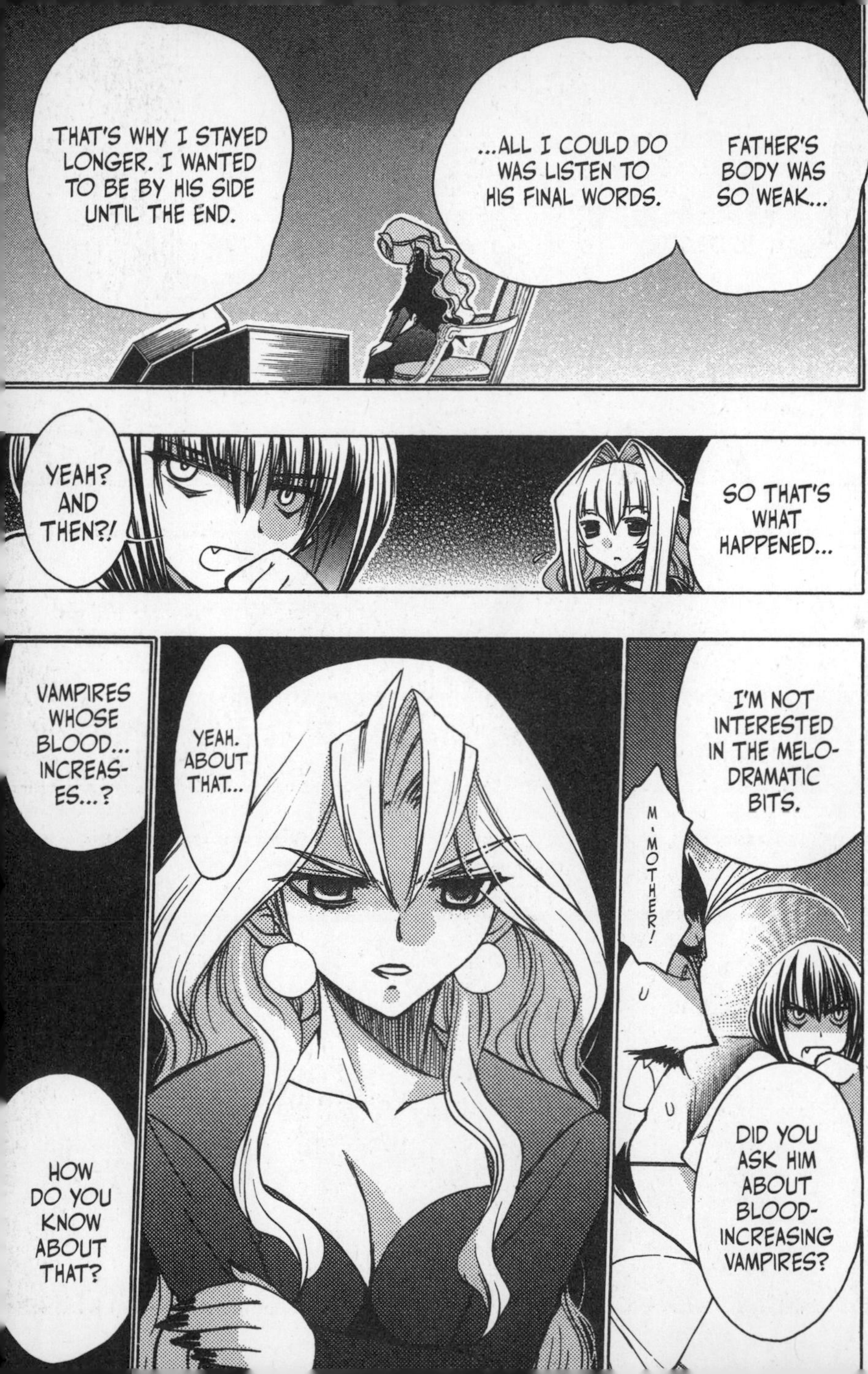
FATHER'S BODY WAS SO WEAK...
...ALL I COULD DO WAS LISTEN TO HIS FINAL WORDS.
THAT'S WHY I STAYED LONGER. I WANTED TO BE BY HIS SIDE UNTIL THE END.
SO THAT'S WHAT HAPPENED...
YEAH? AND THEN?!
I'M NOT INTERESTED IN THE MELO-DRAMATIC BITS.
M-MOTHER!
DID YOU ASK HIM ABOUT BLOOD-INCREASING VAMPIRES?
YEAH. ABOUT THAT...
VAMPIRES WHOSE BLOOD... INCREASES-ES...?
HOW DO YOU KNOW ABOUT THAT?

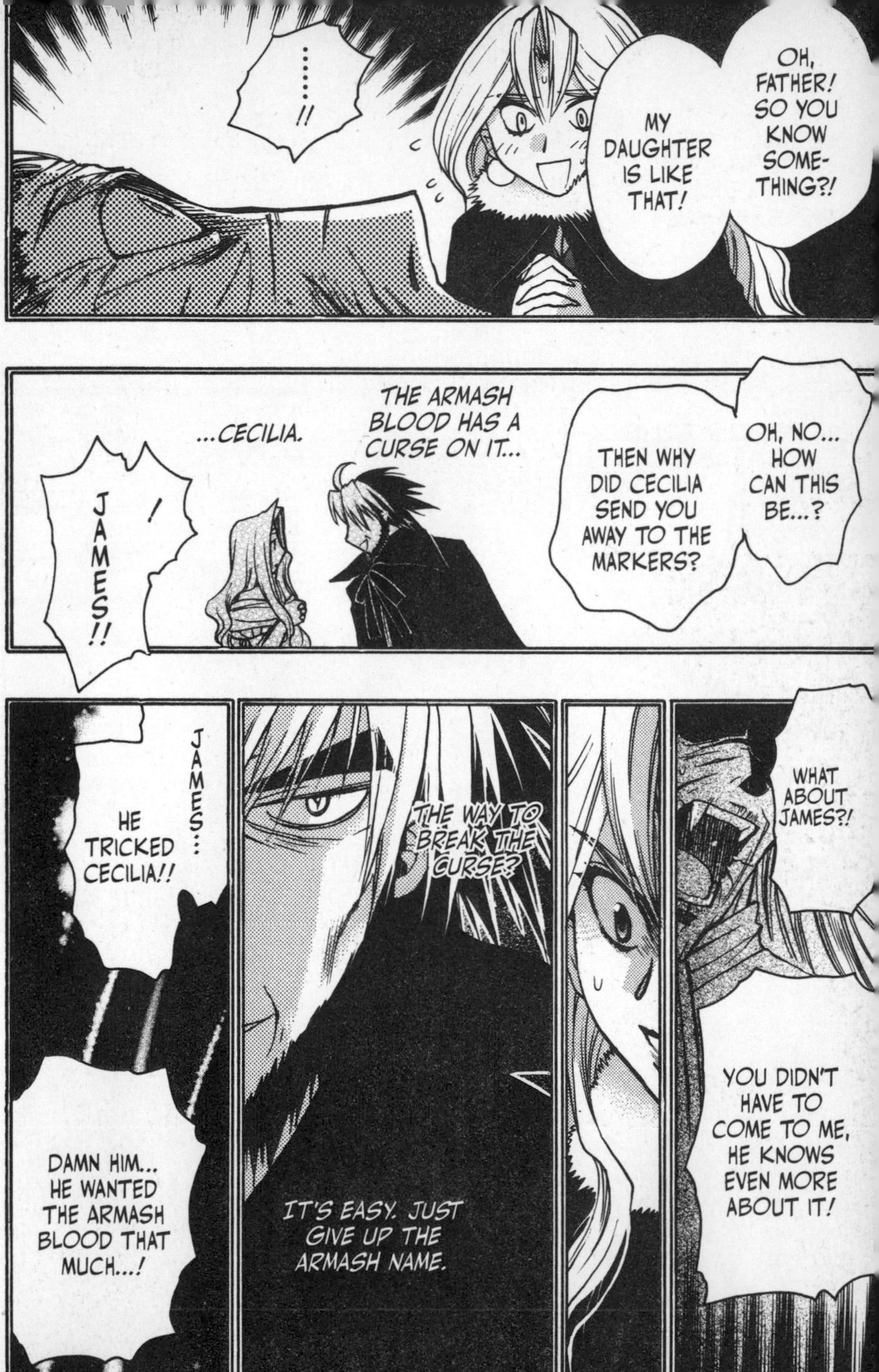
OH, FATHER! SO YOU KNOW SOME-THING?!
MY DAUGHTER IS LIKE THAT!
......!!
OH, NO... HOW CAN THIS BE...?
THEN WHY DID CECILIA SEND YOU AWAY TO THE MARKERS?
THE ARMASH BLOOD HAS A CURSE ON IT...
...CECILIA.
!
JAMES!!
WHAT ABOUT JAMES?!
YOU DIDN'T HAVE TO COME TO ME, HE KNOWS EVEN MORE ABOUT IT!
THE WAY TO BREAK THE CURSE?
IT'S EASY. JUST GIVE UP THE ARMASH NAME.
JAMES...
HE TRICKED CECILIA!!
DAMN HIM... HE WANTED THE ARMASH BLOOD THAT MUCH...!

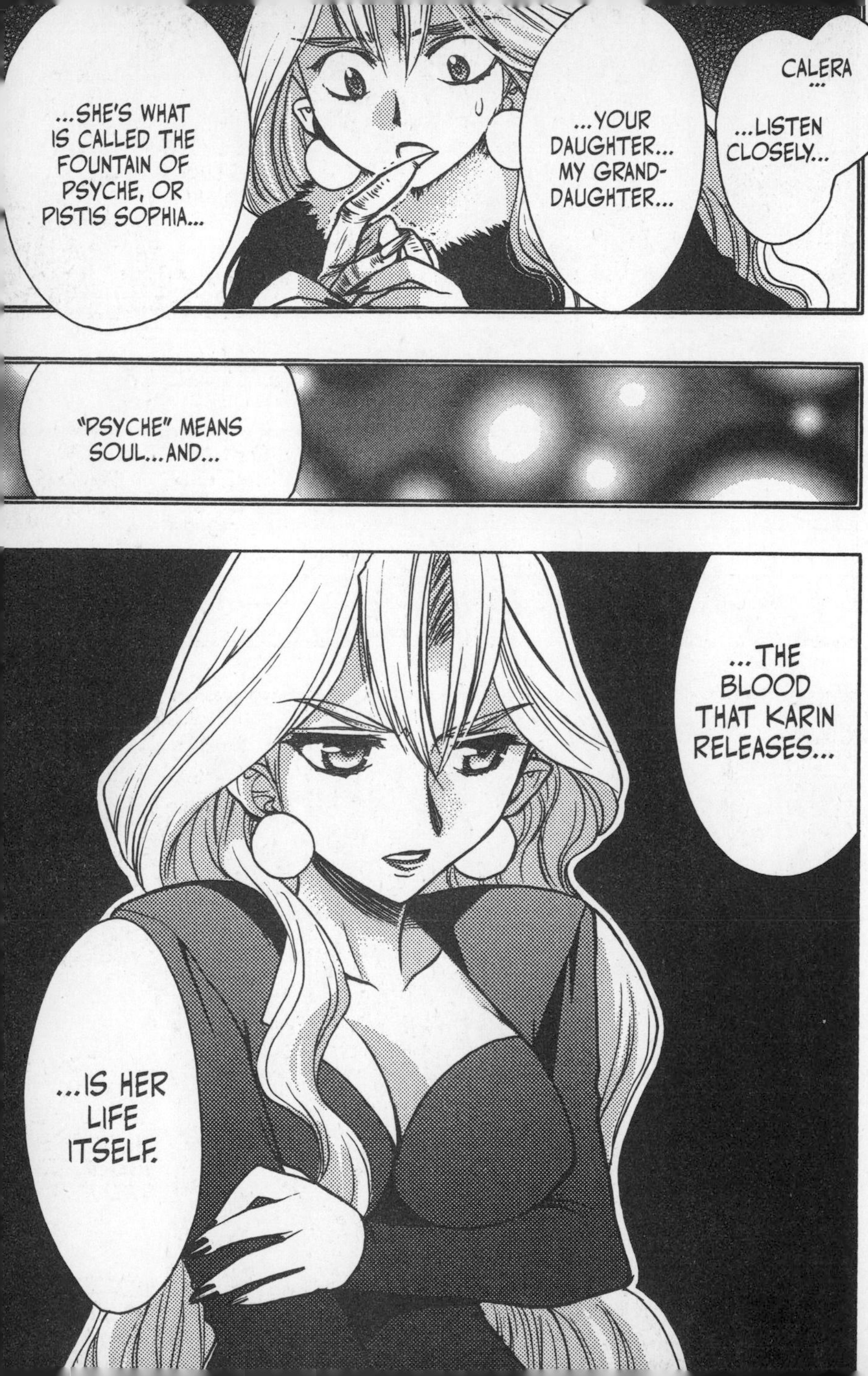
CALERA ... ...LISTEN CLOSELY...
...YOUR DAUGHTER... MY GRAND-DAUGHTER...
...SHE'S WHAT IS CALLED THE FOUNTAIN OF PSYCHE, OR PISTIS SOPHIA...
"PSYCHE" MEANS SOUL...AND...
...THE BLOOD THAT KARIN RELEASES...
...IS HER LIFE ITSELF.

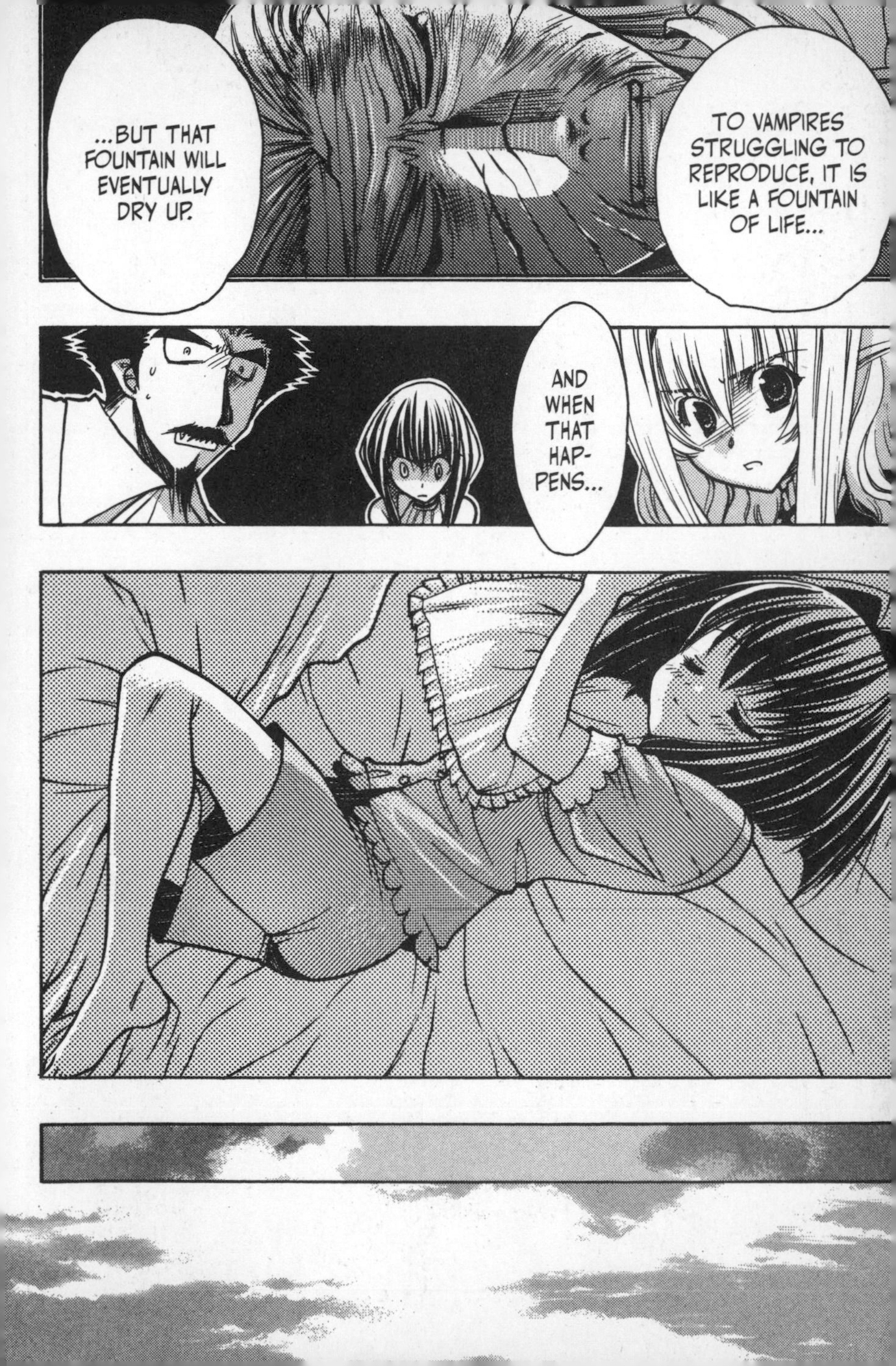
TO VAMPIRES STRUGGLING TO REPRODUCE, IT IS LIKE A FOUNTAIN OF LIFE...
...BUT THAT FOUNTAIN WILL EVENTUALLY DRY UP.
AND WHEN THAT HAP-PENS...

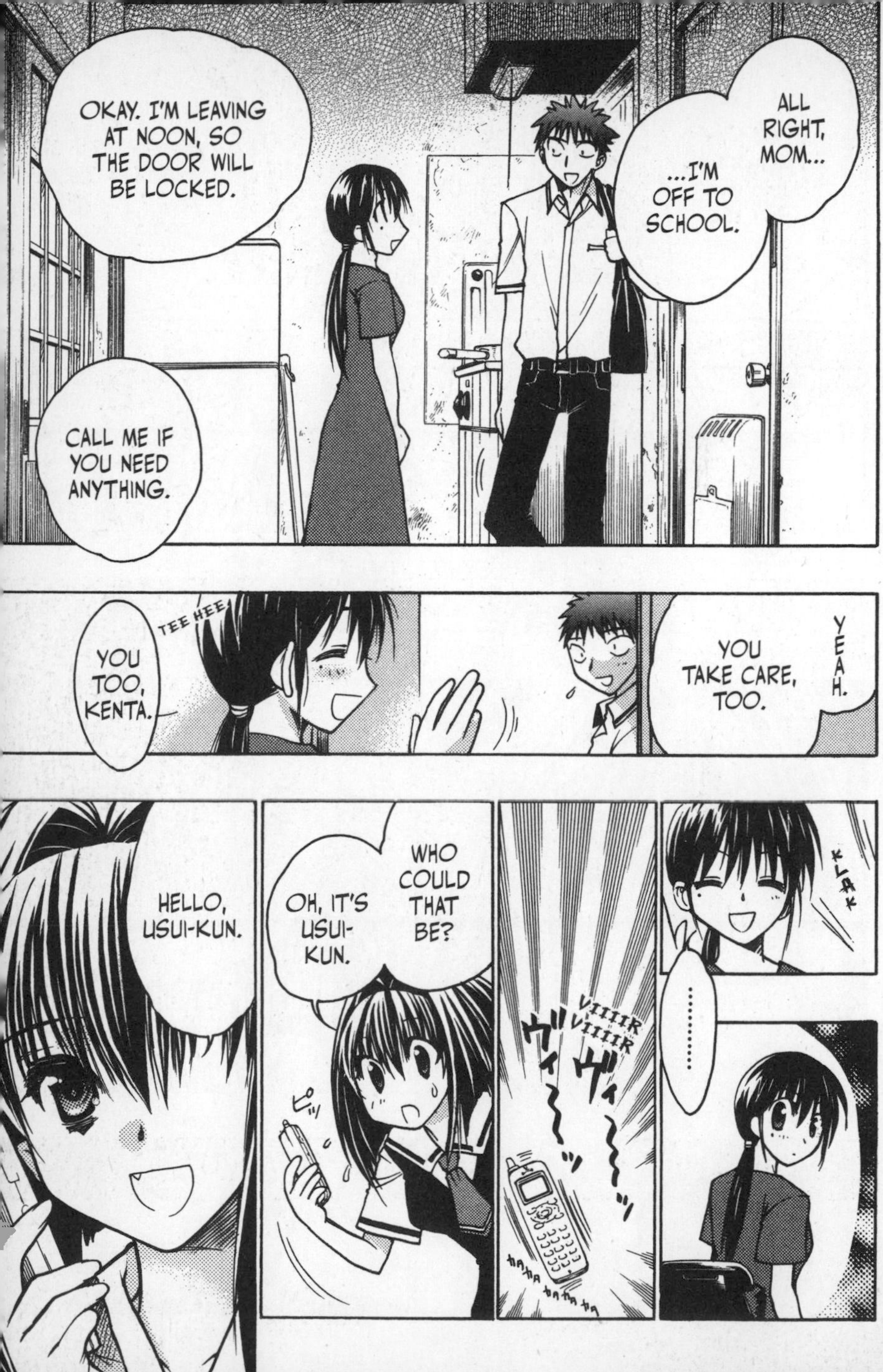
ALL RIGHT, MOM...
...I'M OFF TO SCHOOL.
OKAY. I'M LEAVING AT NOON, SO THE DOOR WILL BE LOCKED.
CALL ME IF YOU NEED ANYTHING.
YEAH.
YOU TAKE CARE, TOO.
TEE HEE.
YOU TOO, KENTA.
KLAK
......
VIIIIR
VIIIIR
WHO COULD THAT BE?
OH, IT'S USUI-KUN.
HELLO, USUI-KUN.

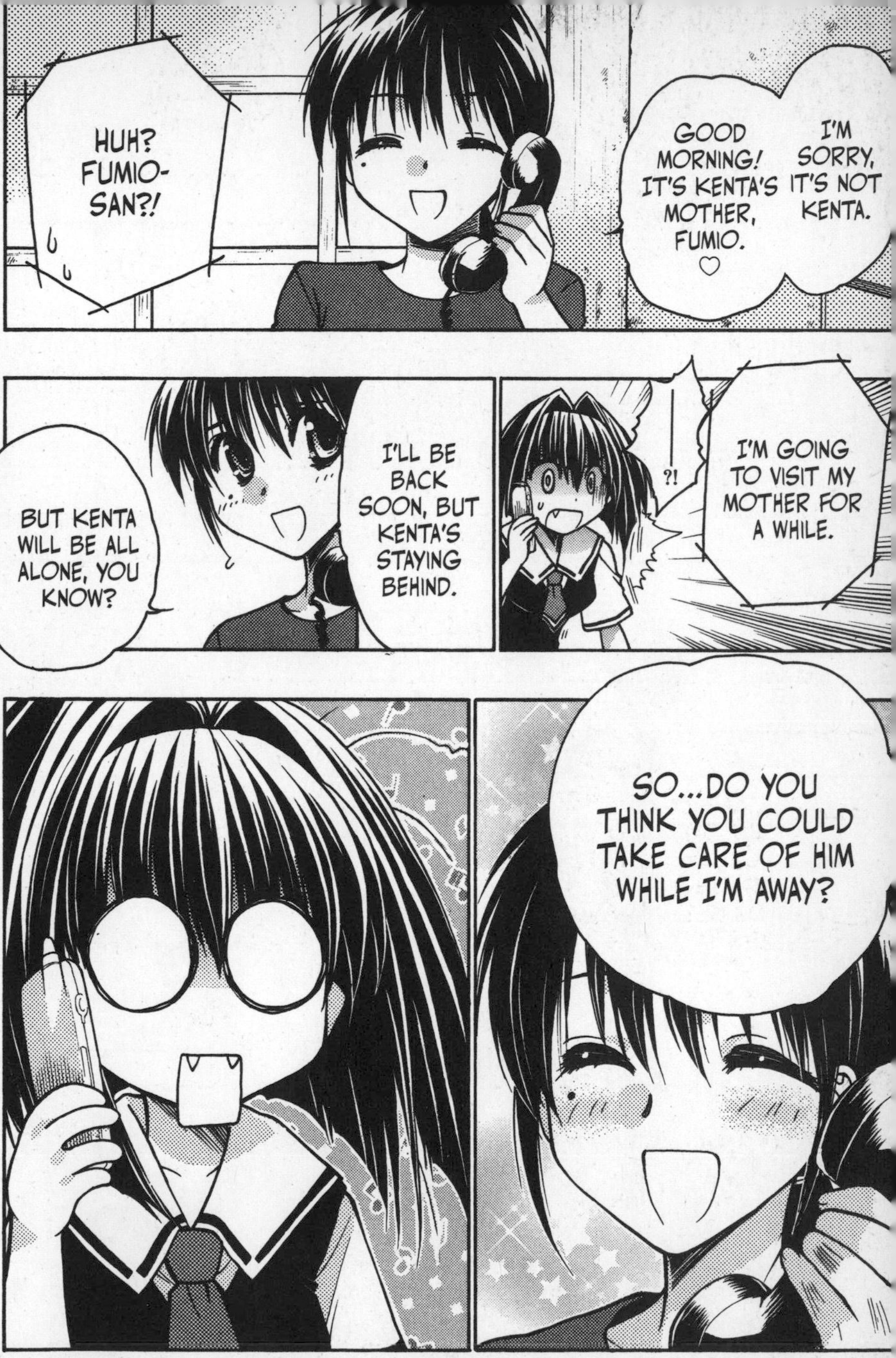
GOOD MORNING! IT'S KENTA'S MOTHER, FUMIO. ♡
I'M SORRY, IT'S NOT KENTA.
HUH? FUMIO-SAN?!
I'M GOING TO VISIT MY MOTHER FOR A WHILE.
?!
I'LL BE BACK SOON, BUT KENTA'S STAYING BEHIND.
BUT KENTA WILL BE ALL ALONE, YOU KNOW?
SO...DO YOU THINK YOU COULD TAKE CARE OF HIM WHILE I'M AWAY?

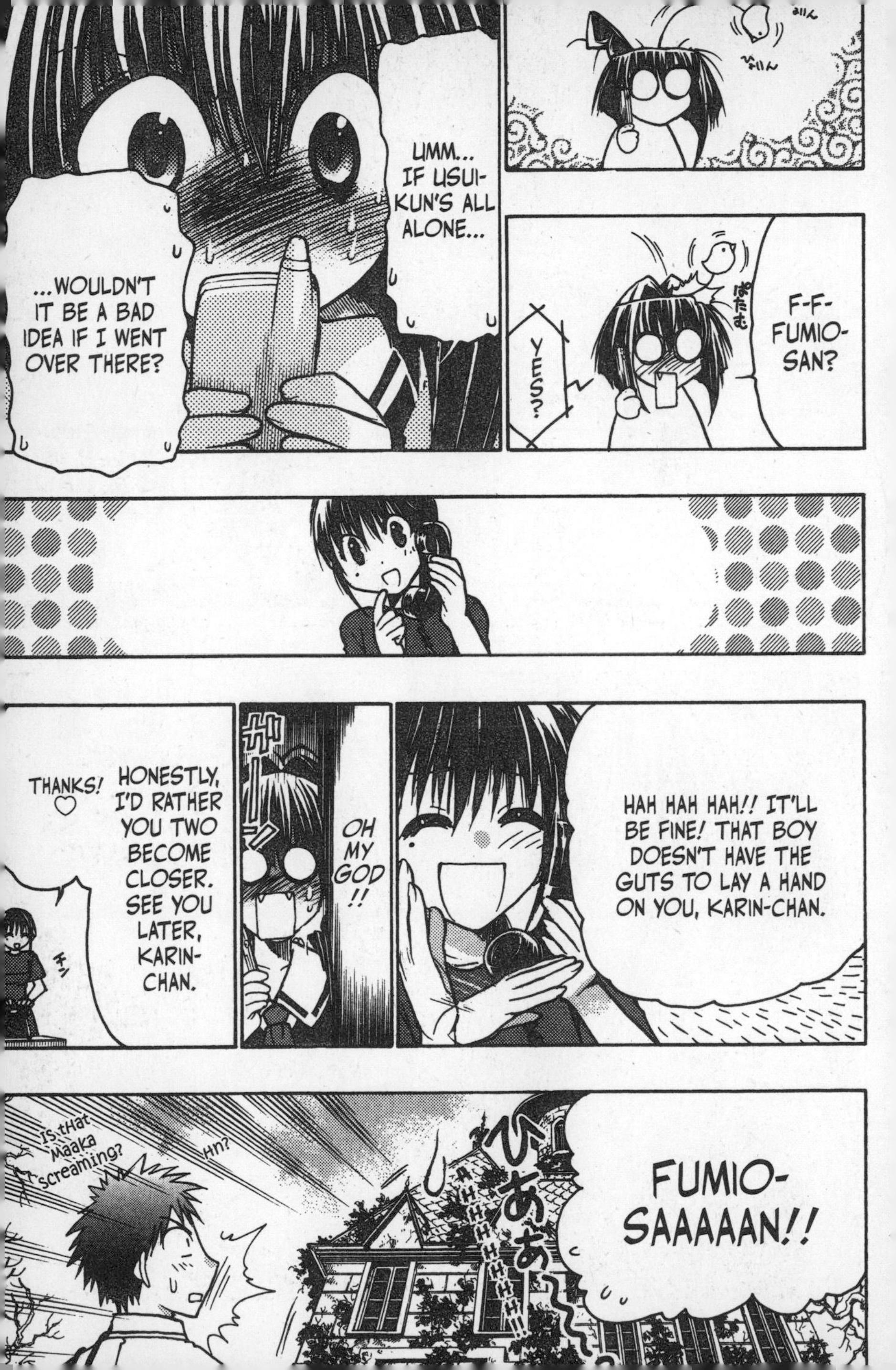
F-F-FUMIO-SAN?
ぱたむ
YES?
UMM... IF USUI-KUN'S ALL ALONE...
...WOULDN'T IT BE A BAD IDEA IF I WENT OVER THERE?
HAH HAH HAH!! IT'LL BE FINE! THAT BOY DOESN'T HAVE THE GUTS TO LAY A HAND ON YOU, KARIN-CHAN.
OH MY GOD!!
HONESTLY, I'D RATHER YOU TWO BECOME CLOSER. SEE YOU LATER, KARIN-CHAN.
THANKS! ♡
チン
FUMIO-SAAAAAN!!
ひあぁ～
AHHHHHHH!!
Hn?
Is that Maaka screaming?

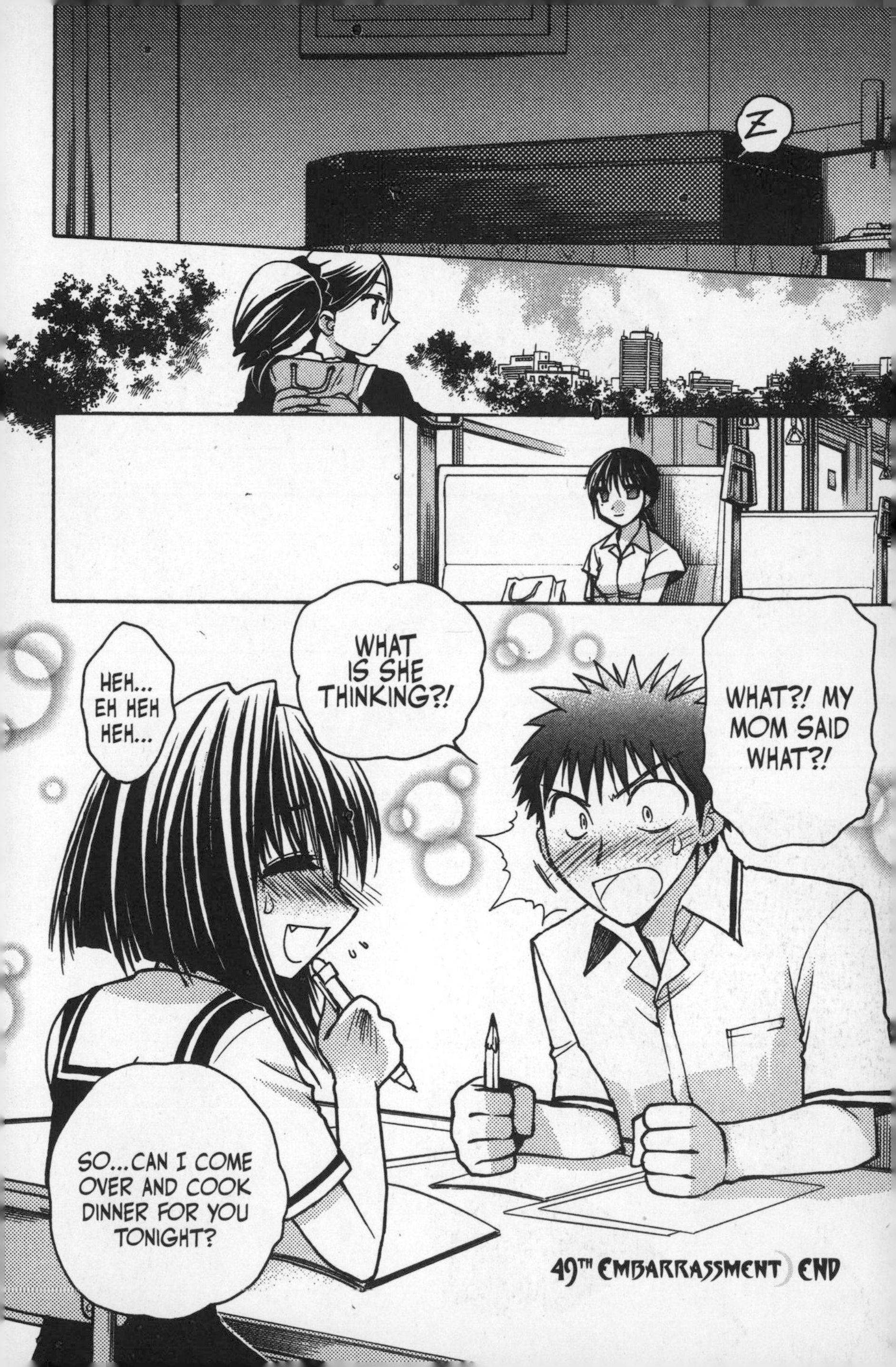
Z
WHAT?! MY MOM SAID WHAT?!
WHAT IS SHE THINKING?!
HEH... EH HEH HEH...
SO...CAN I COME OVER AND COOK DINNER FOR YOU TONIGHT?
49TH EMBARRASSMENT END

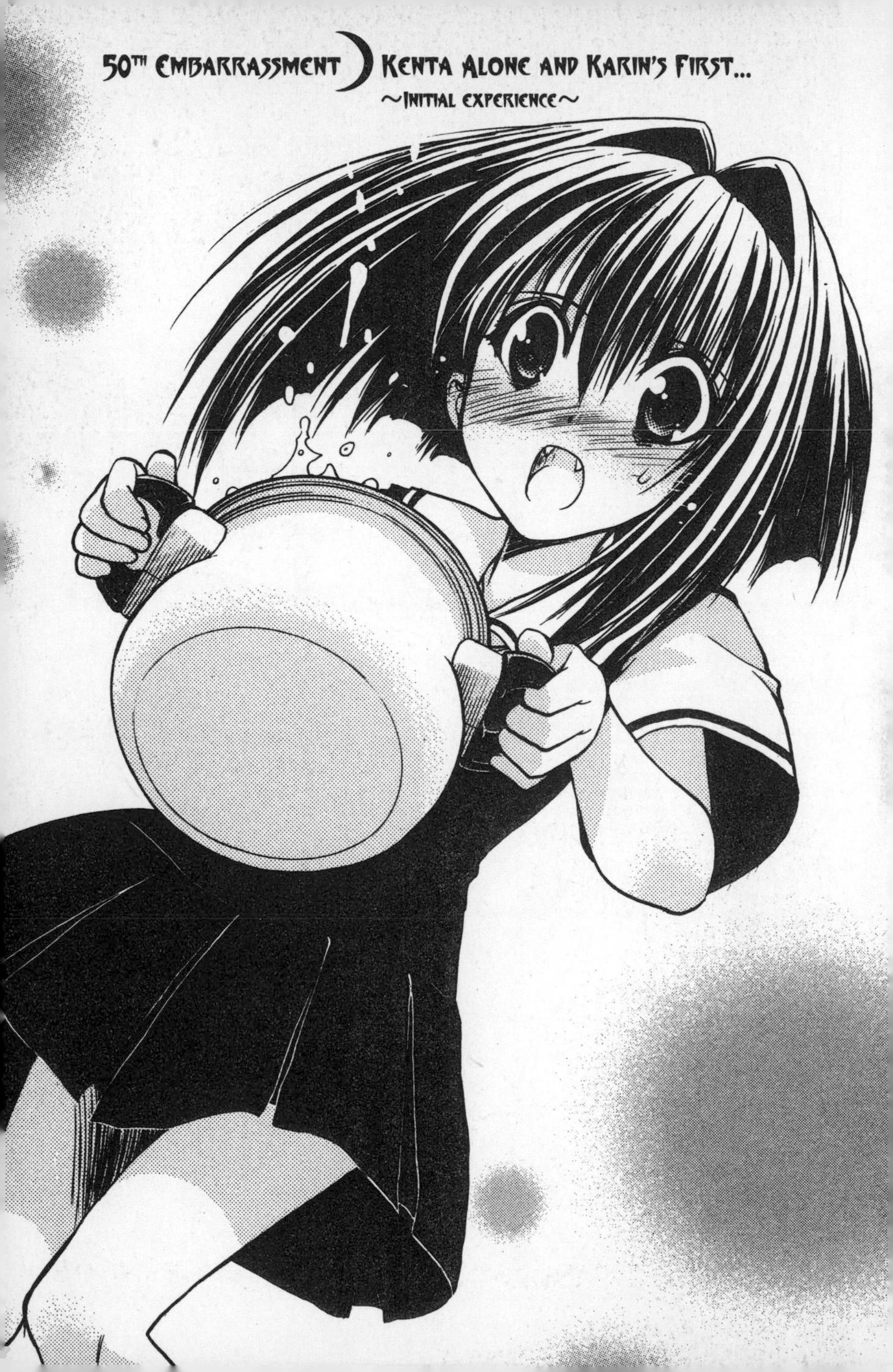
50TH EMBARRASSMENT) KENTA ALONE AND KARIN'S FIRST...
~INITIAL EXPERIENCE~

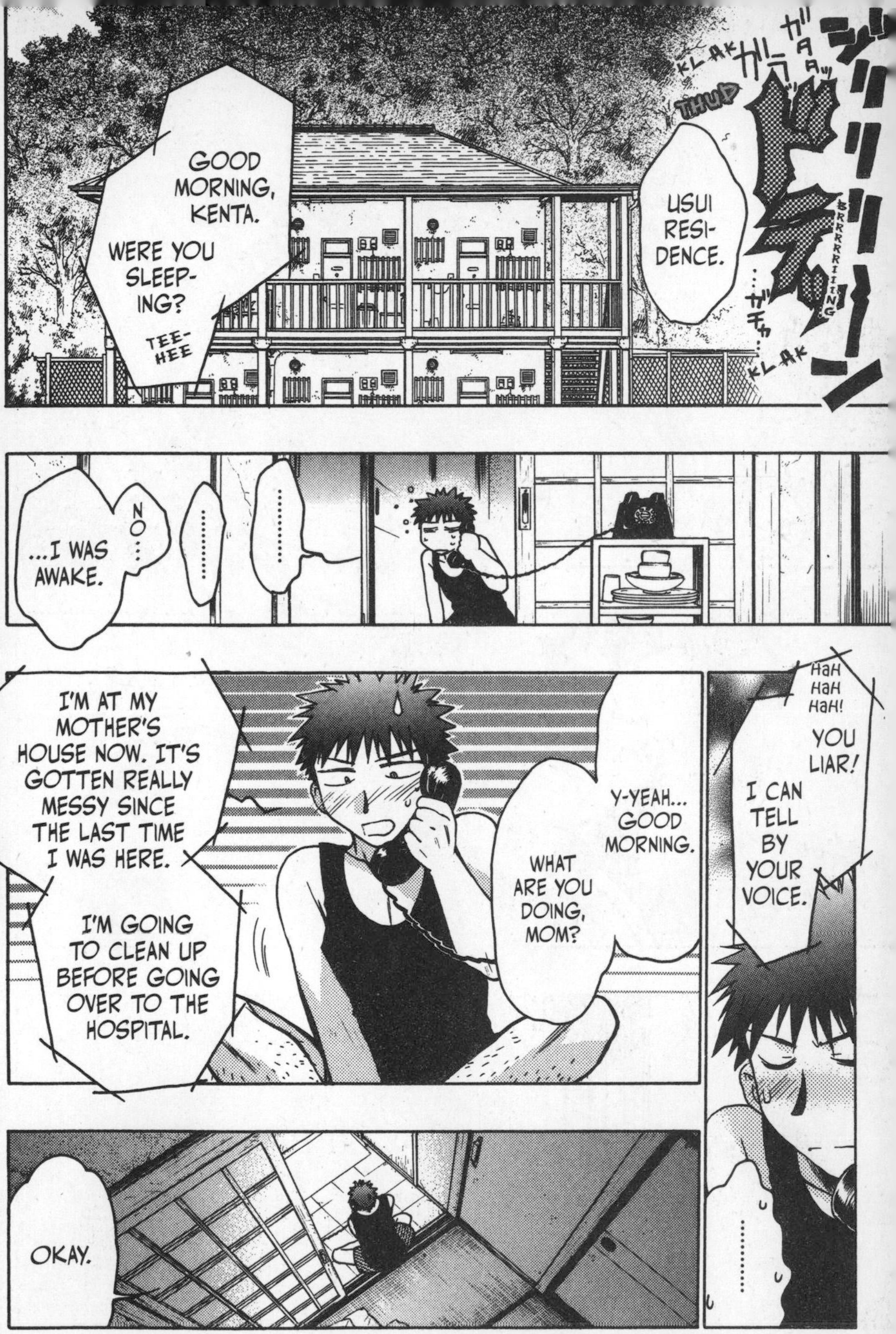
KLAK
THUD
BRRRRRIIING
KLAK
USUI RESI-DENCE.
GOOD MORNING, KENTA.
WERE YOU SLEEP-ING?
TEE-HEE
....
....
NO...
...I WAS AWAKE.
HAH HAH HAH!
YOU LIAR!
I CAN TELL BY YOUR VOICE.
Y-YEAH... GOOD MORNING.
WHAT ARE YOU DOING, MOM?
I'M AT MY MOTHER'S HOUSE NOW. IT'S GOTTEN REALLY MESSY SINCE THE LAST TIME I WAS HERE.
I'M GOING TO CLEAN UP BEFORE GOING OVER TO THE HOSPITAL.
....
OKAY.

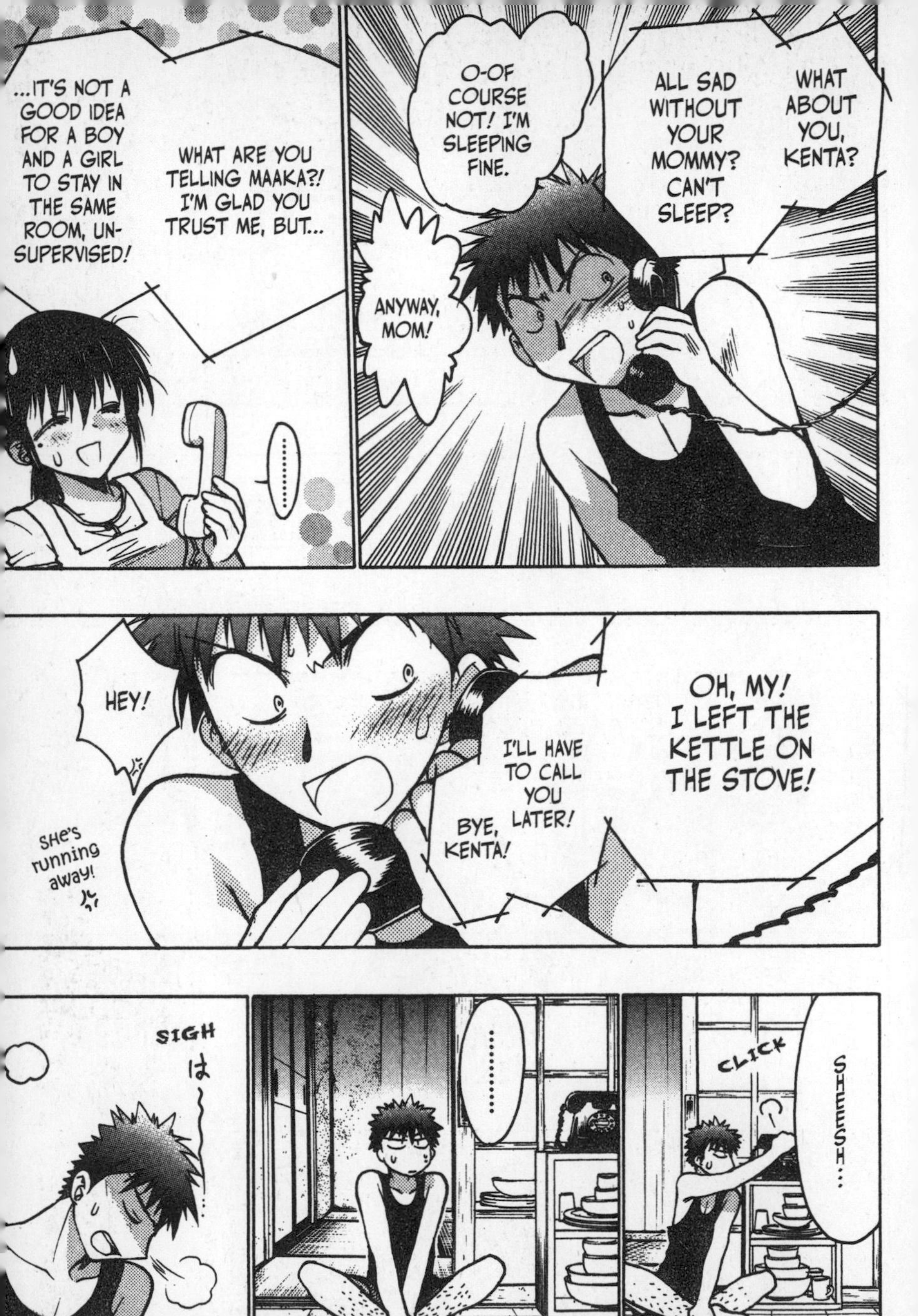
WHAT ABOUT YOU, KENTA?
ALL SAD WITHOUT YOUR MOMMY? CAN'T SLEEP?
O-OF COURSE NOT! I'M SLEEPING FINE.
ANYWAY, MOM!
WHAT ARE YOU TELLING MAAKA?! I'M GLAD YOU TRUST ME, BUT...
...IT'S NOT A GOOD IDEA FOR A BOY AND A GIRL TO STAY IN THE SAME ROOM, UN-SUPERVISED!
......
OH, MY! I LEFT THE KETTLE ON THE STOVE!
I'LL HAVE TO CALL YOU LATER!
BYE, KENTA!
HEY!
SHE'S running away!
SHEESH...
CLICK
......
SIGH
は~…

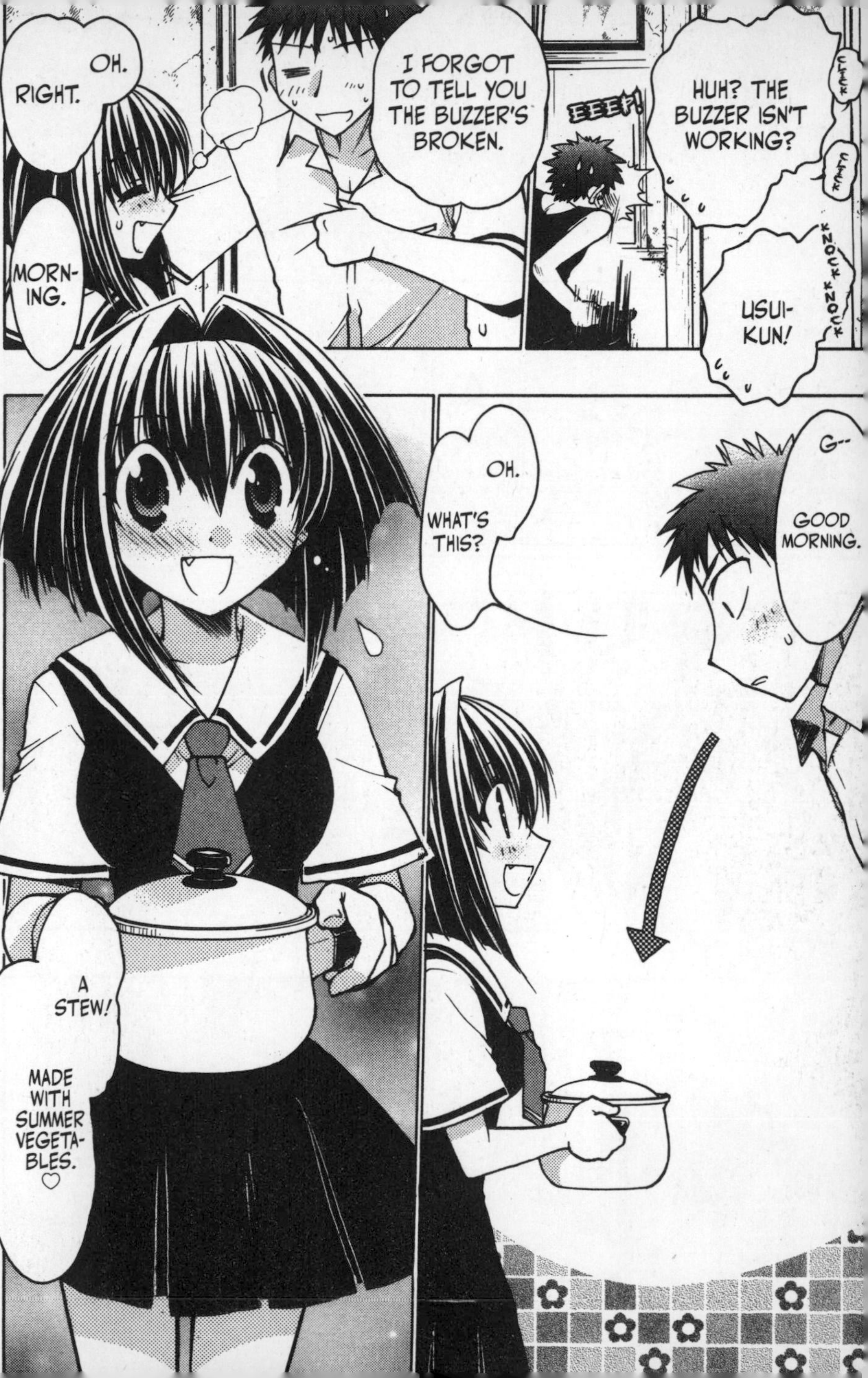
CLICK
CLICK
HUH? THE BUZZER ISN'T WORKING?
EEEP!
KNOCK KNOCK
USUI-KUN!
I FORGOT TO TELL YOU THE BUZZER'S BROKEN.
OH. RIGHT.
MORNING.
G-- GOOD MORNING.
OH. WHAT'S THIS?
A STEW!
MADE WITH SUMMER VEGETABLES. ♡

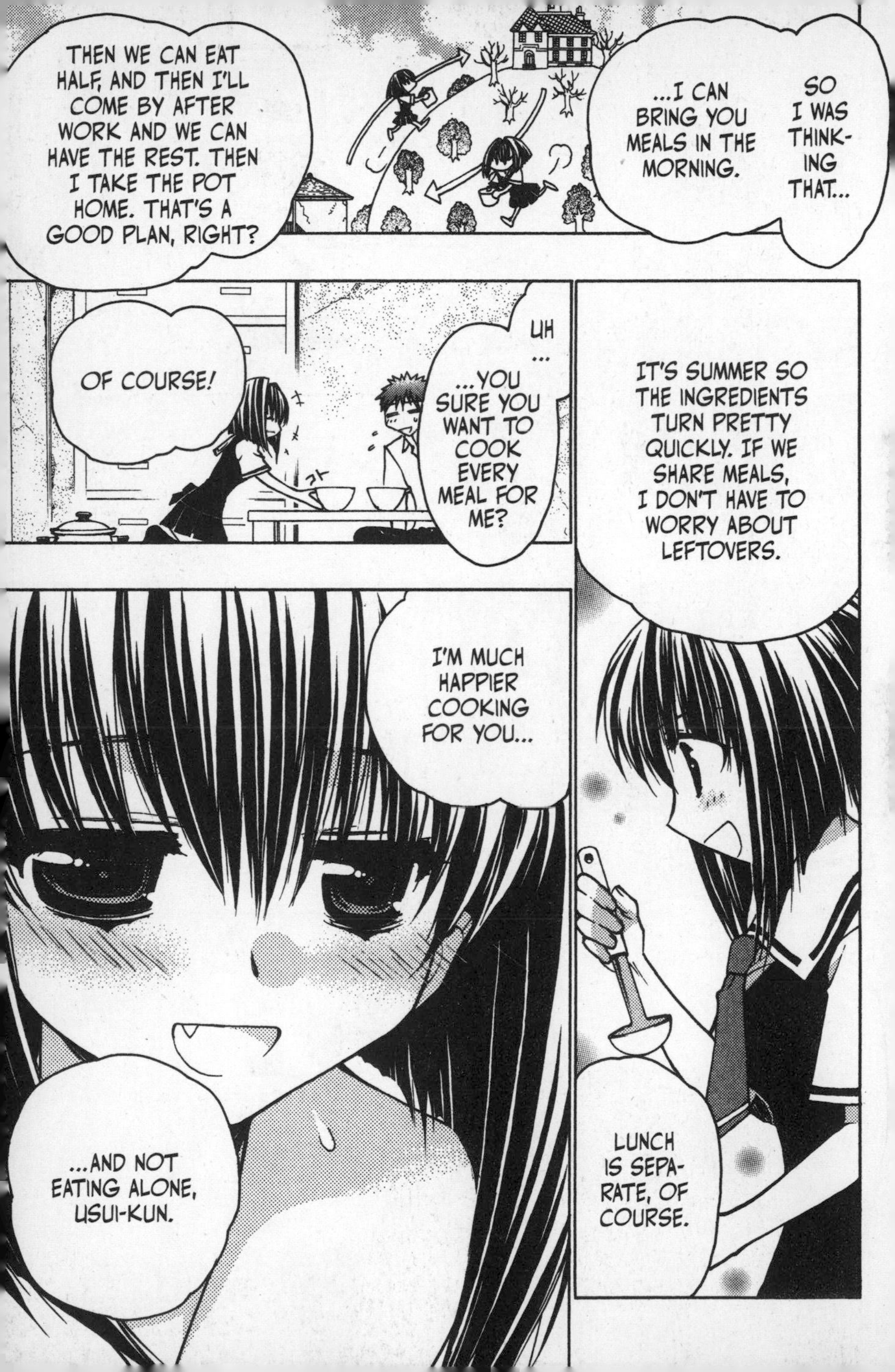
SO I WAS THINKING THAT...
...I CAN BRING YOU MEALS IN THE MORNING.
THEN WE CAN EAT HALF, AND THEN I'LL COME BY AFTER WORK AND WE CAN HAVE THE REST. THEN I TAKE THE POT HOME. THAT'S A GOOD PLAN, RIGHT?
IT'S SUMMER SO THE INGREDIENTS TURN PRETTY QUICKLY. IF WE SHARE MEALS, I DON'T HAVE TO WORRY ABOUT LEFTOVERS.
UH ...
...YOU SURE YOU WANT TO COOK EVERY MEAL FOR ME?
OF COURSE!
LUNCH IS SEPARATE, OF COURSE.
I'M MUCH HAPPIER COOKING FOR YOU...
...AND NOT EATING ALONE, USUI-KUN.

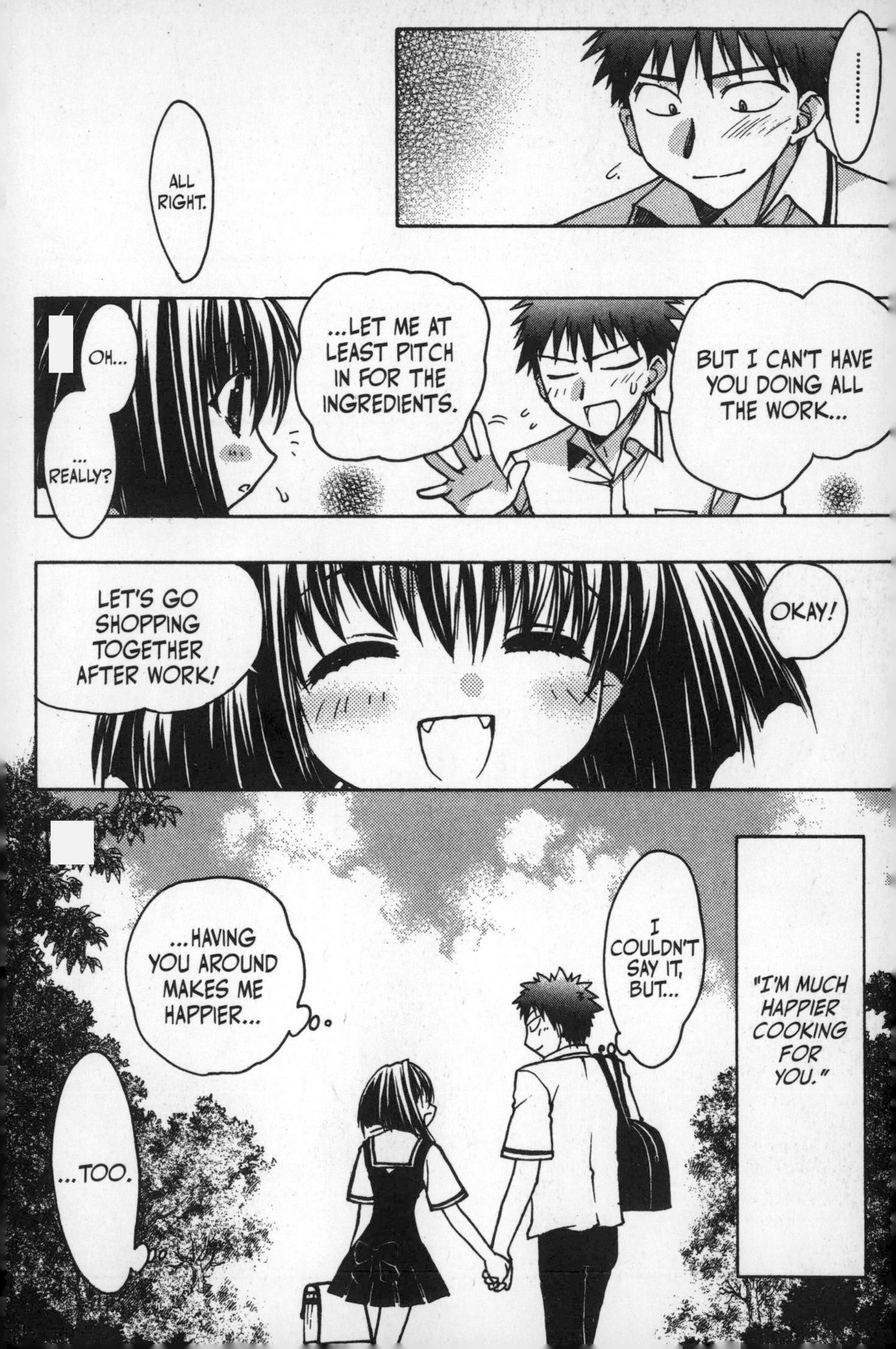
......
ALL RIGHT.
BUT I CAN'T HAVE YOU DOING ALL THE WORK...
...LET ME AT LEAST PITCH IN FOR THE INGREDIENTS.
OH...
... REALLY?
OKAY!
LET'S GO SHOPPING TOGETHER AFTER WORK!
"I'M MUCH HAPPIER COOKING FOR YOU."
I COULDN'T SAY IT, BUT...
...HAVING YOU AROUND MAKES ME HAPPIER...
...TOO.

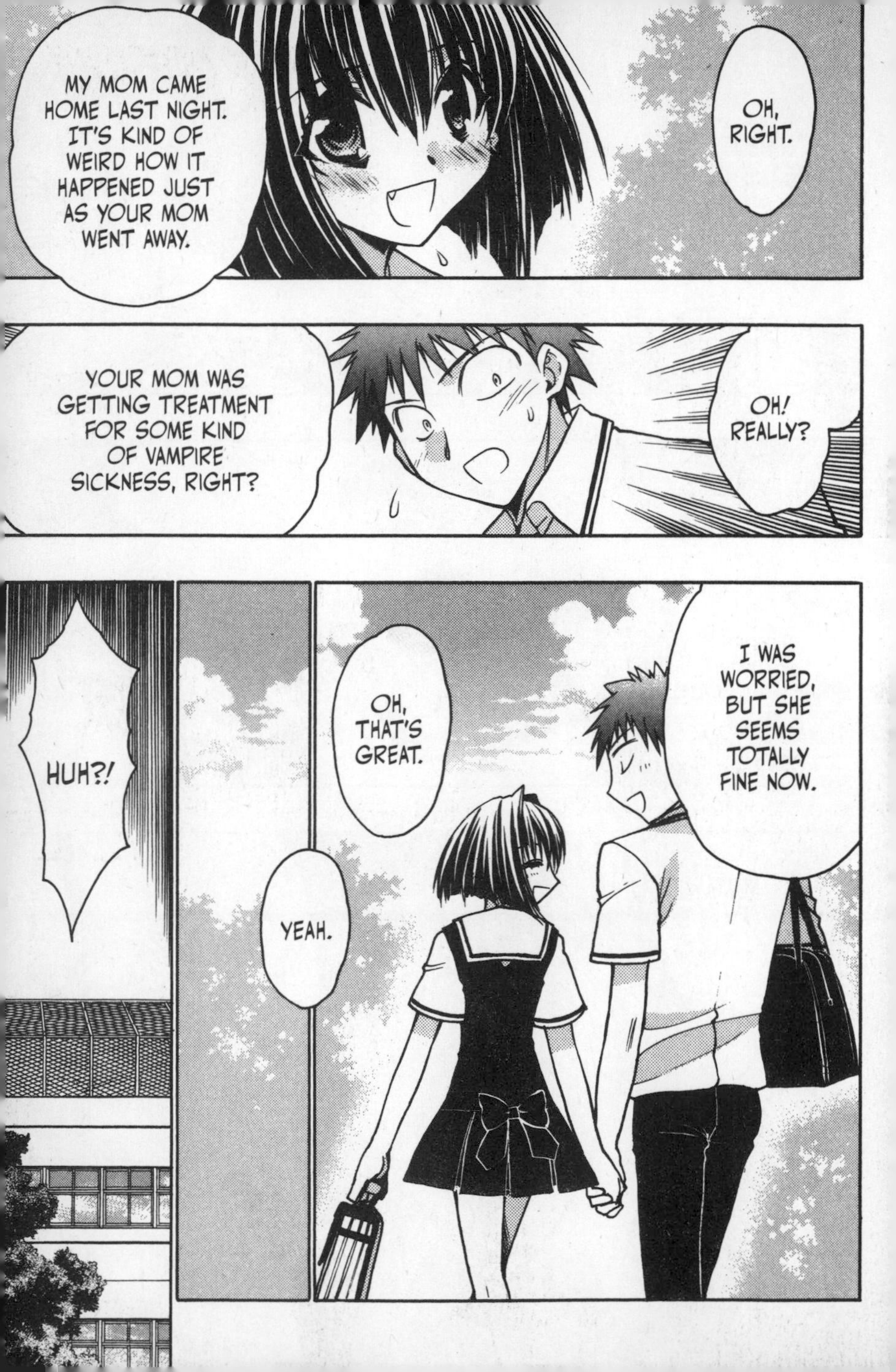

OH, RIGHT.
MY MOM CAME HOME LAST NIGHT. IT'S KIND OF WEIRD HOW IT HAPPENED JUST AS YOUR MOM WENT AWAY.
OH! REALLY?
YOUR MOM WAS GETTING TREATMENT FOR SOME KIND OF VAMPIRE SICKNESS, RIGHT?
I WAS WORRIED, BUT SHE SEEMS TOTALLY FINE NOW.
OH, THAT'S GREAT.
YEAH.
HUH?!

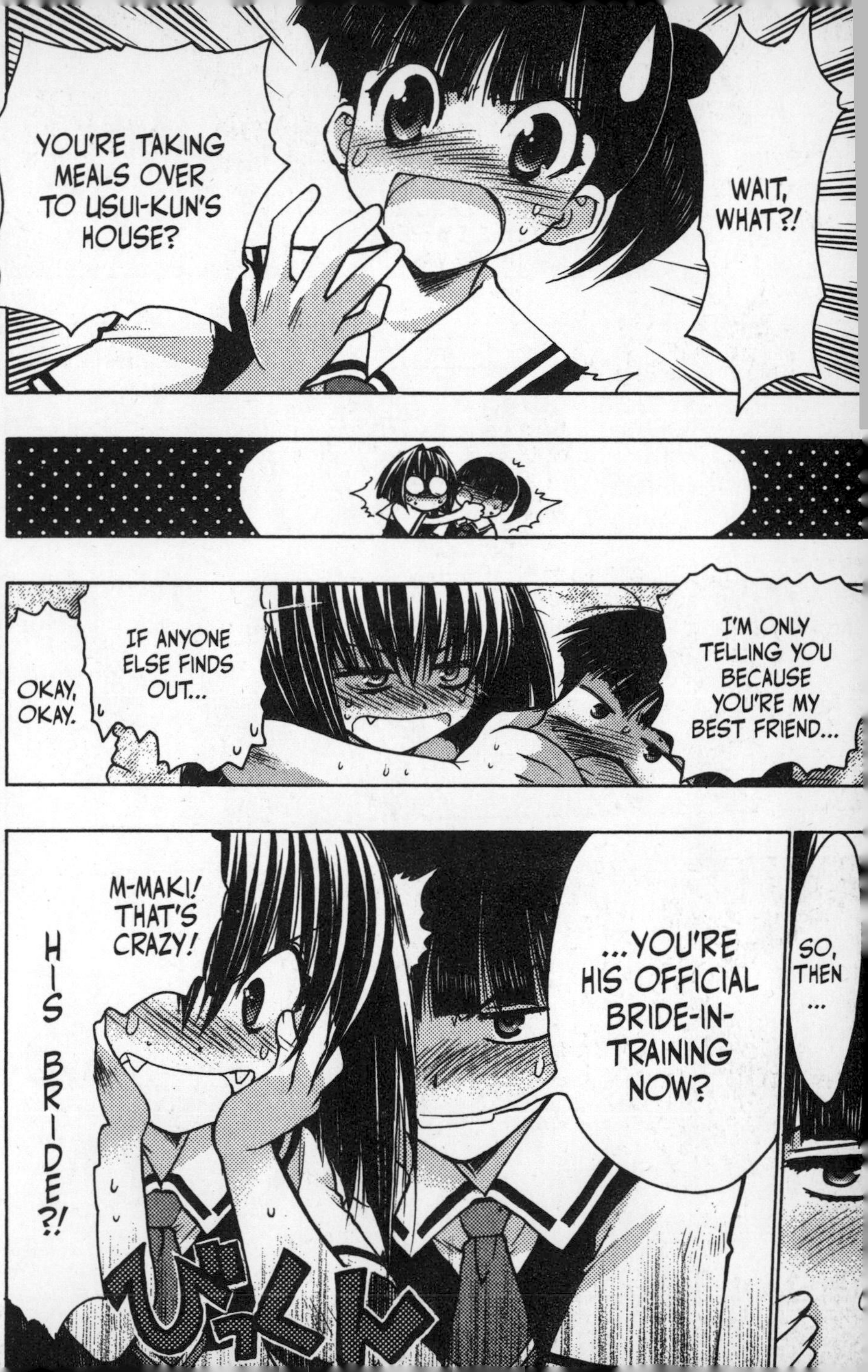
WAIT, WHAT?!
YOU'RE TAKING MEALS OVER TO USUI-KUN'S HOUSE?
I'M ONLY TELLING YOU BECAUSE YOU'RE MY BEST FRIEND...
IF ANYONE ELSE FINDS OUT...
OKAY, OKAY.
SO, THEN ...
...YOU'RE HIS OFFICIAL BRIDE-IN-TRAINING NOW?
M-MAKI! THAT'S CRAZY!
HIS BRIDE?!

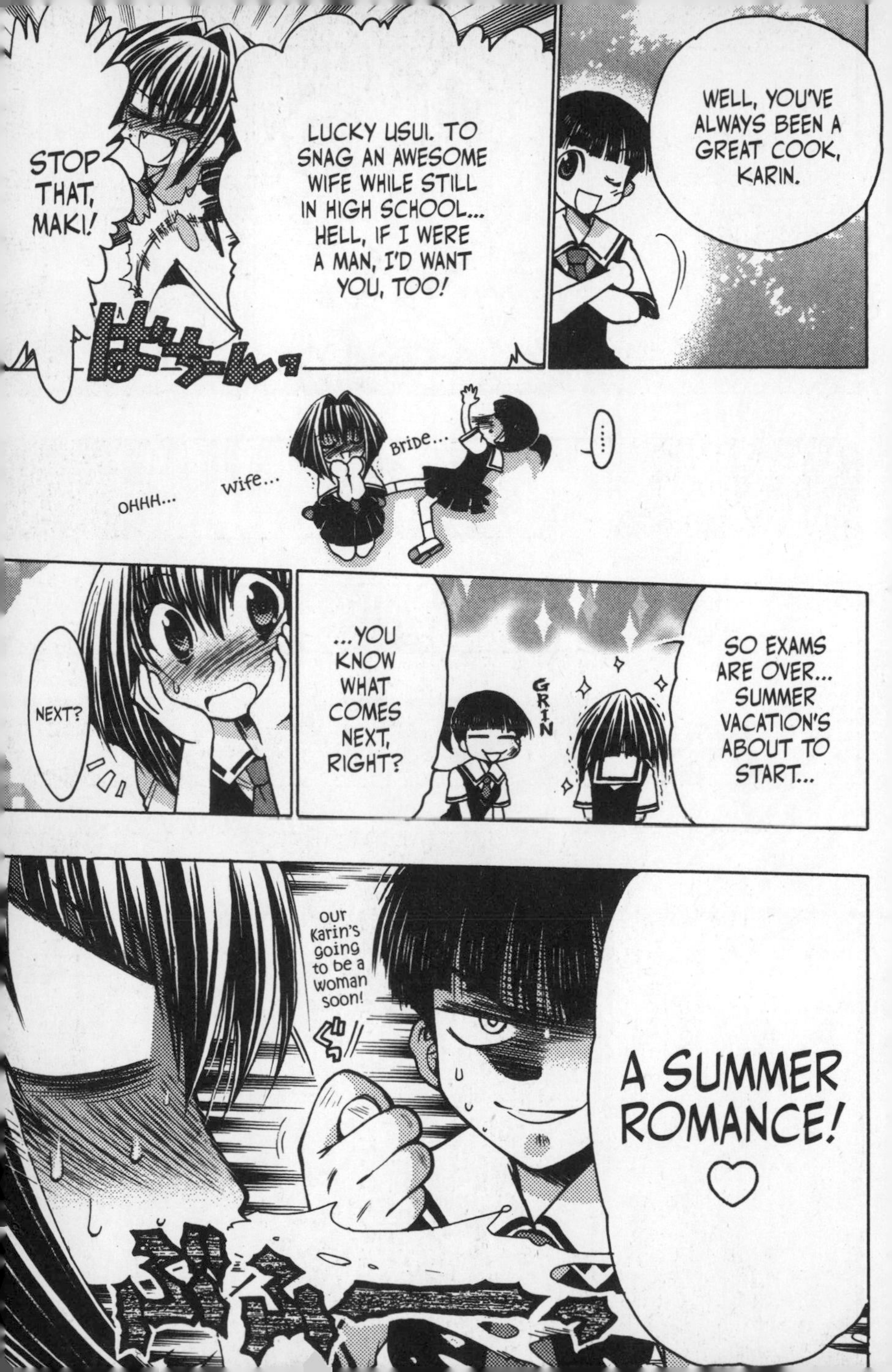
WELL, YOU'VE ALWAYS BEEN A GREAT COOK, KARIN.
LUCKY USUI. TO SNAG AN AWESOME WIFE WHILE STILL IN HIGH SCHOOL... HELL, IF I WERE A MAN, I'D WANT YOU, TOO!
STOP THAT, MAKI!
...
Bride...
wife...
OHHH...
SO EXAMS ARE OVER... SUMMER VACATION'S ABOUT TO START...
GRIN
...YOU KNOW WHAT COMES NEXT, RIGHT?
NEXT?
A SUMMER ROMANCE!
Our Karin's going to be a woman soon!

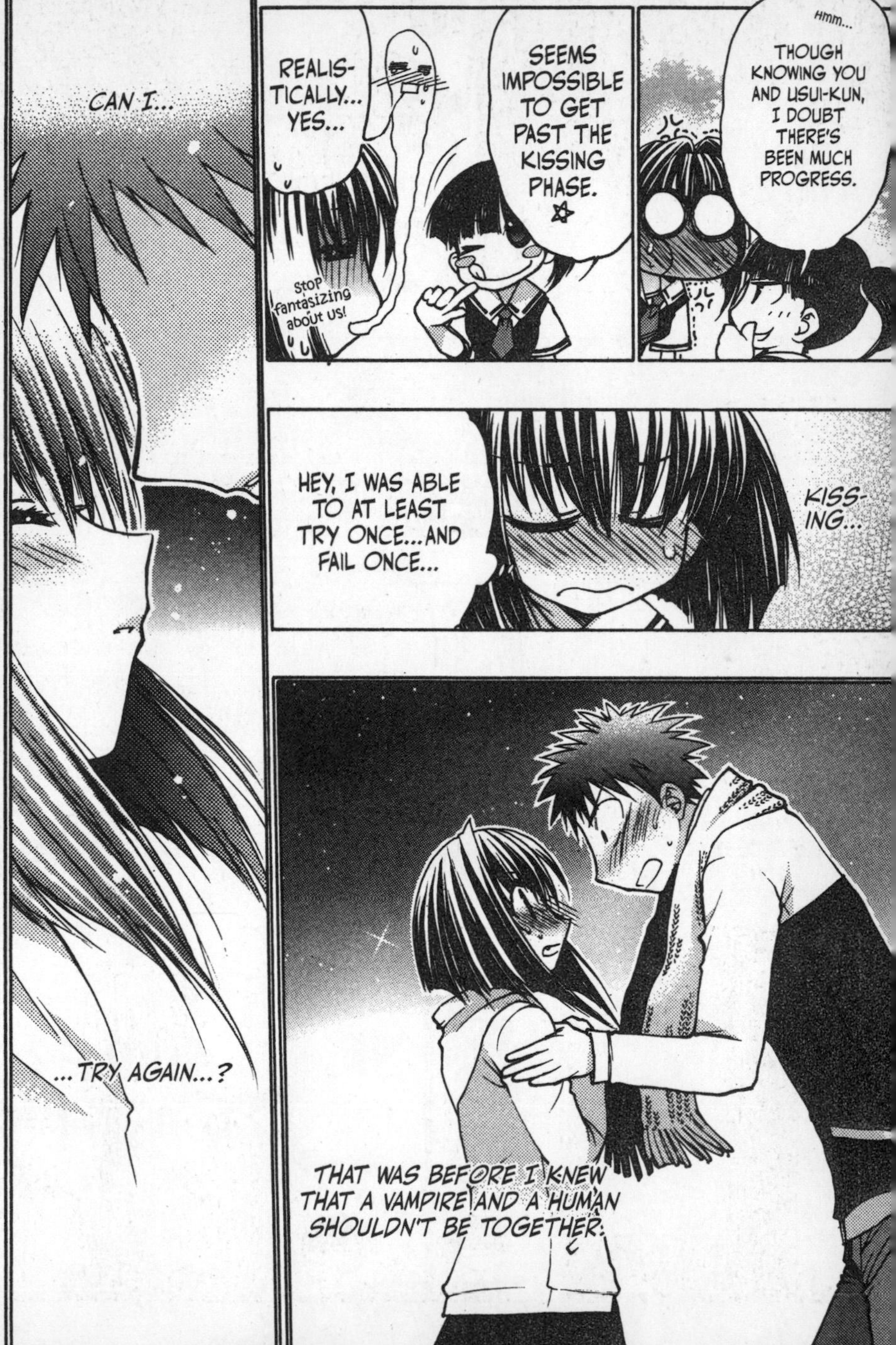
Hmm...
THOUGH KNOWING YOU AND USUI-KUN, I DOUBT THERE'S BEEN MUCH PROGRESS.
SEEMS IMPOSSIBLE TO GET PAST THE KISSING PHASE.
REALIS-TICALLY... YES...
Stop fantasizing about us!
KISS-ING...
HEY, I WAS ABLE TO AT LEAST TRY ONCE...AND FAIL ONCE...
THAT WAS BEFORE I KNEW THAT A VAMPIRE AND A HUMAN SHOULDN'T BE TOGETHER.
CAN I...
...TRY AGAIN...?

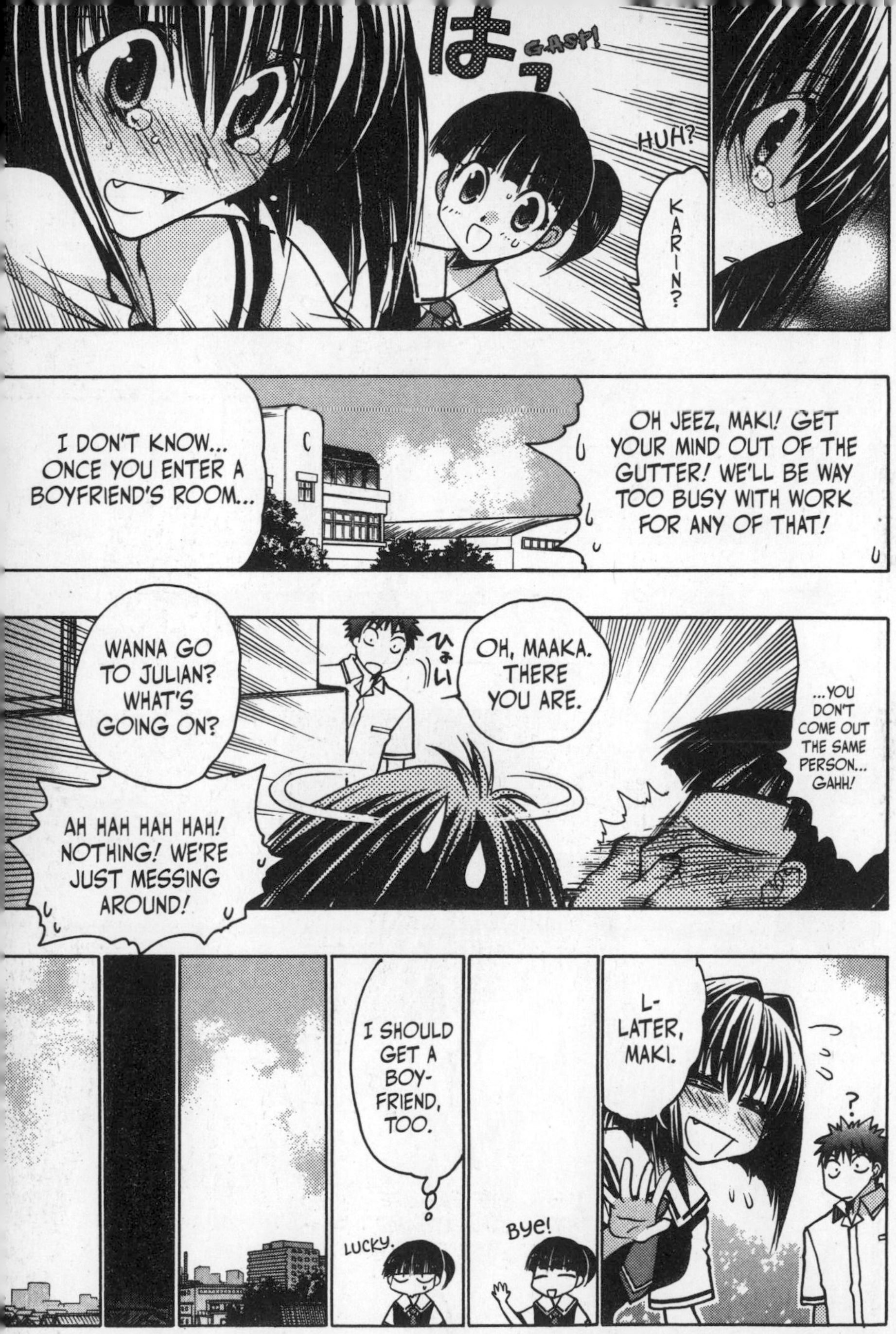
HUH?
KARIN?
はっ GASP!
OH JEEZ, MAKI! GET YOUR MIND OUT OF THE GUTTER! WE'LL BE WAY TOO BUSY WITH WORK FOR ANY OF THAT!
I DON'T KNOW... ONCE YOU ENTER A BOYFRIEND'S ROOM...
...YOU DON'T COME OUT THE SAME PERSON... GAHH!
OH, MAAKA. THERE YOU ARE.
ひょい
WANNA GO TO JULIAN? WHAT'S GOING ON?
AH HAH HAH HAH! NOTHING! WE'RE JUST MESSING AROUND!
?
L-LATER, MAKI.
BYE!
I SHOULD GET A BOY-FRIEND, TOO.
LUCKY.

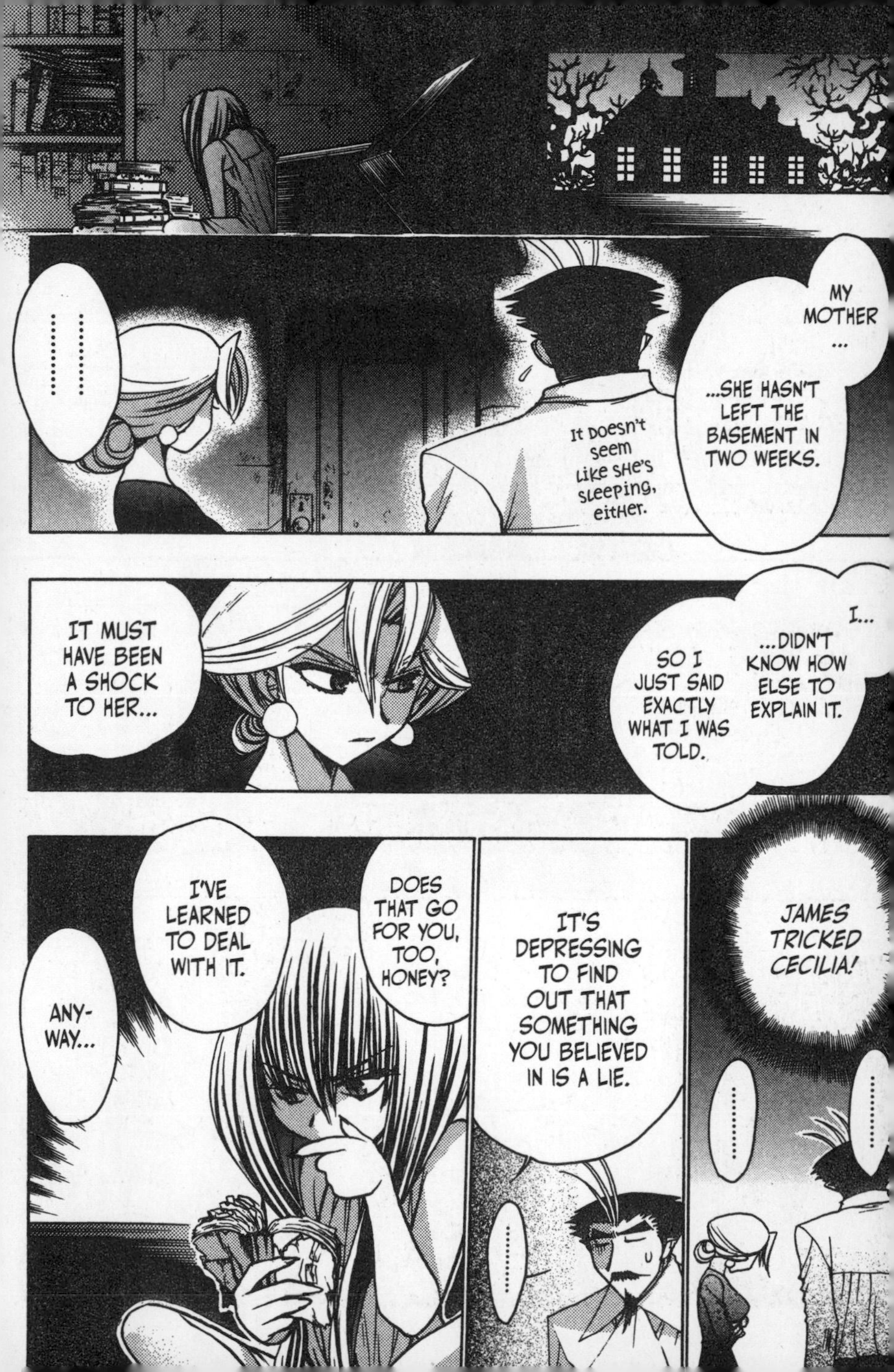
MY MOTHER ...
...SHE HASN'T LEFT THE BASEMENT IN TWO WEEKS.
It Doesn't seem like SHe's sleeping, eitHer.
....
I...
...DIDN'T KNOW HOW ELSE TO EXPLAIN IT.
SO I JUST SAID EXACTLY WHAT I WAS TOLD.
IT MUST HAVE BEEN A SHOCK TO HER...
JAMES TRICKED CECILIA!
....
....
IT'S DEPRESSING TO FIND OUT THAT SOMETHING YOU BELIEVED IN IS A LIE.
......
DOES THAT GO FOR YOU, TOO, HONEY?
I'VE LEARNED TO DEAL WITH IT.
ANY-WAY...

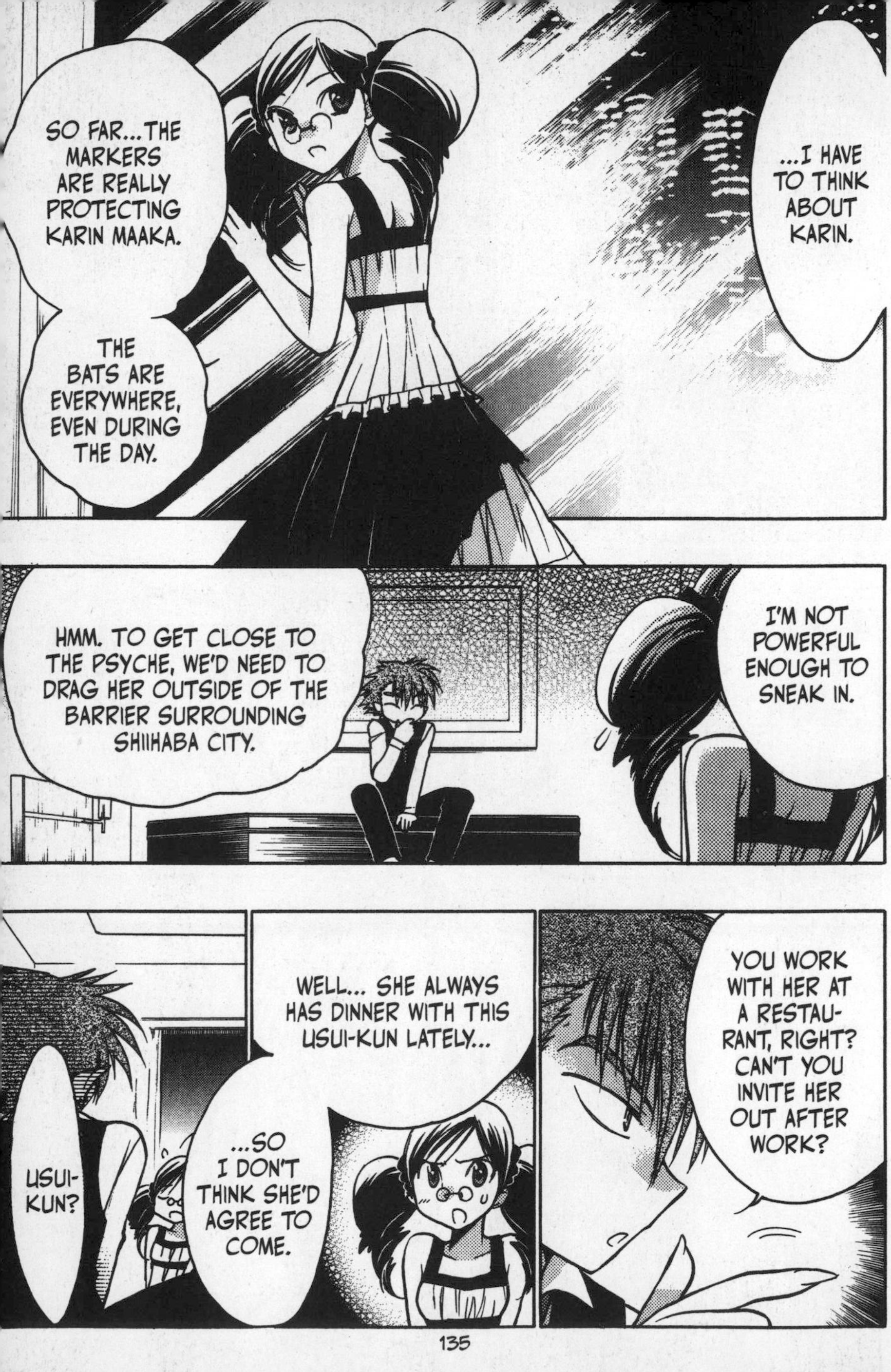
...I HAVE TO THINK ABOUT KARIN.
SO FAR...THE MARKERS ARE REALLY PROTECTING KARIN MAAKA.
THE BATS ARE EVERYWHERE, EVEN DURING THE DAY.
I'M NOT POWERFUL ENOUGH TO SNEAK IN.
HMM. TO GET CLOSE TO THE PSYCHE, WE'D NEED TO DRAG HER OUTSIDE OF THE BARRIER SURROUNDING SHIIHABA CITY.
YOU WORK WITH HER AT A RESTAU-RANT, RIGHT? CAN'T YOU INVITE HER OUT AFTER WORK?
WELL... SHE ALWAYS HAS DINNER WITH THIS USUI-KUN LATELY...
...SO I DON'T THINK SHE'D AGREE TO COME.
USUI-KUN?

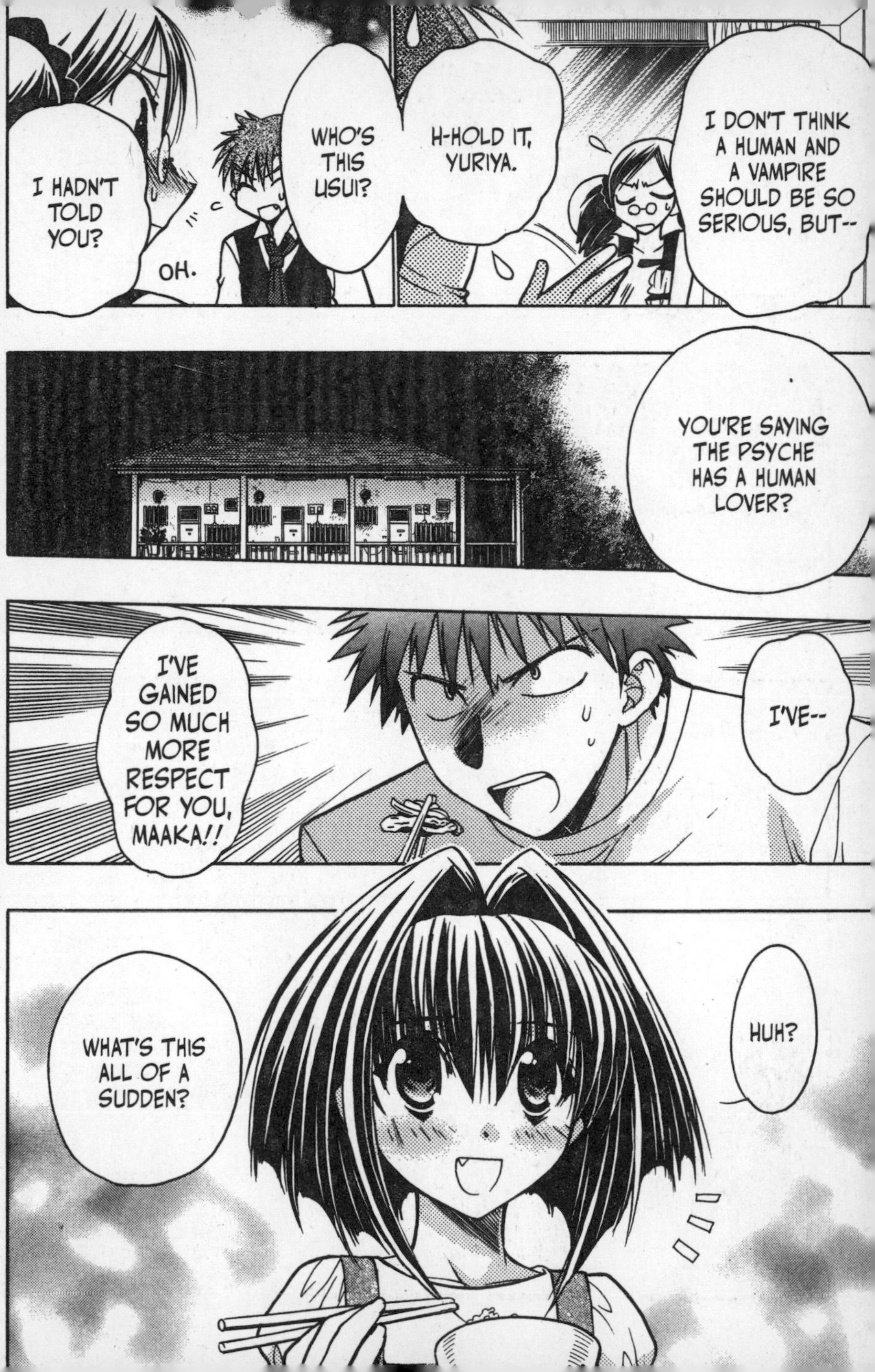
I DON'T THINK A HUMAN AND A VAMPIRE SHOULD BE SO SERIOUS, BUT--
H-HOLD IT, YURIYA.
WHO'S THIS USUI?
OH.
I HADN'T TOLD YOU?
YOU'RE SAYING THE PSYCHE HAS A HUMAN LOVER?
I'VE--
I'VE GAINED SO MUCH MORE RESPECT FOR YOU, MAAKA!!
HUH?
WHAT'S THIS ALL OF A SUDDEN?

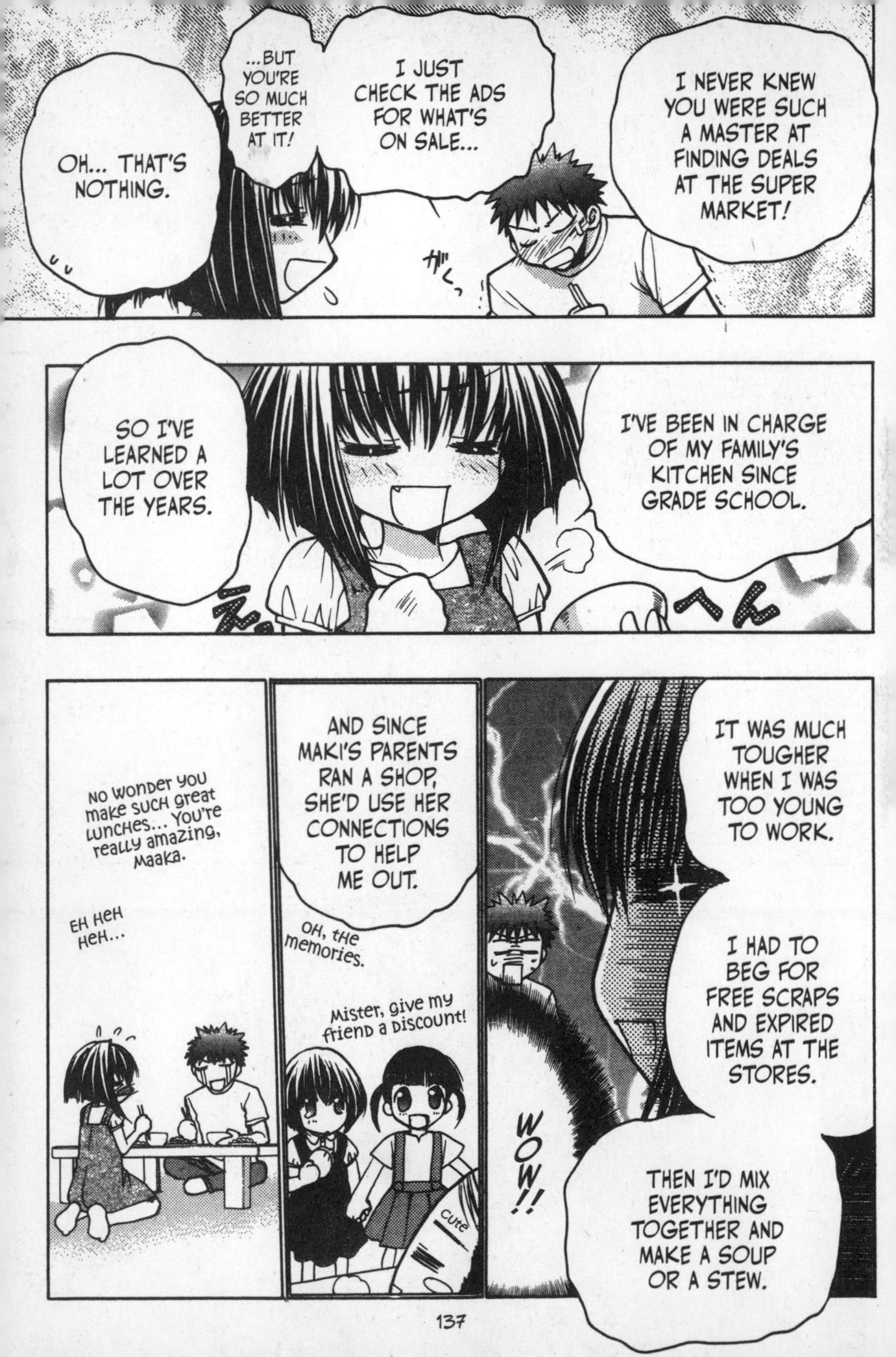
I NEVER KNEW YOU WERE SUCH A MASTER AT FINDING DEALS AT THE SUPER MARKET!
I JUST CHECK THE ADS FOR WHAT'S ON SALE...
...BUT YOU'RE SO MUCH BETTER AT IT!
OH... THAT'S NOTHING.
I'VE BEEN IN CHARGE OF MY FAMILY'S KITCHEN SINCE GRADE SCHOOL.
へん
SO I'VE LEARNED A LOT OVER THE YEARS.
IT WAS MUCH TOUGHER WHEN I WAS TOO YOUNG TO WORK.
I HAD TO BEG FOR FREE SCRAPS AND EXPIRED ITEMS AT THE STORES.
THEN I'D MIX EVERYTHING TOGETHER AND MAKE A SOUP OR A STEW.
WOW!!
AND SINCE MAKI'S PARENTS RAN A SHOP, SHE'D USE HER CONNECTIONS TO HELP ME OUT.
OH, THE memories.
Mister, give my friend a Discount!
Cute
No wonder you make such great lunches... You're really amazing, Maaka.
EH HEH HEH...

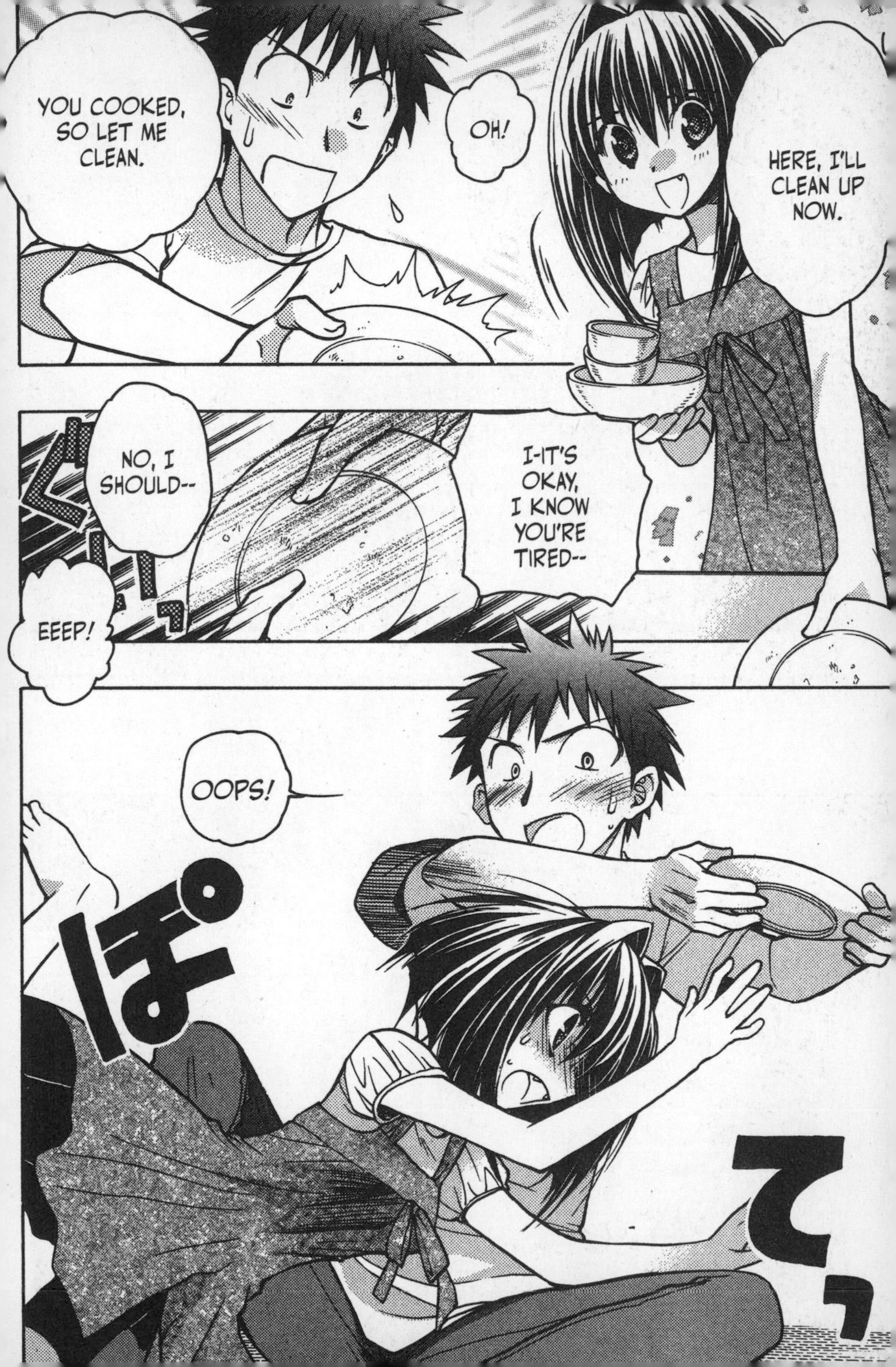
HERE, I'LL CLEAN UP NOW.
OH!
YOU COOKED, SO LET ME CLEAN.
I-IT'S OKAY, I KNOW YOU'RE TIRED--
NO, I SHOULD--
EEEP!
OOPS!
ぽ
て

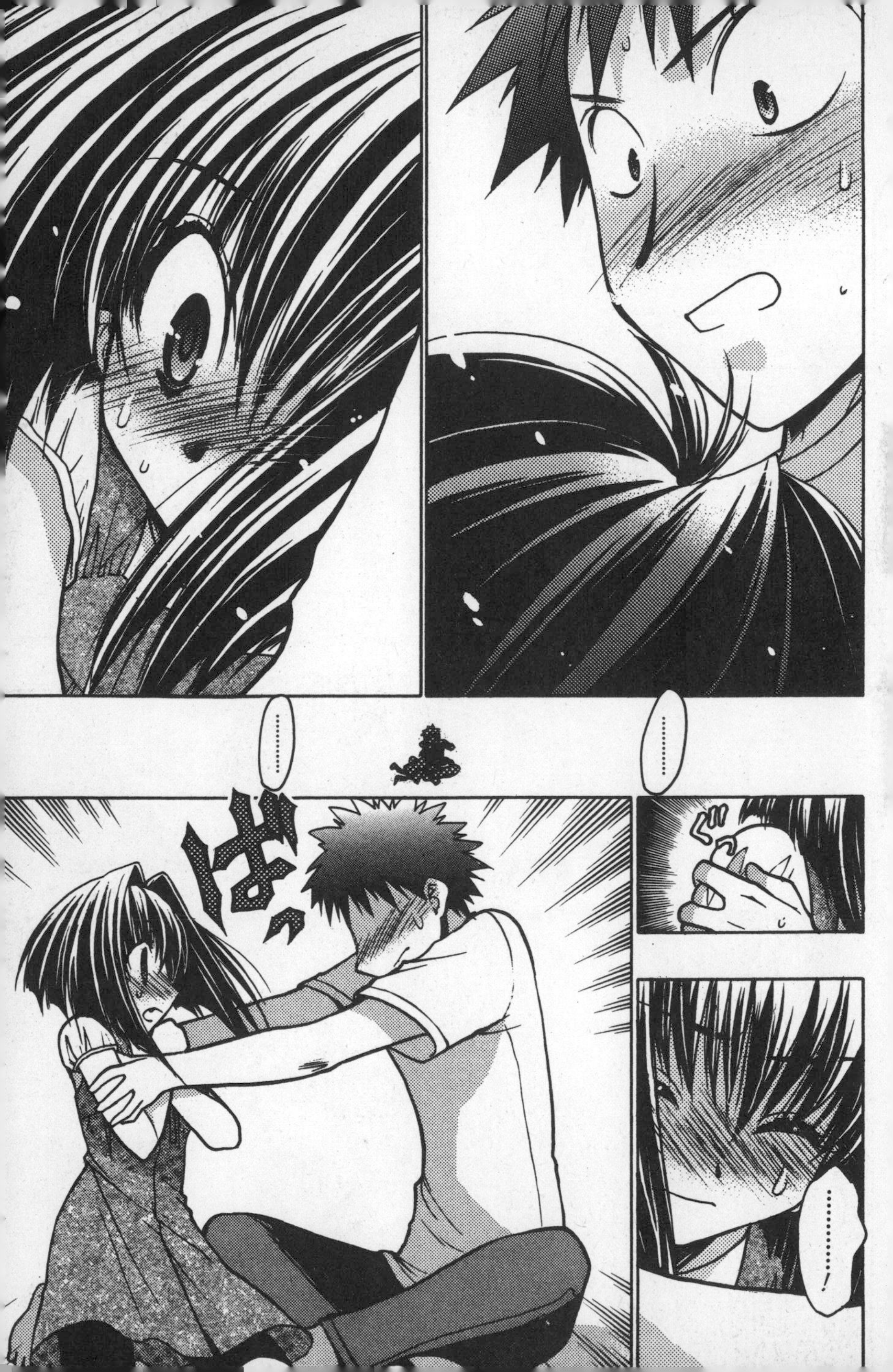
……
……
ぐ
……!
ばっ

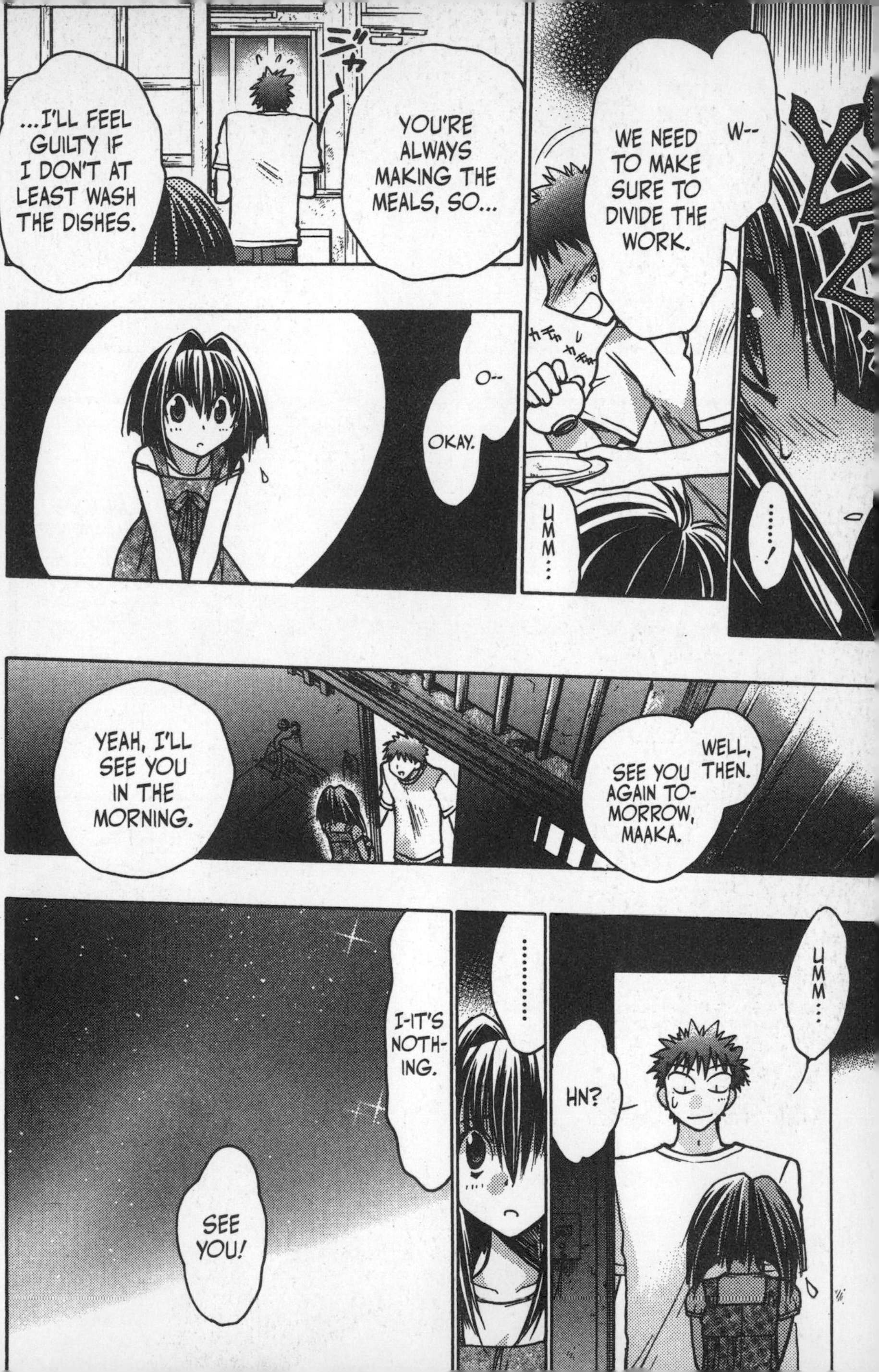
W--
WE NEED TO MAKE SURE TO DIVIDE THE WORK.
YOU'RE ALWAYS MAKING THE MEALS, SO...
...I'LL FEEL GUILTY IF I DON'T AT LEAST WASH THE DISHES.
......!
UMM...
O--
OKAY.
WELL, THEN.
SEE YOU AGAIN TO-MORROW, MAAKA.
YEAH, I'LL SEE YOU IN THE MORNING.
UMM...
HN?
....
I-IT'S NOTHING.
SEE YOU!

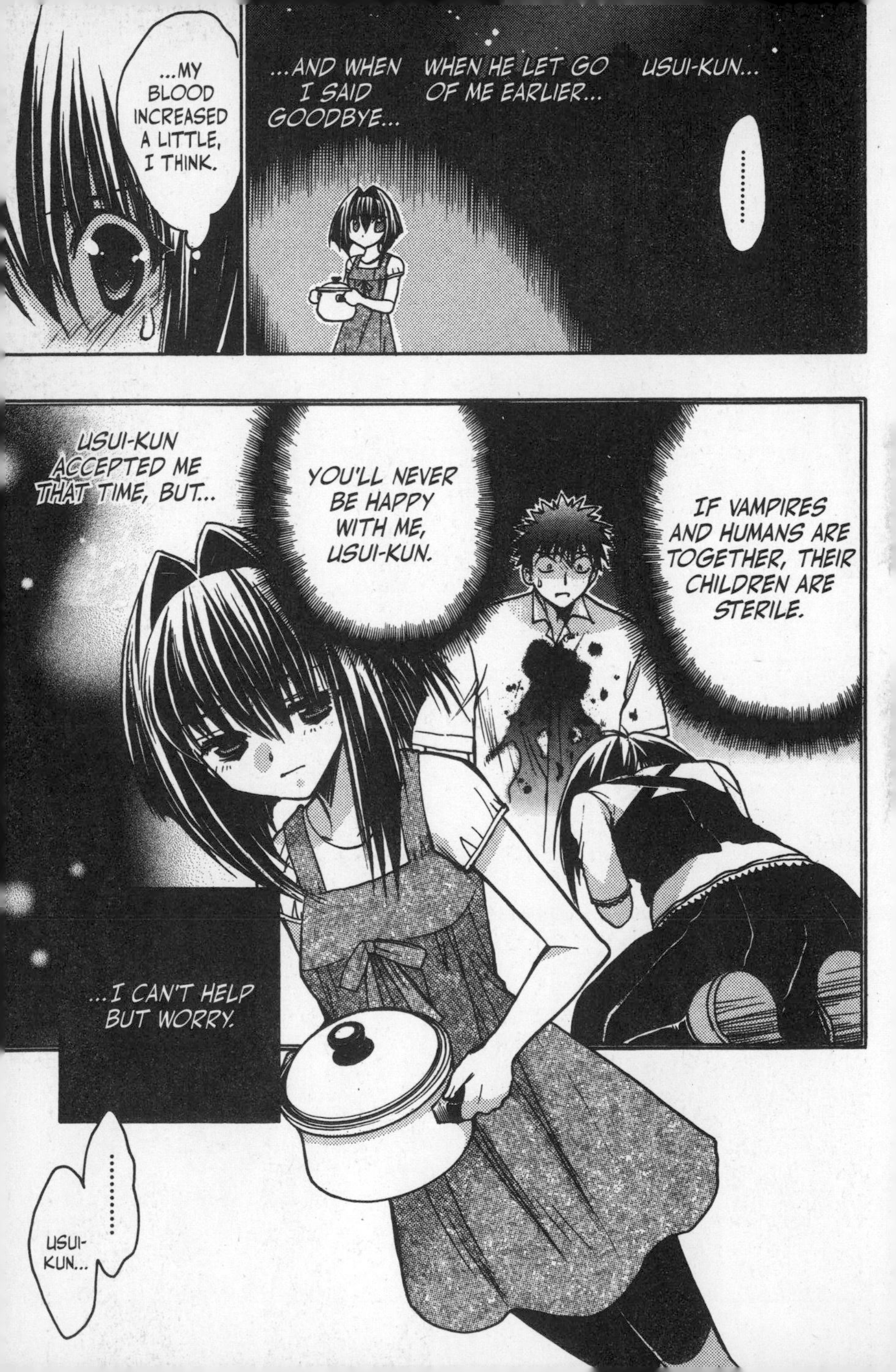
USUI-KUN...
......
WHEN HE LET GO OF ME EARLIER...
...AND WHEN I SAID GOODBYE...
...MY BLOOD INCREASED A LITTLE, I THINK.
IF VAMPIRES AND HUMANS ARE TOGETHER, THEIR CHILDREN ARE STERILE.
YOU'LL NEVER BE HAPPY WITH ME, USUI-KUN.
USUI-KUN ACCEPTED ME THAT TIME, BUT...
...I CAN'T HELP BUT WORRY.
......
USUI-KUN...

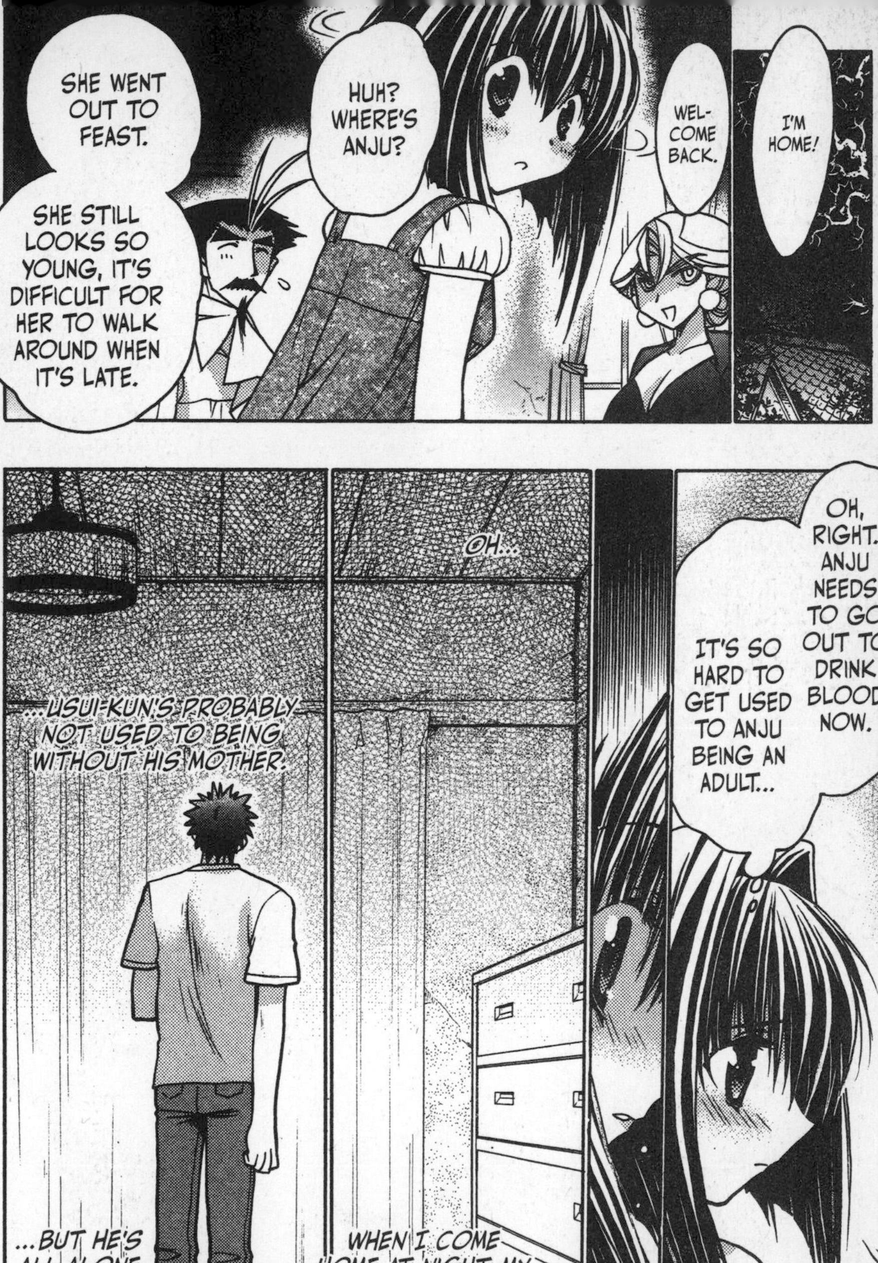
I'M HOME!
WEL-COME BACK.
HUH? WHERE'S ANJU?
SHE WENT OUT TO FEAST.
SHE STILL LOOKS SO YOUNG, IT'S DIFFICULT FOR HER TO WALK AROUND WHEN IT'S LATE.
OH, RIGHT. ANJU NEEDS TO GO OUT TO DRINK BLOOD NOW.
IT'S SO HARD TO GET USED TO ANJU BEING AN ADULT...
OH...
WHEN I COME HOME AT NIGHT, MY FAMILY'S AWAKE...
...USUI-KUN'S PROBABLY NOT USED TO BEING WITHOUT HIS MOTHER.
...BUT HE'S ALL ALONE NOW...

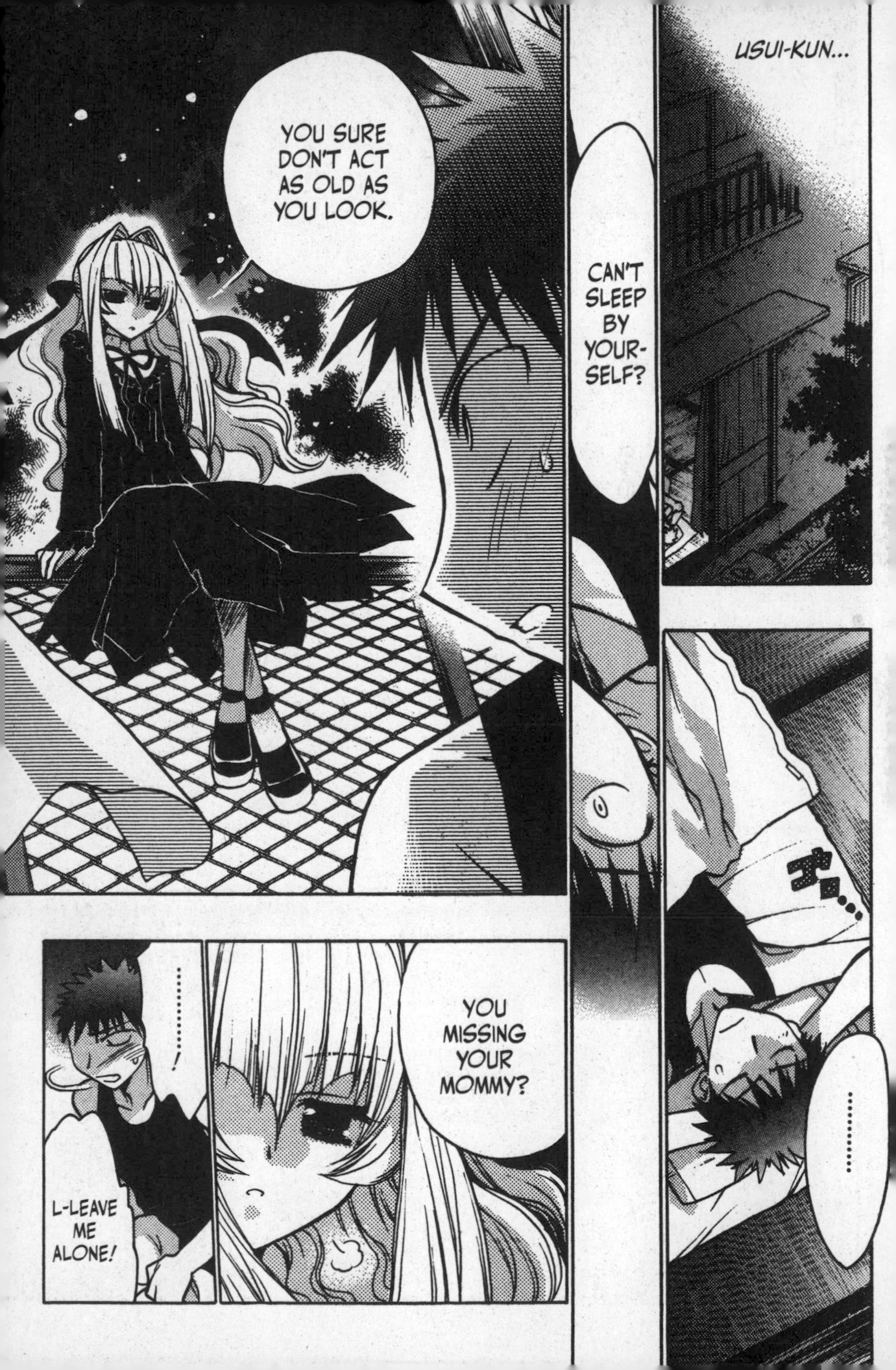
USUI-KUN...
CAN'T SLEEP BY YOUR-SELF?
YOU SURE DON'T ACT AS OLD AS YOU LOOK.
....
YOU MISSING YOUR MOMMY?
......!
L-LEAVE ME ALONE!

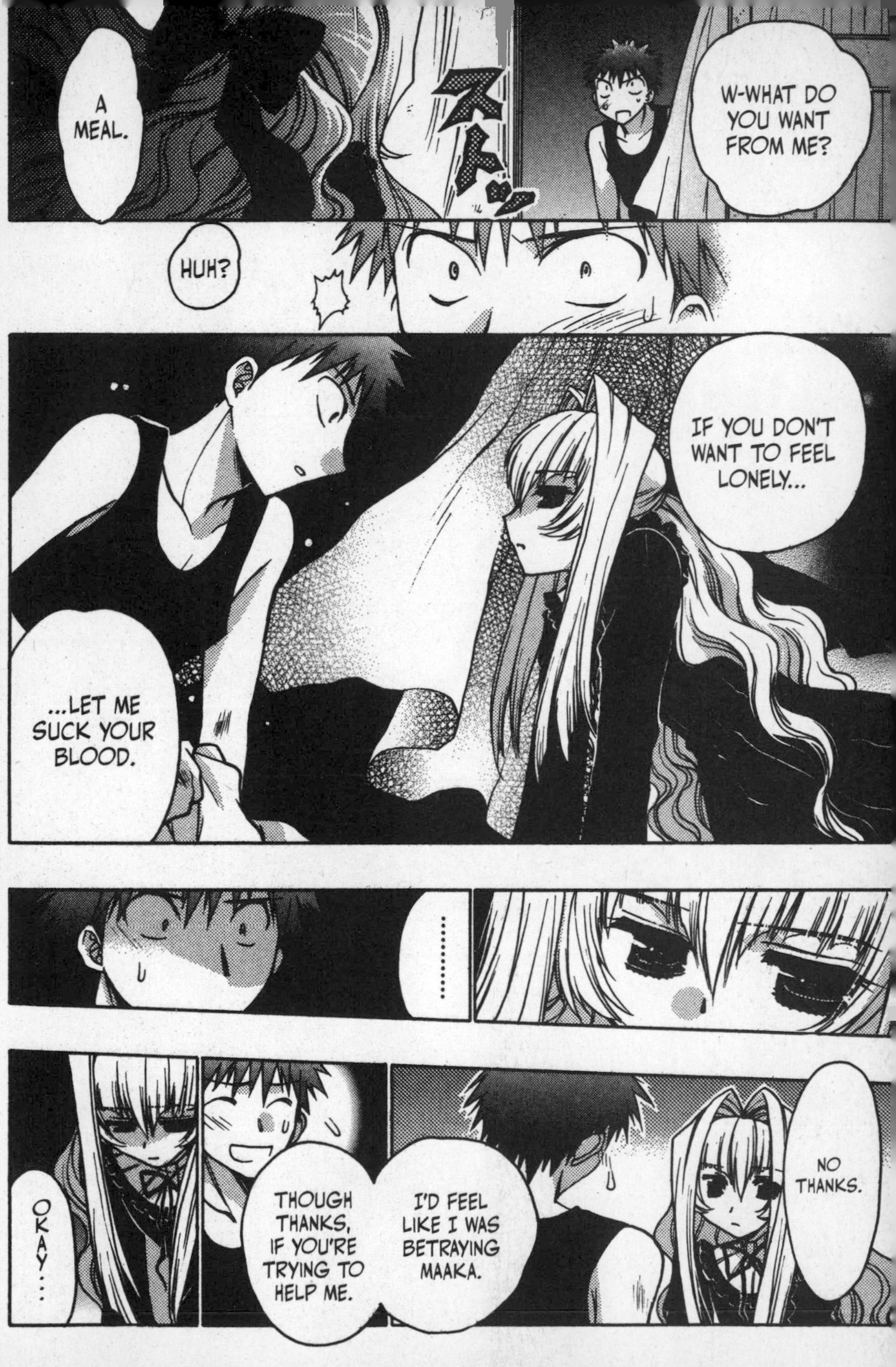
W-WHAT DO YOU WANT FROM ME?
A MEAL.
HUH?
IF YOU DON'T WANT TO FEEL LONELY...
...LET ME SUCK YOUR BLOOD.
......
NO THANKS.
I'D FEEL LIKE I WAS BETRAYING MAAKA.
THOUGH THANKS, IF YOU'RE TRYING TO HELP ME.
OKAY...

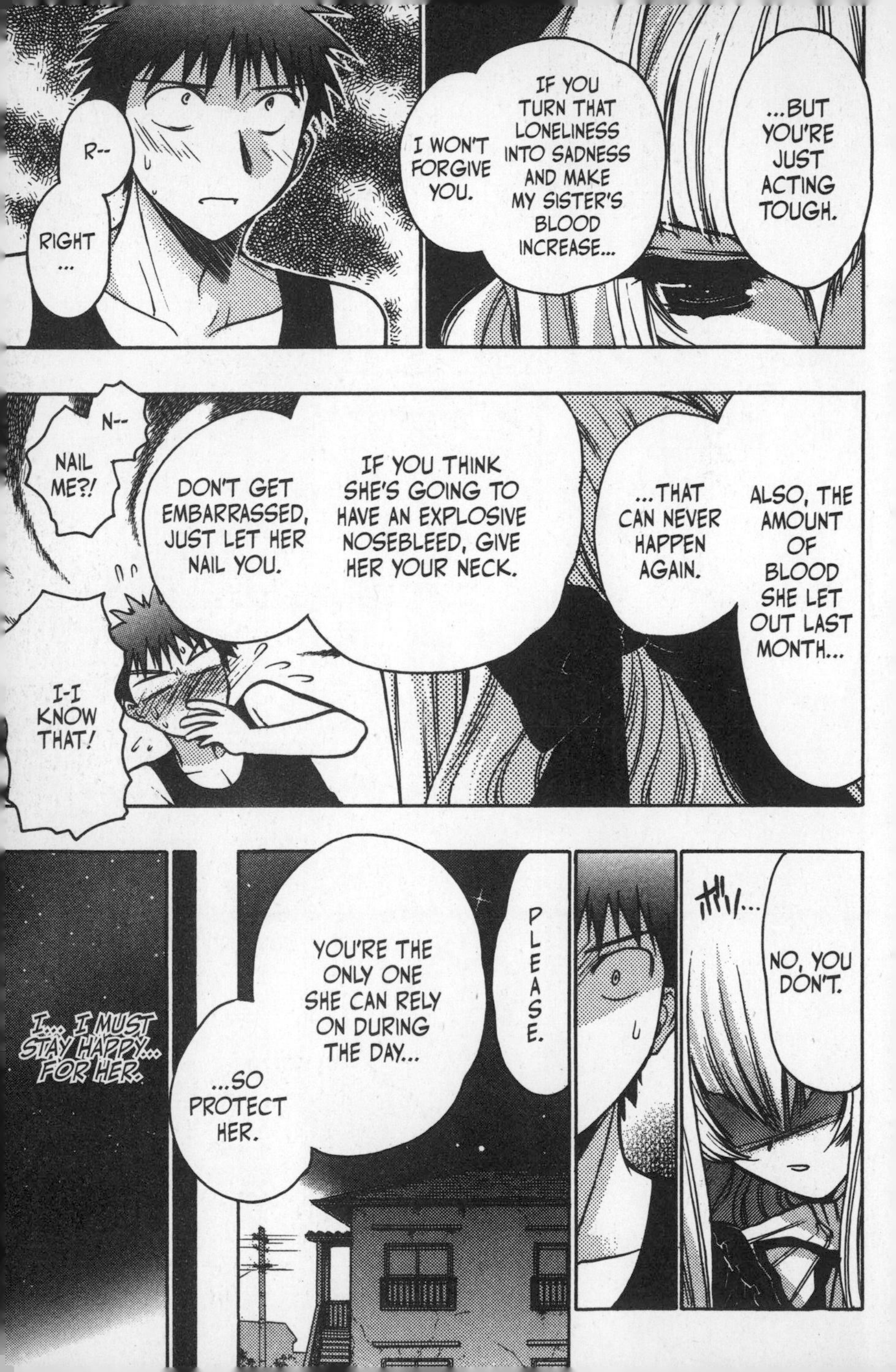
...BUT YOU'RE JUST ACTING TOUGH.
IF YOU TURN THAT LONELINESS INTO SADNESS AND MAKE MY SISTER'S BLOOD INCREASE...
I WON'T FORGIVE YOU.
R--
RIGHT ...
ALSO, THE AMOUNT OF BLOOD SHE LET OUT LAST MONTH...
...THAT CAN NEVER HAPPEN AGAIN.
IF YOU THINK SHE'S GOING TO HAVE AN EXPLOSIVE NOSEBLEED, GIVE HER YOUR NECK.
DON'T GET EMBARRASSED, JUST LET HER NAIL YOU.
N--
NAIL ME?!
I-I KNOW THAT!
NO, YOU DON'T.
PLEASE.
YOU'RE THE ONLY ONE SHE CAN RELY ON DURING THE DAY...
...SO PROTECT HER.
I... I MUST STAY HAPPY... FOR HER.

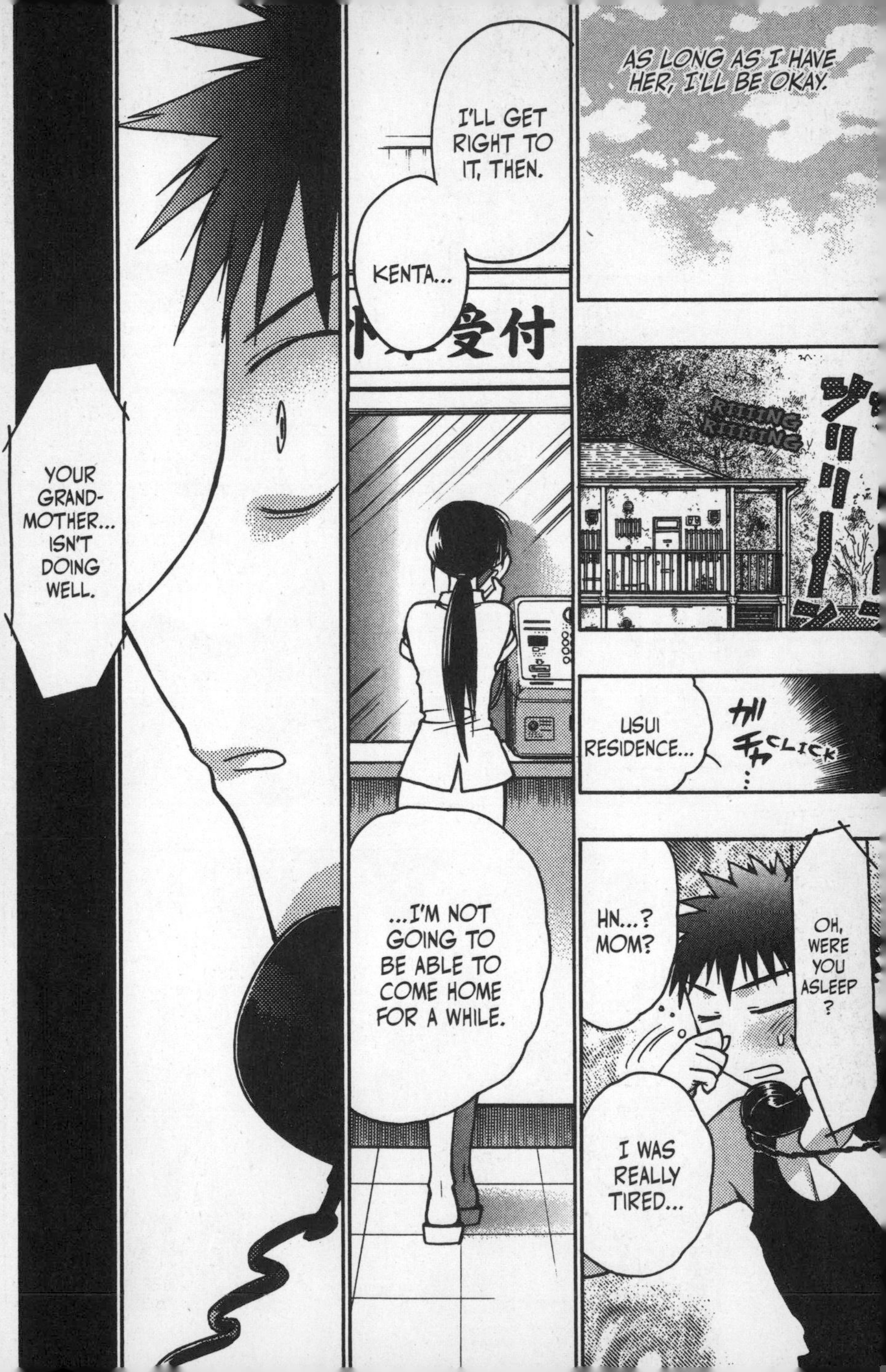
AS LONG AS I HAVE HER, I'LL BE OKAY.
RIIIING RIIIING
USUI RESIDENCE...
CLICK
OH, WERE YOU ASLEEP?
HN...? MOM?
I WAS REALLY TIRED...
I'LL GET RIGHT TO IT, THEN.
KENTA...
...I'M NOT GOING TO BE ABLE TO COME HOME FOR A WHILE.
YOUR GRANDMOTHER... ISN'T DOING WELL.

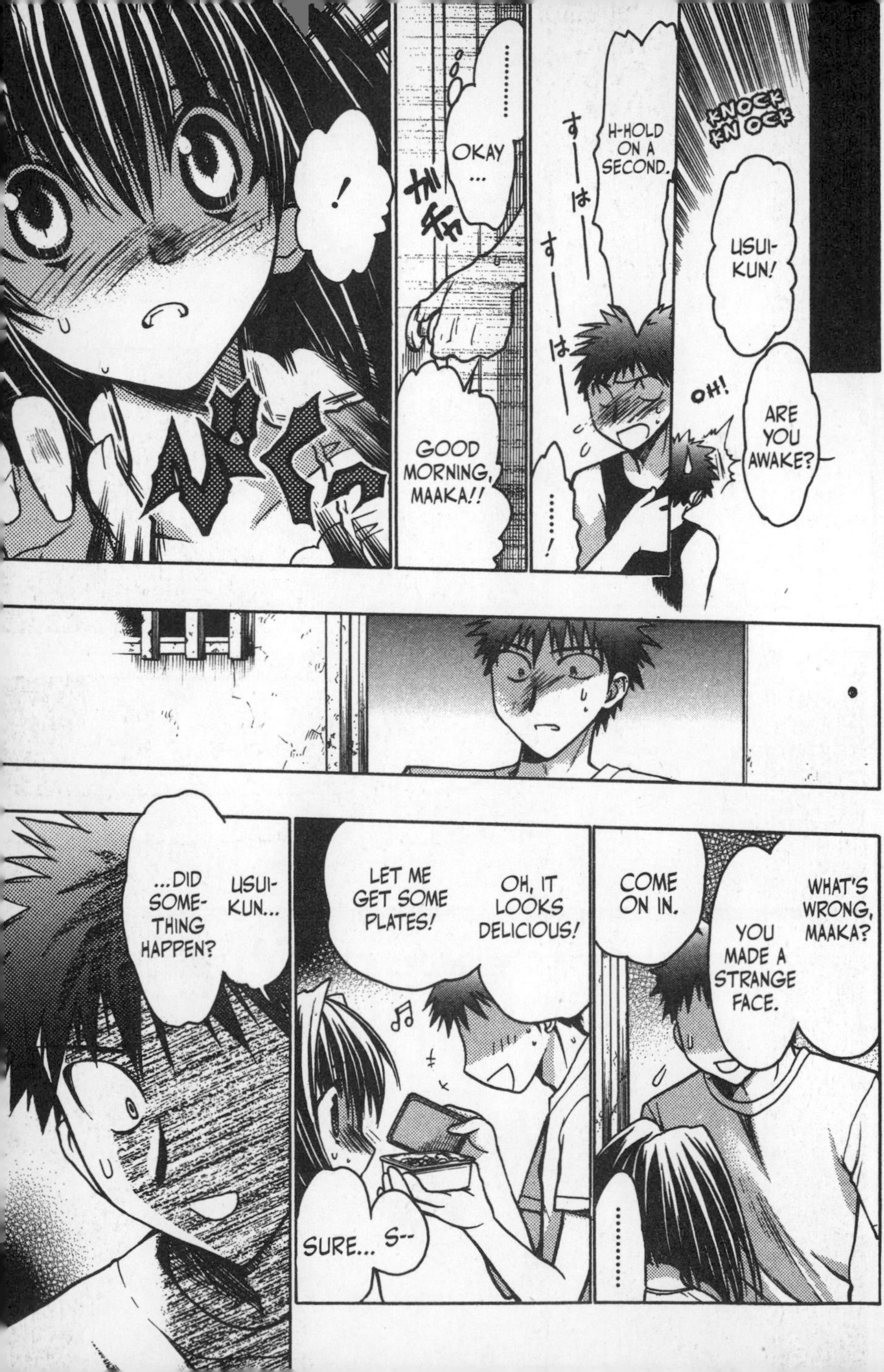
KNOCK KNOCK
USUI-KUN!
OH!
ARE YOU AWAKE?
H-HOLD ON A SECOND.
すーはー
すーはー
......!
......
OKAY ...
ガチャ
GOOD MORNING, MAAKA!!
!
WHAT'S WRONG, MAAKA?
YOU MADE A STRANGE FACE.
COME ON IN.
......
OH, IT LOOKS DELICIOUS!
LET ME GET SOME PLATES!
SURE... S--
USUI-KUN...
...DID SOMETHING HAPPEN?

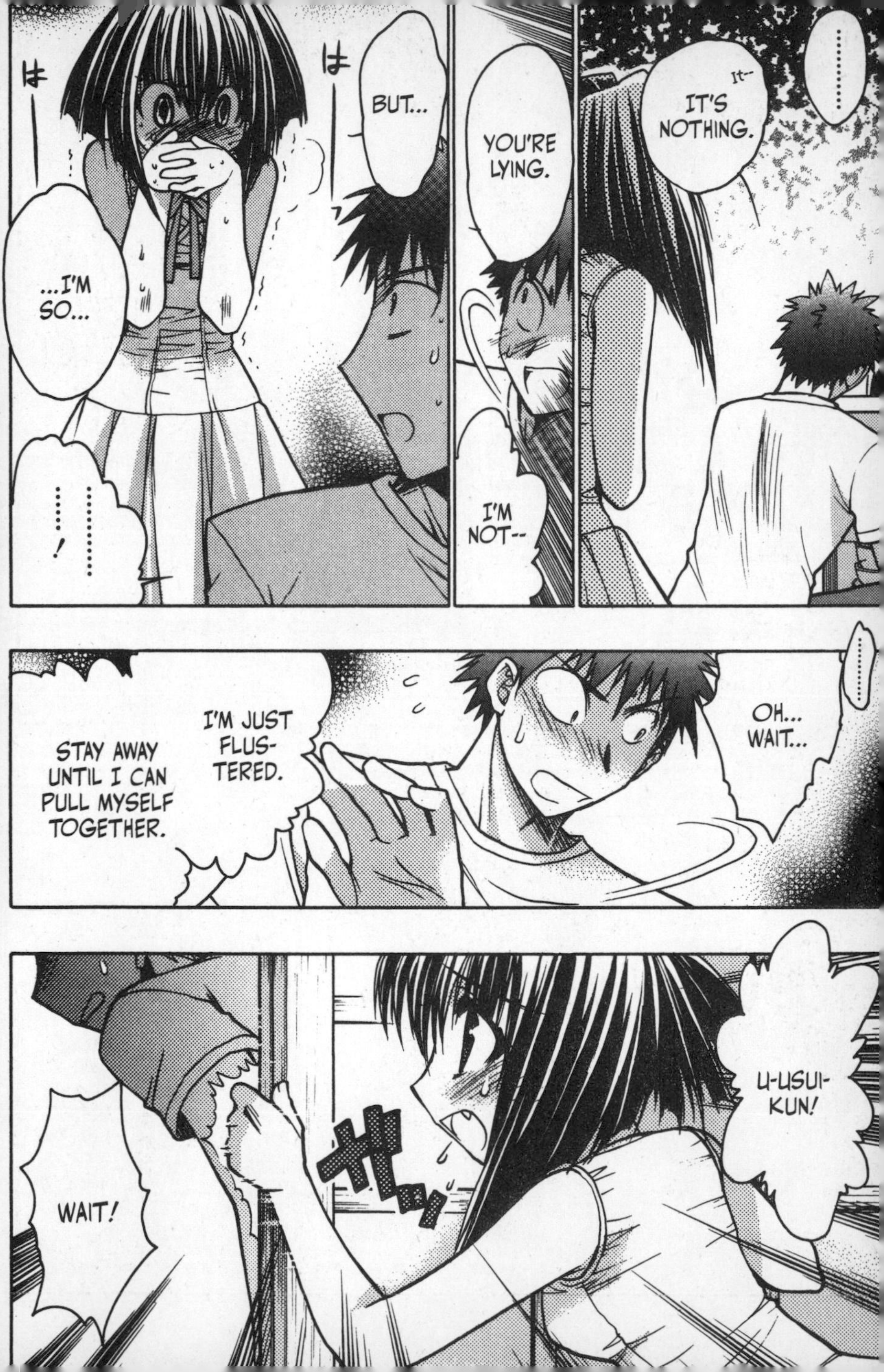
......
It--
IT'S NOTHING.
YOU'RE LYING.
I'M NOT--
BUT...
は
は
...I'M SO...
......!
......
OH... WAIT...
I'M JUST FLUS-TERED.
STAY AWAY UNTIL I CAN PULL MYSELF TOGETHER.
U-USUI-KUN!
ザッ
WAIT!

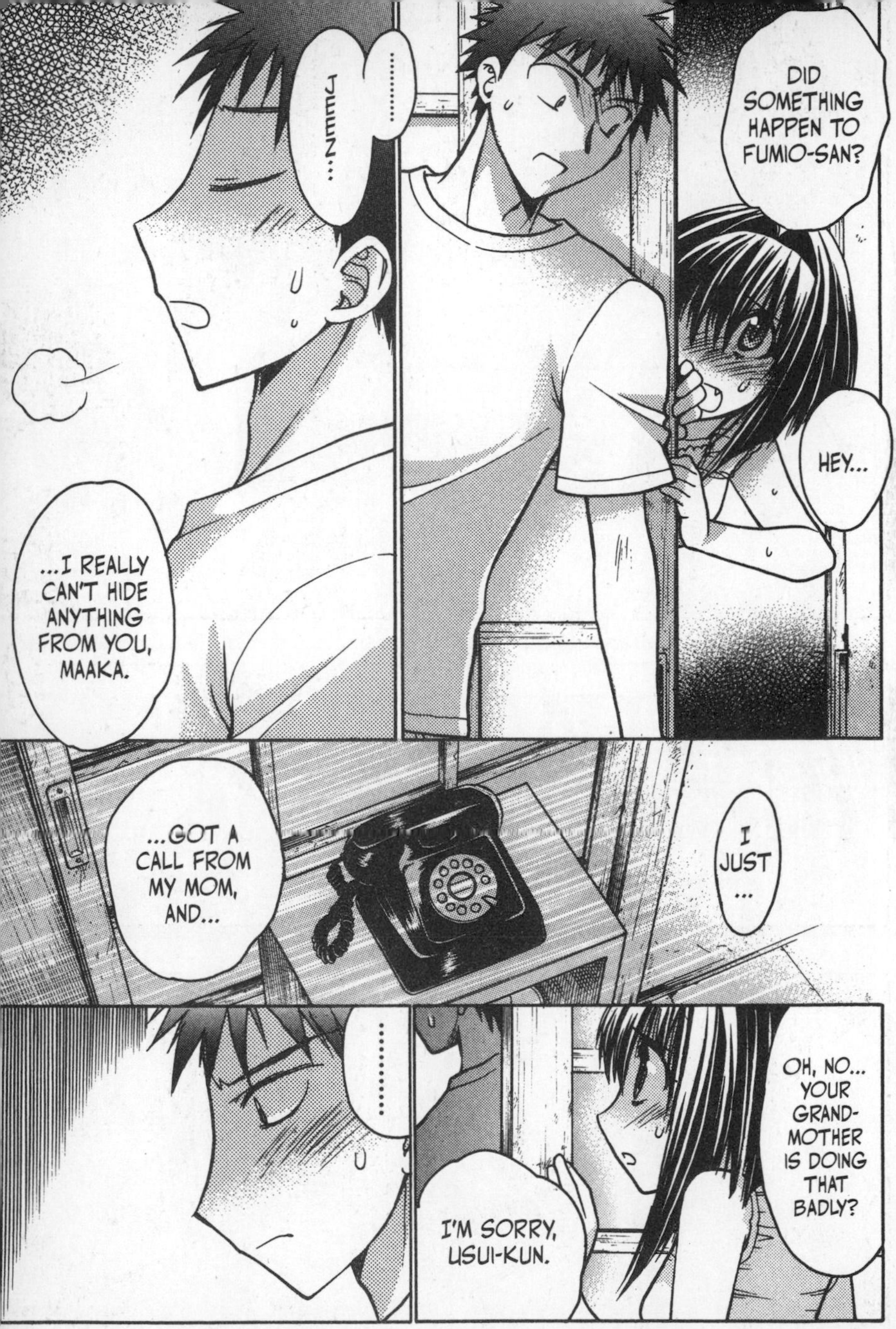
DID SOMETHING HAPPEN TO FUMIO-SAN?
HEY...
....
JEEZ...
...I REALLY CAN'T HIDE ANYTHING FROM YOU, MAAKA.
I JUST ...
...GOT A CALL FROM MY MOM, AND...
OH, NO... YOUR GRAND-MOTHER IS DOING THAT BADLY?
I'M SORRY, USUI-KUN.
....

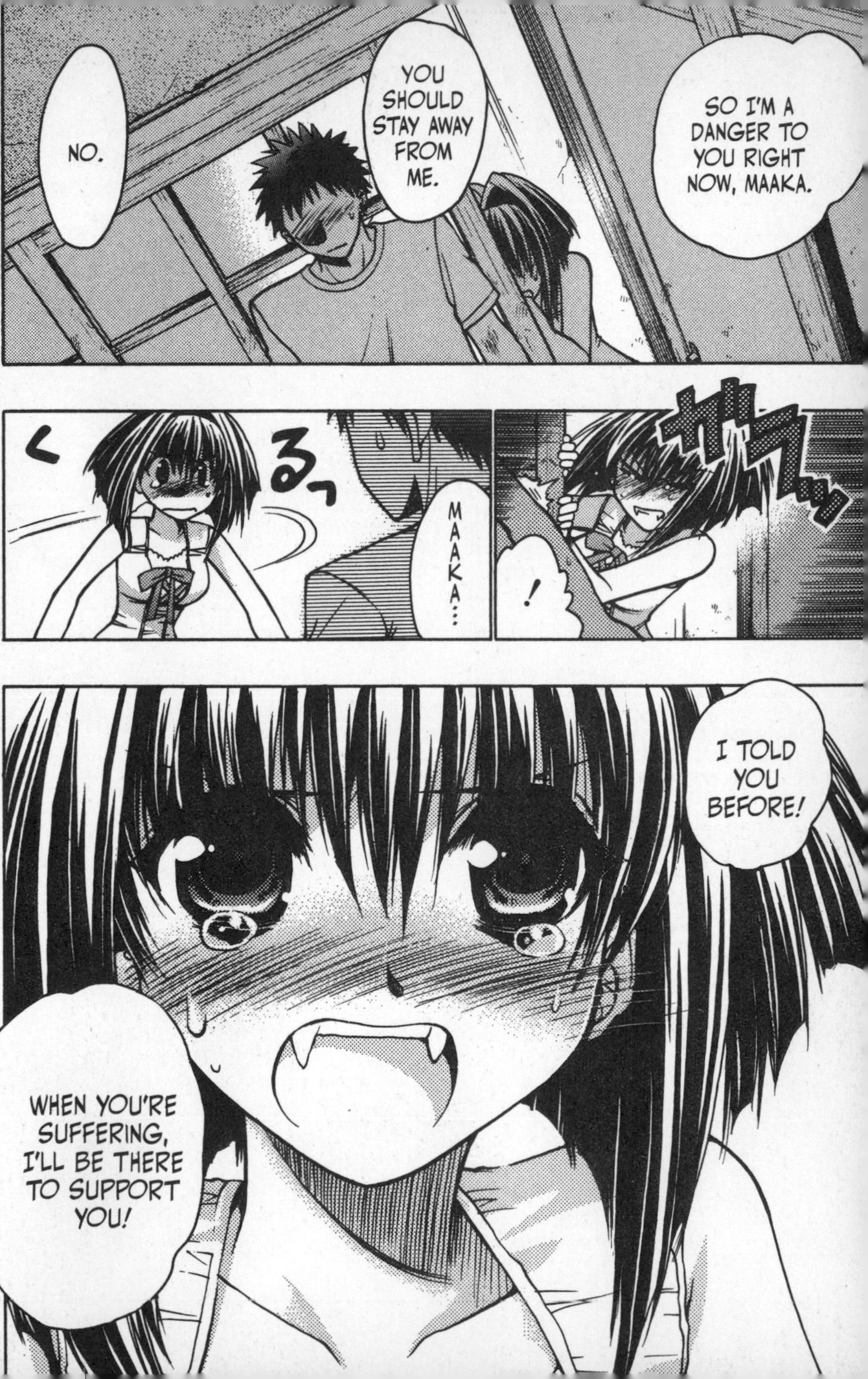
SO I'M A DANGER TO YOU RIGHT NOW, MAAKA.
YOU SHOULD STAY AWAY FROM ME.
NO.
!
MAAKA...
くるっ
I TOLD YOU BEFORE!
WHEN YOU'RE SUFFERING, I'LL BE THERE TO SUPPORT YOU!

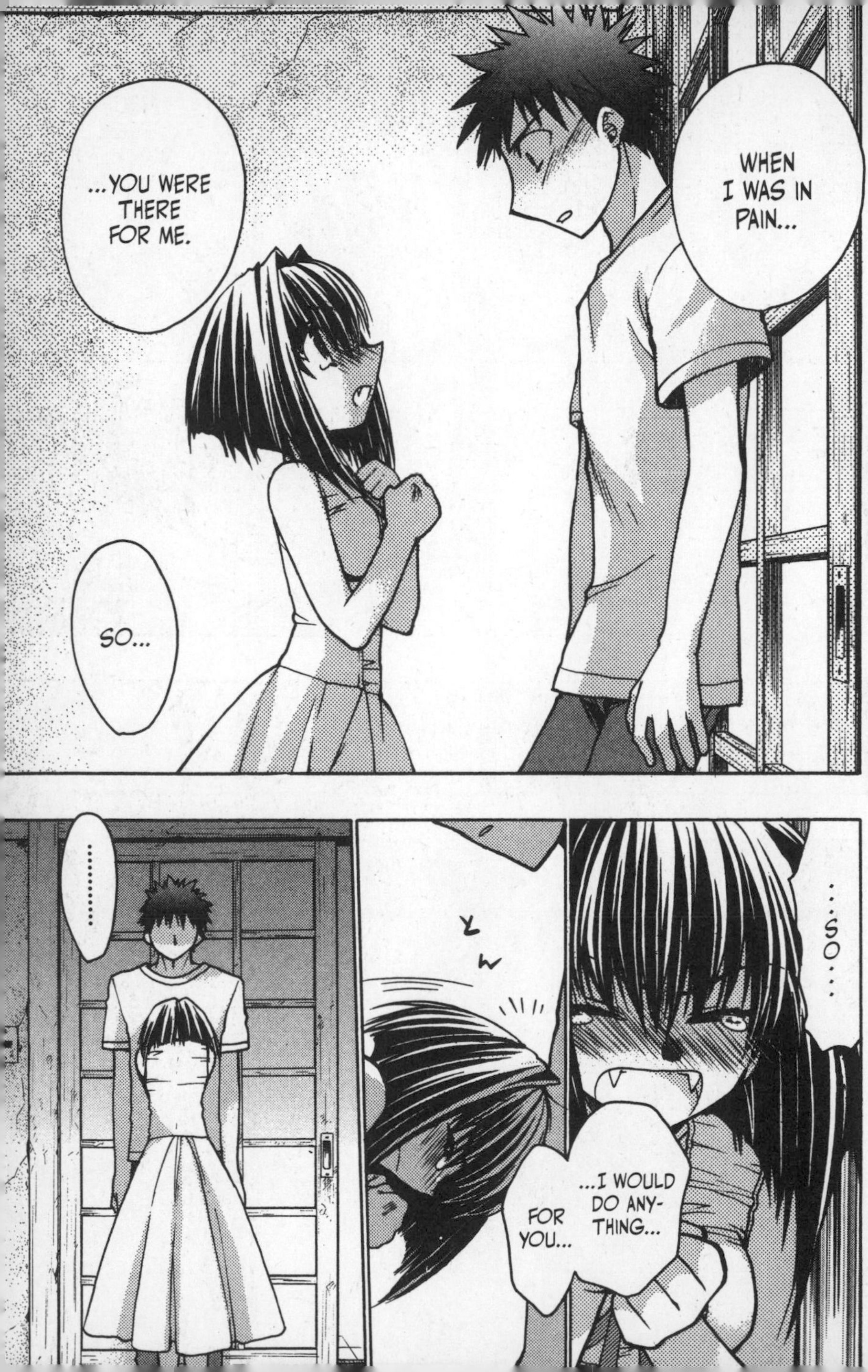
WHEN I WAS IN PAIN...
...YOU WERE THERE FOR ME.
SO...
...SO...
...I WOULD DO ANY- THING...
FOR YOU...
....

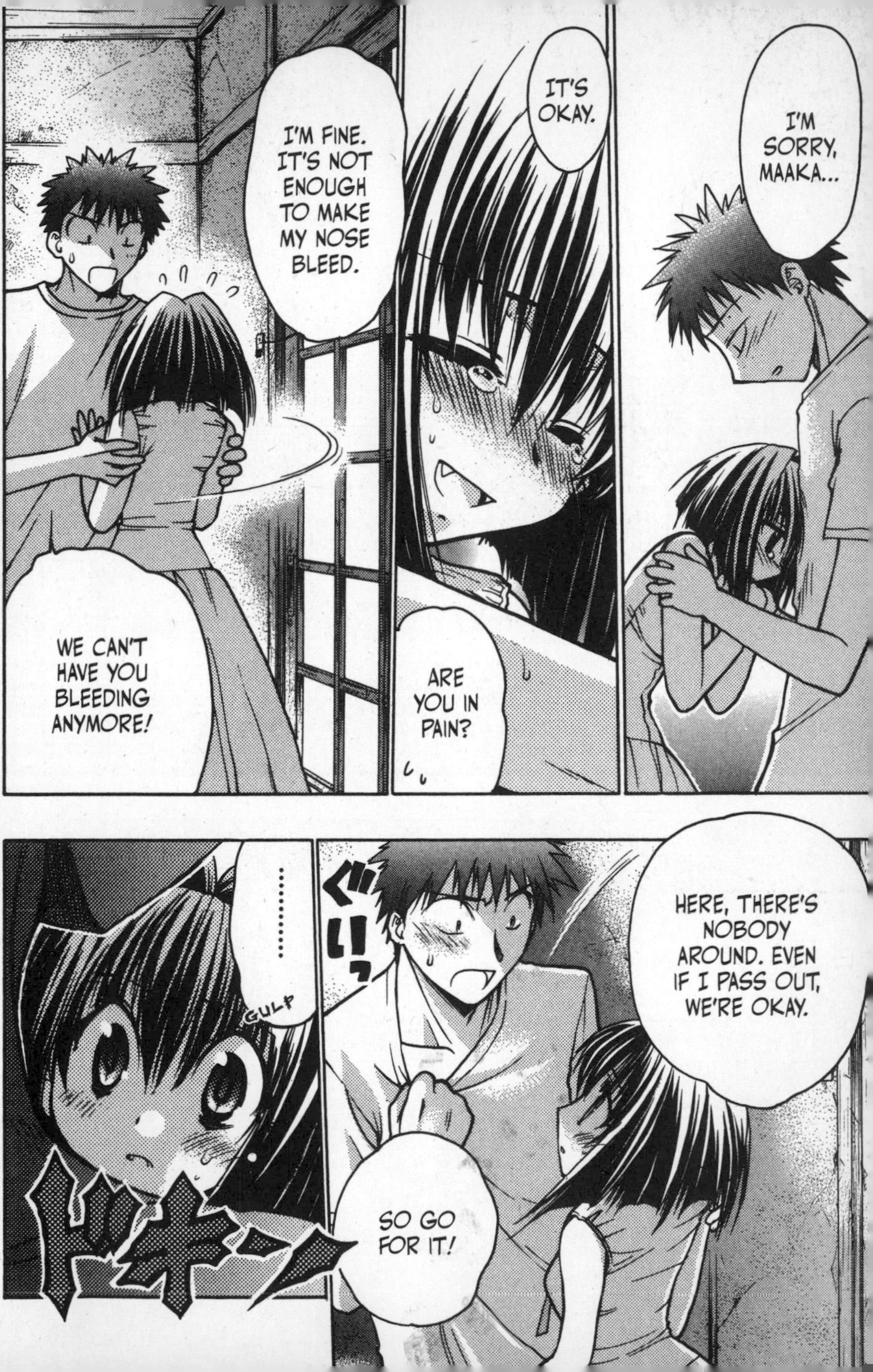
I'M SORRY, MAAKA...
IT'S OKAY.
ARE YOU IN PAIN?
I'M FINE. IT'S NOT ENOUGH TO MAKE MY NOSE BLEED.
WE CAN'T HAVE YOU BLEEDING ANYMORE!
HERE, THERE'S NOBODY AROUND. EVEN IF I PASS OUT, WE'RE OKAY.
SO GO FOR IT!
ぐいっ
......
GULP
ドキーン

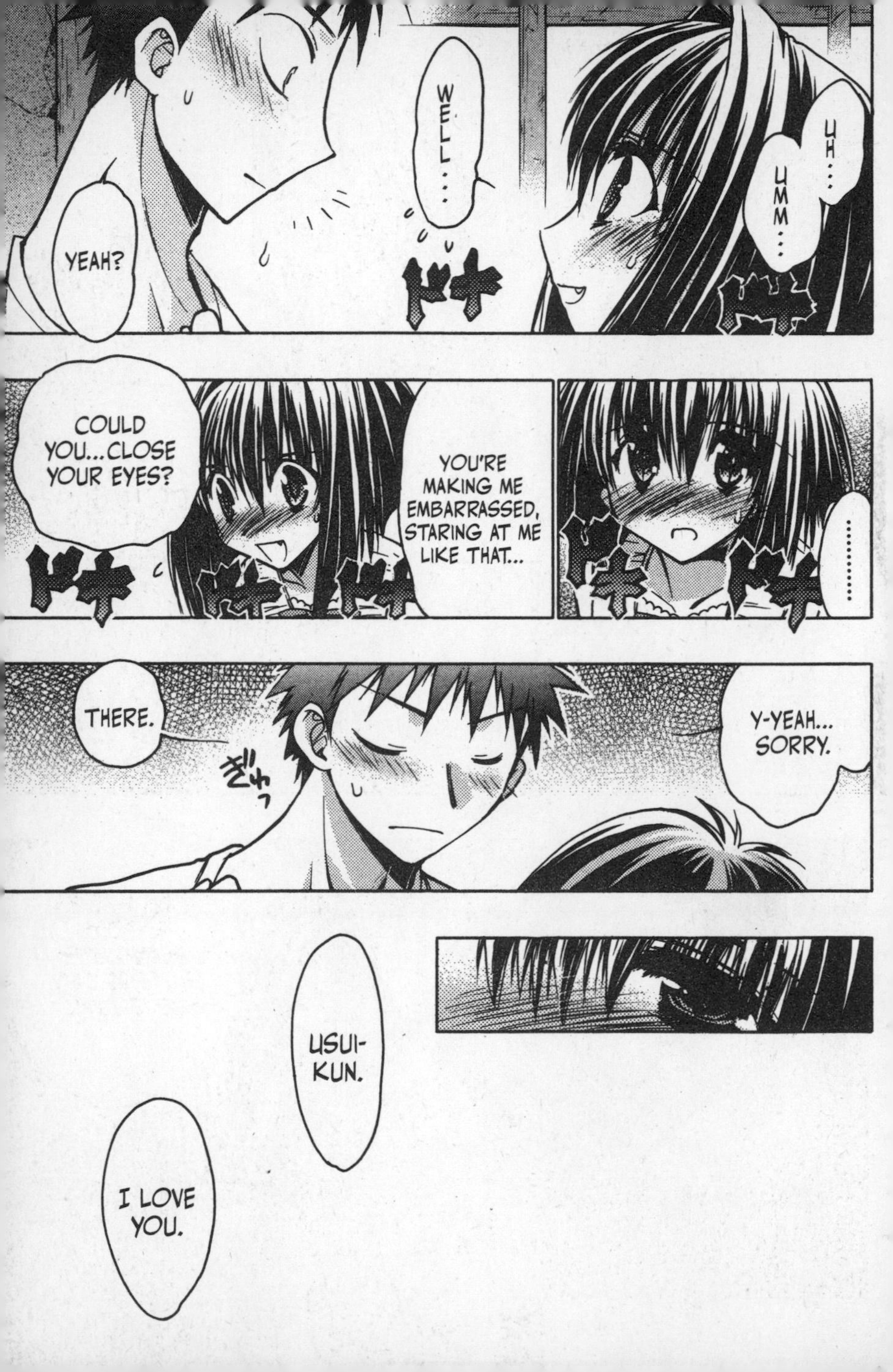
UH... UMM...
ドキ
WELL...
ドキ
YEAH?
......
ドキ ドキ
YOU'RE MAKING ME EMBARRASSED, STARING AT ME LIKE THAT...
ドキ ドキ
COULD YOU...CLOSE YOUR EYES?
ドキ
Y-YEAH... SORRY.
ぎゅっ
THERE.
USUI-KUN.
I LOVE YOU.

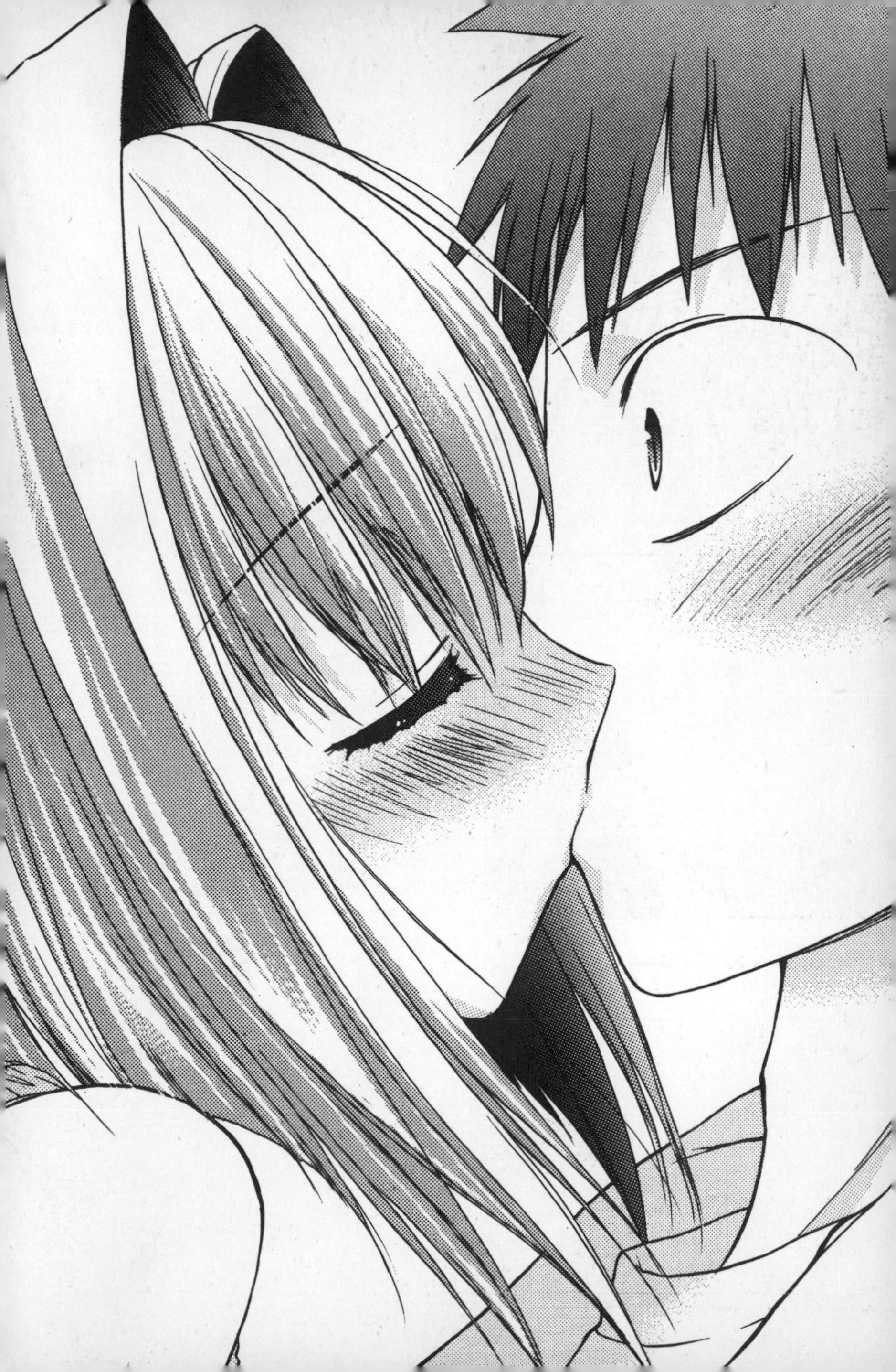

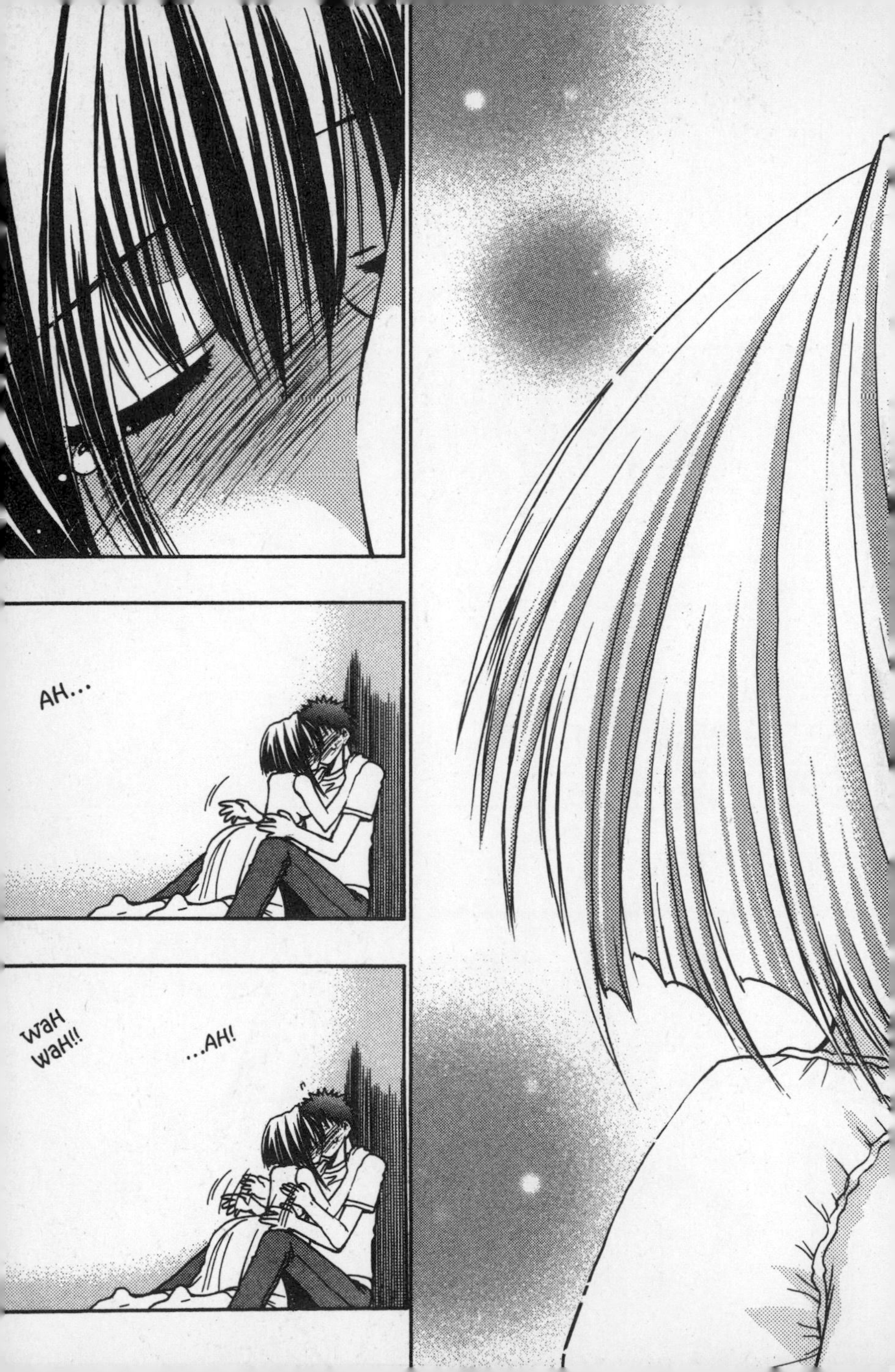
AH...
WAH WAH!!
...AH!

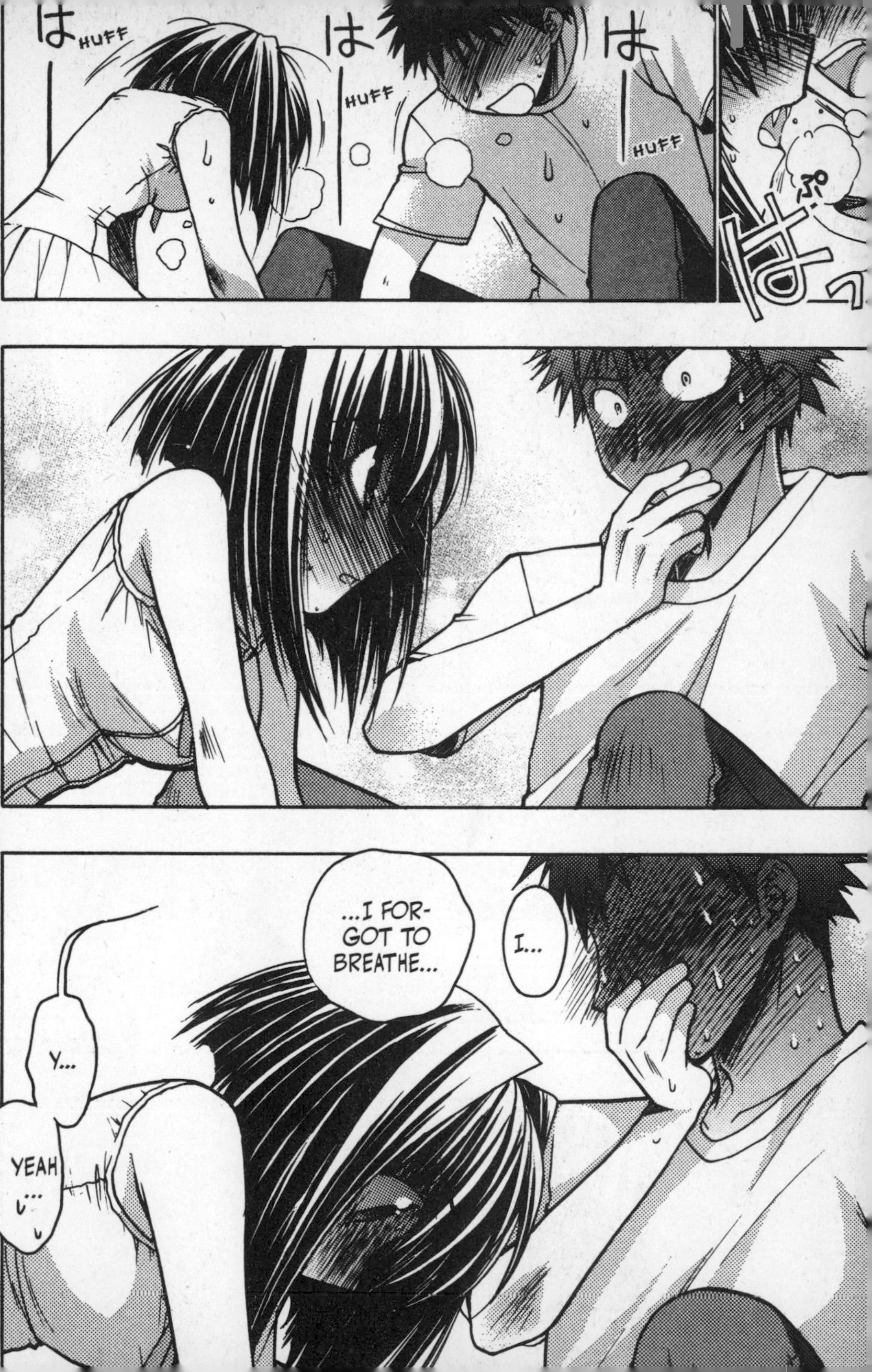

ぷはっ
は
HUFF
は
HUFF
は
HUFF
I...
...I FOR-GOT TO BREATHE...
Y...
YEAH...

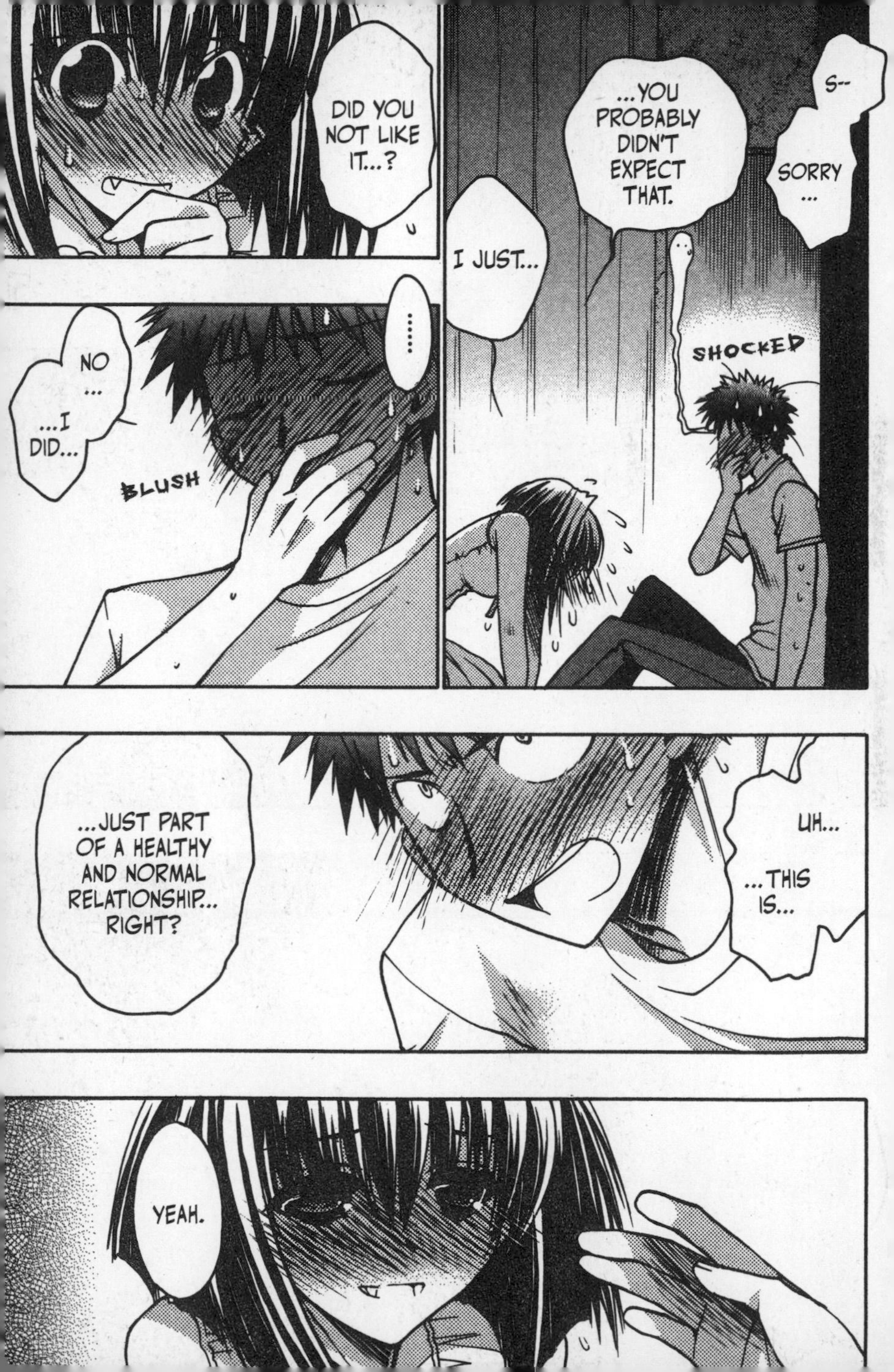

S--
SORRY...
...YOU PROBABLY DIDN'T EXPECT THAT.
I JUST...
SHOCKED
DID YOU NOT LIKE IT...?
......
NO... ...I DID...
BLUSH
UH... ...THIS IS...
...JUST PART OF A HEALTHY AND NORMAL RELATIONSHIP... RIGHT?
YEAH.

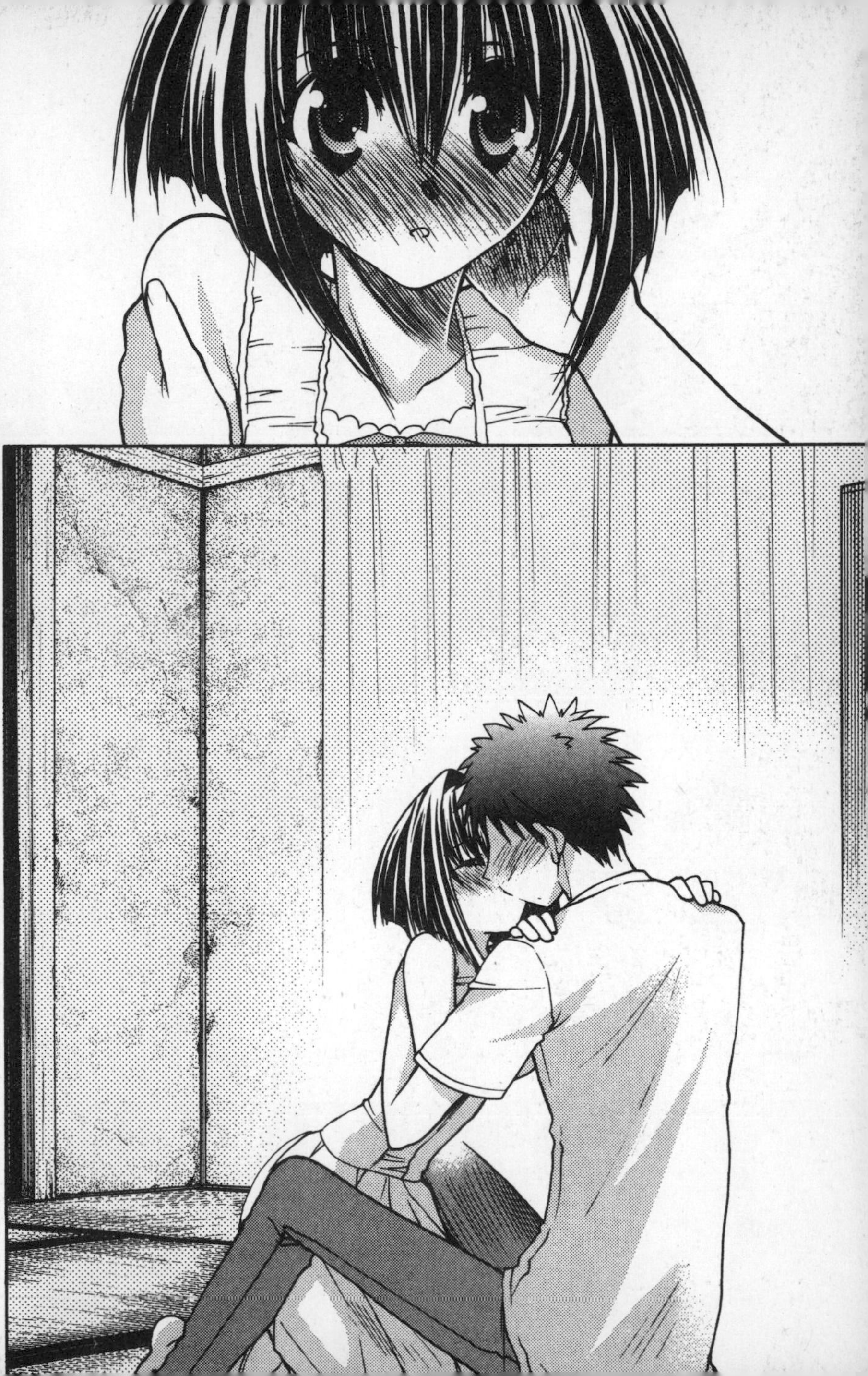

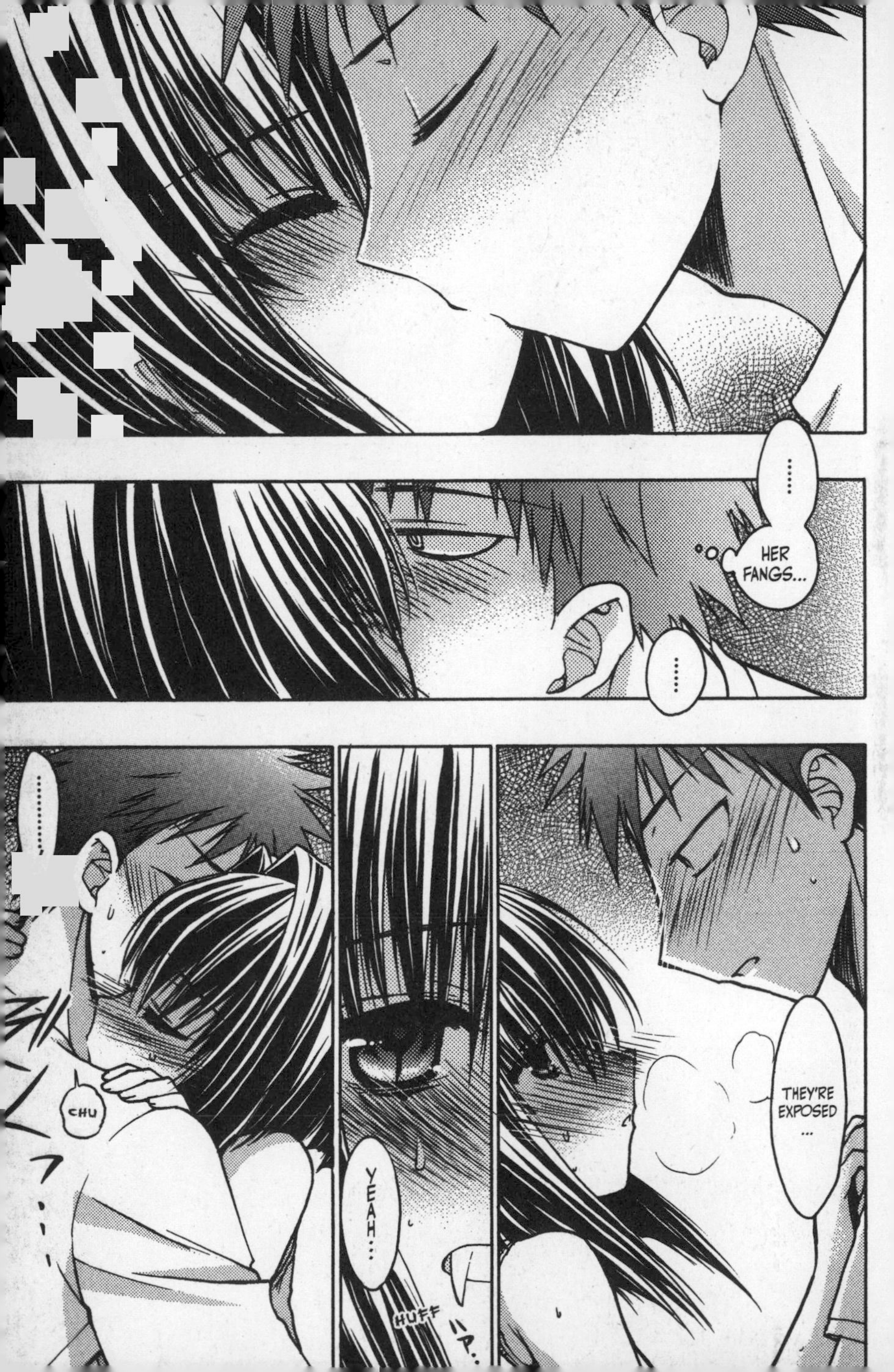
......
HER FANGS...
......
THEY'RE EXPOSED ...
YEAH...
HUFF
......
CHU

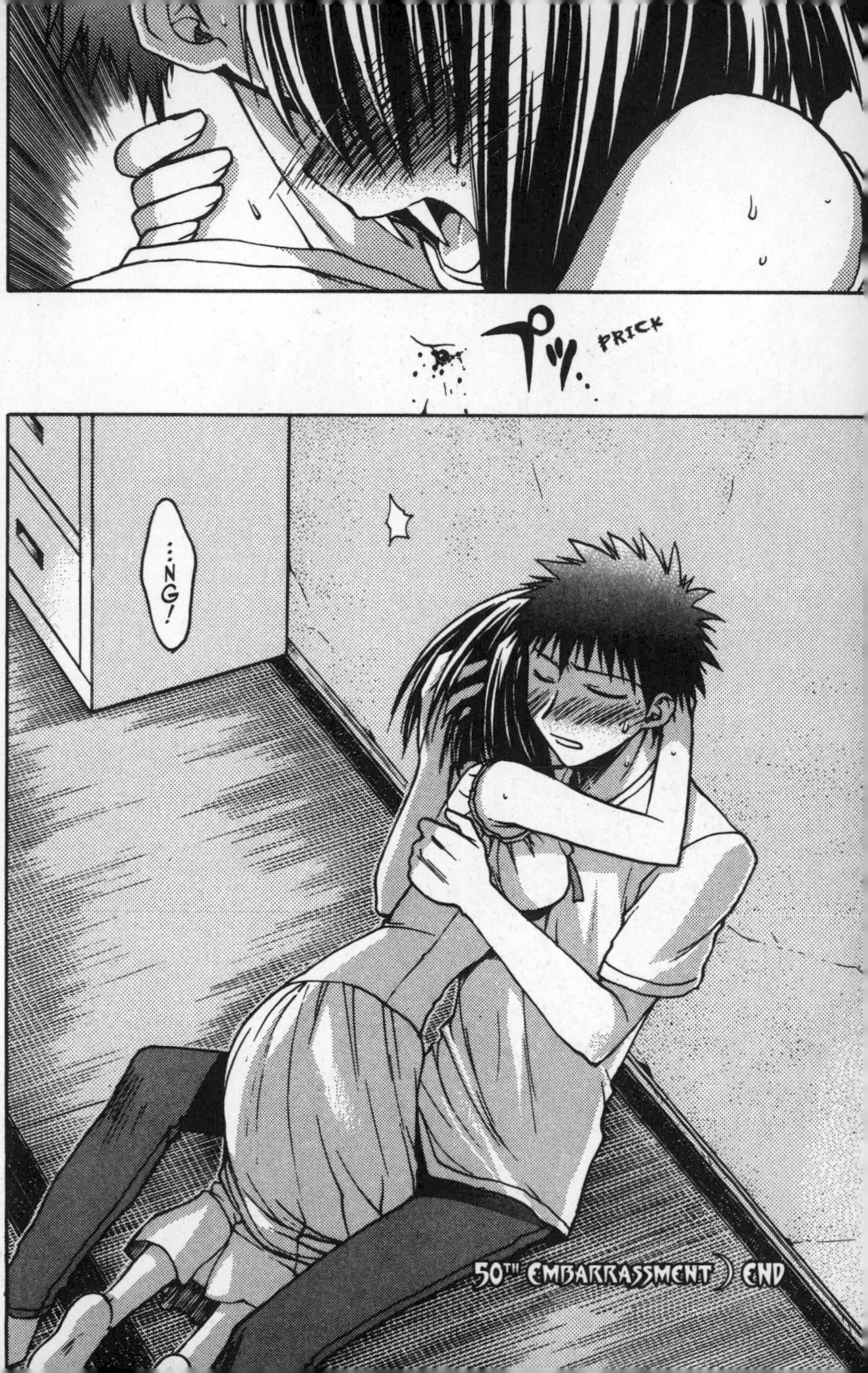
プッ
PRICK
...NG!
50TH EMBARRASSMENT END

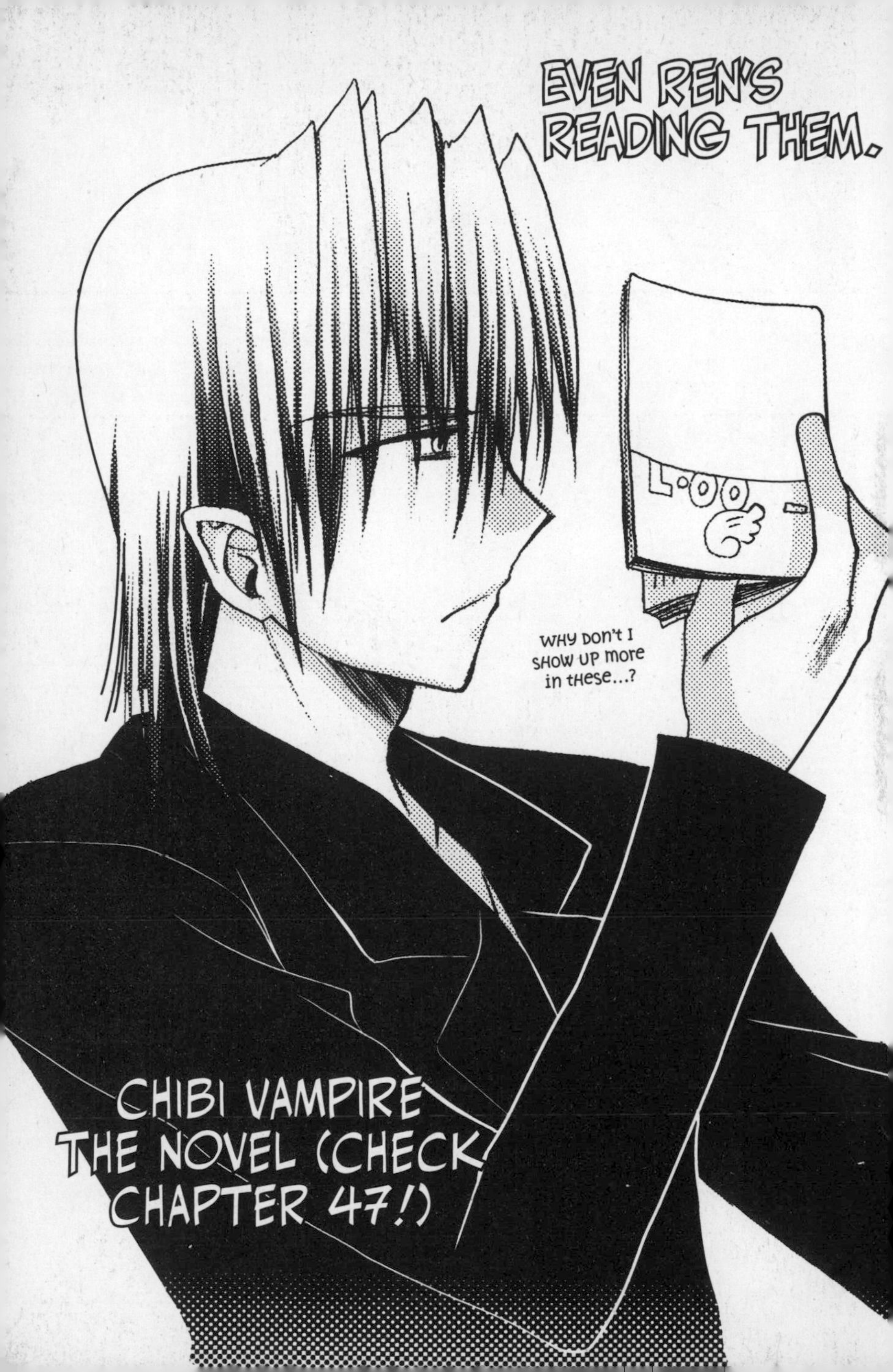
EVEN REN'S READING THEM.
L·OO
WHY DON'T I SHOW UP MORE IN THESE...?
CHIBI VAMPIRE THE NOVEL (CHECK CHAPTER 47!)

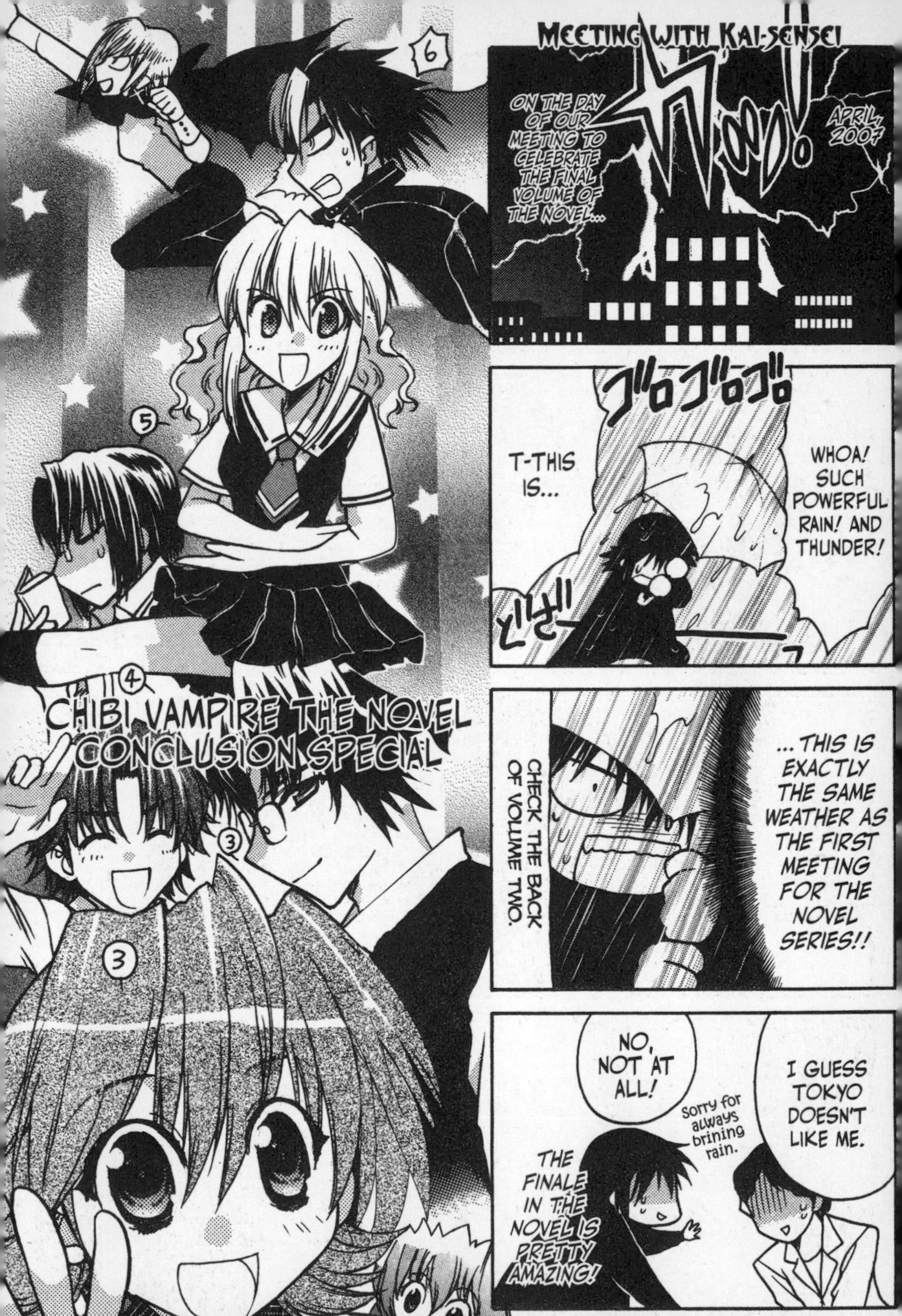
CHIBI VAMPIRE THE NOVEL
CONCLUSION SPECIAL
6
5
4
3
3
MEETING WITH KAI-SENSEI
ON THE DAY OF OUR MEETING TO CELEBRATE THE FINAL VOLUME OF THE NOVEL...
APRIL, 2007
WHOA! SUCH POWERFUL RAIN! AND THUNDER!
T-THIS IS...
...THIS IS EXACTLY THE SAME WEATHER AS THE FIRST MEETING FOR THE NOVEL SERIES!!
CHECK THE BACK OF VOLUME TWO.
I GUESS TOKYO DOESN'T LIKE ME.
NO, NOT AT ALL!
Sorry for always brining rain.
THE FINALE IN THE NOVEL IS PRETTY AMAZING!

KAI-SENSEI, THANK YOU FOR THE HARD WORK OVER THESE LAST FOUR YEARS!

OUT OF POCKET

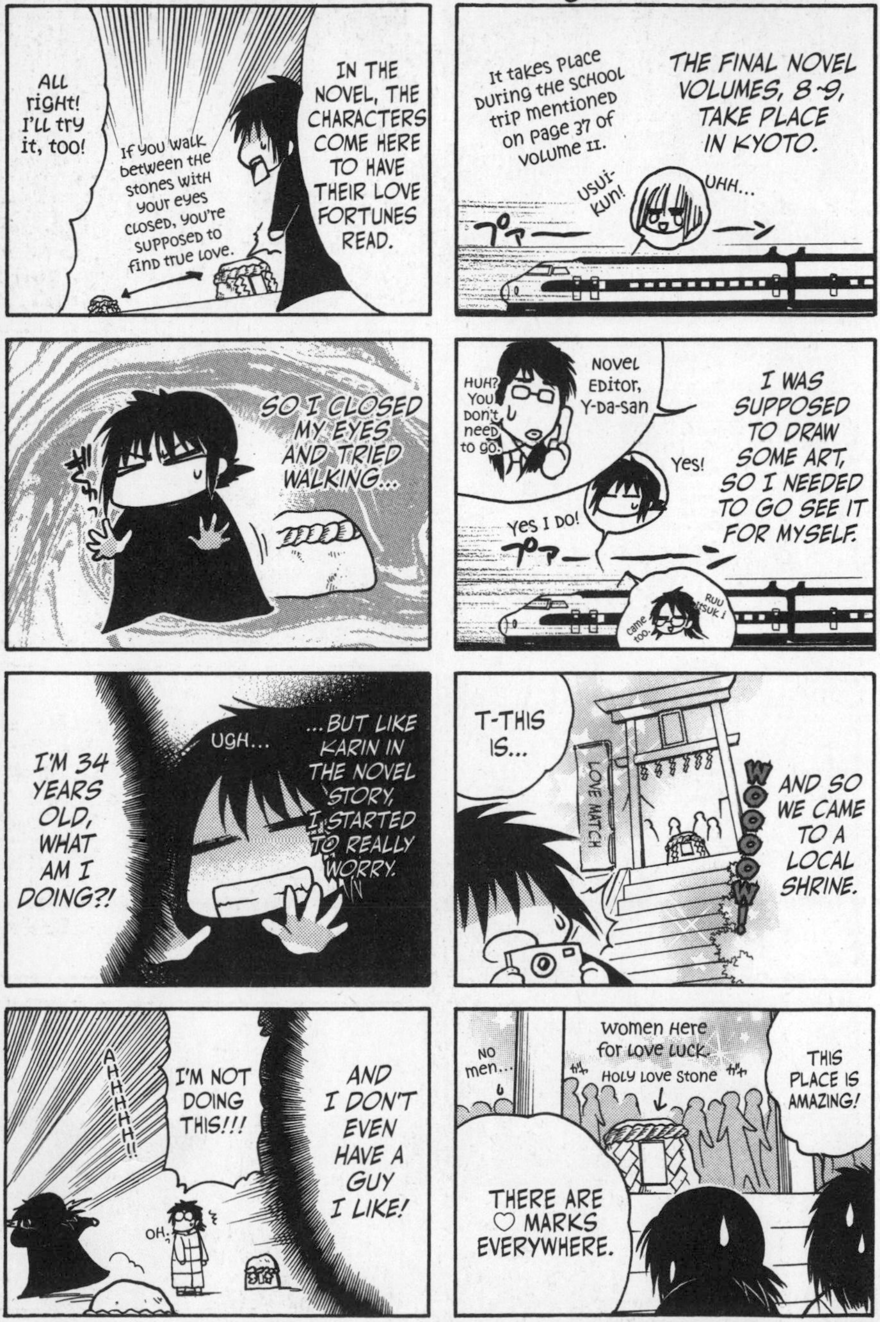
THE FINAL NOVEL VOLUMES, 8~9, TAKE PLACE IN KYOTO.
It takes place during the school trip mentioned on page 37 of volume 11.
UHH...
USUI-KUN!
I WAS SUPPOSED TO DRAW SOME ART, SO I NEEDED TO GO SEE IT FOR MYSELF.
Novel Editor, Y-da-san
HUH? You don't need to go.
Yes!
Yes I do!
RUU ITSUKI came too.
AND SO WE CAME TO A LOCAL SHRINE.
WOOOOOW!
LOVE MATCH
T-THIS IS...
THIS PLACE IS AMAZING!
Women here for love luck.
Holy Love Stone
No men...
THERE ARE ♡ MARKS EVERYWHERE.
IN THE NOVEL, THE CHARACTERS COME HERE TO HAVE THEIR LOVE FORTUNES READ.
If you walk between the stones with your eyes closed, you're supposed to find true love.
All right! I'll try it, too!
SO I CLOSED MY EYES AND TRIED WALKING...
...BUT LIKE KARIN IN THE NOVEL STORY, I STARTED TO REALLY WORRY.
UGH...
I'M 34 YEARS OLD, WHAT AM I DOING?!
AND I DON'T EVEN HAVE A GUY I LIKE!
I'M NOT DOING THIS!!!
AHHHHH!!
OH.

I'm really glad I got to see this.

EMA ①

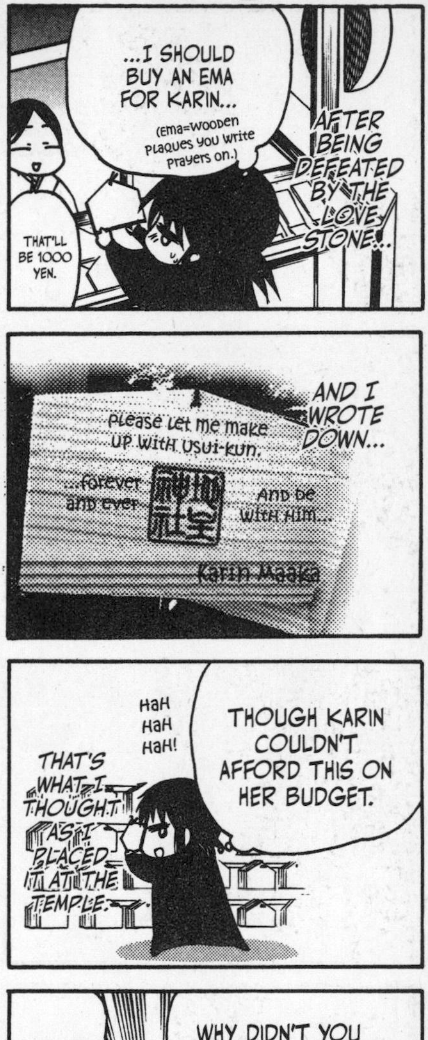

...I SHOULD BUY AN EMA FOR KARIN...
(Ema=wooden plaques you write prayers on.)
AFTER BEING DEFEATED BY THE LOVE STONE...
THAT'LL BE 1000 YEN.
AND I WROTE DOWN...
Please let me make up with Usui-kun.
...forever and ever
And be with him...
Karin Maaka
THOUGH KARIN COULDN'T AFFORD THIS ON HER BUDGET.
HAH HAH HAH!
THAT'S WHAT I THOUGHT AS I PLACED IT AT THE TEMPLE.
WHY DIDN'T YOU BRING IT BACK?! WE COULD HAVE GIVEN IT AWAY IN A FAN CONTEST!
OOPS!
It would have been a rare item!
MY EDITOR, S-O.

EMA ②

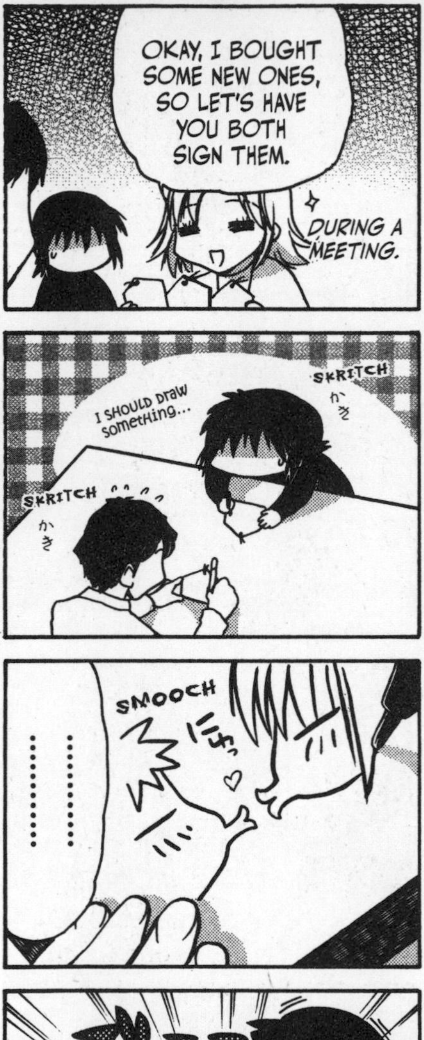

OKAY, I BOUGHT SOME NEW ONES, SO LET'S HAVE YOU BOTH SIGN THEM.
DURING A MEETING.
SKRITCH
かき
I should draw something...
SKRITCH
かき
SMOOCH
....
....
!

I couldn't stop laughing...

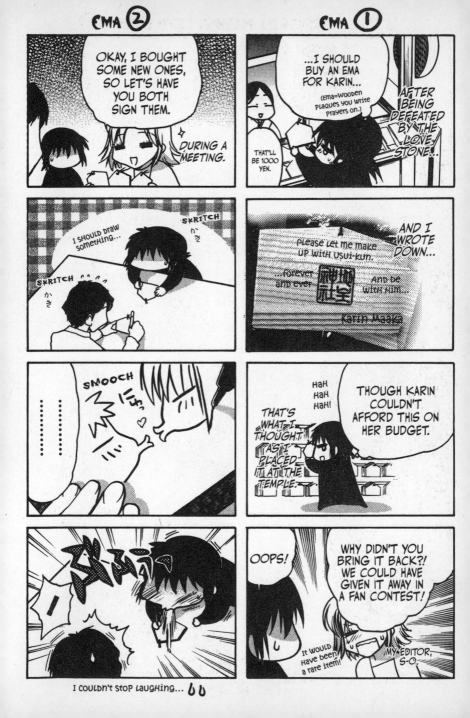

LET'S END THINGS BY MESSING WITH USUI-KUN

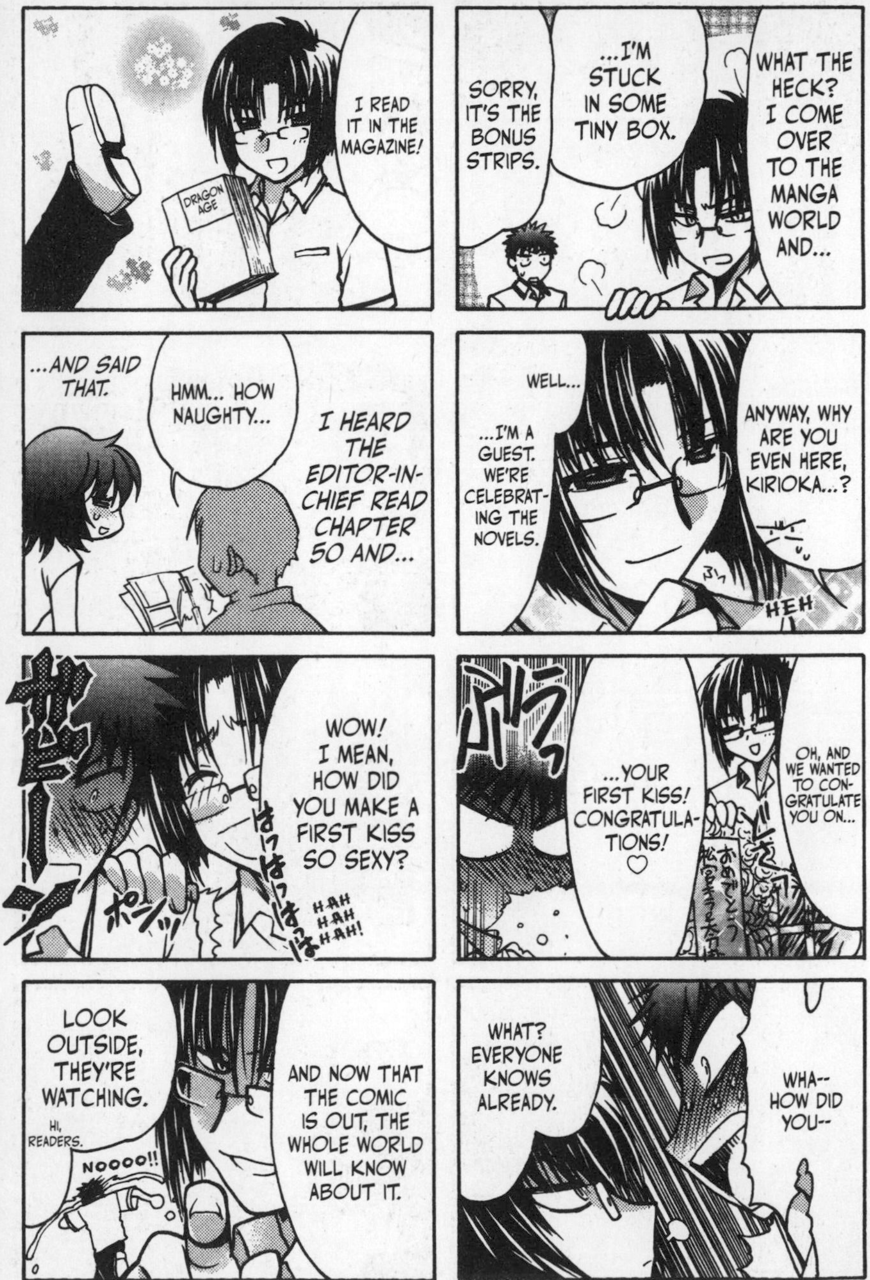
WHAT THE HECK? I COME OVER TO THE MANGA WORLD AND...
...I'M STUCK IN SOME TINY BOX.
SORRY, IT'S THE BONUS STRIPS.
ANYWAY, WHY ARE YOU EVEN HERE, KIRIOKA...?
HEH
WELL...
...I'M A GUEST. WE'RE CELEBRATING THE NOVELS.
OH, AND WE WANTED TO CONGRATULATE YOU ON...
...YOUR FIRST KISS! CONGRATULATIONS! ♡
WHA-- HOW DID YOU--
WHAT? EVERYONE KNOWS ALREADY.
I READ IT IN THE MAGAZINE!
DRAGON AGE
I HEARD THE EDITOR-IN-CHIEF READ CHAPTER 50 AND...
HMM... HOW NAUGHTY...
...AND SAID THAT.
WOW! I MEAN, HOW DID YOU MAKE A FIRST KISS SO SEXY?
HAH HAH HAH!
AND NOW THAT THE COMIC IS OUT, THE WHOLE WORLD WILL KNOW ABOUT IT.
LOOK OUTSIDE, THEY'RE WATCHING.
HI, READERS.
NOOOO!!

NOW THEY KNOW WHAT A PERVERT YOU ARE...

I'M SORRY...

IN OUR NEXT VOLUME...

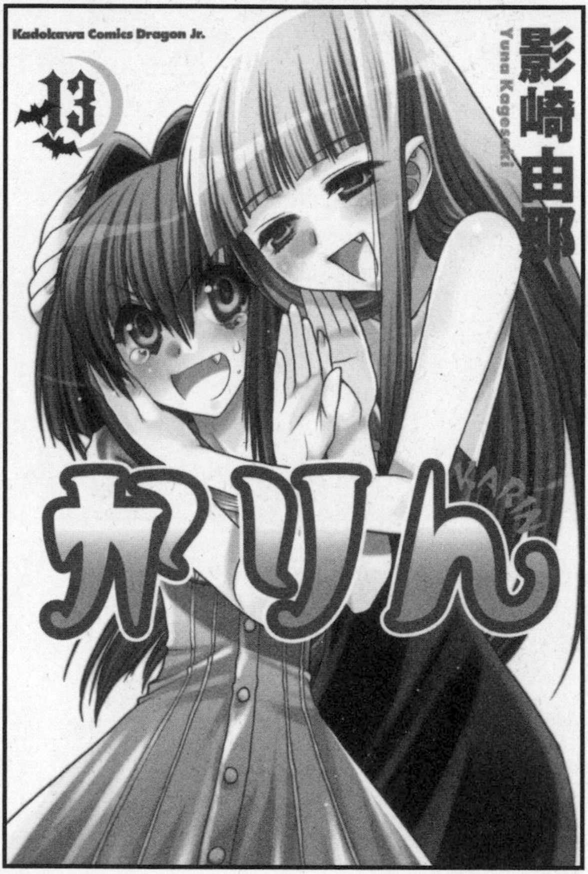
Kadokawa Comics Dragon Jr.
13
影崎由那
Yuna Kageasaki
かりん
KARIN

KARIN FINALLY GETS HER FIRST KISS WITH KENTA AND IS ON TOP OF THE WORLD! BUT TROUBLE IS BREWING AS THE UNFRIENDLY VAMPIRES ARE COMING TO TOWN TO UNCOVER KARIN'S SECRETS. WHEN AN ALL-OUT WAR BETWEEN VAMPIRES BREAKS OUT OVER KARIN, WILL KENTA BE THE ONE TO SAVE HER OR WILL HIS LOVE BE LOST FOREVER?

Can't Move from Under the Bed

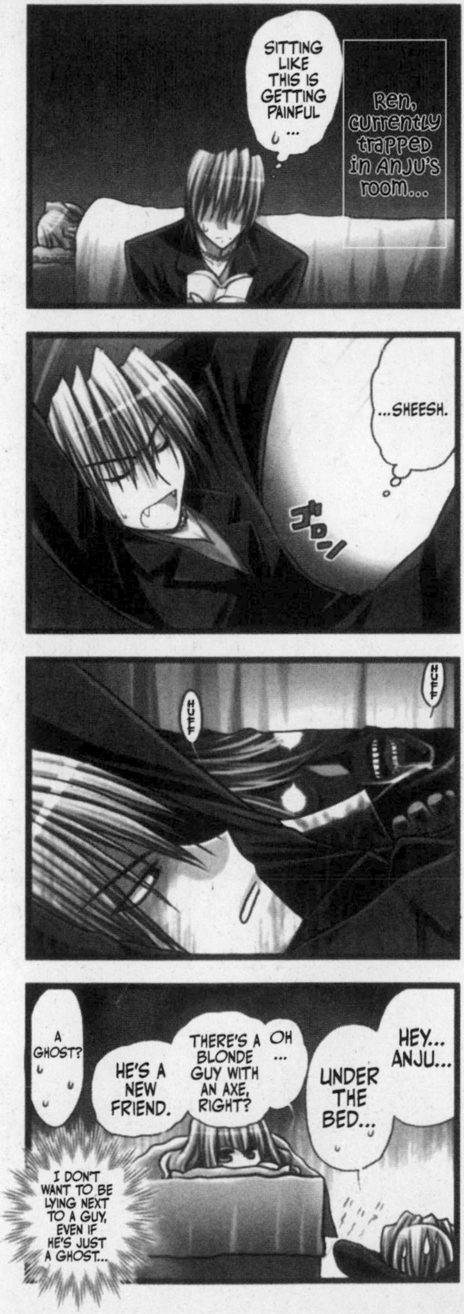

Ren, currently trapped in Anju's room...
SITTING LIKE THIS IS GETTING PAINFUL ...
...SHEESH.
ゴロン
HUFF
HUFF
HEY... ANJU...
UNDER THE BED...
OH ...
THERE'S A BLONDE GUY WITH AN AXE, RIGHT?
HE'S A NEW FRIEND.
A GHOST?
I DON'T WANT TO BE LYING NEXT TO A GUY, EVEN IF HE'S JUST A GHOST...

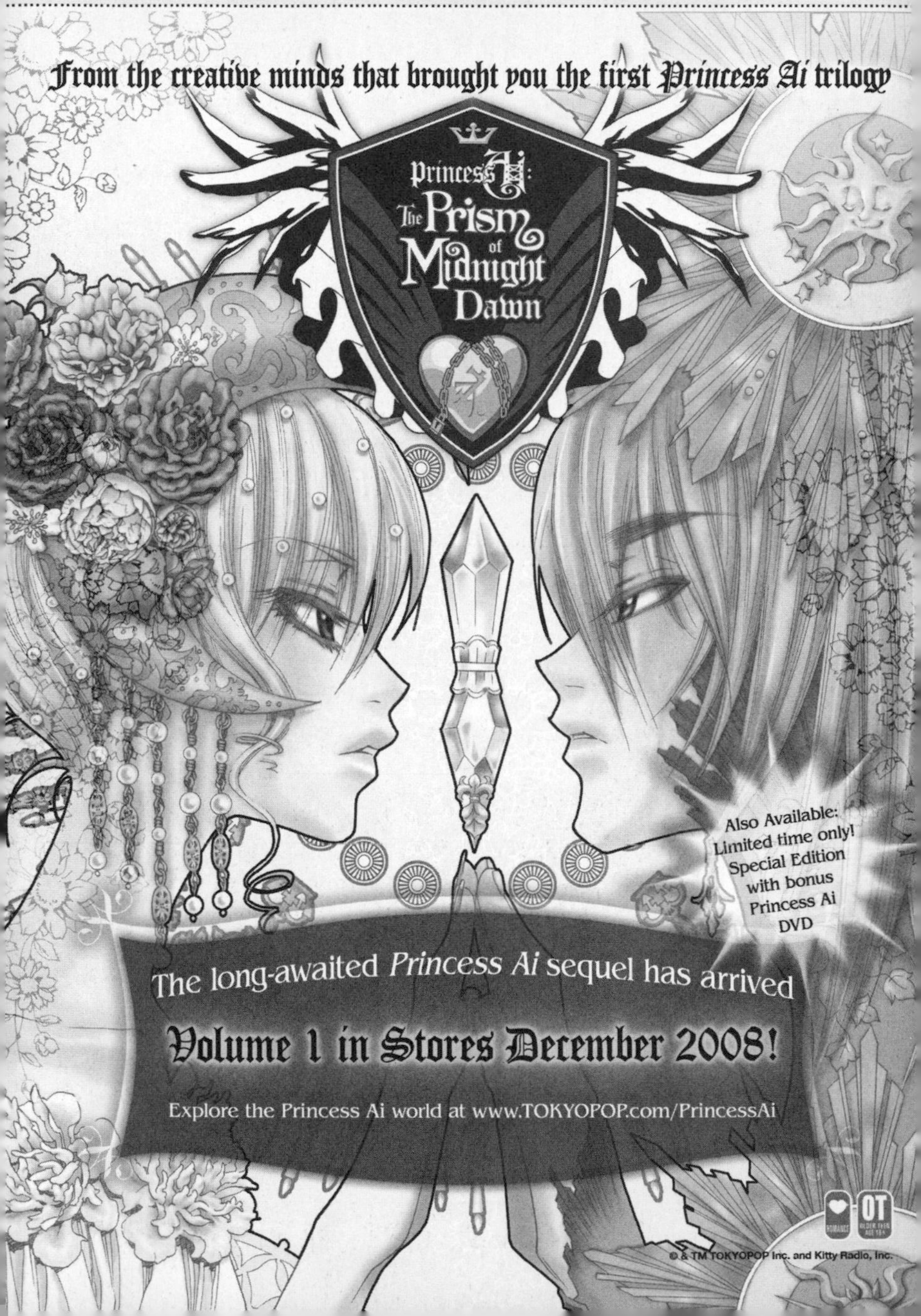
From the creative minds that brought you the first Princess Ai trilogy
Princess Ai: The Prism of Midnight Dawn
Also Available: Limited time only! Special Edition with bonus Princess Ai DVD
The long-awaited Princess Ai sequel has arrived
Volume 1 in Stores December 2008!
Explore the Princess Ai world at www.TOKYOPOP.com/PrincessAi
OT
© & TM TOKYOPOP Inc. and Kitty Radio, Inc.

INCLUDES A PREVIEW OF FRUITS BASKET VOL. 22 (MARCH 2009)

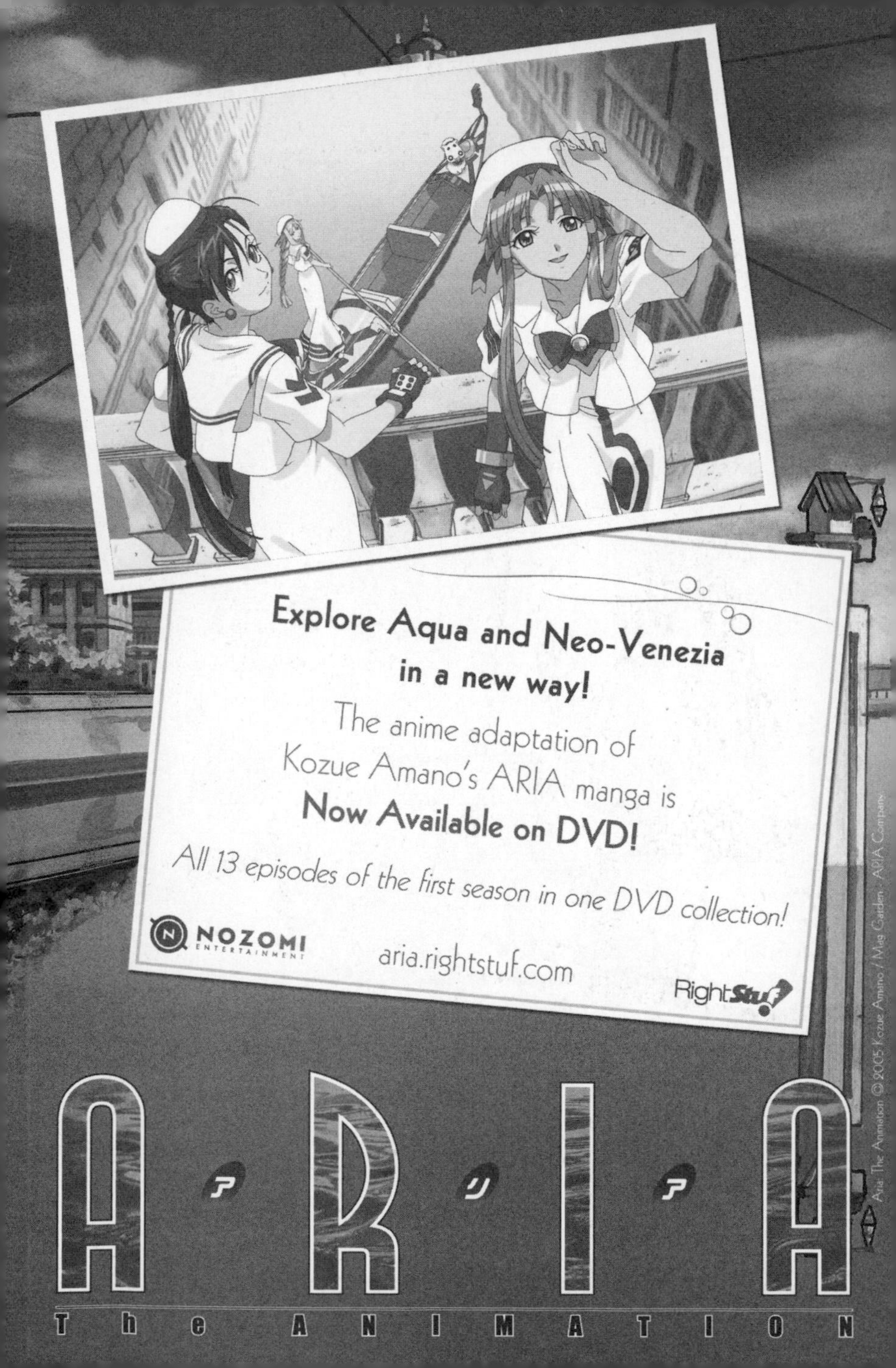

Explore Aqua and Neo-Venezia
in a new way!
The anime adaptation of
Kozue Amano's ARIA manga is
Now Available on DVD!
All 13 episodes of the first season in one DVD collection!
NOZOMI ENTERTAINMENT
aria.rightstuf.com
RightStuf!
ARIA
アリア
The ANIMATION
Aria The Animation © 2005 Kozue Amano / Mag Garden · ARIA Company

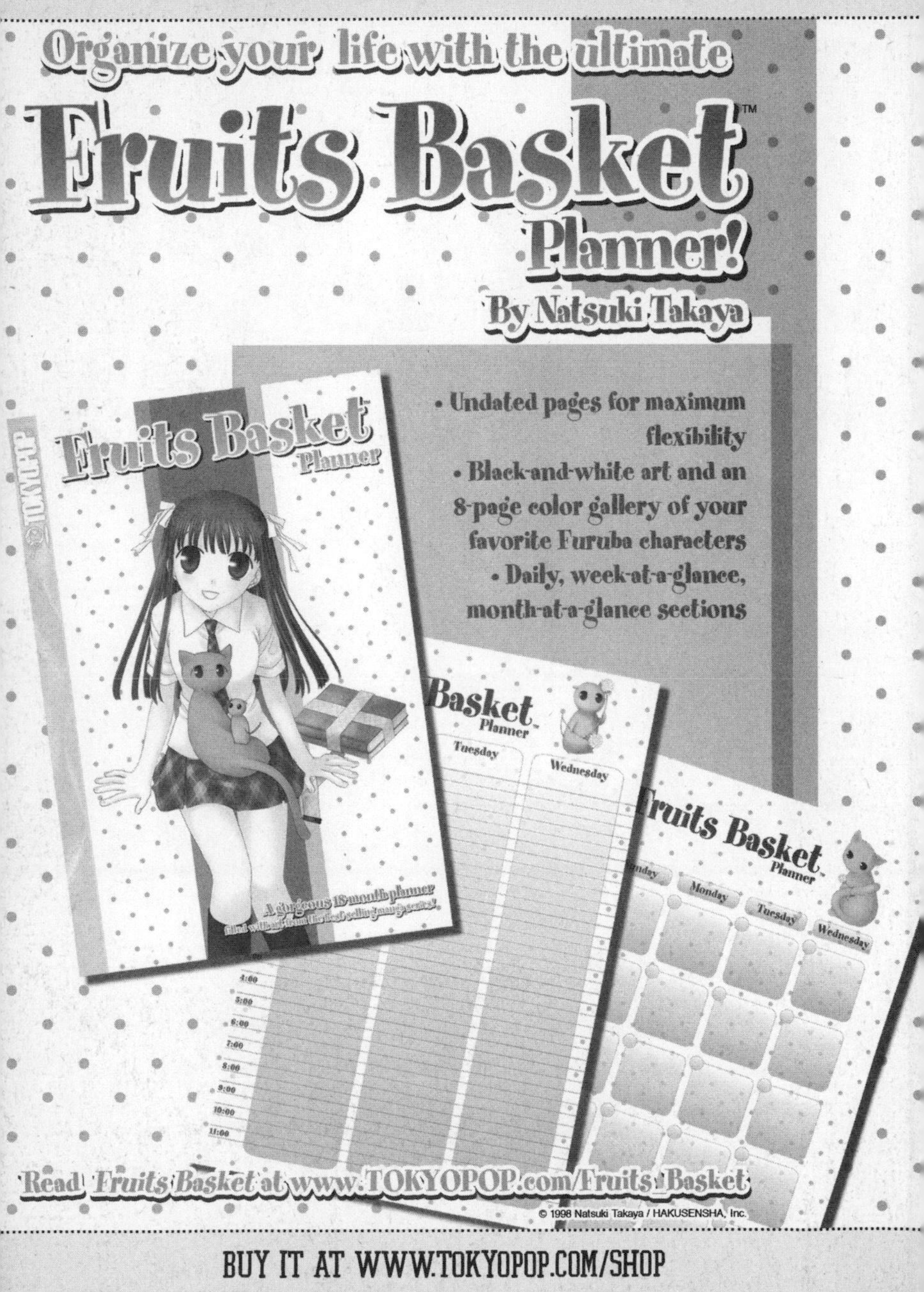
Organize your life with the ultimate
Fruits Basket™
Planner!
By Natsuki Takaya
• Undated pages for maximum flexibility
• Black-and-white art and an 8-page color gallery of your favorite Furuba characters
• Daily, week-at-a-glance, month-at-a-glance sections
Fruits Basket™ Planner
TOKYOPOP
A gorgeous 18-month planner
Basket™ Planner
Tuesday
Wednesday
4:00
5:00
6:00
7:00
8:00
9:00
10:00
11:00
Fruits Basket™ Planner
Monday
Tuesday
Wednesday
Read Fruits Basket at www.TOKYOPOP.com/Fruits_Basket
© 1998 Natsuki Takaya / HAKUSENSHA, Inc.

BUY IT AT WWW.TOKYOPOP.COM/SHOP